DISCOVERY

DISCOVERY:
Theory, Practice, and Problems

Roger S. Haydock
Professor and Clinical Director
William Mitchell College of Law
Member, Minnesota Bar

David F. Herr
Member, Minnesota Bar
Adjunct Clinical Professor of Law
William Mitchell College of Law

Little, Brown and Company
Boston   *Toronto*

Library of Congress Catalog Card Number 82-083731
ISBN Number 0-316-35162-8

Sixth Printing

EB

Published simultaneously in Canada
by Little, Brown & Company (Canada) Limited

Printed in the United States of America

To Cherie
and
to Julia

SUMMARY OF CONTENTS

CONTENTS

Contents

Chapter 2
DEPOSITIONS   *87*

Contents

Chapter 4

REQUESTS FOR PRODUCTION AND
PHYSICAL EXAMINATIONS   *231*

PREFACE

Discovery touches many law-school courses. This book is designed to provide you with the information you need in whatever substantive, procedural, skills, or clinic course you are participating in. Discovery itself is a fundamental segment of civil procedure; its rules occupy a significant portion of a procedural course. The practice of discovery is an essential component of a litigation course; its procedures provide litigators with a vital arsenal of strategies and tactics to employ in their cases. The existence and availability of discoverable information is indispensable to the trial itself, providing the trial lawyer with the necessary witnesses and documents to prove a case. Understanding both the conceptual and pragmatic elements of discovery will increase your knowledge, comprehension, and appreciation of many legal experiences.

We convey this information to you as one lawyer to another. For purposes of this book, we consider you to be an attorney (relax, bar examiners), and we ask that you consider yourself the same. Viewing yourself as a litigator may enhance your understanding and recall of the materials. The more you can see yourself as a lawyer representing a client, or the more you act like an attorney in a skills course or like a litigator in a clinic, the more likely you will absorb these materials and achieve the goals that underlie the book. We hope this book will allow you to understand some of the intricacies of substantive law problems, to solve procedural dilemmas, to practice taking depositions and drafting discovery documents, to bolster your confidence and competence, and to allay some of the anxiety and tension that naturally afflict the novice at law.

Discovery practice may not be what it seems to be or what you think it is. As you read and digest these materials, you may become knowledgeable, informed, curious, surprised, pleased, and shocked. The materials may cause you to wwwhhh, sigh, tsk, mutter, and guffaw. Not everything in the practical world of discovery will comport with your notions of the legal profession, the adversary system, the role of lawyers, and our system of justice. Since this book presents a variety of alternative strategies, tactics, and techniques that are employed in the real world, we present both the way things are and the way things should be. In part, your task as an attorney will be to find a means to make both ways coincide. We employ the integrated approach to professional responsibility and interpose throughout the book ethical comments, concerns, questions, and suggestions.

Discovery practice occurs in the office and between attorneys. It seldom reaches the judicial forum. Cases that do proceed to court are resolved at the lower-court level and may go unreported and unnoticed. We know many of you are involved in a clinic course, clerk for a law firm or judge, or know more than you should. We ask you to assist us with future editions of this book. We invite you to send us copies of any orders, motions, forms, letters, happenings, anecdotes, corrections, and approaches to discovery practice that have escaped our attention and notice.* We conclude with the hope that this book enhances your understanding of the law and brings you nearer to the excitement and adventure—the discovery—that awaits you as a lawyer. It's true.

Roger S. Haydock
David F. Herr

June 1, 1982

---

*Correspondence may be sent to the authors at William Mitchell Law Clinic, William Mitchell College of Law, 875 Summit Avenue, Saint Paul, Minnesota, 55105.

ACKNOWLEDGMENTS

The experience of writing a book resembles most other life experiences. We had occasions of joy, anxiety, mirth, pain, laughter, frustration, missed deadlines, another chapter?, misplaced footnotes, satisfaction, who wrote this?, parallel ideas, what color cover?, and delight. We are pleased this book is being published, in part because we hope it contributes to the education of law students and lawyers and in part because this book is a testament to the notion that authors can grow from the support, assistance, ideas, and love of others. We first want to acknowledge that phenomenon.

Many individuals provided us with this experience. We list some of them to thank them publicly.

Deborah Hoch, Diane Dube, and Mark Thompson ably researched discovery law, corrected our footnotes, and edited chapters. Alberta Dowlin, Stephanie Martin, Gloria Karbo, Lynnette Shanahan, and Betty Wade typed and word-processed the countless drafts. Geoffrey Peters, Robert Oliphant, Melvin Goldberg, and John Sonsteng provided their support. Richard Ruvelson, Margaret Kaiser, and Gayle Hendley supplied additional research. Our editors, Richard Heuser, Michael West, and Nancy Campbell, also have provided invaluable assistance with the publication of this book.

Other colleagues, lawyers, and judges provided their ideas and comments. Numerous clients afforded us the opportunity to develop discovery tactics. Many law students from William Mitchell College of Law questioned and challenged the materials and participated in the exercises in this book, and our colleagues both praised and assaulted our earlier efforts.

Roger's Acknowledgments: Cherie, Marni, Marci, and Jeffrey especially assisted me during the creation of this book. Their support and love made this adventure more meaningful. Sue and Sil Haydock helped me become a law student. The faculty of William Mitchell and their support of clinical education and materials prodded me on. Our friends, especially our Marriage Encounter friends, including Jack and Sue Hood, helped me become a discoverer.

David's Acknowledgments: This book, or at least my contribution to it, would not have been possible without the guidance and encouragement of so many. Professor Michael Steenson tried to teach me to write, and Professor Bill Danforth taught me to enjoy that nemesis of most law students, procedure. The attorneys of my firm, Maslon Edelman Borman & Brand, have given abundant support and assistance. My friends have given the most, and I thank them.

This book would not exist without the help of everyone noted here, and of many others. They should share the credit. We, of course, must take the blame for any inaccuracies, inconsistencies, or other shortcomings. Or, at least, each of us can accept the blame on behalf of his co-author, whose fault it must have been.

R.S.H.
D.F.H.

DISCOVERY

INTRODUCTION

Oh, do not ask, "What is it?"
Let us go and make our visit.
T. S. Eliot
The Love Song of J. Alfred Prufrock

Burning with curiosity she went in after the rabbit down a hole under the
hedge, never once considering how in the world she was to get out again.
Lewis Carroll
Alice's Adventures in Wonderland

You are about to join J. Alfred and Alice in exploring the world of discovery. This book explains and analyzes discovery rules, procedures, court decisions, strategies, tactics, and techniques. It mixes practice with theory. You will learn how and why attorneys seek information and respond to discovery requests. You will learn how to go into the hole and ask questions and how to get out with discoverable information.

There is no one way to "practice" discovery. We tend to do things, including discovery, our own way. Sure, there are rules and regulations, commas and colons, citations and sanctions, but by and large discovery practice varies significantly from attorney to attorney and from case to case. While there are some mechanical, black-and-white rules that we all follow (you have 30 days to respond) and while there are some commonly accepted tactical decisions (prepare your deponent thoroughly), still the bulk of discovery practice consists of judgmental and strategic decisions about which road to take: to the right, to the left, or to Mandalay? What accounts for this diversity of discovery practice? Plenty. The following paragraphs will set forth some of the factors that account for the "plenty."

Discovery Theory. Each rule has its own theories supporting its existence. Sometimes the rules have alternative rationales or a set of underlying assumptions that may or may not be realistic, practical, or accurate. A practicing attorney must be aware of the philosophy that underlies the discovery rules in order effectively to interpret and apply them. An attorney must understand both why the rules exist as well as how the rules apply. A discovering lawyer must be both a legal philosopher and a legal artist. That is not always understood by all practitioners.

Cooperative Discovery. Modern discovery practice encourages attorneys to be friends during the exchange of discovery information. The make-up and tenor of the current rules openly promote, support, cajole, and push attorneys into establishing a cooperative discovery exchange. Some local federal district rules mandate that the attorneys actually talk to each other about bartering discovery information. This approach is the clear preference of those who ordain discovery rules and of the majority of attorneys who implement them. It will be a major theme of this book.

Informal Exchanges. In many cases, it takes only 20 cents and a seven-digit number to obtain basic factual information from an opposing attorney. In other cases, it takes only 20 cents and an envelope to disclose all documents and things, except the smoking paper. This informal telephone and letter exchange of information and documents stems in part from the cooperative nature of discovery and in part, of course, from the approach taken by the lawyers.

Lawyer Control. The present discovery system places the initiation, use, and response to discovery in the control of the lawyers. They can do what they want, within reason. Judges are there primarily to enforce discovery methods only if the attorneys are unable to resolve their disputes by mutual stipulation.

Stipulation Power. Discovery Rule 29 allows attorneys almost unfettered discretion to modify, change, alter, tinker with, or transubstantiate any or all of the discovery rules and procedures, by themselves, without resort to a court order. They need only agree, and their stipulation becomes the governing rule and procedure. The courts encourage the use of this power.

Judicial Differences. Anyone who knows of two federal or state judges who have an identical approach to discovery may first call the authors collect and then call Ripley's Believe It or Not. Different judges, even in the same district or county, have varying approaches to discovery requests, responses, and pretrial procedures. How they view the role of discovery within the adversary system affects their decisions.

Introduction

The Adversary System.   "One that contends with, opposes, or resists: the enemy." That is a dictionary adversary. The nature and extent of that contention, opposition, and resistance will vary from attorney to attorney and from case to case. Nonetheless, the discovery process (which preaches cooperation) often occurs in the midst of a battle, within a litigation war (with "enemies" in some cases). Resolving that confrontation can be achieved with the ease of putting a parallelogram peg into a hexagonal hole.

The Role of the Attorney.   Lawyers view their roles in the litigation process differently, from the style of a Billy Martin, to a John Denver, to the Wizard of Oz. And the same attorney will often view his or her role differently at various stages of the same or different cases.

The Best Interests of the Client.   What the client wants, what the client needs, what interests the client has: these and other counseling matters influence the progress of a case. The client's choice of available legal options will affect what an attorney can and cannot do through discovery.

The Stake.   What is the case worth? What value does the attorney place on a case? Does the potential recovery or remedy justify X amount of discovery? Or Y amount of discovery?

Time.   Sometimes there is no time to pursue timely discovery. But these should be limited to the few instances in which clients involve an attorney in an untimely fashion — for instance, at the last second.

Arguable Interpretive Differences.   Attorneys on opposite sides of the case naturally tend to interpret the law differently. This is due in large measure to the demonstrable truth that statutes, cases, and discovery rules can be read from left to right and can be interpreted from right to left, particularly when applied to cases with two or more varying stories.

Varying Stories.   "He was going at least 63 miles per hour." "No, it was a she, and she was going about 24.5 kilometers per hour." Differing accounts, varying perspectives, conflicting interests, and different people. Having different attorneys representing divergent viewpoints inevitably leads to differing views regarding the importance and relevance of and need for certain discovery information. Investigating, discovering, and proving who is right costs money.

Costs.   They include discovery expenses and attorney's fees. Attorneys with clients can dream about discovery. But only attorneys with clients with sufficient money or resources can afford to implement discovery. Discovery is often expensive, and these expenses may well preclude extensive inquiries and disclosures. The panoply of discovery devices usually contains at least one inexpensive device to obtain information.

Wallpapering. What is it? It is that abhorent *modus operandi* of some attorneys, who truckload reams of discovery requests to the opposing attorney, enough to wallpaper the other attorney's office, hallway, and summer retreat.

Gaming. A tactic used by some attorneys, gaming is designed to undercut the purpose and value of discovery by playing games with the process. Sometimes it's totally ignoring discovery requests; other times it's incomplete or self-serving discovery responses; and other times it's the wholesale delivery of discovery information interspersed with tons of irrelevant junk. (See Wallpapering.)

Surprise! A thorough use of discovery methods practically eliminates the possibility of a major surprise occurring in the trial of a case. Some attorneys prefer to maintain some surprise information for the trial, and will do their best not to reveal such information during discovery. Other attorneys prefer disclosing such information to the other side, even if not requested, to strengthen the discloser's negotiation position. Because some 90 to 96 percent of civil cases are resolved through negotiated settlements, there may not be much reason to save something especially worthwhile for the trial.

"Oh, My Goodness." Many cases have some bit of information that, if disclosed to the other side, causes the disclosing attorney to say silently: "Oh, my goodness." This information will be somehow harmful to a disclosing party and accordingly weaken a party's case. Discovery works both ways and requires the disclosure of both helpful and harmful information. All data must be disclosed if appropriately requested. Oh, my goodness and all.

Lawyer Inaction. Sometimes lawyers don't do something because they don't know what to do or how to do it. This inaction results from a lack of even moderate competence or a lack of sufficient confidence or a lack of adequate experience. What we know or don't know about discovery practice clearly influences our approach to discovery. We want to avoid the knots in our stomach, the weakening of our knees, the sweat in our palms, the shudder of our body, the quavering of our voice, and the whisper in our ear, "What have you just done? Why didn't you go to dental school?" The same afflictions that ravage lawyers ravage law students in clinical programs. Clinicians, supervisory attorneys, and student attorneys do not talk about this phenomenon often enough (unless it happens to someone else) or about what effect it has on a case or client; and there is precious little in the legal literature. But we have all experienced the phenomenon and know the toll it has taken and takes on our decisionmaking. Law students will sometimes be able to overcome these feelings and emotions by out-preparing the other side, by relying on their natural interest and enthusiasm to carry them through, by resorting to the power generated by the competitive genes that initially brought them to law school, and by praying to the Force.

There Is Plenty More.

These factors and others account for the varying approaches taken by attorneys on seemingly similar cases. This is not to say that there does not exist a substantial amount of agreement among lawyers on how best to proceed in many cases, but it does recognize the reality of disparity of discovery approaches. The rules and procedures are there; their interpretation and application need to be made by you.

What rules, decisions, and practice? The Federal Rules of Civil Procedure relating to discovery and federal court practice will be the primary focus of this book. There is, in actuality, little difference between those rules and the discovery rules of many states. Similarity also obtains between federal and state practice, even in those states that have not modeled their rules after the federal rules. Admittedly, the captions are different and the courthouses are blocks or cities apart, but many discovery tactics and strategies are the same in both systems.

Chapter 1 explains the scope of discovery. Chapter 2 details the intricacies of deposition practice. Chapter 3 explains interrogatories, while Chapter 4 describes a related discovery device, requests for production, and also focuses on medical examinations. Chapter 5 deciphers requests for admissions in the context of an interview with the world's only known "admitter." Chapter 6 concludes the book with an explanation of enforcement sanctions.

Studying these chapters should initiate you into the do's and don'ts, the why's and wherefore's of discovery law.[1] But learning the strategy of discovery also involves practice in analyzing situations, formulating questions and responses, deciding which lines and means of inquiry to

---

[1]More detailed treatment of complex discovery, discovery in special proceedings (such as administrative hearings and arbitration), foreign discovery, and proposed discovery reforms appears in R. Haydock & D. Herr, Discovery Practice (1982), Chapters 9-12. The Federal Rules of Civil Procedure that relate directly to discovery include Rules 26, 28-37, and 45. Authoritative general works on discovery are listed in the Bibliography at the end of this volume, along with treatises, books, and articles that pertain specifically to the topics of each chapter in this book.

pursue, and advising your clients. To develop these skills, you can tackle the problems we have placed in the last section of each chapter. For instance, the problems that end Chapter 1 and relate to the scope of discovery ask you to analyze factual situations involving relevancy, privilege, lawyer mental impressions, trial preparation materials, witness statements, experts, and supplemental information. They should afford you, the law student, with opportunities to apply the legal doctrines to typical discovery situations, to understand better the application of the discovery rules, to assume the roles of advocate and judge, and to review the major concepts treated in the chapter.

Those problems that follow the remaining chapters are slightly different; they are designed to provide practice opportunities that involve you directly in the discovery process. You will draft interrogatories, requests for production, requests for admissions, and responses to these requests. You will prepare and plan depositions, take a deposition, represent a deponent, and be engaged in other discovery procedures. Your instructor will provide the structure and setting for these problems.

To provide the factual settings for these problems, we have supplied three hypothetical case files in Appendix A. The first case, a consumer contract and breach of warranty action, *American Campers v. Summers,* is a complete, self-contained case with a factual memo, pleadings, and documents. The second hypothetical case, a personal-injury action, *Bellows v. Norris,* contains information, pleadings, and documents common to both parties. This case also forms the basis for depositions and discovery problems that require each party to retain confidential information. The Supplement to this book contains confidential facts that your instructor will give to you to prepare the problems. The third case, *Graham v. Turkel,* a legal malpractice case, provides a factual setting for expert discovery and some of its problems also employ confidential information available to your instructor in the Supplement.

All of the problems and the hypothetical cases they draw upon occur in the mythical jurisdiction of the State of Summit, County of Little, City of Mitchell. This jurisdiction has adopted the Federal Rules of Civil Procedure and the Federal Rules of Evidence. The relevant substantive state laws appear in the legal memoranda included in each case file. These memos provide you with the basic law necessary to conduct discovery. Your instructor may have you apply other or additional laws from another jurisdiction.

Some of the problems, particularly the depositions, may require you

Introduction

or your deponent to provide detailed information that does not appear in the case files. You and your deponent may add such facts if it is reasonable that an attorney or a client would know of such facts and remember them. The details you add must be consistent with the facts given and cannot distort or exaggerate the situation.

This book is based in part upon our experience, teaching, clinical practice, our colleagues' tales, the insights of others, common sense, and a dash of humor. This introduction and occasional comments may seem irreverent to some of you, out of place to others, and humorous to still others. Only the last response is encouraged. Sometimes we take ourselves and what we do too seriously (just think of final exams), and an occasional light tone puts some things in perspective.

Chapter 1
THE SCOPE

Ask and you shall receive. Seek and you shall find.

Matthew 7:7

§1.1 PURPOSES OF DISCOVERY

Discovery rules and procedures have evolved over the years to serve many functions in the litigation process. Major purposes include:

1. *Supplementation of pleadings.* The Federal Rules of Civil Procedure authorize simple and brief pleading "notice" and include Rules 26 through 37 as the means to determine and sift the supporting facts.

2. *Early and thorough disclosure of information by all sides.* This exchange of facts provides both sides with information more efficiently and effectively than if each had to reconstruct a case unaided by the other.

3. *Some equalizing of the investigative resources of both sides without allowing one side to take undue advantage of the other.* Current rules do not allow for the wholesale disclosure of materials; instead, they balance one side's need for facts with the other side's ability to supply them.

4. *Limited exploration into the adversary's camp to discover its perceptions of the facts and case.* The rules permit a requesting party to uncover what the responding party perceives the facts, issues, strengths, and weaknesses of the case to be.

5. *Documentation of testimony and preservation of documents.* Discovery devices establish the knowledge or lack of knowledge of a witness or party and locate and identify tangible evidence for later use.

6. *Isolation of issues and determination of material and undisputed facts.* This discovery function mimics pretrial conferences and motions for summary judgment, in order further to narrow discovery efforts and to obviate unnecessary litigation.

7. *Promotion of negotiated settlements.* Discovery allows exchanges of information, opinions, conclusions, claims, and defenses and provides each side with the opportunity to observe the demeanor and responses of witnesses and verify the authenticity of documents. These functions facilitate the realistic assessment of the value of a case.

8. *Fostering of trial verdicts based upon accurate presentations and informal arguments, not on surmise and surprise.* Discovery procedures allow the trial lawyer to be better prepared and to be a more effective advocate, increasing the likelihood that a verdict will be correct and fair.

9. *Providing an economical method of resolving disputes.* This presumes that the attorneys who implement the rules use them appropriately and that the judges who apply the rules interpret them properly.

All of these functions are essential to the maintenance of our current litigation system. It is fair to ask which came first — the purposes or the system. The answer, of course, is both, because neither could exist without the other. Discovery is an integral part of the litigation process and the acceptance of that view will make this chapter and this book more understandable and useful. For many lawyers discovery merely gets in the way of going to trial, and that attitude accounts for much of the misuse of discovery devices. Discovery for other lawyers seems to be the best way to avoid or delay going to trial, and that attitude, too, accounts for its share of the abuse of discovery procedures. But for most lawyers, discovery constitutes an effective, efficient, and economical means of representing a client involved in litigation, a perspective which in itself fosters such a system.

All nine purposes are invaluable to everyday litigation practice. Discovery allows an attorney to know as much about a case, with limitations, as the opposing attorney knows. The facts, opinions, conclusions, theories, and even trial preparation materials in some cases are there for the asking. Discovery permits a lawyer to review and probe the good, the bad, and the indifferent from the safety of his or her office before settlement, and long before trial. Just as trial lawyers develop their own systems of trial notebooks, which they use to present and argue a case at trial, so also discovery provides attorneys with a system to develop a case to present and argue during negotiations. A thorough use of discovery leaves few reasons for two reasonable attorneys seeking to satisfy their clients' best interests to decide to go to trial instead of negotiating a settlement.

The present formalized discovery system promotes the use of informal discovery exchanges by lawyers. The very existence of the rules encourages lawyers to use more efficient and economical means to exchange information. Bilateral trading of documents, cooperative bartering of information, mutual alteration of procedures, and informal enforcement of the rules, all have come about because the discovery rule procedures are somewhat more costly, more formal, and less efficient. Discovery practice often precedes formalized discovery theory.

Newton discovered long ago, in another context, that every advantage has a disadvantage. So also with discovery. It can be expensive. It may cause delay. It may force the other side to prepare a case better. It may prompt the other side to react with additional discovery, and it can be abused. The continuing review of discovery rules and the constant monitoring of discovery practice will lead to more evolutionary and innovative changes, and to the further elimination of abusive situations.

A danger lurks in simply relying on the rules and what may appear to be a reasonable application of them. The danger lies in the failure to apply the theories and rationales supporting the particular rule. An understanding and application of the reasons for the rule is the best way of determining how the rule should be interpreted and applied. Some of the rules have been adopted based upon a set of assumptions that may or may not be present in the specific facts and circumstances of a case. The rules therefore should not be applied automatically or mechanically; they require the understanding of a legal philosopher and the application of a legal artist. A practitioner has to be both.

§1.2 SCOPE OF DISCOVERY

Rule 26 defines the boundaries of what is and what is not discoverable. Subsections of Rule 26 define the limits and impose restrictions on the scope of discovery relating to:

1.	Methods	26(a)
2.	Relevancy	26(b)(1)
3.	Privilege	26(b)(1)
4.	Insurance	26(b)(2)
5.	Trial Preparation Materials	26(b)(3)
6.	Mental Impressions	26(b)(3)
7.	Witness Statements	26(b)(3)

8.	Expert Opinions	26(b)(4)
9.	Protective Orders	26(c)
10.	Sequence and Timing of Discovery	26(d)
11.	Supplementation of Responses	26(e)
12.	Discovery Conferences	26(f)
13.	The LSAT score of the opposing lawyer	

This chapter explores these provisions of Rule 26, some other provisions which involve procedural matters, and some discovery strategies relating to the scope of discovery. Chapter 7 will explain court discovery conferences. Only professional jealousy explains the discoverability of LSAT scores.

§1.3 METHODS OF DISCOVERY

Rule 26 outlines five major devices available for discovery:

1. Depositions upon oral examinations or written questions;
2. Written interrogatories;
3. Production of documents or things or permission to enter upon land or other property, for inspection and other purposes;
4. Physical and mental examinations;
5. Requests for admissions.

Although these devices will be explained in detail in separate chapters, a summary description of each will provide a better understanding of the applications of Rule 26.

Depositions. A deposition is a sworn statement made by a deponent before a notary or other officer authorized to administer oaths. The deponent may be a party or any person who has information. The deposition is usually conducted orally, the attorney who requested the deposition typically examining and cross-examining the deponent, with the opposing attorney in attendance. The questions and answers are usually transcribed and later prepared in transcript form. A deposition may be conducted using written questions submitted by the requesting attorney and read to the deponent by the officer.

Written interrogatories. Interrogatories are written questions submitted to a party to be answered in writing under oath. This discovery device is particularly suitable for information involving specific factual data or witness and document information.

Production of documents. A party may require another party to provide documents and tangible things for inspection and copying or to permit entry onto land or access to other property for inspection, testing, or sampling. A party may be able to obtain the same access to documents, things, and land from a non-party through a subpoena duces tecum under Rule 45.

Physical and mental examinations. A party may be able to obtain a physical or mental examination of another party if the condition of that person is in controversy and if there exists good cause for an examination. These types of examinations usually occur in personal injury litigation.

Requests for admissions. Responses to requests for admissions determine the truth of certain matters and the genuineness of documents. This device not only discovers information, but also narrows the disputed issues for trial.

The provisions of Rule 26 relating to the scope of discovery apply, with some exceptions, with equal force to all five of these devices. The extent of what is and what is not discoverable is virtually the same, regardless of the device used to obtain the information. Each device has some inherent limitations that affect the practical scope of discovery, but what cannot be obtained through one discovery device can usually be obtained through another.

§1.4 RELEVANCY: WHAT IS DISCOVERABLE

Rule 26(b)(1) explains what is discoverable:

> *In General.* Parties may obtain discovery regarding any matter, not privileged, which is relevant to the subject matter involved in the pending action, whether it relates to the claim or defense of the party seeking discovery or to the claim or defense of any other party, including the existence, description, nature, custody, condition and location of any books, documents, or other tangible things and the identity and location of persons having knowledge of any discoverable matter. It is not ground for objection that the information sought will be inadmissible at

the trial if the information sought appears reasonably calculated to lead
to the discovery of admissible evidence.

This rule and interpretive case law provide vast leeway to discover
nearly everything there is to know about a case. Granting or denying
discovery is a matter within the broad discretion of the trial court.[1] The
party who opposes discovery carries a "heavy burden" of showing why
discovery should be disallowed.[2] We all know that discovery may
constitute a "fishing expedition."[3] What we need to know is what
kind and how many fish we can catch, so we need to explain the four
specific standards which define the scope of discoverable information.
   1. *Non-privileged matter relevant to the subject matter involved in the pending action.* Courts have construed this clause liberally,[4] declaring that
this rule envisions generally unrestricted access to sources of information.[5] The term *subject matter* relates to any matter in a case; it does not
limit itself to the merits of a case, nor does it distinguish between
substantive concerns and procedural matters.[6] Questions about liability and damages, jurisdiction and venue, have been held to be clearly
discoverable.[7]
   Court descriptions have further broadened the boundaries of relevancy. The term *relevant* encompasses any matter "that bears on or that
reasonably could lead to other matter that could bear on any issue that
is or may be in the case."[8] Requests for discovery should be considered
relevant if there is any possibility that information sought may be
relevant to the subject matter of the action.[9]
   Opinions, contentions, and conclusions have also been declared
discoverable under related rules. Rule 33(b) specifically provides that
an interrogatory will not be objectionable merely because a question
involves an opinion or contention; Rule 36 permits requests for admis-

§1.4   [1]*See, e.g.,* Pettway v. American Cast Iron Pipe Co., 576 F.2d 1157 (10th Cir.
1978), *cert. denied,* 439 U.S. 1115 (1979).
   [2]*See* Blankenship v. Hearst Corp., 519 F.2d 418, 429 (9th Cir. 1975).
   [3]Hickman v. Taylor, 329 U.S. 495, 507 (1947).
   [4]Mitsui & Co. v. Puerto Rico Water Resources Auth., 79 F.R.D. 72, 80 (D.P.R. 1978).
   [5]Heathman v. United States Dist. Ct. for Cent. Dist. Cal., 503 F.2d 1032, 1035 (9th
Cir. 1974).
   [6] 4 Moore's Federal Practice ¶26.56[1], at 26-117 (2d ed. 1980) (hereinafter cited as
Moore's Federal Practice).
   [7]*See* Sinclair Refining Co. v. Jenkins Petroleum Process Co., 289 U.S. 689, 691-696
(1933).
   [8]Oppenheimer Fund, Inc. v. Sanders, 437 U.S. 340, 351 (1978).
   [9]Detweiler Bros. v. John Graham & Co., 412 F. Supp. 416, 422 (E.D. Wash. 1976),
citing 8 C. Wright & A. Miller, Federal Practice and Procedure §2008, at 47 (1970).

sions that involve opinions of fact. The "matter" discoverable under Rule 26 includes opinion and conclusions questions. Any discovery device may be used to obtain such information.[10]

The discovery standard of relevancy is not limited by the evidentiary standard of relevancy.[11] It is much broader in scope and encompasses any information that relates to the subject matter of a case regardless of its admissibility at trial.[12] This includes information exclusively within the knowledge or possession of the other side and information already known to the discovering party,[13] as well as information equally available to the interrogator as a matter of public record.[14] This latter type of request for known information is consistent with the discovery theory that knowing what others know and what they know that others know is useful and appropriate information. This type of information has been held to be discoverable not because it necessarily produces new information but because it permits a party to verify facts for use as admission requests, an equally valid discovery purpose.[15]

It is difficult to define relevancy systematically because the variety of legal and factual settings provide an infinite number of questions relating to it. Numerous examples that help define the line between the relevant and the irrelevant appear in other publications.[16]

Limits are placed on the kind and number of discoverable fish. The Supreme Court recently reminded the trial courts to "not neglect their power to restrict discovery where" appropriate.[17] The rules do not permit a party "to roam in shadow zones of relevancy and to explore matter which does not presently appear germane on the theory that it might conceivably become so."[18] Questions regarding the plaintiff's motives in instituting a lawsuit and in fee arrangements will usually be held irrelevant, but not in all cases.[19] Questions concerning discussions between the plaintiff and his, her, or its attorney prior to the

[10] 4 Moore's Federal Practice ¶26.56[3], at 26-168 (2d ed. 1980).
[11] Fed. R. Civ. P. 26(b), Notes of Advisory Comm. — 1946 Amendments, reprinted in 28 U.S.C.A. 153.
[12] Freeman v. Seligson, 405 F.2d 1326, 1335 (D.C. Cir. 1968).
[13] See 8 C. Wright & A. Miller, Federal Practice and Procedure §2014, at 110-111 (1971, Supp. 1980).
[14] Petruska v. Johns-Manville, 83 F.R.D. 32, 35 (E.D. Pa. 1979).
[15] Wilmington Country Club v. Horwath & Horwath, 46 F.R.D. 65, 66 (E.D. Pa. 1969).
[16] See 4 Moore's Federal Practice ¶26.56[1].
[17] Herbert v. Lando, 441 U.S. 153, 177 (1979).
[18] In re Surety Assn. of America, 388 F.2d 412, 414 (2d Cir. 1967), quoting Broadway & Ninety-Sixth St. Realty Co. v. Loew's, Inc., 21 F.R.D. 347, 352 (S.D.N.Y. 1958).
[19] See 4 Moore's Federal Practice ¶26.52[2], at 26-157 to -160 (2d ed. 1980).

filing of the complaint, the manner in which plaintiffs were solicited, fee arrangements, and other information concerning the institution of the action have been denied, because it was "difficult to see how an inquiry into the circumstances surrounding the instigation of the action could affect the substance of the claim."[20]

Courts will balance the competing interests of parties in deciding whether to order disclosure of certain information. The interests of one party may outweigh the discovery interests of another party, especially when the use of the discoverable information serves only a limited purpose. One court has held that a discovery request for information for use as possible impeachment material at trial does not outweigh another party's interest in preserving the privacy of certain information.[21]

But no single definition delineates the exact boundaries of discovery. No one test determines the appropriateness of discovery requests. We seem to be left with analogies as the final determinant:

> The exactitude of discovery, the lawyer's tool for factfinding, properly lies somewhere between the acuity of the surgeon's scalpel and the carpenter's hammer. Ideally, the lawyer probes for facts with the precision and delicacy of a cardiologist incising the aorta to receive a by-pass vehicle. Realistically, the lawyer's factfinding search shares a closer propinquity with the carpenter's trade and pounds much more bluntly.[22]

2. *Matters relating to the claim or defense of any party.* This phrase makes it clear that the range of subject matter extends to claims and defenses asserted by any party, including the party seeking discovery. Controverted issues involving jurisdictional matters will be an appropriate area for discovery.[23] Damage claims as well as liability issues are discoverable.[24] The subject matter of "potential" issues that may be available to a party may also be discoverable.[25] Matters supporting additional claims or defenses may be uncovered through discovery, and a party may seek information to ferret out these possible claims or defenses.

---

[20]Foremost Promotions, Inc. v. Pabst Brewing Co., 15 F.R.D. 128, 130 (N.D. Ill. 1953).

[21]Williams v. Thomas Jefferson Univ., 343 F. Supp. 1131, 1132 (E.D. Pa. 1972).

[22]Roesberg v. Johns-Manville Corp., 28 Fed. R. Serv. 2d 1170, 1183 (E.D. Pa. 1972).

[23]Data Disc, Inc. v. Systems Technology Assocs., Inc., 557 F.2d 1280, 1285 (9th Cir. 1977).

[24]General Instrument Corp. v. General Diode Corp., 41 F.R.D. 1, 3 (D. Mass. 1966).

[25]Manual of Federal Practice §5.24, at 300 (R. Fischer, ed., 2d ed. 1979).

Information involving "similar" transactions may also be discoverable.[26] The practices or policies of a party similar to the acts or conduct involved in the pending claims or defenses may be discoverable if they show some habit or pattern. Materials and information that accrue after a lawsuit has ensued may also be discoverable. The time span of the discoverable subject matter of a case may be extended to include events after the litigation began. A case involving continuing claims or defenses will make such post-complaint matter relevant. Discovery may also be available regarding matters involved in motions to reopen or vacate a judgment under Rule 60[27] and to enforce a judgment by examining a judgment debtor to determine assets.[28]

One proposal to amend the discovery rules suggested limiting the scope of discovery to any matter "relevant to the issues raised" by any party rather than to the "subject matter" of the case.[29] Another suggestion proposed that the phrase "relevant to the subject matter" be replaced with the standard "relevant to the issues raised by the claims and defenses of any party."[30] The rejection of these proposals by the Supreme Court maintains the current broad scope of discovery. The Supreme Court recently reaffirmed the broad scope of discovery extending beyond the issues raised by pleadings, because discovery helps define and clarify issues and because discovery assists in shaping the merits.[31]

Specific claims and issues will, however, affect the discoverability of some information. Inquiries into the financial status of a party will usually be disallowed unless there is a specific claim of punitive damages against that party for reckless or wanton conduct.[32] Information about the claims of non-parties may become relevant to a case if the habits, prior conduct, or past practices of a party are in issue.[33] Discovery relating to class-action considerations including the existence and scope of the class will be allowed to resolve class determination.[34]

---

[26]See Laufman v. Oakley Bldg. & Loan Co., 72 F.R.D. 116, 120 (S.D. Ohio 1976).

[27]H.K. Porter Co. v. Goodyear Tire & Rubber Co., 536 F.2d 1115, 1122 (6th Cir. 1976).

[28]Caisson Corp. v. County West Building Corp., 62 F.R.D. 331 (E.D. Pa. 1974).

[29]Advisory Committee on Civil Rules, Preliminary Draft of Proposed Amendments to the Federal Rules of Civil Procedure (March 1978), reprinted in 77 F.R.D. 613, 626-627 (1978).

[30]See American Bar Association, Section of Litigation, Report of the Special Committee for the Study of Discovery Abuse (1977).

[31]Oppenheimer Fund, Inc. v. Sanders, 437 U.S. 340, 351 (1978).

[32]Renshaw v. Ravert, 82 F.R.D. 361, 363 (E.D. Pa. 1979).

[33]Johnson v. W.H. Stewart Co., 75 F.R.D. 541, 543 (W.D. Okla. 1976).

[34]Kamm v. California City Dev. Co., 509 F.2d 205, 210 (9th Cir. 1975).

Discovery directed to individually named class members will usually be permitted, but discovery directed to class members will be denied[35] unless such information is necessary to resolve an issue[36] or is unavailable from the representative parties.[37]

A recent addition to Rule 26 provides another means to establish the scope of discovery. Rule 26(f) permits discovery conferences and allows a judge to restrict the extent of discovery by identifying the issues, establishing a discovery plan, and setting limits on discovery. This relatively new format provides another means for an attorney to attempt to limit discovery by seeking such a conference and persuading a judge or magistrate to establish reasonable bounds.

3. *The existence, description, nature, custody, condition, and location of documents and tangible things, and the identity and location of persons having knowledge of any discoverable matter.* This clause clarifies that tangible things are discoverable and that individuals as sources of information are also discoverable. These individuals need not necessarily have firsthand information. It is sufficient if they have knowledge of any discoverable information, which includes hearsay sources.[38] This provision does not refer to inquiries into the "contents" of documents because the first factor, which allows discovery of subject matter, includes the contents of documents.

4. *Information reasonably calculated to lead to the discovery of admissible evidence.* This standard further broadens the scope of discovery by stating that both inadmissable and admissable evidence is discoverable and that information likely to lead to admissible evidence is also discoverable. This includes any type of trial evidence, including impeachment information and any sources or leads about potential trial evidence.[39] Indeed, one of the benefits resulting from a broad scope of discovery is this opportunity to explore, discover, and establish new information that supports another theory or that bolsters a previously unsupported allegation.

These four standards, when applied together, create an exceedingly broad scope of discoverable information. The "reasonably calculated" standard, when joined with the "subject matter" standard, provides a

---

[35]*See* Wainwright v. Kraft Co. Corp., 54 F.R.D. 532 (N.D. Ga. 1972).

[36]Gardner v. Awards Marketing Corp., 55 F.R.D. 460 (C.D. Utah 1972).

[37]*See* Dellums v. Powell, 566 F.2d 167, 186 (D.C. Cir. 1977).

[38]Fed. R. Civ. P. 26(b), Notes of Advisory Comm. — 1946 Amendments, reprinted in 28 U.S.C.A. 154.

[39]*See* 8 C. Wright & A. Miller, Federal Practice and Procedure §2015, at 113-121 (1970).

requesting attorney with rule-sanctioned reasons to justify and support requests for information relating to almost anything about a case. There are limits, of course. Rule 26 subsections narrow this broad scope; legitimate objections to certain information also narrow the scope. These limitations reflect the balanced discovery philosophy that if a party wants to go discovery fishing, that party ought to catch no more than a reasonable and sufficient limit. The Supreme Court recently emphasized the need for reasonable discovery restraints by declaring that the discovery provisions must be applied " 'to secure the just, speedy, and inexpensive determination of every action.' "[40]

These rules, cases, and definitions frame the theory of the scope of discovery. Practice, experience, and economics frame the practicalities of the extent of discovery. These practicalities in turn frame three specific approaches to what is discoverable.

First, you can ask for everything you want to discover, whether you professionally believe it to be discoverable or not. The experience of many attorneys confirms that what one attorney thinks to be discoverable another lawyer believes never to be discoverable. The broad standards of Rule 26 account for the wide divergence of opinion regarding the discoverability of various types of information. Sometimes there will be a collective opinion regarding some information, confirmable in a published judicial decision. More often the professional opinions of practitioners and the myriad of unreported and unknown lower-court opinions determine what is or is not discoverable in a specific case. Some practitioners believe that the identities of witnesses for trial are usually discoverable through interrogatories; the weight of authority holds otherwise.[41] Some lawyers believe that a party always has an obligation to supplement all discovery responses; Rule 26(e) states otherwise. Still other attorneys believe that a party's income tax return is ordinarily discoverable; court decisions indicate the contrary.[42] These differences in approach to practice become magnified when local customs, specialized traditions, and the adversary process add other factors. Your doubts about the discoverability of something

[40]Herbert v. Lando, 441 U.S. 153, 177 (1979), *quoting* Fed. R. Civ. P. 1.

[41]Compare Brennan v. Engineered Prods., Inc., 506 F.2d 299, 303 n.2 (8th Cir. 1974) *with* Lloyd v. Cessna Aircraft Co., 434 F. Supp. 4, 8 (E.D. Tenn. 1976).

[42]The Advisory Committee Notes state that a party's income tax return is generally not privileged. Fed. R. Civ. P. 26(b), Notes of Advisory Comm. — 1970 Amendments. However, courts have held that a party's interest in privacy outweighs the other party's discovery interests, Wiesenberger v. W.E. Hutton & Co., 35 F.R.D. 556, 557 (S.D.N.Y. 1964).

may not match your adversaries' doubts. Ask and you may receive.

Second, you can ask only for those things you have the time and finances to pursue. Your time and your client's finances will determine the practical extent of discovery in a case. The theoretical scope of discovery will be limited by the actualities of economics and strategy. If you ask for something, you need to consider the costs involved in your taking the time necessary to follow through and read or decipher information, or to spend the day perusing files of materials. The availability of support staff and the strengths and weaknesses of a case will also determine the extent of discovery. The peculiarities of the adversary system as applied to a case will also affect discovery. Local restrictions on the number of interrogatories, the termination of discovery at a set time before trial, and the scope of pretrial conference orders may affect what is requested.

Third, you can ask for information you intend to obtain through court order if your request is refused by the opposing attorney. Most judges, when confronted with the issue of whether to allow something to be discovered, permit such discovery — for several reasons. One, the rules clearly favor liberal disclosures, and judges like to follow the rules. Two, reported opinions allowing discovery outnumber cases prohibiting discovery, and judges like to go with the numbers. Three, an attorney who takes the time and effort to prepare a motion, memorandum, and proposed order, all for some bit of information, must be convinced that he or she is right and must really want the information. Judges will respect that conviction and may not want to second-guess that judgment. Four, courts recognize that the value of the information sought usually outweighs the burden discovery places on the responding party, and courts like to weigh things. Five, there is less likelihood of being reversed on appeal if discovery is permitted than if it is not permitted, and judges do not like to think themselves wrong. Seek and you may find.

§1.5   PRIVILEGE

§1.5.1   Analysis

Rule 26(b)(1) explicitly declares privileged matter to be non-discoverable. Privilege in discovery contexts is the same as that defined by the rules of evidence.[1] No general privilege secures a person from providing information, but the law of evidence has established specific privileges that permit a person to withhold information in certain reasonably well-defined circumstances. What is and what is not privileged for discovery purposes is defined by constitutional provisions, statutory law, common law, the rules of evidence, and cases interpreting them.

This section outlines privileged information encountered in discovery in both federal and state proceedings. Detailed analysis of federal case law, state decisional and statutory laws, and uniform rules on privileges appear in considerable detail elsewhere,[2] so our purpose is to summarize the status of federal and state law privileges in order to inform you regarding proper discovery requests and responses.

The existence of a privilege is one of the few claims that will legitimately stonewall discovery inquiries. Attorneys therefore need to become familiar with the limits of privilege to determine just what information can properly be sought and when objections and refusals to respond can properly be interposed. But familiarity can be difficult to achieve because the law of privileges seems to be constantly developing. There is no common agreement defining the present status of privileges, and this lack of consensus compounds the confusion surrounding many privileges.

The rule of privilege provides protection to communications occurring in privileged relationships. The following elements usually need to be present to create a privilege, though they do not apply in all situations nor to all privileges:

1. The communication must originate in confidence with an understanding that the information will not be disclosed;
2. The element of confidentiality must be essential to a full and satisfactory maintenance of a relationship between individuals or must serve a vital governmental or public need;
3. This relationship or need must be one which in the opinion of the community ought to be fostered;
4. The injury that would occur by disclosure must outweigh any

§1.5 [1]Mitchell v. Roma, 265 F.2d 633, 636 (3d Cir. 1959).

[2]J. Weinstein & M. Berger, Weinstein's Evidence (1980); 4 Moore's Federal Practice ¶26.60-.66 (2d ed. 1980); 8 J. Wigmore, Evidence in Trials at Common Law §§2190-2396 (McNaughton rev. 1961) (hereinafter cited as Wigmore, Evidence); 8 C. Wright & A. Miller, Federal Practice and Procedure §§2016-2034 (1970).

benefit gained by the disposition of litigation based upon the information.[3]

Courts review these and other factors in deciding the propriety of an asserted privilege.[4] The following questions and responses explore some of these factors. Not all privileges or situations will involve these questions; some circumstances will involve other criteria. These questions do, however, provide a framework for an initial analysis of the existence and applicability of a privilege.

1. *Was the information intended to be a confidential communication?* The basic rationale for privileges is the need to retain the confidential character of the information. This confidentiality must usually be present to support the existence of a privilege, although, for example, it need not be present to create a marital testimony privilege between spouses.

2. *Was the privilege properly asserted?* A party must usually refuse to reveal the information voluntarily. The disclosure of such data, even with an objection, may well constitute a waiver of the privilege. A party may not assert a privilege during discovery and plan to waive that privilege at trial.

3. *Who is the holder of the privilege?* The privilege is a personal right and usually belongs to the person who communicates the information. Some privileges will belong to someone else; for example, the informer's privilege belongs to the government. The holder can assert the privilege, and often the individual or organization who received the information can assert it on behalf of that person. For example, the client is the holder of the attorney-client privilege, and either the client, or the attorney on behalf of the client, may assert the privilege.

4. *Is the information discoverable from another source?* Information which is communicated in a confidential manner may be obtainable from another source. Data communicated to a government agency, for example, will be protected but may be obtainable or provided to another source, such as an independent investigator. An attorney may not be compelled to disclose facts his or her client has communicated, but the client may be deposed regarding such facts.

5. *Are the data discoverable through another discovery device?* Information obtainable through a discovery device that does not breach a

---

[3] 8 Wigmore, Evidence §2285 (McNaughton rev. 1961).
[4] *See* United States v. Nixon, 418 U.S. 683, 707-713 (1974).

confidence will be preferred to a method that delves into privileged matter.

6. *Does another privilege protect the data?* Information not sheltered by one privilege may be protected under another privilege. For example, the attorney-client privilege may not protect certain communications, while the privilege against self-incrimination may.

7. *Has the party claiming the privilege maintained the confidential nature of the information?* The privileged data will lose their protected status if the party claiming the privilege voluntarily discloses such information to a non-privileged source.

8. *Has the privilege been waived in whole or in part through some disclosure?* The person who holds the privilege is the one who may waive it. Inadvertent disclosure may or may not result in a waiver. Partial disclosure of the subject matter of a topic will usually constitute a waiver of the entire subject matter. Some situations will permit selective declaration of a privilege. For example, the privilege against self-incrimination may be selectively asserted.[5]

9. *Which party has the burden to establish the existence of the privilege?* The party claiming the privilege has the burden to show its existence and application through facts and persuasion.

10. *Is the motion seeking disclosure or protection properly before the court?* The party seeking disclosure will bring a Rule 37 motion. A party seeking protection will seek a Rule 26 motion. Courts, by local rule, standing order, or expectations, may require the attorneys to attempt to resolve the dispute before seeking judicial relief.

11. *Has the requesting party proved a need for the information?* The information must otherwise be discoverable under the provisions of Rule 26(b), and it may be necessary for the party seeking the information to explain why the information is needed.

12. *What are the interests of the party seeking discovery?* Usually the requesting party needs the information for the litigation. The party's interest is that of having access to information to be able to assess the case accurately and to prepare the issues for trial properly.

13. *What are the interests of the party claiming the privilege?* These interests parallel the interests in keeping certain communications confidential: to preserve the integrity of relationships or to further governmental interests. The exact interest will depend upon the particular privilege.

---

[5] *See* In re Master Key Litigation, 507 F.2d 292, 294 (9th Cir. 1974).

14. *What are the interests of the public?* Discovery and testimonial exclusionary rules and privileges contravene the fundamental principal that "the public has a right to every man's evidence."[6] A countervailing public interest may be promoted by protecting certain communications. These conflicting public interests must be weighed.

15. *Which interests prevail?* The existence and applicability of privileges will be strictly construed. Courts will create or apply them only in situations where the rationale for non-disclosure transcends the "normally predominant principle of utilizing all rational means for ascertaining truth."[7] The courts will weigh all the competing interests and decide what is protected and what must be disclosed.

16. *Have the parties provided enough information through affidavits and memos regarding the privilege?* Parties can assist judges in weighing these competing interests by providing the court with the facts of the situation and by explaining their positions.

17. *Is an in camera inspection of the privileged matter necessary?* A judge may need to review the communicated information to determine whether indeed it falls within a privileged classification. Federal Rule of Evidence 104(a) suggests this procedure may be improper in some cases, but judges will be inclined to review the allegedly privileged matter and then excise the privileged matter from the non-privileged matter.

18. *Is the privilege absolute or qualified?* The application of almost any privilege to a specific situation will render that privilege qualified and not absolute. The court determines the extent of the qualifications in its assessment of the competing interests of the parties and public.

20. *Will a protective order permitting limited disclosure protect the privileged information?* Rule 26(c) provides the court with discretion to shape an order limiting the disclosure of privileged information. This opportunity is used, for example, with some frequency regarding trade secrets.

21. *What privilege law applies? Federal common law? Federal statutory law? State law? Which state law?* Evidence Rule 501 provides the answers and case law interprets this rule.

22. *Why was this case assigned to me in the first place?*

The courts and parties will review these and other questions in determining the existence and applicability of a privilege. The following subsections explain the sources of privileges in the federal system.

---

[6]United States v. Bryan, 339 U.S. 323, 331 (1950), *quoting* 8 Wigmore, Evidence §2192 (McNaughton rev. 1961).
[7]Elkins v. United States, 364 U.S. 206, 234 (1960).

Federal Evidence Rule 501 lists the various sources of privilege for federal cases:

1. The United States Constitution;
2. Acts of Congress;
3. Rules prescribed by the Supreme Court;
4. Common law interpreted in light of reason and experience.

§1.5.2 Privilege under the United States Constitution

Privileges based upon constitutional rights include protection against self-incrimination, the right of privacy, and governmental secrecy.[8]

Non-party witnesses may refuse to disclose information if that information may incriminate them. A non-party deponent or a person responding to a subpoena duces tecum may decide not to disclose certain incriminating materials. The asserted privilege in many of these situations may well be absolute and, if so, a Rule 37 motion brought by the requesting party will be denied.

The Fifth Amendment privilege is a personal privilege; it allows a person to refuse to provide testimony or information against himself or herself. The privilege does not protect information or documents in the possession of a third party,[9] however, even including the client's attorney. Nor can the privilege be claimed by a corporation.

A party may or may not be able effectively to assert a self-incrimination privilege in a civil suit. Though a party can never be forced to waive a privilege, courts have held that a party cannot both seek affirmative relief and assert a privilege to block inquiries about those affirmative claims.[10] These holdings reflect the trial rule that a witness cannot testify on direct examination and then claim a privilege on cross-examination about matters made relevant by the direct. The trial rule is based on the rationale that a party cannot assert a privilege as a shield if the party is using the information to wield a sword.

Nevertheless, the assertion of a privilege by a plaintiff will not automatically justify dismissal of an action. While some courts have imposed such a sanction against a party who sought affirmative

[8]Campbell v. Gerrans, 592 F.2d 1054, 1056 (9th Cir. 1979).
[9]Couch v. United States, 409 U.S. 322, 328, 331 (1973).
[10]*See* Kastigar v. United States, 406 U.S. 441 (1972).

relief,[11] others have balanced the interests of the competing parties and imposed less restrictive alternatives.[12]

The right to privacy forms a more obscure penumbra of privilege rights. In practice, the right to privacy may be raised as an objection to a discovery question seeking information about a party's personal or financial matters. In theory, the right stems from a variety of constitutional provisions including the First, Fifth, and Fourteenth Amendments. In discovery, the specific area of privacy invaded depends upon the circumstances of the party and upon the specific request.

Those courts that have considered privileges based upon privacy appear to expend little effort in analyzing the precise nature of privacy rights. Instead, they labor to balance whatever those privacy rights might be with the opposition's legitimate and compelling need to obtain the information.[13] The typical balancing tests employ several factors:

1. The scope of the invasion of privacy. The broader the breach of confidentiality, the less likely the discovery will be permitted; the narrower the breach of privacy the more likely the request will be granted.
2. The needs of the opposition for the information. The more necessary the information is, the more likely it will be obtainable; the less vital it is, the less likely it will be available.
3. The status of the person or corporation claiming the privilege. If the claimant is a party, it is more likely that discovery will be allowed; if not a party, it is less likely to be allowed.
4. The availability of the information from another source. If a source is exclusive, it is more likely that the source will be required to disclose the information; if there are other sources, it is less likely that the requested source will be forced to disclose the information.
5. The specific kind of privacy invaded. The more "sacred" the right, the less likely it will be revealed; the less vital the privilege, the more likely it will be revealed. A "sacred" right might include freedom of the press and rights of reporters not to

[11]See Kisting v. Westchester Fire Ins. Co., 290 F. Supp. 141 (W.D. Wis. 1968).
[12]Campbell v. Gerrans, 592 F.2d 1054 (9th Cir. 1979).
[13]Lora v. Board of Educ. of the City of New York, 74 F.R.D. 565, 576-577 (E.D.N.Y. 1977).

divulge sources of information. A less vital interest might be confidential financial records.

Discovery that has sought access to government information has been opposed by the governmental claims of constitutional privileges. Typical claims include military secrets, executive privilege, and state secrets. The Supreme Court has recognized that these claims are not absolute.[14] Such information is discoverable under limited circumstances and can be protected through the provisions of a protective order.[15]

§1.5.3   Privilege under Acts of Congress and State Legislatures

Congress and state legislatures have adopted and will continue to adopt statutes creating privileges in certain specific situations. Many of these statutes do not directly create an evidentiary privilege, but rather prohibit governmental agencies or employees from disclosing reported information to individuals or the general public. Specific categories include: accident reports, trade secrets, confidential information, statistics, "insider" information, immunity, information about national defense and security, and the privacy and identity of the reporter of the information. These privileges are usually qualified and not absolute; some but not all such information may be discoverable.[16]

§1.5.4   Privilege under Supreme Court Rules

The United States Supreme Court and state supreme courts have promulgated rules that restrict the disclosure of information. Various sections of the Federal Rules of Civil Procedure restrict the disclosure of discovery information in a way parallel to the characteristics of a privilege. Rule 26(b)(3) limits the scope of discovery involving trial preparation materials and work product. Rule 26(b)(4) restricts dis-

[14]United States v. Nixon, 418 U.S. 683, 712 (1974).
[15]Dellums v. Powell, 561 F.2d 242 (D.C. Cir. 1977).
[16]*See* Association for Women in Science v. Califano, 566 F.2d 339, 346 (D.C. Cir. 1977).

coverable information concerning experts. Rule 26(c) provides a court with discretion to protect a party from any discovery causing annoyance, embarrassment, oppression, or undue burden or expense. Rule 35, which provides for physical and mental examinations of parties, operates as a waiver of the common law physician-patient privilege. State civil procedure rules have similar provisions.

These rules cannot be properly identified as privileges, but they have been described as providing "qualified immunity from discovery."[17] By whatever name, they continue to restrict certain types of information from disclosure.

§1.5.5 Common Law Privileges

Federal Rule of Evidence 501 establishes privileges based on "the common law as interpreted by the courts of the United States in the light of reason and experience." In 1972 the Supreme Court submitted to Congress a number of specific privileges contained in its proposed Rule 501 to create a detailed set of privilege rules and standards. Congress decided not to enact these specific privileges because the legislators, lawyers, commentators, and evidence experts could not agree about which privileges should be created, codified, modified, or eliminated. Congress instead adopted Rule 501 "to provide the courts with flexibility to develop rules of privileges on a case-by-case basis."[18] The proposals contained in Rules 502 through 513, even though rejected by Congress, have significant effect on this development. These proposed rules act as "standards" that federal courts may employ as "comprehensive guide[s] to the federal law of privileges."[19]

Federal courts are also free to reject the suggestions contained in the proposed rules. The Supreme Court did so in *Trammel v. United States* by redefining the scope of the husband-wife privilege.[20]

The following subsections summarize the extent of the attorney-client privilege specifically and outline the status of other specific privileges derived from these proposed rules and from common law, state statutes, and state decisional law.

---

[17]Kirkland v. Morton Salt Co., 46 F.R.D. 28, 30 (N.D. Ga. 1968).
[18]Trammel v. United States, 445 U.S. 40, 47 (1980).
[19]Weinstein's Evidence ¶501[03] at 501-28.
[20]445 U.S. 40 (1980).

§1.5.6   Attorney-Client Privilege

The attorney-client privilege is the oldest of the privileges involving confidential communications. The privilege encourages "full and frank communication between attorneys and their clients and promote[s] broader public interests in the observance of law and administration of justice." It recognizes that "sound legal advice or advocacy . . . depends upon the lawyer being fully informed by the client."[21] The privilege exists between a client and his, her, or its attorney. A client has a privilege to refuse to disclose and to prevent any other person from disclosing confidential communications with a lawyer or a representative of the lawyer. The character of this privilege raises several questions regarding the applicability and extension:

1. *Is the information that is communicated privileged?* No. A client can be questioned about what he or she knows, even though that knowledge has been communicated to his or her lawyer, unless, of course, there exists another claim of privilege, such as self-incrimination. The mere fact that a client communicates certain information to an attorney does not enshroud that information with the privilege. "The privilege only protects disclosure of communications; it does not protect disclosure of the underlying facts by those who communicated with the attorney."[22] "For example, the client may not be asked a question: 'What did you tell your attorney about the amount claimed as a business expense?' But he may be asked the question, 'Did you spend the amount claimed as a business expense for meals or for travel?' " As one court has stated, "The client cannot be compelled to answer the question, 'What did you say or write to the attorney?' but may not refuse to disclose any relevant fact within his knowledge merely because he incorporated a statement of such fact into his communication to his attorney."[23] The form of the discovery question affects the application of the privilege.

2. *Does the privilege extend to the identity of a client?* Not normally.[24] But the identity of a client is usually privileged if disclosure would implicate the client.

3. *Does the privilege cover fee arrangements between an attorney and a*

---

[21]Upjohn Co. v. United States, 449 U.S. 383 (1981).
[22]Upjohn Co. v. United States, 449 U.S. 383, 395 (1981).
[23]City of Philadelphia v. Westinghouse Elec. Corp., 205 F. Supp. 830, 831 (E.D. Pa. 1962), *quoted with approval,* in Upjohn Co. v. United States, 449 U.S. 383, 395-396 (1981).
[24]United States v. Hodge & Zweig, 548 F.2d 1347, 1353 (9th Cir. 1977).

client? Not usually.[25] But the privilege will protect such fee information to avoid incriminating the client.

4. *Are written communications privileged?* Yes, to the extent that any of the contents are privileged.[26] The mere transfer of any materials or documents or tangible things from a client to his or her lawyer does not render these items confidential. A Rule 34 request for production will compel the production of factual documents whether they are in the attorney's possession or the client's possession.

5. *Are communications by the lawyer privileged?* Yes, if the requirements of the rule are fulfilled.[27] The privilege normally extends both to the client's communication and to the attorney's response and advice.[28] The mere communicating of legal advice does not preclude that legal theorizing from being discovered. Rules 33 and 36 permit discovery concerning matters which relate the law to the facts involved.

6. *Are acts of the client that are observed by his or her attorney privileged?* Usually. Information communicated in any form will be privileged as long as the other facets of the privilege rule are met. The act of rolling up a sleeve to show a lawyer a hidden scar is part and parcel of the privileged communication.[29]

7. *Does the privilege extend to communications inadvertently overheard by eavesdroppers?* Perhaps. The client may be able to invoke the privilege to prevent testimony by a third person who overhears a communication intended to be confidential.[30]

8. *Who may claim the privilege?* The privilege belongs to and is for the benefit of the client, not the attorney. The client determines when the privilege is to be asserted or waived. The attorney typically raises it on behalf of the client.[31]

9. *What is the status of the privilege with regard to corporate clients?* This question has not been authoritatively answered. A corporate client functions differently from an individual client, and this fact affects communications and confidentiality. Corporations have many individuals of different status with relevant information about a case;

[25]*See* United States v. Ponder, 475 F.2d 37, 39 (5th Cir. 1973).

[26]Colton v. United States, 306 F.2d 633, 639 (2d Cir.), *cert. denied,* 371 U.S. 951 (1962).

[27]Mead Data Central, Inc. v. United States Dept. of the Air Force, 566 F.2d 242, 254 & n.25 (D.C. Cir. 1977).

[28]Upjohn Co. v. United States, 449 U.S. 383 (1981).

[29]McCormick's Evidence §89, at 183 (1972).

[30]*See* McCormick's Evidence §75 (1972).

[31]United States v. Baskes, 442 F. Supp. 322, 327 (N.D. Ill. 1977).

much of this information involves both business and legal concerns; and many of the corporate agents, as well as the employees, may be eyewitnesses to an event. Courts have faced these problems and have developed a number of alternative approaches to apply the attorney-client privilege to corporate clients:

1. *The unlimited approach.* All confidential communications between a corporate officer, employee, or director with an attorney create a privilege.[32]
2. *The subject-matter test.* Communications are privileged if (a) an employee makes the communication at the direction of his or her supervisor, and (b) the subject matter is related to the employee's job duties.[33]
3. *The modified subject-matter test.* Five requirements must be met to establish the attorney-client corporate privilege under this approach:
   (a) The communication is made for the purpose of securing legal advice;
   (b) The employee making the communication does so with the direction of his or her corporate superior;
   (c) The superior makes the request so that the corporation could secure legal advice;
   (d) The subject matter of the communication is within the scope of the employee's corporate duties; and
   (e) The communication is not disseminated beyond those persons who, because of the corporate structure, need to know its contents.[34]
4. *The Upjohn approach.* The Supreme Court recently reviewed the corporate client privilege and declined to establish a firm rule concerning its scope.[35] The decision rejected lower-court decisions that attempted to restrict the scope of the privilege, but it did not delineate specific factors. The communications protected by the Court were matters within the employee's corporate duties and were elicited through confidential interviews with lawyers. The concurring opinion of Chief Justice Burger suggested the following detailed criteria as creating a privilege:

[32]United States v. United Shoe Mach. Corp., 89 F. Supp. 357, 358 (D. Mass. 1950).
[33]Harper & Row Publishers, Inc. v. Decker, 423 F.2d 487, 492 (7th Cir. 1970).
[34]Diversified Indus., Inc. v. Meredith, 572 F.2d 596, 609 (8th Cir. 1978).
[35]Upjohn Co. v. United States, 449 U.S. 383 (1981).

The attorney must be one authorized by the management to inquire into the subject and must be seeking information to assist counsel in performing any of the following functions: (a) evaluating whether the employee's conduct has bound or would bind the corporation; (b) assessing the legal consequences, if any, of that conduct; or (c) formulating appropriate legal responses to actions that have been or may be taken by others with regard to that conduct.[36]

10. *In what situations will the privilege not exist?* No privilege arises in situations in which a client seeks legal advice to commit a crime or fraud, an attorney commits malpractice, or a client fails to pay an attorney for professional services.[37]

11. *When does the attorney-client privilege terminate?* The privilege lasts forever; it survives even after the attorney-client relationship ends. The privilege also extends beyond the client's death. The client or a personal representative may waive all or part of the privileged communications. Certain conduct by a client will also operate as a waiver; for example, a client who reviews documents to refresh recollection waives the privilege as to those documents.[38]

§1.5.7 Other Specific Privileges

The following privileges apply in the various situations that give rise to confidential communications. Not all these privileges are recognized by all jurisdictions. The privileges designated 1 through 9 below represent the more commonly accepted privileges in federal and state courts. The remaining privileges represent situations that act as a bar to disclosure in some state jurisdictions.

1. Marital spousal privileges are of two types: a privilege not to testify against a spouse regarding any information, and a privilege not to disclose confidential communications between

---

[36]Upjohn Co. v. United States, 449 U.S. 383, 403 (1981) (Burger, C.J., concurring), *citing with approval* Diversified Indus., Inc. v. Meredith, 572 F.2d 596 (8th Cir. 1978), *and* Harper & Row Publishers, Inc. v. Decker, 423 F.2d 487 (7th Cir. 1970).

[37]*See* In re Doe, 551 F.2d 899, 900–901 (2d Cir. 1977).

[38]Bailey v. Meister Brau, Inc., 57 F.R.D. 11, 13 (N.D. Ill. 1972).

spouses. The former privilege as recently defined by the Supreme Court for federal cases is available only to the witness spouse and the other spouse can neither compel nor foreclose testimony.[39] The interspousal privilege affords protections to confidential marital communications and neither spouse can disclose such information without the consent of the other.[40]

2. Communications with clergy will be deemed privileged to protect the confidence of the disclosures.[41]

3. Trade secrets and other confidential business communications will be protected by privileged status.[42]

4. Political vote privileges protect a voter from disclosing his or her vote.[43]

5. The required-report privilege protects the confidentiality of reports and returns required by law to be filed with the government.[44]

6. Governmental privileges exist for (a) military, diplomatic, and state secrets, (b) governmental opinions and recommendations, (c) investigatory law enforcement files, (d) and freedom-of-information exemptions.[45]

7. The identity of an informer will also be protected by a privilege.[46]

8. A general physician-patient privilege has been created by case law and statute. Many exceptions to this privilege have been developed that narrow the privilege severely.[47]

9. A limited psychotherapist-patient privilege covers confidential personal revelations of a patient.[48]

10. An optometrist-patient privilege operates similarly to the physician-patient privileges.[49]

---

[39]Trammel v. United States, 445 U.S. 40, 53 (1980).
[40]Trammel v. United States, 445 U.S. 40, 51 (1980).
[41]Wolfe v. United States, 291 U.S. 7, 14 (1934).
[42]Advisory Committee's Note to Proposed Evidence Rule 508, 56 F.R.D. 248 (1973).
[43]8 Wigmore, Evidence §2214, at 163–164 (McNaughton rev. 1961).
[44]Association for Women in Science v. Califano, 566 F.2d 339, 344 (D.C. Cir. 1977).
[45]See McCormick's Evidence §107 (1972).
[46]Carl Zeiss Stiftung v. V.E.B. Carl Zeiss, Jena, 40 F.R.D. 318, 331 (D.D.C. 1966), aff'd, 384 F.2d 979 (D.C. Cir.), cert. denied, 389 U.S. 952 (1967).
[47]See United States v. Meagher, 531 F.2d 752, 753 (5th Cir. 1976).
[48]Standard 504 contained in proposed Fed. R. Evid. 504.
[49]Rev. Wash. Code §18.53.200 (1980).

11.   The hospital-and-medical-review-committee privilege is applicable to staff discussions evaluating the adequacy of provisions for hospital care.[50]

12.   A grand-jury privilege provides protection and secrecy to grand-jury testimony.[51]

13.   The teacher-pupil privilege restricts disclosures of communications between teachers and their students.[52]

14.   The social service and juvenile workers and children privilege protects communications between probation and welfare workers and juveniles.[53]

15.   A counselor-pupil privilege applies to communications between licensed counselors and school students.[54]

16.   An accountant-client privilege applies to communications between a professional accountant and his or her client.[55]

17.   A scholar's privilege has been recognized in federal court decisions to promote the free flow of confidential information and sources necessary to scholarly research.[56]

18.   Tax returns enjoy a qualified privilege, protecting against disclosure, unless such information is vital and unavailable from any other source.[57]

19.   Business privileges protect confidential business contracts, customer lists, and other business matters.[58]

20.   A judicial privilege protects persons engaged in judicial decisionmaking processes (including governmental officials and judges and juries) from disclosing the mental processes employed in formulating judgments.[59]

21.   Qualified privileges exist for news sources, usually based on "shield" laws or First Amendment protections.[60] Editorial

[50]Bredice v. Doctors Hosp., Inc. 50 F.R.D. 249 (D.D.C. 1970).
[51]Rev. Wash. Code §10.27.090 (1980).
[52]Nev. Rev. Stat. §49.291 (1973).
[53]N.M.R. Evid. 509.
[54]Nev. Rev. Stat. §49.290 (1973).
[55]Couch v. United States, 409 U.S. 322 (1973).
[56]United States v. I.B.M. Corp., 83 F.R.D. 92 (S.D.N.Y. 1979).
[57]Federal Sav. & Loan Ins. Corp. v. Krueger, 55 F.R.D. 512 (N.D. Ill. 1972).
[58]See Maritime Cinema Serv. Corp. v. Movies EN Route, Inc., 60 F.R.D. 587 (S.D.N.Y. 1973).
[59]These persons may have to disclose factual matters. Standard Packaging Corp. v. Curwood Inc., 365 F. Supp. 134, 136 (N.D. Ill. 1973).
[60]See, e.g., 12 Okla. Stat. Ann. §2506 (1980); Branzburg v. Hayes, 408 U.S. 665 (1972).

processes and mental impressions have been held discoverable in libel cases.[61]

§1.6   INSURANCE AGREEMENTS

Rule 26(b)(2) clearly allows the discovery of insurance policies and provisions:

> *Insurance Agreements.* A party may obtain discovery of the existence and contents of any insurance agreement under which any person carrying on an insurance business may be liable to satisfy part or all of a judgment which may be entered in the action or to indemnify or reimburse for payments made to satisfy the judgment. Information concerning the insurance agreement is not by reason of disclosure admissible in evidence at trial. For purposes of this paragraph, an application for insurance shall not be treated as part of an insurance agreement.

Yes, Santa Claus is discoverable. What are the reasons for this? (1) Because insurance is an asset created specifically to satisfy the claim; (2) because the insurance company ordinarily controls the litigation; (3) because information about coverage is available only from defendant or his insurer; and (4) because disclosure does not involve a significant invasion of privacy.[1]

These rationales do not extend to other potential assets of a party. Other assets that may be available to satisfy a judgment become a proper subject for discovery only after a trial in a supplementary proceeding to enforce the judgment.[2] Insurance coverage differs from other assets because it is the insurance carrier and not the insured who coordinates and controls the defense of claims, and because all attorneys in the action will be able to make a realistic appraisal of a case based upon the facts and not upon speculation. The amount of coverage will affect the timing of settlement and the avoidance of unneces-

[61]Herbert v. Lando, 441 U.S. 153 (1979).
§1.6 [1]Fed. R. Civ. P. 26(b)(2), Notes of Advisory Comm. — 1970 Amendments, reprinted in 28 U.S.C.A. 155.
[2]K. Sinclair, Federal Civil Practice 539 (1980).

sary litigation. A moderate coverage policy will encourage a settlement not exceeding its limits. A large coverage policy may delay a reasonable settlement. Money has a way of strengthening the merits of some cases.

A series of interrogatory questions will usually uncover information about the existence of insurance. A Rule 34 request for production will reveal the policy itself. These discovery requests should be routine questions in all cases. Why? Because insurance policies may provide coverage. Homeowners' policies are a particularly fertile ground for the imaginative attorney to reap benefits for his or her client. Other insurance policies may have funds available for unusual circumstances. That's why.

§1.7 TRIAL PREPARATION MATERIALS

§1.7.1 Introduction

Courts over the past decades have considered discovery requests seeking the disclosure of every imaginable type of information. Cases considering these requests include the seminal decision of *Hickman v. Taylor*,[1] which spawned the "work-product" doctrine. Subsequent judicial decisions developed the scope of work product by applying other doctrines such as "qualified privilege," "good cause," "relevancy," and "litigation materials."[2] The 1970 amendments to the discovery rules codified some of these decisions and created the "trial preparation materials" rule.

There continues to exist a fair amount of confusion regarding what is and what is not discoverable from efforts made and materials prepared in anticipation of litigation or for trial. This confusion stems in part from the use and misuse of various terms, including *work product.* This term means different things to different lawyers, judges, and

_____

§1.7   [1]329 U.S. 495 (1947).

[2]The Supreme Court has declared the trial preparation work-product doctrine a qualified privilege. United States v. Nobles, 422 U.S. 225, 237-238 (1975). Circuit and district court judges frequently fail to define precisely or accurately the doctrine they employ to allow or restrict discovery. See Fed. R. Civ. P. 26(b)(3), Notes of Advisory Comm. — 1970 Amendments.

justices.[3] The Supreme Court has contributed both to the continuing vitality of the work-product doctrine and to the confusion surrounding its definition. The Court in a recent review of the work-product rule stated that the doctrine "has been *substantially* incorporated in Federal Rule of Civil Procedure 26(b)(3)" and then only 47 words later stated that "Rule 26(b)(3) *codifies* the work-product doctrine."[4] It is indeed fair to ask: Which is it?

This section will avoid such confusion by employing the terminology defined in Rule 26(b)(3) and by avoiding other terms manufactured by well-meaning jurists and commentators. This rule does not contain the phrases *good cause* or *work product*. We begin with a true/-false analysis of this matrix and continue with an elaboration of Rule 26 provisions.

True or False?

1. Trial Preparation materials are documents and tangible things prepared in anticipation of litigation or for trial.

True. Anyone who can think knows that.

2. Trial preparation materials are discoverable only upon a showing of substantial need and undue hardship under Rule 26.

True. Anyone who can read knows that.

3. Documents and tangible things not trial preparation materials are discoverable through a Rule 34 request.

Maybe. Maybe not. Some documents and tangible things may not be discoverable because they are irrelevant or privileged. Other documents and tangible things will be discoverable merely for the asking.

4. Documents containing the written impressions, conclusions, opinions and legal theories of an attorney are never discoverable through discovery.

True. Period.

5. A party or witness cannot obtain a copy of a statement made by that party or witness.

False.

---

[3]The term *work product* was coined in the argument of the Hickman v. Taylor case before the Third Circuit. The Court of Appeals thought the phrase accurately described what the court held to be excluded from discovery. Hickman v. Taylor, 153 F.2d 212, 223 (3d Cir. 1945).

[4]Upjohn Co. v. United States, 449 U.S. 383, 398-399 (1981) (emphasis added).

6. Witness statements and investigative file materials are not discoverable.

Some are. Some are not. It depends.

Rule 26(b)(3)

[A] party may obtain discovery of documents and tangible things otherwise discoverable . . .

This provision limits the scope of the rule to the disclosure of written documents or tangible things. Other forms of discovery requests are not covered. Some materials will not be discoverable because they may be irrelevant as defined by Rule 26(b)(1) or because they contain privileged matter. A Rule 34 request will produce all other documents or tangible objects unless they are trial preparation materials.

. . . prepared in anticipation of litigation or for trial for that party or by or for that party's representative (including his attorney, consultant, surety, indemnitor, insurer, or agent) . . .

This clause is the rule's definition of trial preparation materials. The definition seems circular: trial preparation materials are materials prepared for trial or in anticipation of litigation. The definition includes materials comprising a case file, including investigation matters, witness statements, file memos, letter correspondence, legal memoranda, lawyer and staff notes, client communications, trial notebooks, and other documents and tangible things. The rule itself does not detail criteria that determine which of these materials will be classified as trial preparation materials in a particular case. Case law has developed factors that, when applied, determine the nature of the materials. These factors can be categorized into three questions:

WHO assembled the materials?

WHEN were the materials gathered?

WHY were the materials collected and for whom?

These three factors are not independent of each other. A court may consider all three factors in determining whether some requests seek trial preparation materials or may decide that one of the factors controls the fate of the materials.

The WHO. The key figure is the lawyer. The presence or involvement of an attorney in the investigation process is a significant factor in classifying the materials. The presence of a lawyer is not a requirement; documents created and gathered by non-lawyers may be trial preparation materials;[7] the involvement of an attorney does not automatically convert materials into trial preparation matters.[8] However, the inclusion of a lawyer may cause materials to be considered to have been prepared in anticipation of litigation.[9]

The WHEN. The time when materials were prepared will affect their classification. Materials gathered during litigation usually become trial preparation materials. Documents and tangible things prepared after a cause of action has arisen but before litigation has been initiated may or may not be trial preparation matters.[10] Materials assembled before the maturation of a legal claim may be trial preparation materials depending upon how imminent the claim was and upon the timing of subsequent litigation.[11]

The WHY. The Federal Advisory Committee Notes add some gloss to the definition of trial preparation materials by excluding three categories of materials according to their assembled purpose: (1) materials assembled "pursuant to public requirements," (2) materials assembled in the "ordinary course of business," and, naturally, (3) materials assembled "for nonlitigation purposes."[12] The first category excludes as trial preparation materials documents that are prepared under a duty pursuant to statute or regulation.[13] The second category eliminates materials because the inherent nature of a business or activity makes such preparation useful or necessary regardless of the existence of litigation or because such materials are customarily collected other than for litigation.[14] The third category by definition excludes materials if the reason they were collected was for a non-litigation purpose.

Need the non-litigation purpose be the primary reason why the materials were gathered? A significant reason? A secondary reason? The answer to these questions has not yet been definitively provided by case law. The "primary purpose" reason appears to be more con-

---

[7]*See* Bredice v. Doctors Hosp., Inc., 50 F.R.D. 249, 251 (D.D.C. 1970).

[8]*See* 4 Moore's Federal Practice ¶26.64[3] (2d ed. Cum. Supp. 1980).

[9]*See* Thomas Organ Co. v. Jadranska Slobodna Plovidba, 54 F.R.D. 367 (N.D. Ill. 1972).

[10]Spaulding v. Denton, 68 F.R.D. 342, 346 (D. Del. 1975).

[11]*See* McDougall v. Dunn, 468 F.2d 468 (4th Cir. 1972).

[12]Fed. R. Civ. P. 26(b)(3), Notes of Advisory Comm. — 1970 Amendments, reprinted in 28 U.S.C.A. 156.

[13]Galambus v. Consolidated Freightways Corp., 64 F.R.D. 468, 472 (N.D. Ind. 1974).

[14]Thomas Organ Co. v. Jadranska Slobodna Plovidba, 54 F.R.D. 367, 371 (N.D. Ill. 1972).

sistent with other provisions of Rule 26 than the other reasons. One indicium of a non-litigation purpose is the tone of the materials: are they impartial and without an adversarial tone? The more partisan the materials are, the more likely they will be declared trial preparation materials.

> [All trial preparation materials will be discoverable only] upon a showing that the party seeking discovery has substantial need of the materials in the preparation of his case and that he is unable without undue hardship to obtain the substantial equivalent of the materials by other means. . . .

A party now has the burden to demonstrate both "substantial need" and "undue hardship" to obtain access to trial preparation materials. A requesting party must first show substantial need by demonstrating that the materials are very important to the preparation of the case,[15] and then showing that the substantial equivalent cannot be obtained without undue hardship. This latter factor has been met in a number of situations. Courts have ordered trial preparation documents to be disclosed when witnesses became unavailable,[16] memories of witnesses faded over time,[17] reports were made contemporaneously with or shortly after an event,[18] witnesses became hostile and antagonistic,[19] or the opposing party possessed surveillance films made of a party.[20]

Courts have ruled that parties fail to demonstrate substantial need and undue hardship if witness statements could be obtained from other sources, such as personal interviews and depositions.[21] The cases that have reviewed requests for trial preparation materials have involved the disclosure of witness statements and correspondence between parties' employees or agents,[22] but not other materials from investigative files. This is because practitioners seek to obtain witness statements and party correspondence rather than other file materials,

[15]Rackers v. Siegfried, 54 F.R.D. 24, 26 (W.D. Mo. 1971).
[16]See Hilton v. Contiship Corp., 16 F.R.D. 453 (S.D.N.Y. 1954).
[17]Teribery v. Norfolk & Western Ry., 68 F.R.D. 46, 48 (W.D. Pa. 1975).
[18]See Gillman v. United States, 53 F.R.D. 316, 319 (S.D.N.Y. 1971).
[19]Mitchell v. Bass, 252 F.2d 513, 518 (8th Cir. 1958); see also Xerox Corp. v. I.B.M. 64 F.R.D. 367 (S.D.N.Y. 1974).
[20]Snead v. American Export-Isbrandtsen Lines, Inc., 59 F.R.D. 148, 151 (E.D. Pa. 1973).
[21]United States v. Chatham City Corp., 72 F.R.D. 640 (S.D. Ga. 1976).
[22]See 4 Moore's Federal Practice ¶26.64[4] (2d ed. 1980).

perceiving that they stand little chance of obtaining other categories of trial preparation materials.

§1.7.2 Witness Statements

Rule 26(b)(3) explicitly makes two types of statements discoverable merely for the asking and without having to show substantial need and undue hardship: (1) a party can obtain his or her own statement from another party; (2) a witness can obtain a copy of his or her statement from any party. This provision of the rule also defines a statement as either "a written statement signed or otherwise adopted or approved by the person making it," or as "a stenographic, mechanical, electrical, or other recording, or a transcription thereof, which is a substantially verbatim recital of an oral statement by the person making it and contemporaneously recorded." These definitions include the following types of statements among others:

1. A statement written and signed by the party or witness;
2. A statement typed by someone else and signed by the party or witness;
3. A statement prepared by a third person and initialed by a party or witness;
4. A statement written by someone else and corrected by a party or witness;
5. A tape-recorded conversation of a party or witness interview;
6. A telephone-recorded interview of a party or witness;
7. A statement of a party or witness in the presence of a court reporter which is later transcribed;
8. Diagrams or drawings made by a party or witness.[23]

Who writes or prepares the statement is irrelevant; the party or witness need only sign, adopt, or approve it. Whether the party or witness is aware of being recorded is irrelevant for purposes of this rule. Whether the statement is made in anticipation of trial or not is also irrelevant.

Investigation decisions determine whether a party or witness statement falls within one or the other categories of this rule. If a recorded

[23]Parker v. Carroll, 20 Fed. R. Serv. 2d 698, 700-701 (D.D.C. 1974).

statement is made during an interview, that statement or a later transcript becomes discoverable. If a recorded statement is not made, a written statement can be prepared after the interview and later signed, adopted, or approved by the witness, making it discoverable. It is an important tactic to decide whether a statement should be preserved and whether it should be preserved in a form that becomes discoverable. This decision will depend upon a myriad of factors in a case, including the type of witness (friendly, neutral, or adverse), the timing of the statement, the purpose for the statement, and other discovery options.

A party who seeks to obtain his or her witness statement from an opponent is entitled as a matter of right under the rules to a copy of any statements that he or she made. All other statements can be obtained from an opponent (unless voluntarily disclosed) only after a showing of need and hardship. Likewise, a litigant can obtain a copy of any witness statement from a witness by persuading the witness to request a copy from an opposing party and then to give a copy of the statement to the litigant.

Certain information obtained from witnesses may not be discoverable. Oral statements made to an attorney by a witness contained in the lawyer's notes and memoranda are not discoverable. The Supreme Court recently declared this information protected as part of "the attorney's mental processes in evaluating the communications."[24]

§1.7.3 Attorney Mental Processes

Some materials are exempt from disclosure. Rule 26(b)(3) provides in part that "the court shall protect against disclosure of the mental impressions, conclusions, opinions, or legal theories of an attorney or other representative of a party concerning the litigation."

This portion of the rule explicitly defines and protects specific categories of trial preparation materials. These categories reflect the holding of the Supreme Court in *Hickman v. Taylor,* which declared secure the mental impressions and beliefs of an attorney.[25] This doctrine protects the effectiveness of the lawyer's work by preserving such materials from discovery. No showing of substantial need or undue hardship will justify its disclosure.

[24]Upjohn Co. v. United States, 449 U.S. 383, 401(1981).
[25]Hickman v. Taylor, 329 U.S. 495, 509-512 (1947).

The "mental impressions" of an attorney need to be distinguished from trial preparation materials and privileged matter. Material that includes factual information, as distinguished from opinion, is trial preparation material discoverable upon a showing of substantial need and undue hardship, whereas the attorney's opinion remains exempt from discovery. Matters discussed between an attorney and a client may be privileged under the attorney-client privilege, whereas mental impressions of an attorney remain protected through Rule 26(b)(3).

Applying the protections of Rule 26 raises three questions:

1. *Is this protection absolute?* No one knows. The Supreme Court recently faced this exact question and declined to answer it. The Court, in *Upjohn Co. v. United States,* did hold that an attorney's mental impressions "cannot be disclosed simply on a showing of substantial need and inability to obtain the equivalent without undue hardship."[26] The Court left open the question whether attorneys' mental impressions may be discoverable in rare situations.

There are limits placed upon an attorney's ability to create exempt materials. One court held that an attorney cannot protect a verbatim witness statement from disclosure by including its text in an evaluative memorandum prepared for litigation.[27] Another court held that an attorney's involvement in creating information does not automatically convert such data into exempt information. One party sought to discover the calculations of damages in a case, and the responding party refused to disclose the calculations, claiming that the information contained attorneys' work efforts. The court rejected this position, stating that even though lawyers developed the information, the damage calculations must be disclosed because that information would be presented at trial.[28] This analysis is consistent with other cases, which declare factual information to be discoverable even if gathered through attorney's efforts.

2. *Does this protection extend to non-written, intangible matters?* While Rule 26(b)(3) explicitly exempts written mental impressions, opinions, conclusions, and legal theories from discovery, Rules 33 and 36 expressly permit the discovery of interrogatory information and admissions relating to the application of law to fact. A Rule 34 request

---

[26]Upjohn Co. v. United States, 449 U.S. 383, 401(1981).

[27]Mervin v. FTC, 591 F.2d 821, 825 (D.C. Cir. 1978).

[28]Wheeling-Pittsburgh Steel Corp. v. Underwriters Laboratories, Inc., 81 F.R.D. 8, 12 (N.D. Ill. 1978).

seeking documents may be properly objected to as requesting materials that are exempt from discovery. An attorney may be obligated to disclose some opinions and legal theories in response to interrogatories under Rule 33(b), but will be entitled to maintain the confidentiality of those memos and documents containing this information which are prepared for internal use.[29]

Case law has extended the protection afforded a lawyer's mental impressions, opinions, conclusions, and legal theories to oral deposition requests. Courts have established certain guidelines detailing the scope of deposition questioning of a deponent. Those guidelines prohibited questions about any matter that revealed "counsel's mental impression" concerning the case, including specific areas and general lines of inquiry discussed by opposing counsel with the deponent, and any facts to which opposing counsel appeared to have attached particular significance during conversations with the deponent.[30]

The Supreme Court in *Upjohn* appears to make no distinction between the forms of the attorney's mental impressions as affecting their discoverability. The materials sought to be discovered in *Upjohn* were notes and memoranda made of oral witness interviews.[31] The Court protected these materials because they revealed attorney's mental processes. The rationale underlying this protection would apply to discovery requests seeking to reveal the attorney's memory of the oral interviews, including interrogatories and depositions.

3. *Can this protection be waived?* Some situations will require the disclosure of protected information. One situation involves the subject matter of a lawsuit. If the mental processes of an attorney are an issue in a case, such as in a legal malpractice case, they will be discoverable. Another situation involves waiver by the statements or conduct of the client or of the attorney acting for the client.

Case law has restricted the extent of waivers by holding that the subject-matter waiver doctrine does not always apply to these protections. This doctrine declares that partial or inadvertent disclosure of some information constitutes a waiver of all information relating to the subject matter.[32] The subject-matter doctrine does apply to the attorney-client privilege and to trial preparation materials that do not con-

---

[29]*See* Natta v. Hogan, 392 F.2d 686, 693 (10th Cir. 1968).
[30]Ford v. Philips Elec. Instruments Co., 82 F.R.D. 359, 360-361 (E.D. Pa. 1979).
[31]Upjohn Co. v. United States, 449 U.S. 383 (1981).
[32]*See, e.g.,* Duplan Corp. v. Deering Milliken Inc., 540 F.2d 1215, 1223 (4th Cir. 1976).

tain an attorney's mental impressions, opinions, conclusions, or legal theories.[33] Courts have not applied the subject-matter waiver to mental impression materials because they have found that inadvertent or partial disclosure can be controlled and that the public policy supporting protection continues to operate even if the protection has been reduced.[34] This means that protected information could be disclosed selectively or inadvertently without constituting a waiver of the protection afforded the preserved materials.

§1.7.4 Practice Considerations

The party claiming that materials are trial preparation materials has the burden to show just that. The party who claims substantial need and undue hardship has that burden to carry. Judges who have some doubts about the status of documents and tangible things have the discretion to review such materials in camera before making a decision.[35]

In sum, the most accurate and reliable measure of the applicability of the trial preparation doctrine continues to be a reasonable and complete reading of Rule 26. This approach triggers the consideration of the following and other questions relating to trial preparation information:

Do the materials sought constitute the mental impressions, opinions, conclusions, or legal theories of an attorney or representative of the party? If so, they are protected from discovery.

Do the documents requested constitute materials prepared in anticipation of litigation or for trial? If so, they are trial preparation materials protected from discovery absent further demands by the other party.

Does the other party claim a substantial need for such materials, which can only be otherwise obtained through undue hardship? If so, such material will be discoverable excluding attorney mental processes.

Does the other party or a witness seek his or her own statement? If so, it will be discoverable.

---

[33]United States v. Nobles, 422 U.S. 225, 238-239 (1975).
[34]United States v. Nobles, 422 U.S. 225, 238-241 (1975); Duplan Corp. v. Deering Milliken Inc., 540 F.2d 1215, 1223 (4th Cir. 1976).
[35]See Hamilton v. Canal Barge Co., 395 F. Supp. 975, 978 (E.D. La. 1974).

§1.8 EXPERTS

§1.8.1 Introduction and Categories of Experts

Discovery concerning experts frequently includes discovery of their identity, their opinions, and facts known to them. Additionally, discovery may include background information on the bases for any opinions and other factors relating to what the experts know.

In understanding the rules governing discovery of experts, it is first important to understand the theoretical basis for even arguing that the materials should *not* be discoverable. The most prevalent reason for objecting to discovery of expert information is a group of vaguely related claims that expert information is privileged[1] or constitutes work product.[2] Both of these arguments have been rejected by the courts, and the discovery of expert information is now governed by the rules without reference to these doctrines, which, even in their most expansive view, do not encompass the facts and opinions held by an expert.

Another traditional reason for objecting to the discovery of expert information is that it would be fundamentally unfair to require a party to disgorge such information. The expert would be paid by one party to develop facts, opinions, and related information for use in the case, but the discovering party would then have access to that information free of charge.[3] This argument has similarly been rejected by courts, which have imposed a requirement that when expert information must be disclosed it may be proper to have the party gaining that information bear an appropriate portion of the cost of developing it.[4]

Rule 26(b)(4) now supersedes these arguments by establishing the provisions, procedures, and standards applicable to expert discovery. The rule defines who is an expert, what can be discovered from an expert and under what circumstances, and how discovery can be obtained. It establishes two categories of experts: experts a party expects to call as witnesses at trial and experts retained or specially employed

§1.8 [1]*See, e.g.,* American Oil Co. v. Pennsylvania Petroleum Prod. Co., 23 F.R.D. 680 (D.R.I. 1959).

[2]*See* Carpenter-Trent Drilling Co. v. Magnolia Petroleum Corp., 23 F.R.D. 257 (D. Neb. 1959).

[3]*See generally* 8 C. Wright & A. Miller, Federal, Practice, and Procedure §2029 (1970).

[4]*See, e.g.,* Seven-Up Bottling Co. v. United States, 39 F.R.D. 1, 2 (D. Colo. 1966).

in anticipation of litigation. The comments to the rule recognize a third category, experts informally consulted but not retained, and also a fourth category, the expert whose information was not acquired in preparation for trial, but rather, as an actor or viewer. Court decisions have created a fifth category regarding experts: the employee expert.

§1.8.2 Trial Experts

Discovery of trial experts is first limited to discovery by interrogatories, and questions relating to the identity, subject matter of the proposed testimony, facts and opinions, and grounds for the opinions to be offered. Since Rule 26(b)(4) applies only to facts known and opinions held that are acquired or developed in anticipation of litigation or for trial, the party may additionally obtain from trial experts any information that relates to background, qualifications, or bias on the part of the witness.[5]

The 26(b)(4)(A)(i) interrogatories may be the only discovery available regarding a trial witness's expert opinions. If any further discovery is sought, the 26(b)(4)(A)(i) interrogatories will be a condition precedent to obtaining that information. A party may not forego interrogatories and seek documents or depositions directly.[6] The rules have no provision for the payment of fees to the expert witness or to a party for expenses incurred in answering the interrogatories permitted under this rule. The apparent reason for not making fees awardable in this situation is that answering these interrogatories does not involve additional preparation from the expert inasmuch as the answers will be prepared by counsel based on information that should already be in the attorney's file.

If, however, additional discovery is permitted beyond the Rule 26(b)(4)(A)(i) interrogatories, then the rule makes the payment of fees and expenses appropriate. Since the mere award of expenses incurred in testifying at a deposition or answering additional interrogatories by an expert does not adequately shift the burden of developing that information to the party obtaining it, the rule will specifically permit an award of a portion of the fees expended in the development of the information. This provision seeks to eliminate any unfairness imposed

[5]*See, e.g.,* Keith v. Van Dorn Plastic Mach. Co., 29 Fed. R. Serv. 2d 671 (E.D. Pa. 1980); United States v. I.B.M. Corp., 84 F.R.D. 651 (S.D.N.Y. 1979).
[6]*See* United States v. I.B.M. Corp., 72 F.R.D. 78 (S.D.N.Y. 1976).

by one party's attempting to ride on another party's coattails in development of expert facts and opinions.

While some courts have stated that an order permitting deposition testimony beyond the fully answered interrogatories should be liberally granted upon an appropriate payment of fees,[7] other courts will require the showing of a substantial need.[8] If a deposition is permitted, it will usually proceed much as cross-examination at trial, though it will frequently be more extensive and more probing.

Rule 26(b)(4)(A)(i) requires answers to interrogatories for experts a party "expects to call" as a witness at trial. Although this phrase is not a precise one, it has not been subject to substantial litigation for a simple reason. The rule is self-enforcing in that if a witness is not disclosed or if the party refused to answer 26(b)(4)(A)(i) interrogatories relating to that expert, that witness should not be permitted to testify at trial.[9] If the interrogatories are answered, but a party feels the answers are inadequate, it is necessary to obtain an order compelling more adequate answers before expert testimony will be barred or limited at trial.[10]

The approach of Rule 26 to discovery from trial experts is not completely satisfactory. The rule does not provide standards for determining the sufficiency of the interrogatory answers it requires; it also fails to give courts any guidance to determine when additional discovery may be appropriate. In practice, courts exercise wide discretion in the area of discovery from trial experts, and attorneys also approach the matter on a case-by-case basis. It is common practice for attorneys to exchange reports from experts, or to stipulate to depositions of all parties' experts in a given case.

The response to 26(b)(4) interrogatories may also guide a court in determining whether to permit discovery of further information, such as requiring the exchange of expert reports or permitting expert depositions. An inadequate interrogatory answer invites a court-ordered deposition. Similarly, courts have been willing to order depositions of trial experts when those experts have not prepared reports or have prepared inadequate reports.[11] Some courts have stated that a deposi-

---

[7]*See, e.g.,* Herbst v. International Tel. & Tel. Corp., 65 F.R.D. 528, 530 (D. Conn. 1975).

[8]*See* Cox v. Fennelly, 40 F.R.D. 1 (S.D.N.Y. 1966).

[9]*See, e.g.,* Taggart v. Vermont Transp. Co., 32 F.R.D. 587 (E.D. Pa. 1963), *aff'd,* 325 F.2d 1022 (3d Cir. 1964).

[10]*See* A.O. Smith v. Viking Corp., 79 F.R.D. 91 (E.D. Wis. 1978).

[11]Beech-Nut Foods Corp. v. Gerber Prods. Co., 29 Fed. R. Serv. 2d 410 (E.D. Pa. 1980).

tion of an expert is not appropriate without a showing of a need for the report or deposition,[12] which in part will be reflected in the answers to the interrogatories.

§1.8.3 Retained or Specially Employed Experts

The discovery rules are substantially more restrictive of discovery from non-testifying experts. Those experts to which this restricted discovery status applies are retained or specially employed by another party in anticipation of litigation or preparation for trial. While the rule speaks of "retained" and "specially employed" experts, it does not include experts who are regular employees of a party. "Retained" means an expert hired as an independent contractor, and "specially employed" means an expert hired as a temporary employee for the case. Specially employed experts do include a full-time employee who is specially assigned to be an expert.

Before any discovery may be obtained of the facts or opinions of the non-testifying retained or specially employed expert, there must be a showing of exceptional circumstances. Rule 26(b)(4)(B) provides the courts with only a limited basis upon which to determine exceptional circumstances: circumstances must make it impracticable to obtain the facts or opinions on the same subject by any other means. Exceptional circumstances that would permit discovery include the lack of available experts because of a severely limited pool of qualified experts or the existence of an expert who has facts that could not be duplicated (such as data obtained from destructive tests of damaged material).[13] The inability to obtain the particular expert's opinions elsewhere is obviously not sufficient grounds to compel further discovery from that expert. If a party can obtain similar facts and opinions from others versed in the area involved, the courts will not order discovery from the expert.[14]

One question which has caused surprising difficulty for the courts is the question of whether the *identity* of the non-testifying retained or specially employed expert may be discovered. The rule does not specifically address this question, and the advisory committee notes shed

---

[12]*See, e.g.,* Wilson v. Resnick, 51 F.R.D. 510 (E.D. Pa. 1970).

[13]*See, e.g.,* Sanford Constr. Co. v. Kaiser Aluminum & Chem. Sales, Inc., 45 F.R.D. 465 (E.D. Ky. 1968).

[14]*See, e.g.,* Marine Petroleum Co. v. Champlin Petroleum Co., 29 Fed. R. Serv. 2d 668 (D.C. Cir. 1980).

little light on it. The notes merely state that: "as an ancillary procedure, a party may on a proper showing require the other party to name
experts retained or specially employed, but not those informally consulted."[15] The committee does not state whether the showing required
in this comment is the full showing of exceptional circumstances or
some lesser showing. The best answer to this question is that the
identity of non-testifying retained or specially employed experts is
usually discoverable. If disclosure might in itself disclose the theories
of an attorney, that attorney's mental impressions, privileged information, or irrelevant matter a strong case can be made for not requiring
that disclosure. On the other hand, in a more conventional situation,
the identity of an expert will reveal nothing other than the name itself.
Courts are reluctant to protect the identity of an expert merely because
that expert was retained and gave an opinion unsatisfactory or unfavorable to the party retaining him, which opinion that party now seeks
to protect by deciding not to call the expert.

Rule 26(b)(4)(C) requires that a party obtaining discovery from a
non-testifying, retained or specially employed expert pay the expert a
reasonable fee for time spent in responding to the discovery as well
as a fair portion of the fees and expenses previously incurred by the
party retaining the expert to develop the expert's facts and opinions.
The purpose is to minimize the unfairness of forced disclosure of
information to an adverse party, as well as compensate the expert.
These provisions reflect the adversary position that one side should
not benefit from any information gained in a "free ride" with the other
side's expert.

§1.8.4 Employee Experts

Experts who are employees of a party are treated as persons with
information under the general provision of Rule 26(b)(1) in most
cases.[16] An employee may be a specially employed expert within the
meaning of Rule 26(b)(4)(A). In order to be a specially employed
expert, the employee must be specifically hired for the litigation. In
most cases experts are part-time consultants who clearly are independent contractors and not employees.

---

[15]Fed. R. Civ. P. 26(b)(4), Notes of Advisory Comm. — 1970 Amendments.
[16]*See* Virginia Elec. & Power Co. v. Sun Shipbuilding & Dry Dock Co., 68 F.R.D. 397,
406 (E.D. Va. 1975).

§1.8.5   The "Actor" Expert

Witnesses who generally acquire their information as an actor or viewer involved in the occurrence or transaction giving rise to the lawsuit are "actor" experts. Often they will be parties to the case, and their expertise or conduct is an issue in the case (as is a defendant physician in a medical malpractice action). They may be called upon to serve three possible roles during discovery: that of an adverse party or agent, that of an eyewitness, and that of an expert. Though their identities and facts known to them will always be discoverable under the general provisions of Rule 26(b), their opinions may or may not be discoverable, depending on the nature of the opinions in question. If asked the basis of the opinion supporting why they did something, they have to respond. If asked an opinion question seeking speculative or conjectural information, they need not respond.[17] Actors may not be required to disclose information gained in anticipation of litigation. A party seeking discoverable information from this category of expert need not pay any fees or expenses. Thus, to the extent their information is not developed in anticipation of litigation or for trial, they are, like the employee expert, treated as any other expert, and their facts and opinions are fully discoverable without limitation.

§1.8.6   The Informally Consulted Expert

The rule governing discovery from the informally consulted expert is simple. There is no discovery. The identity, opinions held, and facts known by such an expert are not discoverable.[18] An "informally consulted" expert is an expert who has been approached by a party or that party's attorney for some information or initial opinion but who will not testify at trial, has not been retained or "specially employed," is not an employee of the party, and is not an actor in the case. Thus, facts held or opinions held by a friend consulted at a cocktail party are not discoverable.[19]

---

[17]Rodriques v. Hrinda, 56 F.R.D. 11, 14 (W.D. Pa. 1972).

[18]*See* Fed. R. Civ. P. 26(b)(4), Notes of Advisory Comm. — 1970 Amendments; Nemetz v. Aye, 63 F.R.D. 66, 68 (W.D. Pa. 1974).

[19]*See, e.g.,* Nemetz v. Aye, 63 F.R.D. 66 (W.D. Pa. 1974).

§1.8.7   Failure to Comply with Expert Discovery Requests

A frequent problem regarding experts involves the proper and timely disclosure of such experts as witnesses in the trial of a case. The trial court has discretion to determine whether or what sanctions will be imposed for the failure to identify expert witnesses. Disclosure of expert trial witnesses may be required either under the rules of discovery or under local rules of practice. The requirements of these rules may not be the same: a judge may rely on either or both in applying sanctions. In addition, the disclosure of experts may be required pursuant to Rule 16, relating to pretrial conferences. Many pretrial orders issued by judges require the identification of all experts expected to testify at trial.

If a party identifies an expert in answer to interrogatories, it is necessary to obtain an order compelling adequate answers before a party may complain about the adequacy of the answers. Thus, if a party identifies an expert and merely states that the expert will "testify concerning the cause of the accident," the other party will not be able to limit that expert's testimony at trial. In all likelihood, however, a court would grant a motion to compel a more adequate answer or, in the event a more adequate answer were not made, would then limit the expert's trial testimony. Obviously, it is impossible to file a motion to compel discovery from an expert who is not identified. The unidentified, undisclosed expert may not be suspected. In view of the manifest unfairness of permitting a party to call a witness to testify at the last minute, courts are ready to bar such an expert's testimony.[20]

Rule 26(e)(1)(B) requires a party to supplement answers to interrogatories relating to experts. A response that a party has not yet engaged an expert or has not determined what experts will be called at trial must be updated. The rule is silent regarding sanctions for failure to supplement, but a court order compelling discovery may be obtained with an alternative sanction imposed in the order, warning that testimony will be excluded if such witnesses are not identified and the appropriate information disclosed.[21] The fact that one party has indicated that it has not yet engaged experts or determined which experts will be called to testify at trial does not relieve the opposing

---

[20]*See* Tabatchnick v. G.D. Searle & Co., 67 F.R.D. 49 (D.N.J. 1975).
[21]Wallace v. Shade Tobacco Growers Agriculture Assn., Inc., 21 Fed. R. Serv. 2d 1130 (D. Mass. 1975).

party from answering appropriate interrogatories relating to retained experts or experts to be called at trial.

§1.9 SUPPLEMENTAL RESPONSES

Rule 26(e) imposes a continuing duty to supplement responses in specific situations. The rule does not impose a general duty to supplement all discovery responses in all circumstances but does require disclosure of additional information in response to previous discovery requests seeking such information in four situations.

1. Supplementary information must be disclosed regarding the identity and location of persons having knowledge of discoverable matters;
2. Additional data must be revealed concerning the identity of each expert witness to be called at trial and the subject matter and substance of such testimony;
3. Amended responses must be made when a party or attorney obtains information that a prior response is incorrect and that a failure to amend would be a knowing concealment;
4. Additional information must be later added if the original response was incomplete at the time made.

These duties to supplement extend to all forms of discovery requests, including interrogatories, depositions, requests for production, and requests for admissions.

The courts within their sound discretion will interpret Rule 26(e) and apply the disclosure duty to appropriate situations.

Rule 26(e)(1) specifically requires the updating of questions that inquire about the identity and location of persons having knowledge of discoverable matter and about the identities and testimony summaries of expert witnesses who will testify at trial. Expert witnesses who will not testify at trial but who have knowledge of discoverable matters fall within the former supplemental requirements, and the subject matter and substance of these expert opinions need only be disclosed if the experts will testify at trial.

The Eighth Circuit has held that the failure to supplement these discovery requests may constitute fundamental unfairness justifying a continuance or the imposition of a sanction upon the offending party.[1] The Fifth Circuit permitted the defendant additional time to prepare for trial when interrogatory answers were supplemented three days before trial, adding new material facts to the case.[2] The Sixth Circuit excluded the testimony of witnesses whose names were added three days before trial to a previous interrogatory request.[3] The Eighth Circuit, meanwhile, has held that the mere failure to supplement these discovery requests may not in itself require the imposition of a sanction, unless the party who lacks the information has suffered undue prejudice as a result of the failure to supplement.[4]

Rule 26(e) requires a response that was incomplete when made to be completed at a later time. Rule 26(e)(2)(A) clearly imposes a duty on a party to correct a response that was incorrect when made. This may occur in situations where the party mistakenly provides a response or bases a response upon some incorrect data. Rule 26(e)(2)(B) specifically imposes a duty on a party to supplement a prior response that is no longer accurate when failure to amend would constitute a knowing concealment. A party breaches this duty by withholding correct information and by failing to amend a prior response.

These provisions impose a continuing obligation on a party to disclose after-acquired information to correct or complete a previous response. Rule 26 nowhere imposes a duty to check the accuracy of previous disclosures, but it does establish the duty to reveal actual knowledge and to prevent knowing concealment by an attorney or party. Information obtained by a party or attorney triggers the rule. Information known to a non-party witness will not trigger disclosure unless the attorney or the party becomes aware of that information and determines that it fits within the scope of Rule 26(e).[5]

Rule 26(e)(3) specifies that additional or alternative duties to supplement responses may be imposed by court order, by stipulation of the parties, or by new requests for supplementation of prior responses. Supplemental discovery requests may not be necessary in all cases because Rule 26 will require supplementation in many situations, but such supplemental requests will still be an appropriate and effective

---

§1.9 [1]Voegeli v. Lewis, 568 F.2d 89, 96 (8th Cir. 1977).
[2]Shelak v. White Motor Co., 581 F.2d 1155, 1160 (5th Cir. 1978).
[3]Davis v. Marathon Oil Co., 528 F.2d 395, 403 (6th Cir. 1976).
[4]Phil Crowley Steel Corp. v. Macomber, Inc., 601 F.2d 342, 344 (8th Cir. 1979).
[5]*See* Havenfield Corp. v. H. & R. Block, Inc., 509 F.2d 1263, 1272 (8th Cir. 1975).

tactic to require disclosure in situations not mandated by Rule 26. Occasionally, the responding party will want to update *sua sponte* some discovery responses to conform the facts to matters to be proved at trial. This practice will be allowed as long as the disclosure occurs a reasonable time before the other party prepares for trial and if no prejudice arises.[6]

The terms and the provisions of Rule 26(e) will continue to be defined by the courts. Rule 26(e) requires that the supplementation of responses must be done "seasonably." The determination of the proper timing of a seasonable supplement will depend upon the facts of the circumstances of each case. One court has declared that supplementation of responses at the time of trial is not seasonable, regardless of whether the time delay was due to failure to prepare for trial or to an intentional purpose to gain the benefit of surprise.[7] Another court has held that supplemental answers were not timely furnished because four months had passed between obtaining the new information and disclosure; the court rejected the defense claim that it did not appreciate the significance of the facts until trial preparation.[8] The more the supplemented responses will affect a party's trial preparation and presentation, resulting in undue prejudice, the more likely the courts will impose some sanction upon failure to comply with Rule 26(e).[9] Local court rules that restrict discovery procedures and that may prevent supplementation of responses at the close of discovery unless good cause is shown may conflict with the policy reasons underlined in Rule 26(e). The reliance of parties on these local rules and the circumstances of each case will determine their applicability.

Although the limits and breadth of Rule 26(e) have not yet been clearly defined, other rules and practice will require the supplementation of information. In effect, a party may obtain information that supplements previous responses:

1. Automatically from a deposing party by the duties imposed on that party under Rule 26(e) to supplement witness names and expert witness information and to correct and complete prior responses;
2. By employing additional discovery requests including a set

[6]*See* Bollard v. Volkswagen of Am., Inc., 56 F.R.D. 569, 578 (W.D. Mo. 1971).
[7]Tabatchnick v. G.D. Searle & Co., 67 F.R.D. 49, 55 (D.N.J. 1975).
[8]Havenfield Corp. v. H. & R. Block, Inc., 509 F.2d 1263, 1272 (8th Cir. 1975).
[9]*See* Kestenbaum v. Falstaff Brewing Corp., 575 F.2d 564, 575 (5th Cir. 1978).

of interrogatories, requests for production, or another deposition;

3. By stipulating with the opposing attorney to supplement and update all or selected discovery requests, the most common being interrogatories and requests for production;
4. By a request during a court conference or pretrial proceeding or by a motion seeking a court order at an earlier point in time;
5. By pouting.

§1.10 PROTECTIVE ORDERS

§1.10.1 Introduction

The discovery rules include a provision protecting attorneys from each other. Rule 26(c) permits a party, or anyone involved in a discovery request, to bring a motion seeking a court order and protection from some aspects of discovery. The movant has the burden to show "good cause" why justice requires protection from "annoyance, embarrassment, oppression, or undue burden or expense."[1] The rule balances one party's need for information with another party's right to certain protections. Indeed, the issue involved with most motions for protective orders "is not whether the court is going to allow parties to embark upon a fishing expedition, but whether the court may make the voyage more pleasant for those who are required to become passengers by the Rules of Civil Procedure."[2]

Information obtained by a party through the discovery process may be used in any way that the law permits, subject to the provisions on protective orders. "The implication is clear that without a protective order, materials obtained in discovery may be used by a party for any purpose. . . ."[3] The movant's burden to show the necessity for a protective order includes a particular and specific demonstration of

§1.10 [1]*See* Reliance Ins. Co. v. Barron's, 428 F. Supp. 200 (S.D.N.Y. 1977) (burden); Lincoln Am. Corp. v. Bryden, 375 F. Supp. 109 (D. Kan. 1973) (annoyance, expense, and embarrassment).

[2]Twin City Fed. Sav. & Loan Assn. v. American Title Ins. Co., 31 F.R.D. 526 (W.D. Mo. 1962).

[3]In re Halkin, 598 F.2d 176, 188 (D.C. Cir. 1979).

facts as distinguished from general and conclusory statements. This demonstration must be made through the submission of affidavits or the introduction of evidence or information supporting the grounds of the motion.[4]

The person seeking the protective order may have to take some steps to preserve the right to obtain the order. A deponent cannot fail to attend a properly noticed deposition and later seek a protective order against such discovery.[5] A party cannot seek protection from interrogatories or requests for productions or admissions without first filing timely and appropriate objections to such requests.[6] Local rules may also affect the right of a party to seek a protective order. The failure to comply with a local rule that requires counsel to confer with the opposing party in good faith to resolve issues before filing motions raises the risk of the protective order's being denied on a procedural basis.[7]

Attorneys will often stipulate to provisions protecting discovery information. These provisions may be incorporated into a stipulation signed by the attorneys or may be incorporated into a proposed order jointly submitted to a court for routine approval. Reasonable attorneys will be able to accommodate each other's needs through stipulations without becoming involved in contested motions for protective orders. The reasons supporting a protective order will usually correspond to the nature and scope of the protective orders sought. Rule 26(c) lists a number of available protective orders. The following subsections discuss them.

§1.10.2 That Discovery Not Be Had

Courts have granted protective orders prohibiting discovery of parties and witnesses because of ill health;[8] if a discovery request is submitted to a party at the eleventh hour, in an untimely fashion;[9] and if

---

[4]*See* Lewis v. Capital Mortgage Inv., 78 F.R.D. 295 (D. Md. 1977).
[5]Hudson Tire Mart, Inc. v. Aetna Cas. & Sur. Co., 518 F.2d 671 (2d Cir. 1975).
[6]4 Moore's Federal Practice ¶26.68, at 26-492 (2d ed. 1980).
[7]Quaker Chair Corp. v. Litton Business Sys., Inc., 71 F.R.D. 527 (S.D.N.Y. 1976).
[8]Celanese Corp. v. Duplan Corp., 502 F.2d 188 (4th Cir. 1974), *cert. denied,* 420 U.S. 929 (1975).
[9]Global Maritime Leasing Panama, Inc. v. M/S *North Breeze,* 451 F. Supp. 965 (D.R.I. 1978).

discovery questions do not pursue legitimate needs, but instead constitute an attempt to take advantage of trial preparation efforts.[10] Courts will preclude discovery from one person until other individuals who appear to have more knowledge of the facts have been examined.[11]

§1.10.3 That Discovery Be Had Only on Specified Terms and Conditions

Courts have explicit power to control the time and place of conducting discovery if the parties themselves are unable to reach agreement.[12] Courts have considered the financial positions of the deponent and the parties in designating a place for the deposition[13] and have declared that the lengthy examination of a sick or elderly deponent may not be permitted.[14] Courts have also scheduled the sequence of discovery in appropriate circumstances, by requiring the taking of a deposition before the disclosure of documents and by requiring responses to interrogatories before the taking of depositions.[15] Simultaneous submission of interrogatories and requests for production have been coordinated by court order in cases involving multiple defendants.[16] Likewise, simultaneous disclosure of discovery information will be ordered, in certain cases, if the information would influence either side's response.[17] Some common discovery orders also include special protective provisions. For example, Rule 35 protective provisions regarding physical examinations frequently include prohibitions against the use of truth serum, hypnosis, and drugs.

Litigants have recently sought protective orders preventing the disclosure of discovery information to the public and to the press. Court rulings have not been uniform in dealing with these issues, and future court decisions will continue to shape the nature and scope of these protective orders.

[10]Schweinert v. Insurance Co. of N. Am., 1 F.R.D. 247 (S.D.N.Y. 1940).
[11]*See* Salter v. Upjohn Co., 593 F.2d 649 (5th Cir. 1979).
[12]Detweiler Bros., Inc. v. John Graham & Co., 412 F. Supp. 416 (E.D. Wash. 1976).
[13]Leist v. Union Oil Co. of California, 82 F.R.D. 203 (E.D. Wis. 1979).
[14]De Wagenknecht v. Stinnes, 243 F.2d 413 (D.C. Cir. 1957).
[15]Smith v. China Merchants Steam Navigation Co., Ltd., 59 F.R.D. 178 (E.D. Pa. 1972).
[16]Rochester Gypsum Coop., Inc. v. National Gypsum Co., 23 Fed. R. Serv. 2d 355 (E.D. Pa. 1976).
[17]Davis v. General Motors Corp., 64 F.R.D. 420 (N.D. Ill. 1974).

The federal circuits appear split regarding the granting or denial of such orders. The Second Circuit has declared that "we entertain no doubt as to the constitutionality of the rule allowing federal courts to forbid the publicizing in advance of trial of information obtained by one party to another by use of the court's processes."[18] The Third Circuit in dicta declared "it may well be, for instance, that the parties and counsel who take advantage of a part of the discovery processes implicitly waive their First Amendment rights to freely disclose or disseminate the information obtained through those processes."[19] But the District of Columbia Circuit in *In re Halkin* declared that:

> an order restraining extra-judicial comment by parties and lawyers has been uniformly held to be a serious restriction of fundamental First Amendment rights. . . .Litigation itself is a form of expression protected by the First Amendment. . . .For the very reasons that have led courts to conclude that lawyers and parties retain their First Amendment rights generally, we conclude that those rights extend to discovery materials.[20]

It is clear that that protective orders will be invalid if they prohibit the disclosure of information obtained other than through discovery. The courts also have made it clear that First Amendment rights attaching to discovery materials will not be absolute:

> First Amendment interests will vary according to the type of expression subject to the order. An order restraining publication of official court records open to the public, or an order restraining political speech implicates different interests than an order restraining commercial information. The interest will also vary according to the timeliness of the expression. An order restraining highly newsworthy information raises a different issue than a temporary restraint of materials having "constant but rarely topical interest."[21]

The *Halkin* decision established three criteria to determine the validity of a protective order in relation to First Amendment rights. "The harm posed by dissemination must be substantial and serious; the restraining order must be narrowly drawn and precise; and there must be no

[18]International Prods. Corp. v. Koons, 325 F.2d 403 (2d Cir. 1963).
[19]Rodgers v. United States Steel Corp., 536 F.2d 1001, 1006 (3d Cir. 1976).
[20]In re Halkin, 598 F.2d 176 (D.C. Cir. 1979).
[21]In re Halkin, 598 F.2d 176, 191 (D.C. Cir. 1979) (footnotes and citations omitted).

alternative means of protecting the public interest which intrudes less directly on expression."[22] The courts will weigh these factors and other circumstances, such as who the parties are and who wishes access to the information, to compose narrow protective orders that balance First Amendment rights with the rights of the parties seeking protection.

§1.10.4   That Discovery Be Had Only by a Particular Method

One court has restricted discovery to interrogatories and denied a party the opportunity to take a deposition, because the interrogatory answers supplied sufficient information in light of the apparent lack of a meritorious claim by the discovering party.[23] Another court ordered a party to proceed by way of an oral deposition rather than by written interrogatories because the court questioned the purpose and motive of the discovering party and because the deposition would be sufficient to produce the information.[24] Courts will be inclined to substitute one mode of discovery for another to protect someone's health, by substituting a written deposition for an oral deposition.[25] Courts base their choice of a discovery device in part upon the interest to be served by the information sought.

§1.10.5   That Certain Matters Not Be Inquired Into

Courts have limited the inquiry of discovery requests to specific, limited topics. Discovery inquiries into privileged matter or burdensome or oppressive requests will be restricted by protective orders.[26] Discovery issues have been limited to those issues raised in a motion for summary judgment.[27]

---

[22]In re Halkin, 598 F.2d 176, 191 (D.C. Cir. 1979).
[23]Shirley v. Chestnut, 603 F.2d 805, 807 (10th Cir. 1979).
[24]Fishman v. A.H. Riise Gift Shop, Inc., 68 F.R.D 704, 705 (D.V.I. 1975).
[25]See J. Underwood, A Guide to Federal Discovery Rules 86 (1980).
[26]See Fed. R. Civ. P. 26(c), Advisory Comm. Notes — 1970 Amendments.
[27]See Scroggins v. Air Cargo, Inc., 534 F.2d 1124, 1133 (5th Cir. 1976).

§1.10.6 That Discovery Be Conducted with No One Present except Persons Designated by the Court

In wrestling with the question of who may be present during a deposition and who may have access to certain discovery information, courts have generally declared that discovery proceedings must take place in public and become part of the public record, unless some compelling reason exists for denying public access to the proceedings.[28] Courts have also claimed for themselves the authority to limit who attends depositions, even excluding parties to a lawsuit.[29] One court recognized that such exclusion should be rarely granted, but itself excluded a party from a deposition to protect the other party from embarrassment or ridicule.[30] Another court precluded deponents from attending the depositions of other deponents because of the subtle and sensitive issues of the case.[31]

Restricting attendance at depositions helps control the dissemination of discovery information when deemed necessary. For example, the disclosure of discovery information has been restricted exclusively to a party's trial counsel for use in preparation of the trial because of the confidential nature of the information.[32] Other courts have ordered information to be disclosed selectively to other participants in the trial process, such as experts.[33]

Non-parties have challenged protective orders that denied them access to certain information. Government investigators, who sometimes need information the access to which has been restricted by a court order, have challenged protective orders denying them information disclosed through discovery. In reviewing these orders, courts balance the government's need for the information with the civil litigant's need for privacy.[34] Parties also have sought to prevent discovery disclosure to non-party individuals on the grounds that such disclosure may foment additional litigation. One court rejected this view and declared that collaboration among lawyers and other persons to dis-

[28]American Tel. & Tel. Co. v. Grady, 594 F.2d 594, 596 (7th Cir. 1979).
[29]Beacon v. R.M. Jones Apartment Rentals, 79 F.R.D. 141, 142 (N.D. Ohio 1978).
[30]Galella v. Onassis, 487 F.2d 986, 997 (S.D.N.Y. 1973).
[31]*See* Beacon v. R.M. Jones Apartment Rentals, 79 F.R.D. 141 (N.D. Ohio 1978) (whether the defendants engaged in unlawful discriminatory housing practices).
[32]Scovill Mfg. Co. v. Sunbeam Corp., 61 F.R.D. 598, 602 (D. Del. 1973).
[33]*See* Gentron Corp. v. H.C. Johnson Agencies, Inc., 79 F.R.D. 415, 418 (E.D. Wis. 1978).
[34]*See* Martindell v. International Tel. & Tel. Corp., 594 F.2d 291 (2d Cir. 1979).

tribute discoverable information is appropriate, may reduce time and money expended in similar proceedings, and promotes "effective, speedy, and efficient representation."[35]

§1.10.7   That a Deposition Be Sealed and Opened Only by Order of the Court

Courts have issued protective orders which require that the discovered information be sealed and filed with the court.[36] This procedure prevents unnecessary disclosure of discovered information. Some courts have adopted local rules that achieve the same result in all cases, or limit the right of persons other than counsel of record to obtain access to the deposition.

§1.10.8   That a Trade Secret or Other Confidential Information Not Be Disclosed or Be Disclosed Only in a Designated Way

Courts have restricted access to trade secret information until such disclosure is necessary to adjudicate the case.[37] The primary factor courts consider in determining the appropriateness of this type of protective order is the degree to which the disclosure of such confidential information will place a party in a significant competitive disadvantage with another party or with competitors.[38] This main factor can be subdivided into four criteria: "(1) the extent to which information is known outside the business; (2) the extent to which information is known to those inside the business; (3) measures taken to guard the secrecy of the information; and (4) the value of the information to the business and its competitors."[39]

---

[35]Patterson v. Ford Motor Co., 85 F.R.D. 152, 154 (W.D. Tex. 1980).

[36]Alloy Cast Steel Co. v. United Steel Workers of Am., 70 F.R.D. 687, 689 (N.D. Ohio 1976).

[37]Lever Bros. Co. v. Procter & Gamble Mfg. Co., 38 F. Supp. 680, 684 (D. Md. 1941).

[38]Parsons v. General Motors Corp., 29 Fed. R. Serv. 2d 175, 177 (N.D. Ga. 1980).

[39]Reliance Ins. Co. v. Barron's, 428 F. Supp. 200, 203 (S.D.N.Y. 1977).

§1.10.9   That Parties Simultaneously File Discovery Responses

This provision is most often involved in patent cases, to prevent one side from being influenced by, and altering its own responses because of, information gained through discovery from the other side. It is available in other situations, however, and may be a useful discovery tool.

§1.10.10   That the Court Make Any Order Which Justice Requires

This catch-all section will occasionally be used by courts to justify protective orders in situations other than the specific situations enumerated in Rule 26(c). The clause reflects the broad discretion a court has to shape discovery and has been used to justify a court's direct supervision of discovery or the appointment of a master to do so.[40]

§1.10.11   Summary

Any party may seek a protective order providing for one or more of the above-enumerated provisions. A non-party in an appropriate case may obtain permission to intervene for the limited purpose of supporting, opposing, or modifying a protective order.[41]

Judges consider various factors when exercising their discretion to grant or deny protective order motions, depending on the facts and circumstances of the particular case. Some general criteria include: (1) the harm caused by the disclosure of information must be substantial and serious, (2) the protective order must be drawn precisely, and (3) there must be no alternative way of protecting the interest of the party seeking the protective order.

Courts also have discretion to modify a protective order.[42] The party or persons seeking modification must either show that the origi-

---

[40]See Fisher v. Harris, Upham & Co., 61 F.R.D. 447 (S.D.N.Y. 1973); Collins & Aikman & Co. v. J.P. Stevens Corp., 51 F.R.D. 219 (D.S.C. 1971).

[41]See, e.g., Martindell v. International Tel. & Tel. Corp., 594 F.2d 291, 294-295 (2d Cir. 1979).

[42]American Tel. & Tel. Co. v. Grady, 594 F.2d 594, 596 (7th Cir. 1979).

nal order was granted improvidently or show some extraordinary circumstance or compelling need requiring disclosure. Parties and witnesses should be entitled to rely upon the enforceability of an original protective order. Courts also have the inherent power to review information in camera or to permit opposing counsel to participate in such in camera proceedings.

Protective orders will reflect the circumstances of a particular case. An order may need to include provisions for abstracts and indexes of classified information,[43] or may require a party or witness to return all documents and copies of discovery information at the close of litigation.[44] Because some provisions of a protective order will be difficult to enforce, courts have considered this fact in determining whether a protective order should be issued at all.

The reasons why someone may obtain a protective order are limited only by the creativity of the attorney seeking protection. The extent of the burden the movant must shoulder will vary depending on the type of relief sought. The more protective the relief, the more persuasive the good-cause showing must be. The reasons that support the court's decision to grant or deny motions are similarly limitless. Judges balance the conflicting interests of the various parties and attempt to fashion a remedy that reflects those interests. Rule 26(c) motions for protective orders will often be a response to a motion under Rule 37 brought by the opposition seeking an order compelling discovery. Rule 37(a) allows the court to enter a protective order upon the denial of a motion to compel discovery even if the objecting party does not move for such a protective order.

§1.11 OVERALL DISCOVERY STRATEGY

§1.11.1 Discovery by Agreement

A substantial amount of discovery is exchanged by agreement of attorneys. Rule 29 encourages such agreement by making any stipula-

---

[43]See Duplan Corp. v. Moulinage et Retorderie de Chavanoz, 509 F.2d 730, 736-737 (4th Cir. 1974), *cert. denied,* 420 U.S. 997 (1975).
[44]Haykel v. G.F.L. Furniture Leasing Co., 76 F.R.D. 386, 391 (N.D. Ga. 1976).

tion, other than one changing certain time limits, enforceable as if it were adopted by rule. Such a stipulation may be equivalent to a court order. Prior to the 1970 amendments, the rules provided that depositions could be taken by stipulation, but the rules did not make specific provision for stipulations relating to other modes of discovery. The 1970 amendments expanded the specific *imprimatur* of the rule to all discovery procedures other than the time limits established in Rules 33, 34, and 36. Federal Rule 29 provides:

> Unless the court orders otherwise, the parties may by written stipulation (1) provide that depositions may be taken before any person, at any time or place, upon any notice, and in any manner and when so taken may be used like other depositions, and (2) modify the procedures provided in these rules for other methods of discovery, except that stipulations extending the time provided in Rules 33, 34 and 36 for responses to discovery may be made only with the approval of the court.

Most depositions are taken under this rule. Attorneys often initially schedule a deposition with a formal notice but then reschedule the time or location of the deposition by agreement with the other lawyer. These agreements will generally be in writing, but not in the form of a formal document. The most common written document in a Rule 29 stipulation is a letter from one attorney to all other counsel of record confirming an oral agreement to reschedule or relocate a deposition.

Stipulations relating to discovery are generally favored by the courts because they foster the flexibility the discovery rules intend to establish. The primary limitation on the use of stipulations is the exception in the rule itself, preventing the use of the rule to extend time limits for interrogatories, requests for production, and requests for admissions. The policy that supports the rule has been articulated in a case denying effect to a stipulation extending such time limits:

> The guiding mandate of the Federal Rules is that "They shall be construed to secure the just, speedy and inexpensive determination of every action." As previously noted, the express provisions in the Rules allowing stipulations aim at this quote. But, if the practice followed by the parties in this case were permitted, the purpose of the Rules would be departed from. Litigants could, as they have done in the past, materially prolong the time for the trial of a case to suit their convenience and interest. The courtesies extended by counsel in such instances, though commendable as professional comity cannot be permitted to interfere with what we think the Rules require. And our conclusion is that the

Rules require court approval to make effective such stipulations as those here involved.[1]

Practice among some attorneys is to ignore both the rule and its rationale and to set their own discovery timetable. Some judges wink at this practice and do nothing to discourage it. A judge may only become aware of it at a time close to trial after the deadlines have passed and may decide to overlook the offense.

Enforcement may also be a problem. A court may impose a sanction *sua sponte* under Rule 37. Unless there has been inordinate delay, causing prejudice to some party, the courts appear to prefer applying the no-harm-no-foul doctrine and frequently choose to ignore any violations of the rule. That may not be as it should be, but it is common. Obviously, in those situations where a trial judge has imposed a discovery cutoff date, or issued other orders relating to discovery, those orders would supersede the provisions of Rule 29.

Judges have the power to alter the time limits applicable to one or more cases by standing order or by local rule. Rule 29 stipulations are frequently used to exchange more interrogatories than those provided by the rules, to allow a medical examination, to exchange expert reports, or to regulate depositions.

The uses of stipulations are endless, and an attorney who approaches discovery with a cooperative attitude may frequently obtain discovery which would not be obtainable by motion. The first effective step in any discovery plan may be asking the opposing lawyer mutually to agree on specific discovery steps. The worst that can happen is that your ideas will be rejected. It will not have been the first time, nor will it be anywhere near the last.

§1.11.2   Planning a Discovery Program

Rule 26(d) provides that discovery methods may be used in any sequence. This provision eliminated the priority system for determining the timing of discovery, which had the party who first noticed or demanded discovery proceeding with discovery before the opposition could proceed. The current provision envisions discovery proceeding

---

§1.11   [1]Orange Theatre Corp. v. Rayherstz Amusement Corp., 130 F.2d, 185, 187 (3d Cir. 1942), *quoted in* 8 C. Wright & A. Miller, Federal Practice and Procedure §2092, at 359-360 (1970).

concurrently, eliminates any fixed priority regarding discovery, and provides courts with the clear power to establish priority if need be.

Practice varies among lawyers regarding the sequence of discovery. Some cases proceed without any set schedule, interrogatories and requests for production exchanges occurring randomly. Other cases include an informal, unwritten schedule resulting in reciprocal discovery exchange. A more formal approach with specific discovery requests being scheduled alternately or in sets can also be used. Rule 26(d) encourages lawyers to arrange their own schedule, one which best suits their and their clients' needs, and discourages court intervention unless reasonable attorneys fail at such arrangements.

When courts have been called upon to establish schedules, they have tended to adopt the traditional scheduling format and permit the party to proceed that has first served formal notice of a deposition or first submitted interrogatories or requests for production or admissions.[2] A compromise approach favored by some courts involves exchanging answers and responses simultaneously and making deposition proceedings and transcripts unavailable to later deponents, in order to reduce the advantage of having available the transcript of an adverse deponent.[3]

Attorneys may now formally seek the assistance of a court in planning and regulating discovery. Rule 26(f) provides a method for convening a discovery conference and involves the active participation of a judge or magistrate in establishing an overall discovery plan. This device is not one that can be routinely requested. It is only available after the attorneys have made good-faith efforts and have been unable to reach accord regarding discovery.

The decision concerning the scope and sequence of discovery should be made very early in the litigation process and usually before investigation is begun, pleadings are drafted, parties are served, motions are brought, stipulations are considered, and discovery is actually begun.

§1.11.3 Investigation

The discovery of trial preparation materials, witness statements, and expert witness information will be determined in large part by

---

[2]Midland Inv. Co. v. Van Alstyne, Noel & Co., 50 F.R.D. 46, 47 (S.D.N.Y. 1970).
[3]*See* McCoy v. General Motors Corp., 33 F.R.D. 354, 355 (W.D. Pa. 1963).

what occurs during the investigation stages. Why and when matters are investigated, whether witness statements are signed or recorded, what questions experts are asked, affect in turn the discoverability by the opposing party of what the investigation reveals. This consideration and the fact that information categorized as trial preparation materials or informally consulted expert opinions will not be readily discoverable by your opponent dictate careful planning of one's investigation.

Some questions you need to consider during the planning stage include:

1. Who do you want to conduct an investigation or interview a witness?
2. Do you want written reports of such investigations, or oral reports?
3. To whom should such reports be addressed or made?
4. How do you want the witnesses' stories preserved? In a written statement? In a tape recording? In an investigator's memo?
5. When should investigations occur? Is litigation anticipated? How can the purpose of the investigation be made clear?
6. Who should contact experts? For what purpose? When?
7. Should you combine and intertwine factual information, reports, and comments with your mental impressions, opinions, conclusions, and legal theories?

Information not discoverable under the rules may always be disclosed voluntarily. Since you will not know the nature (helpful or harmful or neutral) of most information until after you obtain it, planning how to obtain data must therefore take into account the potential discoverability of such data. You may be able to save investigation time and resources by delaying the gathering of information and using discovery devices after litigation has commenced. Only Paul Drake can investigate without considering the effect it has on discovery. Unless you are Paul Drake, consider its impact and plan accordingly.

§1.11.4 Pleadings

Pleadings affect current discovery practice. First, more detailed and complete pleadings make clearer the extent of the subject matter for discovery purposes. Second, the admission of certain allegations in a pleading may well remove the subject matter area relating to that admission from the scope of discovery. Third, pleading allegations may be phrased like a request for admission, forcing the other side to admit certain things early in the case. Fourth, the inclusion of some allegations may force the other side into having to disclose some information or legal theory in a responsive pleading.

§1.11.5 Parties

The number of parties in a case significantly affects the scope of discovery, since interrogatories, requests for production, and requests for admissions may be served only on a party to a case. Though depositions may be had both of parties and non-parties, non-party witnesses must be personally subpoenaed. Again, some responses made by an adverse party in discovery responses may be used at trial and as an admission. So the more parties to a case, the more discovery there may be to counter. Another consideration is that the inclusion of a witness as a party may preclude obtaining that witness's statement. Still other considerations in the inclusion and exclusion of parties to a case, besides discovery considerations, include: a party to a case incurs a natural interest in the outcome of the case and that may affect the validity of his or her testimony at trial; fewer parties mean fewer adversaries; more opposing attorneys affect the negotiation process and mean more cross-examination at trial; and more parties may make more money available for damages.

§1.11.6 Motions

Discovery has an effect on motion practice, and vice versa. A motion to dismiss under Rule 12(b) may eliminate some allegations in a pleading and reduce the scope of the subject matter for discovery purposes. A motion for judgment on the pleadings under Rule 12(c) may well dispose of the entire case. A motion for a more definite statement under Rule 12(e) may parallel the functions that interrogatories serve, by forcing additional disclosure of facts and conclusions, but it will rarely be as effective. Courts grant this motion only to allow a party to draft a responsive pleading, not to prepare for trial.[4] Courts commonly deny such a motion because interrogatories are a better way of supplementing the pleadings.

[4]Richards v. Mark C. Walker & Sons, 9 F.R.D. 563, 564 (D. Neb. 1949); Kellogg Co. v. National Biscuit Co., 38 F. Supp. 643, 648 (D.N.J. 1941).

A motion for summary judgment under Rule 56 will disclose information through the accompanying affidavits. Discovery may continue after the service of a summary judgment motion to obtain information useful to decide the motion. Depositions of an adverse party and other discovery methods may be used to support summary judgment motions. The opposing attorney may find it difficult if not impossible to contradict the admissions and statements appearing in these discovery responses because they come directly from his or her own client. These and other motions need to be considered in planning discovery strategy.

§1.11.7 Factual Stipulations

The process of discovery may be supplanted or supplemented by stipulations between attorneys regarding the facts. The decision whether to suggest, accept, reject, or modify a fact stipulation proposal depends upon the accuracy and completeness of the stipulation, the amount of time and expenses saved, and the impact such a proposal has upon strategic considerations. Such stipulations may be drafted as formal, written agreements, or read into a deposition transcript, or included as part of a pretrial agreement, or reserved for the trial record. The attorneys are free to reach any reasonable agreement regarding the effect the stipulation has on evidentiary, trial, and other litigation elements.[5] The components of such agreements may include some of the following alternative statements, in addition to factual recitals:

1. The witness, if asked the proper questions, would testify that . . .;
2. The facts may be received as evidence at the trial without the laying of any additional foundation;
3. The documents are authentic, genuine, and admissible as evidence;
4. The contents of the stipulation constitute evidence for trial and may be introduced as evidence at the request of either party;
5. Neither party may object to the introduction or receipt of the facts as evidence;

[5]*See* Seay v. International Assn. of Machinists, 360 F. Supp. 123 (C.D. Cal. 1973).

6. The parties waive all objections to the introduction and receipt of the contents of the stipulation as evidence;
7. The contents of this stipulation may be received in evidence on behalf of any party as permitted by the Federal Rules of Evidence, to the same extent as if the witness so testified at a deposition or preliminary hearing or motion hearing or trial;
8. The facts recited in this stipulation remain subject to evidentiary objections interposed by either party.

§1.12 PRE-COMPLAINT DISCOVERY: RULE 27

§1.12.1 Introduction

There are two situations in which it would be helpful, if not essential, to engage in some discovery prior to the formal initiation of litigation. One circumstance involves insufficient information with which to frame a pleading. Another involves the preservation of evidence that may not be available later. The rules do not provide any mechanism to obtain discovery in the former situation, but do provide a pre-litigation device to preserve testimony through Rule 27.

If you do not have sufficient data to frame a complaint, you have to do the best you can in drafting a complaint and then proceed with discovery to obtain the required information; you can then follow discovery with the drafting of an amended complaint. Notice pleading allows for skeleton complaints, and you will ordinarily be able to obtain sufficient discovery before being dismissed. Even if a motion to dismiss is successful, you can still serve an amended complaint and try again.

Rule 27 is not available to obtain facts with which to base a complaint where there exists no prospective loss of testimony. Courts have continually denied petitions under Rule 27 on the grounds that the rule cannot be used for the purpose of ascertaining facts to be used in drafting a complaint.[1] Injustice does not result from these rulings, since common discovery proceedings under Rules 30 through 37 will be available after the filing of a skeleton complaint to ascertain all the facts needed.

§1.12   [1]In re Gurnsey, 223 F. Supp. 359 (D.D.C. 1963).

In the second situation, Rule 27 does allow for taking a pre-complaint deposition for the purpose of perpetuating testimony and preserving evidence. Situations arise that delay the formal start of a lawsuit, causing potential trial evidence to become irrevocably lost. A Rule 27 proceeding is an ancillary or auxiliary procedure to prevent a delay of justice by preserving testimony that would otherwise be lost before the matter to which it relates can become ripe for a judicial determination.[2] Rule 27 provides a means to preserve evidence through oral and written depositions, Rule 34 inspections, and Rule 35 compulsory physical examinations. Since Rule 27 is not itself a discovery device, but serves the limited purpose of preserving evidence,[3] the use of various discovery devices will be limited to such purposes.

§1.12.2 Procedures

In the arsenal of discovery devices available to the practitioner, Rule 27 has limited use. The rule's procedures will be most useful to preserve some specific bit of information or evidence likely to be lost unless it is preserved. This narrow utility contrasts significantly with the broad, liberal use of discovery devices after litigation has ensued. Three specific procedural conditions must be met before its provisions become operational:

1. The matter must be "cognizable in any court in the United States. . . ." At the time of the filing of the petition, the expected action must fall within the jurisdiction of the federal courts. A Rule 27 proceeding must be supported by the jurisdictional grounds of the underlying anticipated lawsuit.

2. The petition must be filed "in the district of the residence of any expected adverse party." This provision determines the proper venue for filling the petition.

3. The petition must contain a caption setting forth the name of the petitioner and other matters. An accepted form is: "In the Matter of the Petition of Yoda to perpetuate the testimony of the Force."

---

[2]De Wagenknecht v. Stinnes, 250 F.2d 414 (D.C. Cir. 1957).
[3]In re Boland, 79 F.R.D. 665 (D.D.C. 1978).

§1.12.3   Contents of the Petition

The petition itself includes the several specific elements outlined in Rule 27 and a request for the specific relief sought. Necessary elements include:

1. Petitioner must expect to be a party to a specific action. Petitioner may be a plaintiff or a potential defendant.

2. Petitioner must presently be unable to bring the action or to cause it to be brought.

3. Petitioner must have an interest in the subject matter of the expected action.

4. Petitioner must state the facts that petitioner desires to establish by the proposed testimony. This statement of facts may be a brief, generalized description that allows the judge to determine whether the facts justify being perpetuated. The scope of such information resembles the scope of discovery under Rule 26 in that the information sought need not be admissible in trial, but only reasonably likely to lead to amissible evidence.

5. Petitioner must enumerate the reasons why petitioner desires to perpetuate the information. This factor requires a demonstration of the likelihood that the evidence sought will be lost or suffer a significant decline in quality because of the unavoidable reasons for delay that prevent the action from presently being brought.

6. Petitioner must supply the names or description of persons expected as adverse parties, and their addresses.

7. Petitioner must list the names and addresses of persons to be examined and describe the substance of the testimony expected to be elicited from each. A general description of the hoped-for information will usually suffice to meet the standard and provide the court with enough information to determine the legitimacy of the petition. This summary, when coupled with the other affidavit facts, provides adequate information to the court.

8. Petitioner must request relief. The petitioner must ask for an order authorizing the petitioner to proceed with the perpetuation of the testimony. The request will commonly be for a deposition, but may also be for written answers to interrogatories, responses to requests for production, or examinations under Rule 35.

§1.12.4 Other Provisions

Rule 27(a)(2) details the provisions regarding notice and service of the petition.

Rule 27(b) also allows proceedings to perpetuate testimony during a pending appeal of an action. This provision recognizes that the lengthy interval between the conclusion of a trial and an appellate judgment may diminish the quantity and quality of evidence. Witnesses may die, physical evidence may deteriorate, memories may fade.

The rule allows a party to seek a motion before a trial court indicating (1) the names and addresses of the persons to be examined and the substance of testimony expected to be elicited; and (2) the reasons for perpetuating such testimony. The rule again specifies that the trial court has discretion to enter an order identical to the orders available in proceedings to perpetuate testimony before an action ensues. The rule makes no distinction regarding different standards to be applied.

§1.13 PROBLEMS

Relevance

1. Petitioner and respondent both seek a dissolution of their marriage. The only contested issue involves custody of their two children, who are six and eight years old. Petitioner claims that respondent has been and is a neglectful and unfit parent. Petitioner submits an interrogatory asking respondent who is a physician, to detail the number of hours that respondent spent working as a doctor over the past four years.

    (a) What reasons would you advance on behalf of the respondent that this information is irrelevant?

    (b) What reasons would you advance on behalf of the petitioner that the information is relevant?

    (c) As a judge, how would you decide and why?

2. The plaintiff has brought a $30,000 negligence action against the defendant, claiming that the defendant ignored a stop sign and

drove through an intersection, hitting plaintiff's car and injuring the plaintiff. The attorney for the defendant has asked during the taking of the plaintiff's deposition whether the plaintiff has ever been arrested or convicted for any criminal or traffic offense.

(a) What reasons would you advance on behalf of the plaintiff that this information is irrelevant?

(b) What reasons would you advance on behalf of the defendant that the information is relevant?

(c) If you were the judge, how would you decide and why?

3. The plaintiff car dealer has brought an action for breach of a retail installment contract, alleging that the defendant consumer has failed to make timely payments. The defendant has asserted affirmative defenses and counterclaims based upon breach of express and implied warranties, claiming the Thunderolds car is defective. The defendant submitted a request for production of documents, asking the plaintiff for copies of all documents, correspondence, and pleadings that contain complaints consumers have communicated to the plaintiff about any car sold by the plaintiff over the past two years.

(a) What reasons would you advance on behalf of the plaintiff that this information is irrelevant?

(b) What reasons would you advance on behalf of the plaintiff that the information is relevant?

(c) What other ways might this request be drafted to make the request more clearly relevant?

4. The plaintiff has brought an employment-discrimination claim against her former employer, alleging that sexual harassment by male co-workers forced her to quit the job. The employer denies this allegation and has submitted an interrogatory asking her to list the names, addresses, and telephone numbers of all men whom she has dated socially since she was 18. The plaintiff is 24 years of age, is single, has never been married, and has frequently dated socially.

(a) What reasons would you advance on behalf of the plaintiff that this information is irrelevant?

(b) What reasons would you advance on behalf of the defendant that this information is relevant?

(c) What other ways might this request be drafted to make the request more clearly relevant?

Privilege

5. During an interview with his attorney, a client relates all the facts of an auto accident to the lawyer. Does the communication of this information render it non-discoverable from the client by an opposing party during the course of subsequent litigation involving the auto accident? Why or why not?

6. During a client interview involving potential medical malpractice claims, an attorney renders legal advice about such litigation to her defendant client.

(a) What privilege protects the information the attorney provides a client?
(b) What type of legal information may be discoverable?
(c) Which discovery devices are available to obtain this type of information?

7. An attorney discusses with her plaintiff client the lawyer fees and expenses involved in commercial litigation.

(a) Will this information be discoverable by the defendant? Explain your answer.
(b) If the fee arrangement were reduced to writing and signed by the plaintiff, would the defendant be able to discover that written fee agreement?

Lawyer Mental Impressions

8. A client, prior to first visiting his attorney, prepares a written statement detailing the facts of his real-estate easement dispute. He gives this memorandum to his attorney, who places it in the law office file.

(a) Is this memo discoverable? Why or why not?
(b) If, during the course of the attorney-client interview, the lawyer obtained additional facts from the client and wrote that

information on the memo, would the memo or that portion of the memo be discoverable? Why or why not?

(c)   If, during the course of the same interview, the attorney wrote down on the memo a summary of the legal advice she discussed with the client, would that memo or any portion of it be discoverable? Why or why not?

9.   An attorney has a conference with his law partner regarding the facts, legal theories, and strategies of a lawsuit the law firm is engaged in. The attorney subsequently prepares a memo summarizing the discussion and places it in the file.

(a)   Is that memo or are any portions of it discoverable by the opposing party? Why or why not?

(b)   Suppose that the attorney has the same discussion with a paralegal, with his office. Is the information discoverable from the paralegal?

(c)   Suppose that the attorney has the same discussion with an independent private investigator hired specifically to investigate the case. Would your answer regarding the discoverability of this information be any different from your response to (b); above? Why or why not?

(d)   The opposing party to the lawsuit deposes that attorney and asks him questions about the facts, legal theories, and strategies of the case. What reasons may the attorney assert in refusing to disclose such information?

10.   During the course of legal research on a case, an attorney makes handwritten notes of citations, case headnotes, and her summaries of the law. Is any of this information discoverable by the opposing party? Why or why not?

Trial Preparation Materials

11.   A client retains an attorney after being injured in an auto accident. Prior to initiating a lawsuit, the attorney personally begins the investigation by interviewing two eyewitnesses, by visiting the scene of the accident, and by summarizing the information in a file memo.

(a) Is that memo or are any portions of it discoverable? Why or why not?

(b) Is the information discoverable from the attorney?

(c) The attorney hires an independent private investigator who conducts the investigation and prepares a memo for the file. If the private investigator retains a copy of the memo and places it in a file in his office, is that copy of the memo discoverable? Why and how, or why not?

12. An employee is injured while working on a job at a factory. Government regulations require the company to investigate the accident and prepare a report, which is then filed in the company's records. Does that report constitute trial preparation materials? Explain your answer.

13. A corporation requires the keeping of personnel, evaluation, and termination records, which are prepared and maintained by supervisors but are kept in the personnel office. An employee is fired and sues the corporation, claiming job discrimination. Are the records maintained by the corporation on that employee trial preparation materials? Why or why not?

14. A supply company receives a telephone call from a business customer complaining that the customer did not receive certain supplies pursuant to its contract with the company. The president of the company orders a manager to prepare and file a written report detailing what happened regarding the alleged undelivered supplies. The president hopes to determine which company employee might be responsible for the error and the extent of the company's potential liability. Three months later the customer sues the company for breach of contract.

(a) Does that report contain trial preparation materials? Why or why not?

(b) If the corporate counsel for the company, not the president, had requested that the manager prepare and file a report for the company records for the same reasons as explained above, would your answer regarding the status of this report as trial preparation material be any different from your response to (a)? Why or why not?

Witness Statements

15.   Sue witnesses an accident in which Jack is injured by a lawn-mower operated by Fran. Jack retains a lawyer who contacts both Sue and Fran on March 1 to obtain their stories.

(a)   On March 1, the attorney prepares a statement in his own handwriting, which Sue signs, and he has Fran write out her story in her own handwriting and date it, but does not have her sign it. Subsequently, Jack sues Fran for negligence. Can Sue or Fran obtain a copy of their own statements? Why and how, or why not?

(b)   Suppose that the attorney does not obtain a written statement from Sue. Instead, the attorney returns to his office on March 1, and several hours later he dictates the story from his notes. Is the dictating tape or a transcript of the tape or the information on the tape discoverable by Fran? Why or why not?

(c)   Suppose that the attorney does not obtain a written statement from Fran. Instead, he contemporaneously records the conversation with Fran on tape without her knowledge or permission. Is that tape or a transcript of the tape or the tape information discoverable by Fran?

16.   A worker at the Mills Company is injured on the job. A co-worker observes the accident and, at the request of a manager, writes down his eyewitness account, signs the statement, and gives it to the manager, who forwards it to the Workers' Compensation Department of the company. The injured worker brings an action against Mills for the injury. Can the co-worker's statement be obtained by the plaintiff through discovery? Why and how, or why not?

17.   A professor at a private university starts a fight with his dean during a charity softball game in October, arguing over which team was the better baseball team. The lawyer to the college requests the dean to write a report of the incident and place it in the professor's university file. The dean does so. In March, the college notifies the professor that he will not receive tenure and refuses to renew his contract. The professor sues the university for breach of contract. Is the dean's statement discoverable by the professor? Explain.

Scope of Discovery

18.   The All Goods Company has monthly management meetings involving the company president, general counsel, secretary, and six division managers; they discuss company matters. A written memorandum of each meeting is prepared by the secretary and distributed to all meeting participants. In October the Everything Corporation, a competitor, sent a letter to the president of All Goods, alleging that some of the company's advertisements constituted deceptive trade practices and detailing the factual bases and legal consequences of the claims. The president jotted some notes on the letter, indicating his reaction to the contents, and distributed copies to all meeting participants. The president then placed two matters on the agenda for the November meeting: (1) the company's general advertising campaign and (2) the letter from Everything Corporation. Both matters were discussed at the November meeting, and the subsequent meeting memorandum contained paragraphs summarizing each discussion. During December the general counsel of the Company requested a memo from the advertising manager regarding her response to the claims in the Everything Corporation letter. The advertising manager then asked each of her three supervisory advertising personnel to submit to her individual memos with their reactions to the letter, which she distributed to them. She received all three memos in December and wrote one reply memo in January to the general counsel. In February, the Everything Corporation sued the All Goods Company, claiming violation of federal and state deceptive-trade-practice statutes. The general counsel then personally interviewed each of the three supervisory advertising personnel and recorded the summaries of the interviews in separate memos placed in his files. The company retained the law firm of Fulton and Flood to defend them in litigation. Fulton personally met with the president of the company and with each of the six division managers and prepared notes of such interviews, which he placed in his office file. Flood personally talked to each of the three supervisory advertising personnel and prepared written file notes in her own handwriting about these conversations. What arguments would you advance on behalf of the plaintiff, Everything Corporation, to obtain all these memos? What arguments would you advance on behalf of defendant, All Goods Company, protecting these documents from disclosure? As the judge, which of the documents would you rule discoverable:

(a)   The October letter from the Everything Corporation containing the handwritten notes by the president of All Goods.

(b) The paragraph summarizing the November meeting discussion.

(c) The three December memos from the advertising personnel to the advertising manager.

(d) The January memo from the advertising manager to the general counsel.

(e) The February interview memos prepared by the general counsel.

(f) The Fulton notes.

(g) The Flood notes.

Expert Information

19. A plaintiff is injured in a boating accident. His treating physician composes a written opinion about the physical condition of the plaintiff at the request of the plaintiff's attorney, who intends to call the doctor as an expert at the trial.

(a) Is that written opinion letter discoverable by the defendant? Why and how, or why not?

(b) If the doctor only gave an oral opinion to the plaintiff's lawyer, would that opinion be discoverable? Why and how, or why not?

20. A chemist at the 4M Company is a full-time employee in the Medical Services Division and was re-assigned to spend one year with a retained outside law firm that represents 4M in a complex antitrust and patent case. She conducts non-destructive tests, provides written test reports to the company and firm, gives oral opinions to the firm, and makes written reports for the company and firm. What is discoverable by the opposition? Why?

21. The Whirlwind Corporation hires an engineer who is a full-time university professor to provide it with an expert opinion regarding one of its products, which is claimed to be defective in a product liability case. The expert provides both written and oral opinions to the corporation counsel.

(a) What is discoverable by the plaintiffs in the product liability case?

(b) If the engineer were hired before the litigation and before the injury occured to the plaintiff, would either the written report or oral opinion, or both, be discoverable in the later litigation? Why or why not?

22. Dr. Chandle has a national reputation as an expert in the treatment of lower-back problems and has been conducting a two-year research treatment program for individuals with lower-back pain. Ron visits him in March, complaining of chronic lower-back pain, and after tests Dr. Chandle accepts him as a patient in the research treatment program, recommends surgery for reduction of his enlarged disc, and performs the surgery in April. Ron continues to experience the same chronic back pain after surgery. Dr. Chandle recommends a physical therapy program for him, but Ron has too much pain and cannot continue with the program. In June, Ron contacts another back specialist, who places Ron on a hanging-traction program. During July, Ron's back pain has subsided and Ron can engage in normal physical activities. In August, Dr. Chandle completes the two-year research project, which has involved 50 patients, and prepares a final report, which he publicly releases. In September, Ron sues Dr. Chandle for medical malpractice. Which of the following will be discoverable by the lawyer for Ron, and why and how?

(a) Results from the March test that Dr. Chandle conducted on Ron.
(b) The surgery X-rays and records.
(c) Dr. Chandle's opinion on why Ron continued to suffer lower-back pain from April through July.
(d) The files and records of the 50 patients involved in the research project.

23. A construction company was sued for negligent installation of a balcony. The company hired two experts, Terry and Dale. Terry submitted a written report that supported the position of the company's engineers. Dale submitted a report that concluded that the construction company's operations were negligent. The company retained Terry as an expert and paid and dismissed Dale.

(a) Can the plaintiff discover the opinions of Dale? Explain.
(b) If the defendant had retained Dale but did not use him or his report for anything further, can the plaintiff discover the opinions of Dale? Why and how, or why not?

Supplemental Information

24. The defendant by answers to interrogatories has provided the opposing attorney with the names of all eyewitnesses to the accident. Subsequent to such answers the defendant learns of another key eyewitness. Must this information be disclosed? Why and how, or why not?

25. The plaintiff has submitted to defendant on May 1 all documents it had, including telephone conversations between the plaintiff and defendant. Subsequent investigation by the plaintiff uncovered another highly relevant telephone message, with notes of a conversation between the parties. Must this information be disclosed? Why and how, or why not?

26. The attorney for the defendant deposed the plaintiff, who testified that she had said nothing to the defendant about a lease on August 10. The plaintiff later advises her attorney that she recalls that she did ask the defendant two questions about the lease on August 10. Must this information be disclosed? Why and how, or why not?

Summaries

27. You supervise the litigation section of your law firm. There has recently been some confusion among the lawyers regarding the application of Rule 26(b)(3) and the creation of trial preparation materials. You decide to draft a concise memo detailing the considerations that will assist the attorneys in determining what documents become trial preparation materials, both before and after litigation. Prepare such a memo.

28. Because of your reputation, you have been asked to address a litigation committee of the federal bar association. You select as your topic Rule 26(b)(3) and what information is exempt from discovery as attorney mental impressions, conclusions, opinions, or legal theories. Prepare a concise memo summarizing considerations that will assist litigators in determining what information falls within the protected attorney mental processes and what falls outside the purview of the rule and so is subject to disclosure.

29. You are a lawyer with a large computer corporation that manufactures, distributes, and sells wholesale and retail in jurisdictions that have adopted Privilege Standard 503. The general counsel for your firm has become concerned with the current developments relating to

the attorney/client privilege as applied to corporations. She has asked you to prepare a concise list of considerations that will assist all corporation lawyers in determining whether their conversations with corporate officers, managers, and employees fall within the range of communications protected by the privilege. Prepare such a memo.

30.   You represent the Energy Preservation Company, a manufacturer and retailer of home insulation designed to insulate homes and reduce energy costs. You have been retained to defend your client in a class-action lawsuit brought by three named plaintiffs and an unspecified number of unnamed class members. The plaintiffs have brought the class action under a state consumer fraud act that permits such actions; they allege that the home insulation did not reduce residential utility expenses. The state rules of civil procedure relating to class actions are identical to Federal Rule 23. The plaintiffs have submitted interrogatories to your client seeking information about customers. You plan to obtain information from the plaintiffs about the alleged claims. Prepare a concise memo explaining:

(a)   What information the plaintiffs can obtain regarding customers.
(b)   What discovery can and should be initiated by you at this stage of the litigation.

Discovery Planning

31.   Consulting the Hypothetical Case Files in Appendix A, prepare a concise memo planning a discovery program for the plaintiff in *American Campers v. Summers.* Your memo should:

(a)   Explain what information you want to obtain.
(b)   Describe the discovery devices you plan to use to obtain that information.
(c)   Explain the sequence of those discovery devices.
(d)   Describe what information might be better obtained through informal investigation.

32.   Plan such a discovery program for the defendant in *American Campers v. Summers.*

33.   Plan such a discovery program for the plaintiff in *Bellow v. Norris.*

34. Plan such a discovery program for the defendant in *Bellow v. Norris.*

35. Plan such a discovery program for the plaintiff in *Graham v. Turkel.*

36. Plan such a discovery program for the defendant in *Graham v. Turkel.*

Chapter 2
DEPOSITIONS

Where Weaver's Needle casts its long shadow at four in the afternoon, there you will find a vein of rose quartz laced with gold wire — and you will be rich beyond your wildest dreams.
— The Legend of the Lost Dutchman Gold Mine and Superstition
Mountain

§2.1 AN OVERVIEW OF THE DEPOSITION PROCESS

§2.1.1 *Advantages of Depositions*

You can search for information by deposing a witness or another party. You may never be able to depose the Lost Dutchman or become all that rich, but depositions do serve several purposes and offer advantages in discovery efforts. Depositions help you to:

1. Explore and obtain information from the other side through prepared and spontaneous, flexible follow-up questions;
2. Determine what a deponent knows and does not know;
3. Pin down a deponent to a particular story;
4. Assess the witness's demeanor to determine what type of trial witness that person would be;
5. Confront an adversary deponent with damaging information or probe the deponent about weaknesses in the case prior to trial;
6. Preserve testimony to be used later as admissions, impeachment evidence, or for other evidentiary or cross-examination purposes at trial.

§2.1.2   Disadvantages of Depositions

Depositions have some disadvantages, though they are usually out-weighed by their advantages:

1. Depositions can be expensive, but they need not be. There are ways to reduce the costs.
2. Depositions may force the other side to prepare or may trigger counter-depositions, but it is poor practice indeed to prepare a case relying on the hope that the other attorney is a stumblebum.
3. Depositions also educate witnesses. Being deposed helps one learn the testifying process as well as what to say and what not to say in testimony. This can be a drawback for the deposing attorney, who in effect makes the adversary deponent a better witness for the trial.
4. A discovery deposition also preserves the testimony of the opposing party or adverse witness, the transcript of which can be used at trial should that deponent be unavailable then.

Yet depositions are the best discovery devices available. They allow you into the other side's camp to gather information, view, understand, and evaluate the opposition, its witnesses, and its case. They should be used (or attempted) in every case, except in those cases in which you can look yourself in the mirror and say, "Even F. Bennett Day Nizer would not depose in this case." So much for the disadvantages.

§2.1.3   Scope of Depositions

Rules 27, 30, 31, and 32 provide the basic procedural framework for taking and using depositions. Of course, they do not regulate all facets and procedures of depositions; custom and common practice provide additional ground rules, particularly on what happens during depositions. These ground rules will vary to some extent from attorney to attorney, from law firm to law firm, and from area to area. Much of internal deposition practice is like situational ethics. Decisions are based upon the circumstances and on the attorney's understanding and application of flexible deposition strategies. This chapter details the civil procedure rules and explains the customs, common practice, accepted ground rules, and specific tactics that fashion and guide deposition proceedings.

There is no right or wrong approach to deposition practice. There may be a generally preferred way, but seldom does an approach rise to indubitable correctness or slump to a sure "oops." When a dispute about some procedure arises between the attorneys, there is no judge or third party present reviewing the goings-on during the deposition: the attorneys have to resolve the matter. They usually will, guided by their understanding of custom, practice, ground rules, strategy considerations and the nature and extent of their cooperative relationship.

Rule 29 specifically allows attorneys to agree to take depositions in any way, shape, or form they desire. If the attorneys cannot work things out, one of them may resort to judicial relief under Rule 37, while the other may seek a protective order under Rule 26(c).

In many situations, however, no clear precedential rule or case law disposes the dispute. Because of the varying customs, practice, and ground rules, it is usually more important for an attorney to have a conscious, purposeful reason to be doing something than to be merely following someone else's advice or reacting to the other side. This chapter provides rationales for conflicting tactics and strategies. The situation will determine which will be best applicable.

§2.1.4 Timing of Depositions

Rule 30(a) states that depositions may be taken without leave of court by a plaintiff 30 days after service of the summons and complaint. Before those 30 days lapse, the plaintiff must seek leave of court to schedule a deposition, except in two situations: if the defendant has served a deposition notice or otherwise sought discovery, or if the deponent will not be available for the deposition after the 30-day period. Rule 32(b)(2) describes the procedure and supporting statements necessary to comply with the latter exception. Such a deposition may not be used against a party if that party shows that he or she was unable to obtain counsel for the deposition. A plaintiff can serve notice of a deposition within the 30-day period without leave of court, as long as the deposition itself is scheduled after that period. A defendant can notice or schedule a deposition any time after receiving a summons and complaint.

Rule 30(b) provides that the attorney taking the deposition has the right to schedule the time for the deposition. Ordinarily, strategy considerations will prompt depositions to be scheduled at the earliest practical time during litigation. Early examination preserves more accurate testimony, permits more time to investigate the facts obtained and to research the issues uncovered, and commits the deponent to testimony early on in the litigation. Further, early deposition may prompt a ready settlement on advantageous terms. Attorneys, especially defense attorneys, may schedule a plaintiff's deposition as soon as possible to evaluate the extent of the claim properly. A successful deposition by the defendant in many of these cases forces an early and economical settlement.

In some situations, however, a deposition should be scheduled later in the litigation. A delayed deposition permits the attorney to be better informed on the areas of inquiry. Investigation may be necessary to prepare properly for the deposition; other discovery devices may produce helpful information. The timing of a deposition may also depend upon other depositions yet to be taken. A deponent at a later deposition may have the advantage of either having attended an earlier deposition or having read the transcript of an earlier deposition, which may influence his or her version of what happened or otherwise affect the testimony. To avoid this problem, depositions of adverse parties or witnesses may be scheduled back to back, on the same or subsequent days. A deposition may need to be taken just before or even during a trial if a witness belatedly becomes available. This latter situation should arise only infrequently.

§2.1.5 Location of Depositions

Rule 30(b)(1) provides that the attorney taking the deposition has the right to specify where it will be held. Plaintiffs and their agents will be required to be available for depositions in the district where the action is pending. Depositions of a corporation's officers or employees will ordinarily be taken at its principal place of business. Special circumstances, such as hardship or financial burden to a party, may also affect the location of a deposition. Depositions are frequently held in the examining attorney's office; often in the court reporter's office; occasionally in a courthouse; sometimes in the opposing attorney's office; and at times in the deponent's office, so that certain documents will be accessible and obtainable. The exact location of the deposition largely depends upon your convenience and what effect you want the location to have on the deponent. Although holding the deposition in your office may be convenient, holding it in a records office may make it more convenient for you to inspect and copy documents obtained through the deposition. Again, holding the deposition in the office of the deponent's attorney may make the deponent comfortable amidst familiar surroundings, whereas holding it in a courthouse may be imposing and threatening to a deponent. Attorneys occasionally wrangle over location. A court reporter's office may offer neutral ground, or a protective order regarding location may be obtained.

§2.1.6   Non-Party Depositions

Deposition notices will not be sufficient to compel the attendance of non-party witnesses to depositions. Service of a Rule 45 subpoena is required to get their attention. The clerk of the district court where the deposition is to be taken issues the subpoena. Rule 45(d)(1) specifies that "[p]roof of service of a notice to take a deposition . . . constitutes sufficient authorization for the issuance of the subpoena by the clerk of district court for the district in which the deposition is to be taken. . . ." It's that simple.

It is almost that simple to schedule the deposition of a non-party witness to be taken in another district. Some of these deponents will be residents of the district in which the deposition is to be located; others will be non-residents. Rule 45(d)(2) explains the difference:

> A resident of the district in which the deposition is to be taken may be required to attend an examination only in the county wherein he resides or is employed or transacts his business in person, or at such other convenient place as is fixed by an order of court. A nonresident of the district may be required to attend only in the county wherein he is served with a subpoena, or within 40 miles from the place of service, or at such other convenient place as is fixed by an order of court.

District courts have broad discretion in designating the location of non-party examinations. Non-party witnesses usually are not required to travel distances just for the convenience of the parties. Corporations are usually deposed at their principal place of business or where the corporate examinee resides. A non-party witness designated as a deponent for a corporation, association, or governmental agency may be able to limit the deposition location to the places authorized by Rule 45(d)(2).

The party seeking the deposition has the burden to show the capacity of the prospective deponent: that is, whether the deponent is a party or non-party. This burden is easily and obviously carried in most situations. But not in all. Occasionally a question will arise as to whether a prospective deponent, usually a corporation's employee, is a non-party witness or an agent of a party. The nature of the relationship between the deponent and the party at the time of the incident and at the time of the deposition determines the answer. A mere employee of a corporation must be subpoenaed to a deposition.

A party who has a relationship with a deponent may have some responsibility for making sure the deponent attends the deposition. A party may be responsible for producing a deponent who is a relative or a former agent, for example, or a former corporate employee whom the party now controls through a wholly-owned subsidiary.

Depositions of non-party witnesses in a lawsuit pending in a state court, other than the state of the deponent's residence, may be arranged pursuant to the subpoena rules of the deponent's jurisdiction. This subpoena process usually mimics the federal procedures and ordinarily provides the examining attorney with an order as a routine matter.

Some practitioners give notice of a non-party deposition with a subpoena duces tecum, which requires the deponent to bring with him or her whatever documents are described in the subpoena. Rules 45(b) and (d) allow a party to schedule a deposition, subpoenaing both the non-party deponent and books, papers, documents, and tangible things to the deposition. This procedure is the only rule-sanctioned process requiring a non-party to provide materials for inspection and copying. Rule 34 is directed solely toward parties; the other discovery rules provide no other means for a party to obtain documents from a non-party. The subpoena duces tecum has to be accompanied with a subpoena for a deposition, a hearing, or a trial. Rule 45 does not permit the issuance of a subpoena duces tecum unless there is also an examination of the person bringing the documents scheduled.

An attorney who only wishes to review documents in the possession of a non-party, and who is faced with a refusal by that non-party to disclose the documents, must schedule a deposition of that non-party and subpoena the documents. Even though the discovering attorney does not plan to examine the deponent, but only plans to review the documents, Rule 30 requires that a formal deposition be scheduled, complete with a court reporter to record the deposition stenographically. Some practitioners stipulate with the opposing lawyer for an informal deposition, which eliminates the need for a court reporter. The "deponent" in these stipulated "depositions" is not examined, but acts essentially as a messenger, who delivers the documents to the office of the requesting lawyer for review. In order to reduce costs, other practitioners circumvent Rule 30 by unilaterally scheduling the delivery of documents without intending to depose the custodian. Opposing lawyers may not be inclined to object because this misuse of Rules 45 and 30 is directed to a non-party and not to their clients, or because they intend to do the same thing to other non-parties. This practice, when clearly a circumvention of the discovery rules, violates the ethical standards of an attorney, who is also an officer of the court.

§2.2 PRELIMINARY DEPOSITION CONSIDERATIONS

The taking of depositions requires the consideration of several matters that affect the deposition. These considerations include proper notice, who can attend a deposition, who can be brought to a deposition, and how to ensure that the deponent brings the necessary documents to the deposition.

§2.2.1 Noticing the Deposition

Rule 30(b) requires the party taking a deposition to provide reasonable written notice to all parties to the action, specifying the time, place, and person to be deposed. Notice to the deponent of four days has been held sufficient, given special circumstances.[1] More time will be required in most cases, and a more reasonable number of days is usually afforded as a matter of professional practice. What is reasonable and sufficient will depend upon the circumstances.

Changes in the scheduled time may be, and routinely are, made by agreement between counsel. Rule 29 permits the lawyers to set their

§2.2 [1]*See* Ramm Indus. Co. v. Chapman Performance Prods. Inc., 18 Fed. R. Serv. 2d 1531 (N.D. Ill. 1974). Some local rules establish a minimum number of days as reasonable notice: ten days (M.D. Fla. Gen. R. 3.02); seven days (E.D. Va. R. 21(G)); five days (D. Kan. R. 17(e)); three days (N.D. Okla. R. 15).

own scheduled date and the time is usually negotiable between the attorneys. A mutually convenient time can be arranged in a variety of ways: a telephone call to the opposing attorney confirming the arrangements with a written notice, a letter to the opposing attorney suggesting a number of alternative times and dates, a cover letter with the formal notice suggesting that the opposing attorney contact you if the time is inconvenient. Rule 30 allows a court to advance or postpone the schedule for cause.

The written notice is sufficient to compel the attendance of a party to the deposition. A subpoena pursuant to Rule 45(a) is necessary to compel the attendance of a non-party deponent. Depositions may be scheduled at any time during regular business hours, and during other hours for good reasons. Recesses will be necessary for rest and recuperation for everyone present at the deposition. Adjournments may become necessary if the deponent needs time to search for some information or make some other inquiries or if the subject matter of the deposition is still developing. You should feel free to discuss deposition format and the timing of recesses, lunch, and other breaks with the other attorney.

Rule 30(g) explains what may happen to the attorney who notices the deposition but fails to appear or fails to obtain the attendance of the court reporter or deponent:

> (1) If the party giving the notice of the taking of a deposition fails to attend and proceed therewith and another party attends in person or by attorney pursuant to the notice, the court may order the party giving the notice to pay to such other party the amount of the reasonable expenses incurred by him and his attorney in so attending, including reasonable attorney's fees.
> (2) If the party giving the notice of the taking of a deposition of a witness fails to serve a subpoena upon him, and the witness because of such failure does not attend, and if another party attends in person or by attorney because he expects the deposition of that witness to be taken, the court may order the party giving the notice to pay to such other party the amount of the reasonable expenses incurred by him and his attorney in so attending, including reasonable attorney's fees.

Reasonable expenses include travel expenses, per diem, and fees for both the deponent and the other attorney(s). If a witness promised to attend the deposition but fails to appear, the examining attorney will be liable for reasonable expenses, unless the witness would not have attended because of illness even if subpoenaed. So set your clock to make sure that you show up, check with the reporter to make certain he or she shows up, and double-check with the deponent.

The rules restrict neither the number of depositions nor the length of a deposition. It is the nature of the beast that one deposition is commonly adequate, but a second or subsequent deposition may be scheduled. Any abuses regarding the number or sequence of depositions may be prevented through a protective order under Rule 26.

An attorney is not required to attend a deposition of a non-party, nor even of a party not his or her client. Rule 30(c) does permit an attorney not attending to submit written questions to be answered by the deponent. But the decision not to attend may have later, unanticipated ramifications. Failure to attend a properly noticed deposition may operate as a waiver of any objection the attorney has to the admissibility of the deposition testimony, because of the lack of sufficient deposition examination of the witness.

§2.2.2 Persons Present at the Deposition

The people present during the deposition are:

1. *The deponent.* All persons who have information relevant to the subject matter or are likely to provide admissible evidence may be deposed. This includes parties, witnesses, and other persons. The problems encountered with identifying corporate deponents is resolved by Rule 30(b)(6):

> A party may in his notice and in a subpoena name as the deponent a public or private corporation or a partnership or association or governmental agency and describe with reasonable particularity the matters on which examination is requested. In that event, the organization so named shall designate one or more officers, directors, or managing agents, or other persons who consent to testify on its behalf, and may set forth, for each person designated, the matters on which he will testify. A subpoena shall advise a non-party organization of its duty to make such a designation. The persons so designated shall testify as to matters known or reasonably available to the organization. This subdivision (6) does not preclude taking a deposition by any other procedure authorized in these rules.

Rule 30(b)(1) solves the further problem of an unknown deponent, by allowing a party to identify the deponent with a "general description sufficient to identify him or the particular class or group to which he belongs."

These rules provide the examining party with the best of all possible discovery worlds. If the examining attorney knows who should be deposed, that person can be designated. If the examining attorney only knows the area to be discovered, the opposing party must designate the person who knows that information. If in the course of the examination, the deposing attorney discovers additional officers, agents, or employees who know something, they can be deposed later. Who could ask for anything more?

2. *The attorney(s)* representing the deponent and the attorneys representing the parties. A deponent who is either a witness or a party has a right to have an attorney present; and all parties to an action have a right to have their respective attorneys present, even though those attorneys may not represent the deponent.

3. *The notary public* who administers the oath and the *officer* who records the testimony. Usually, this will be one and the same — the court reporter. This person(s) can have someone assist him or her during the deposition, for instance, to operate a tape recorder or a video camera.

4. *The parties* (individual parties and officers of corporate parties) to an action have a right to sit in during all depositions. Rule 30(b)(1) requires that a deposition notice be provided each party, implying that all parties have a right to be there. The prevailing view is that parties have an absolute right to be present during a deposition.[2] They have a right to be present during all stages of a trial, and the logical extension of this right would include deposition proceedings. They often do not attend because there is no reason to. A court has discretion to limit a party's attendance, but this limiting order is issued only rarely, as in the case of a party who may ridicule or harass a party deponent.[3]

Sometimes strategic reasons dictate having parties there. For example, their presence may assist in obtaining complete and accurate testimony from the deponent (the deponent may be the only other eyewitness), or their presence may help them prepare for their own deposition. Conversely, there are reasons not to have a party present. For instance, a party may react to some of the testimony and disrupt the deposition, or a party may expect his or her attorney to be aggressive rather than conciliatory, thereby affecting the attorney's perform-

[2]*See* Annot., 70 A.L.R.2d 685, 752-753 (1960).
[3]*See, e.g.,* Gallella v. Onassis, 487 F.2d 986, 997 (2d Cir. 1973).

ance. Sometimes there are even reasons to object to a party's being present. The attorney representing the deponent may object to the influence the party's presence has on the deponent (the party may be the deponent's employer) or may object to the party's being present during confidential testimony. The only way to bar another party's attendance, however, is to obtain a protective order under Rule 26(c)(5).

A corporation, association, or governmental agency may be able to have two individuals present during a deposition. One person would be designated to represent the organization as a party representative. Another person would be designated as the representative deponent pursuant to Rule 30(b)(6).

5. *Third persons.* May third persons (witnesses, interested persons, or just plain members of the public) attend a deposition? Is a deposition a public hearing? Can tickets be sold? First, Rule 26(c)(5) permits protective orders allowing a deposition to proceed "with no one present except persons designated by the court." This implies that anybody may attend unless restricted by a protective order. Further, Rule 29 allows attorneys to establish their own rules for the conduct of the deposition, thus implying that the attorneys may mutually exclude whomever they want from a deposition. But the attorney's power to exclude may be limited: the court reporter at the deposition is a court officer and may be the one deciding who may or may not attend. The rules are silent on this matter, with no indication one way or the other. Some commentators believe that the court reporter has no such right.[4]

Some courts have declared depositions to be private proceedings closed to the public. A 1912 decision held that preliminary proceedings to a trial, including depositions, are private.[5] In 1913, a federal statute was enacted, rejecting this view and specifically declaring depositions in antitrust matters to be open to the public.[6] This special statute does not apply to any other type of deposition. One court has declared that this limited statute is clear evidence of congressional intent to preserve the public nature of depositions.[7] This same court reasoned that deposition inquiries may probe into all sorts of information, much of which will be inadmissible at trial.

---

[4]*See, e.g.,* 2 J. Hetland & O. Adamson, Minnesota Practice 12 (1970); Queen City Brewing Co. v. Duncan, 42 F.R.D. 32, 33 (D. Md. 1966).

[5]United States v. United Shoe Mach. Co., 198 F. 870, 876 (D. Mass. 1912).

[6]Publicity in Taking Evidence Act, 15 U.S.C. §30 (1976) (depositions for use in suits in equity open to the public).

[7]*See* United States v. I.B.M. Corp., 82 F.R.D. 183, 185 (S.D.N.Y. 1979).

The deposition's purpose is markedly different from trial and subject to different protections. The trial judge determines what is admissible and so protects parties from the indiscriminate disclosure of irrelevant private information. But no one determines the relevancy of discovery information. This would support the conclusion that such information should be deemed private until disclosed at trial, but that the public has a right to be present unless a court rules otherwise. Courts have restricted the attendance of individuals present at depositions because of privacy considerations, because the examining party seeks to obtain the independent recollection of a deponent without influence by other depositions, and because such a person would be properly excluded from hearing such testimony at trial. This last reasoning fails to take into account the availability of the deposition transcript to such a witness.

Usually, third persons will not attend a deposition, and ordinarily attorneys do not invite them. However, somebody — an interested observer, a member of the press, or a member of the general public — may want to attend. More often, an attorney wants a third person present for tactical reasons (to influence the deponent), while an opposing attorney objects to that person's being present, also for tactical reasons (to avoid their becoming familiar with the testimony). Rule 26 allows attorneys mutually to restrict the attendance of third persons to a deposition, but if they are unable to agree on who should be present, they will either have to compromise the dispute or seek a protective order or a Rule 37 sanction. Courts that issue such orders must balance the First Amendment rights of the third person (usually the press) with the privacy rights of the litigant. Courts have restricted attendance of a third person (a newsperson) at a deposition and sealed the subsequent transcript.[8] Courts, including the Supreme Court, also have denied third persons access to information in criminal cases, protecting the defendant's right to a fair trial through prior restraint.[9]

Before a deposition, you will need to consider several tactical questions relating to the persons present at the deposition: Whose presence would favorably affect the deposition in your client's behalf? Should you advise the opposing attorney of your intentions? Should you assume that anyone may attend, unless the opposing attorney has obtained a protective order or has asked you to agree mutually to

[8]Times Newspapers, Ltd. (of Great Britain) v. McDonnell Douglas Corp., 387 F. Supp. 189, 197 (C.D. Cal. 1974).
[9]Nebraska Press Assn. v. Stuart, 427 U.S. 539 (1976).

exclude all but essential individuals? Should you ask the opposing attorney whom he or she plans to invite to the deposition? Should your deposition notice indicate whom you will bring? Should you advise the deposing attorney that you are bringing someone else besides the deponent to the deposition?

§2.2.3   Ensuring Production of Documents and Materials

You may want a deponent to bring some documents or tangible things to the deposition. Rule 30(b)(5) allows you to compel the disclosure of such documents from a party at a deposition, by attaching to the deposition notice a Rule 34 request for production of documents or tangible things. Rule 45(b) permits you to compel disclosure from a non-party deponent by serving a subpoena duces tecum commanding the person to bring the designated documents and tangible things to the deposition. Rules 34 and 45 operate in a similar fashion, not only to allow inspection, but also to permit the copying of documents. Rule 45 also allows a court to modify or quash an unreasonable or oppressive subpoena, or to condition the disclosure of such materials on the advancement, by the examining party and to the deponent, of the reasonable costs of production.

Using one or the other of the document disclosure methods may prove very revealing and prevent frustration at the deposition. You will have the opportunity to review documents with the deponent and to receive an explanation of their contents from the deponent. You will also be able to avoid the response from some deponents, "Golly, by now the smoking paper is back on my office desk engulfed in flame."

§2.3   RECORDING THE DEPOSITION

Rules 28(a) and 28(c) require that an officer authorized to administer oaths be present for the taking of a deposition and that this officer cannot be a relative, employee, or attorney of any of the parties or attorneys or otherwise be financially interested in the action. Rule 30(c) requires that testimony be taken stenographically or by some other means ordered by a court or mutually agreed upon by the attorneys. This disinterested court officer is usually a court reporter, who records the testimony by means of a stenotype machine or occasionally by shorthand; he or she is typically from an independent court reporting firm. Rule 30(c) allows someone other than the officer who put the witness under oath to record the testimony, as long as this other person is under the direction of the officer and the officer is personally present. The party who notices the deposition will pay for the officer's time.

But there is no requirement that a recorded deposition be transcribed. Rule 30(c) provides, "If requested by one of the parties, the testimony shall be transcribed." Rule 30(f)(2) states, "Upon payment of reasonable charges therefor, the officer shall furnish a copy of the deposition to any party or to the deponent." Thus, neither party is obliged to have the deposition transcribed. The party who does request a transcription is the party who pays for the original filed with the court and for his or her own copy. The party not requesting transcription can use the court copy, the other side's copy, or pay the reporter for a copy.

§2.3.1   *Telephone Depositions*

Rule 30(b)(7) specifically authorizes telephone depositions by written stipulation or court order. Rule 29 permits an attorney to agree to telephone depositions and clearly authorizes judges to order such depositions at the request of a party. The rule also restricts the location of a telephone deposition to the district within which the deponent answers the questions, that is, where the deponent is when responding.

The purpose of the rule is to publicize and encourage the use of telephone depositions. Such depositions are an ideal way to obtain information efficiently and economically. What about effectively? The decided disadvantage is the lack of visual means to determine the deponent's credibility. That will have to await a new Law Wars technology.

Telephone depositions take place as conference calls and follow procedures similar to ordinary face-to-face depositions. The officer swearing in the deponent may be on the telephone with the examining attorney or in the room with the deponent. Placement depends in part upon how the deposition is recorded, by stenographic recording or through electronic recording.

§2.3.2   Electronic Recording of Depositions

Rule 30(b)(4) specifically allows for other than stenographic recordings, by stipulation or court order. It requires that these stipulations or orders designate:

1. The person before whom the deposition is taken;
2. The means of recording the deposition;
3. The means of preserving and filing the deposition;
4. And other provisions to "assure that the recorded testimony will be accurate and trustworthy."

Tape recorders and videotape equipment are two electronic devices used to record depositions.[1] A number of courts have encouraged such uses, recognizing the benefits of their lower costs. Judges usually grant orders for the use of electronic devices unless the opposing lawyer can show prejudice, excessive costs, or undue burden. One circuit has held that the range of the trial court's discretion to order electronic recording is limited to determining whether safeguards will reasonably ensure accuracy.[2] If so, the order must be granted. If not, it must be denied. Another circuit has disagreed with this reasoning, holding that other factors can be relied upon in exercising discretion, as in any other discovery order.[3]

In the pioneer days of electronic depositions, some courts limited the use of videotape depositions to special circumstances,[4] such as the unavailability of the deponent to testify at trial. Rule 30 now delineates the nature and scope of any necessary court order; it clearly supports the use of electronically recorded depositions. As one court puts it:

> The Court should not be like an ostrich, sticking its head in the sand and being oblivious to advances in technology which can aid in the judicial process. In a situation where the plaintiffs seek the testimony of an essential witness who may not otherwise be available for trial, the video

§2.3   [1]*See* Carter v. Joseph Bancroft & Sons Co., 360 F. Supp. 1103, 1111 (E.D. Pa. 1973); Carson v. Burlington Northern, Inc., 52 F.R.D. 492 (D. Neb. 1971).

[2]Colonial Times, Inc. v. Gasch, 509 F.2d 517, 522 (D.C. Cir. 1975).

[3]International Union v. National Caucus of Labor Committees, 525 F.2d 323, 326 (2d Cir. 1975).

[4]Perry v. Mohawk Rubber Co., 63 F.R.D. 603, 604-605 (D.S.C. 1974), *aff'd without opinion,* 529 F.2d 516 (4th Cir. 1976).

taped deposition should be allowed to give the fact finders greater insight by allowing them to observe the witness' demeanor and manner of testifying.[5]

The technical problems some attorneys associate with electronic recordings can be overcome. Traditional stenographic recording has its own shortcomings with its elements of human error: a human listens to the testimony, a human records the testimony, a human dictates, and a human then types the testimony. The margin for error in ordinary proceedings equals or exceeds the potential errors in mechanical recordings. Some attorneys believe and judge tape recordings to be an inadequate means of recording data: they can be doctored, sound can be difficult to identify, there may be electronically inaudible voices, background noise may cause interference, it can be difficult to locate a segment of testimony, and unknown or undetected mechanical failures can cause the loss of testimony. All these problems can be prevented with proper equipment and safeguards.

Typical safeguards that will assure accuracy and trustworthiness include the following provisions:[6]

1. Two tape recorders should be used to record the entire deposition, in case one mechanically fails.

2. The recording equipment should be of high quality and tested before being used.

3. The person who operates and monitors the equipment should not otherwise participate in the interrogation process. This person need not be someone independent of the party taking the deposition, but such independent status will increase the appearance of accuracy.

4. The oath or affirmation should be administered by a notary public or other person authorized to do so by law. The notary may be from the office of a party.

5. The speakers should identify themselves whenever necessary for clarity of the record.

6. The original tape recording should be labeled, placed in a sealed envelope, and immediately delivered to the court.

7. A transcript should be made, which the deponent reads and

[5]In re Daniels, 69 F.R.D. 579, 581 (N.D. Ga. 1975).
[6]Courts have adopted these provisions in their court orders: Barham v. I.D.M. Corp., 78 F.R.D. 340 (N.D. Ohio 1978); Lucas v. Curran, 62 F.R.D. 336, 338 (E.D. Pa. 1974).

signs and the original of which is filed with the court, with copies provided to counsel.

8. Objections to the accuracy or the trustworthiness of the transcripts should be made within ten days after they are filed with the court.

9. The court should rule on any objections by reviewing the original tape and transcripts.

10. Rule 30(b)(4) permits a party to arrange to have a stenographic recording at his or her own expense, in addition to the electronic recording. While this may provide another safeguard system, it also increases the cost and reduces the value of a separate recorded transcript.

11. An attorney may record a deposition with his or her own tape recorder, in addition to stenographic recording, as long as the recording is unobtrusive and does not interfere with the deposition.

12. An attorney can bring along another stenographer in an unofficial capacity to record testimony taken down stenographically, or in any other way, by the official reporter.

Rule 30(b)(4) court orders will usually include these and other safeguards. Perhaps the stiffest resistance electronic recording receives comes from attorneys who are not noted for the zeal with which they embrace changes. Three or four years of law school takes its toll.

§2.3.3 Videotaped Depositions

Videotaped depositions provide an excellent technique for preserving the testimony of a witness who will not be available for trial. Videotaped recordings have some distinct advantages over conventional stenographic recordings. They show facial expressions, physical posture, demeanor, reactions, exhibits, all in living black and white or color. A videotaped deposition preserves not only what is said, but how it is said, as well as the setting, atmosphere, and conduct of the proceedings. You need only attend a deposition and later read the bare transcript, comparing it to what really happened during the deposition, to realize the night-and-day difference. The videotaped deposition can significantly strengthen the negotiation posture of a case and significantly affect trial results. Showing a videotape to a jury will have substantially more impact than the mere reading (unless you are a

Tracy or a Hepburn) of a transcript. Both stenographic and electronic recordings can capture the testimony of a deposition, but only a video-tape can recreate the tears, tension, and tactics.

The rules relating to stenographic depositions apply with equal force to videotaped depositions, but the procedures differ. More consideration must be given to preparing witnesses, because their demeanor will be visible. Deponents need to be prepared as if they were going to appear on television, which in effect they will. They need to select wearing apparel that not only will improve their appearance at the deposition, but will also be appropriate for color videotape. The presence of a camera will make some deponents more nervous, while others may become preoccupied with the camera rather than focused on the attorney's questions. These and other factors need to be reviewed with the deponent before he or she appears in front of the cameras.

Careful consideration must also be given to the placement of people and equipment. A professional technical crew is necessary to place and operate the camera(s) and the recorder, and to monitor the recording. The equipment is not difficult to operate, but there is a difference between a novice and a professional. The better the technicians, the better the videotaped deposition. The camera or cameras will capture all of the events, including the questioning, the responses, the objections, and any discussion.

There exists a Uniform Audio-Visual Deposition Act, which regulates the procedures to be employed in a videotaped deposition.[7] The act provides that any deposition may be recorded by audio-visual means without a simultaneous stenographic record and without approval of the opposing party or a court. Another party is entitled to make a stenographic or audio record (if it bears the expense) and is also entitled to a copy of the videotape recording (at no expense). The act further dictates that the audio-visual record is an official record, along with any transcript later prepared by an official court reporter; that such a deposition may be used for any purpose and under any circumstances in which a stenographic deposition may be used; and that the notice of subpoena for videotaped deposition must state that the deposition will be recorded by audio-visual means.

The procedures to be observed during the deposition, as detailed by the act, include:

[7]Uniform Audio-Visual Deposition Act, reprinted in 12 Uniform Laws Annotated 11 (Supp. 1981).

1. The deposition must begin with statements explaining the identity of the operator, case, deponent, the date, time, and place, parties, and any stipulations.
2. Counsel must identify themselves on camera.
3. The oath must be administered on camera.
4. The ending of one tape and the beginning of another tape must be announced on the audio recording portion.
5. The deposition must end with statements that the deposition has concluded and with any stipulations regarding custody of the tapes or exhibits.
6. The deposition must be indexed by a time generator or another method established by court rules. A video counter will provide an external means of indexing the deposition and may be enhanced with a timer indicating the length of segments. A time-date generator provides an internal indexing means, by placing the elapsed tape time in minutes and seconds, and the date, if necessary, in one corner of each frame of the videotape.
7. Objections and instructions not to answer, and other comments by the deponent's counsel, will proceed as in a stenographic recorded deposition.
8. The video recording may be edited or altered only by court order or approval.
9. The original recording, any later edited copies, and all exhibits must be immediately filed with the court.
10. Reasonable expenses incurred with a videotaped deposition may be taxed as costs.

The act finally provides that the Supreme Court can establish additional standards for audio-visual deposition recordings.

Since there is usually no going off the record in a video deposition, everything will be recorded, and the videotape may require editing for appropriate use during trial. Equipment currently on the market makes editing relatively easy. The time-date generator provides an index for any objectionable section; sections can be located by high-speed playback machines, which compress the recording into a much shorter period of time while maintaining an understandable audio.

Videotapes may be edited in a number of ways. The operator can black out the objectionable part, suppressing both the audio and video portions, and proceed to the next segment at either normal speed or fast-forward. This method may cause the operator to under- or overshoot the next segment, creating some delay and perhaps confusion.

The operator can black out the audio portion only, and allow the video image to remain. This procedure will be distracting to the jurors and will not be appropriate for long edits. The operator could also opt to make a second videocassette, omitting all objectionable matter. This process can be expensive and must be planned in advance of the trial, but is the most effective way.

Continuing technical advances will ease the fears judges and lawyers have of mechanical things and make videotaped depositions more reliable and effective than traditional stenographic recordings. Costs are still a barrier to widespread video use and will continue to be a major factor until videotape equipment becomes as commonplace in law firms as yellow-page advertisements.

§2.3.4   Reducing the Cost

The costs of depositions include the charge for the court reporter during the deposition and for the transcription of the testimony after the deposition. Court reporters charge an hourly or daily rate for the deposition and a per-page rate for the transcript. The bulk of the recording costs will ordinarily be involved in the transcription expenses, unless you have a deponent who spells words during the deposition. Deposition costs may be advanced by the attorney as long as the client remains ultimately liable for such costs.

The preceding sections have, in bits and pieces, suggested ways of reducing deposition costs (excluding attorney's fees). A deposition need not be transcribed. An attorney anticipating this can take notes during a deposition to record and remember vital information. Ordering a transcript can be delayed until a later stage of the case, and then only if necessary. An attorney can use the deposition filed with the court instead of ordering an individual copy. The attorneys together could order the deposition transcribed and split the costs; they could agree that a deposition of a certain deponent should be taken and split all costs for the deposition. Such a deponent may be important to both sides, may refuse to speak to either side, or may be unavailable for the trial and yet have information both parties need. The attorneys could stipulate to modify the deposition proceedings and to employ a notary public to conduct a tape-recorded deposition. The rules now allow and encourage telephone depositions where appropriate. Judges are inclined to issue orders altering the traditional deposition to reduce costs.

Some attorneys are willing to bargain away some discovery rights to gain the agreement of opposing counsel to take an inexpensive deposition. For example, an examining attorney may agree to waive the right to submit any interrogatories on the topics covered by the deposition. This type of agreement, in the appropriate case, will allow for sufficient discovery, while saving the expenses involved seeking a Rule 37 order.

The extent of cost reduction depends upon the creativity and willingness of the attorneys involved to reduce expenses. Both parties may gain through cooperative approaches—cost reductions may justify taking a deposition in a case involving a client with insufficient funds or little at stake.

Federal statute 28 U.S.C. §1915 provides indigent civil litigants with an opportunity to proceed *in forma pauperis.* Subdivision (a) provides, "Any court of the United States may authorize the commencement, prosecution, or defense of any suit, action or proceeding . . . without prepayment of fees and costs or security. . . ." This provision affords the district court broad discretion in determining the applicability of the statute to a case.[8] Such fees or costs advanced by the court will be taxed as costs and reimbursed to the court, should the *in forma pauperis* party prevail. The statute does not explicitly permit depositions to be funded. It is up to the court in each action to exercise its discretion and decide whether or not to advance costs for depositions and pretrial discovery.[9] Courts have authorized the payment of costs of taking, transcribing, and making copies of depositions.[10] Some courts impose a burden on the indigent party to provide the court with information enabling it to determine the reasonableness and necessity for pretrial discovery costs.[11] The specific criteria applied vary from court to court. A motion, affidavit of indigency, a proposed order, and perhaps an attorney affidavit, ordinarily are sufficient for a motion hearing on your request.

Courts have discretion to order that costs be shared or borne by the opposing party. Some districts have local rules which allocate costs. A party may have to pay for the travel costs of the opposing deponent, and a reasonable attorney's fee for the opposing lawyer, if a deposition

---

[8]Jones v. Morris, 590 F.2d 684, 687 (7th Cir. 1979).

[9]*See* Ebenhart v. Power, 309 F. Supp. 660, 661 (S.D.N.Y. 1969).

[10]*See* Douglas v. Green, 327 F.2d 661, 662 (6th Cir. 1964) (appellant must show a need for such copies).

[11]*See* United States v. Banks, 369 F. Supp. 951, 955 (M.D. Pa. 1974).

occurs beyond a certain distance from the courthouse. The party taking the deposition ordinarily pays the associated expenses of transcription and filing. A district court has discretion to require one party to bear the deposition costs of another party, particularly if the examining party has raised important public issues or has no financial resources.[12]

Some deposition costs will be reimbursable to a prevailing party (or to the court if the party proceeded in forma pauperis). Court reporter fees "for all or any part of the stenographic transcript necessarily obtained for use in the case" may be taxed as costs.[13] The stenographic transcript includes depositions and related costs. The trial court has the discretion to tax as costs those deposition expenses reasonably necessary to the case.[14]

Rule 54(d) outlines recoverable costs and provides that they may be taxed by the clerk on one day's notice and may be reviewed by the court upon a motion served within five days after such notice. The prevailing party typically completes a form provided by the clerk, who then decides who pays what, subject to court review.

§2.3.5 The Record

The reporting officer at the deposition has the responsibility under the rules to record all testimony and all objections occurring during the deposition. Ordinarily a reporter will record everything said by anyone present. The attorneys should make certain that such a record is accurate and complete by:

1. Speaking clearly;
2. Having the deponent speak clearly;
3. Proceeding at a pace appropriate for the reporter;
4. Spelling difficult names and words (or providing a written list of them);
5. Allowing a deponent to finish an answer without interruption (unless the interruption is intentional);
6. Reducing all conduct, gestures, and inaudible responses to

[12]See Haymes v. Smith, 73 F.R.D. 572, 575 (W.D.N.Y. 1976).
[13]28 U.S.C. §1920(2) (1976).
[14]Bailey v. Meister Brau, Inc., 535 F.2d 982, 996 (7th Cir. 1976).

verbal descriptions, noting for the record what the witness or attorney did;

7. Avoiding superfluous comments, ("O.K., now, let me ask you this," "I see," "Strike that"), repeating answers, and unnecessary arguments ("I object and let me read three pages from Wigmore that will explain why . . .");
8. Not asking multiple questions;
9. Refraining from asking negative pregnant questions such as, "Then you didn't apply the brakes until after the impact, did you?" (a yes or no answer establishes nothing definite);
10. Not throwing Federal 2d Reporters at each other.

Everything that goes on during a deposition should be recorded. There are occasions when going off the record will be necessary or be requested by an attorney. If the attorneys agree to go off the record, the court reporter will abide by their request. If one attorney requests going off the record but the other attorney refuses, the court reporter should continue to record. The reporter is an officer of the court for purposes of the deposition and does not have an obligation to obey either attorney. The fact that one attorney has noticed the deposition and hired the reporter does not give that attorney an employer's right to order the reporter to do things.

Going back on the record will occur when either attorney or both attorneys suggest it; a reporter will record the suggestion. Occasionally statements are made, agreements are reached, or things are done off the record that must be included on the record. Whenever these situations occur, one attorney need only verbalize or summarize on the record what happened off the record and obtain the recorded "agreed" from the other attorney.

§2.3.6   Court Reporters and Depositions

Court reporters are an integral part of a deposition. They provide another perspective on depositions and attorney involvement. Some of their more telling observations, obtained from interviews, follow:

1. The abilities of court reporters vary as much as the abilities of attorneys, and the accuracy and completeness of the resulting record and deposition transcript depend in part on the abilities of the reporter.
2. The advent of recording equipment has proven beyond a doubt

that court reporters make mistakes. Some of the errors are within their control; some are not. The deposition process itself builds in mistakes and guarantees that human errors will occur. Consider all the possibilities of error in this sequence of events:

(a) The deponent says something aloud, sometimes imperfectly;
(b) The reporter transcribes the statement accurately, while simultaneously listening to more talk;
(c) The reporter reads and interprets those notes;
(d) The reporter dictates the contents into a tape recorder;
(e) The typist listens carefully to the dictated recording;
(f) The typist types everything accurately and completely.

Moreover, all reporters have particular difficulties with words that sound like other words, with lengthy numbers, with troublesome language, with peculiar information, and with technical data. Mistakes are inevitable.

3. Some reporters will use tape recorders, along with their steno machine, as a reference source, if they have difficulty with their transcription. And court reporters usually have no objection if an attorney brings a tape recorder (although the other attorney may object).

4. Life should be made as easy as possible for court reporters by doing simple things, like providing them with a copy of the deposition notice containing the necessary information, allowing them the choice of where to sit, spelling difficult names or words during the deposition, furnishing them with a glossary of technical terms, providing them with a copy of anything that is read into the record, allowing them a break at least every 90 minutes, and asking them at the end of the deposition if they need anything for preparation of the record.

5. Court reporters may or may not transcribe everything they hear "on the record" and may or may not "edit" the final transcript. Approaches vary. Some court reporters record everything they hear, including "private" conversations between a deponent and his or her counsel, if they are still on the record and if they are within earshot of the reporter. Others do not record such conversations, nor do they record offhand statements that in their opinion have no bearing on the deposition. Should they transcribe these things, they may edit them when they read and dictate their notes.

6. Some court reporters may voluntarily "clean up" the transcript. They may eliminate false starts by an attorney, occasions when an

attorney misspeaks, or unnecessary examining habits such as "O.K., I see, let me ask you this." Some will eliminate lengthier comments by lawyers, such as repeating an answer or a partial, unfinished question. Most will edit statements and comments made by a deponent only rarely. They may alter the sequence of an answer that a deponent completes while the attorney is still asking the question. This occurs with "yes or no" answers or short responses. That is, the deponent may respond before the attorney has finished asking the question. The reporter then places the response after the question, and not in the middle of it.

7. Court reporters do tend to listen to the attorney who has hired them. Many obey that attorney outright. The reporter may side with the hiring attorney during deposition incidents, including conflicts between the attorneys about going off the record, or breaks, or what the deponent just said or did. Court reporters realize that if they do not do things the way the hiring attorney expects, they will not be employed again, and that some other loyal and obedient court reporter will be hired. There are limits, however, since court reporters also realize their obligations not to compromise the accuracy or completeness of a deposition nor the integrity of the system.

8. Some court reporters do not do anything unless they are told to. They do not swear in a deponent unless asked; they do not mark a document unless asked; they do not go back on the record after going off the record unless they are told. Other court reporters may suggest something be done, if in their opinion one of the attorneys has made a procedural mistake.

9. All court reporters charge about the same: an hourly or daily rate plus an amount for the original transcription and one copy. An average deposition produces about 40 pages of transcript per hour.

10. Most court reporters believe that the attorneys involved have the primary obligation and burden to arrange and preserve a "recordable situation" during a deposition. But there is another perspective: court reporters are officers of the court and also have an obligation and burden to ensure that a deposition results in an accurate and complete recording. This requires the court reporter to be impartial, a sometimes-difficult position for someone who is being paid by only one (usually) of the parties. Court reporters have varying understandings of their roles and loyalties during a deposition, understandings that lead to their varying approaches on the above and related elements of a deposition.

§2.4   PREPARING FOR THE DEPOSITION

From your first law-school exam you know that you had to prepare thoroughly for the questions and the answers in order to do well. So also with a deposition.

Preparation of a case requires familiarity with your file and all other sources of factual information and legal claims and defenses relating to the case. Preparation also requires a grasp of the applicable legal doctrines and overall discovery strategies. Further, it demands knowledge of both the subject matter of the deposition and what the deponent knows about that topic. This includes experts and lay witnesses. If the deponent is an eyewitness to an auto accident, you should be familiar with the location, site, topography, area and other matters relating to the accident. If a deponent is an expert engineer, then you should be versed in whatever specialized engineering area the deposition will cover.

An assessment of the deponent is extremely beneficial to proper preparation of the case. Your best source of information may be your own client or a friendly witness who knows the deponent. You should seek whatever information will assist you: gauge the deponent's ability to communicate, degree of common sense, amount of education, extent of sophistication, stability of emotional reactions, physical appearance, and any particular strengths or weaknesses relevant to the deposition. If you do not have access to anyone with such information, you will then be limited to making these and other determinations during the early stages of the deposition.

Preparation further requires a determination of the purpose or purposes of the deposition. There may be more than one purpose. There may be a primary purpose with secondary considerations. The purpose may even change during a deposition. Because depositions serve countless specific purposes in a case, their length varies. You may schedule a one-week deposition for one deponent, and only a 30-minute deposition for another, to elicit some bit of information or to pin down a deponent on some matter. But an initial decision must be reached regarding why you are taking a deposition and what goals you hope to achieve.

With assessments of the factual, legal, and personality aspects of the deposition, you can now decide upon the approach to take toward the deponent and your overall strategy. Different purposes necessitate different approaches and different strategies. If you want to obtain reams of information, then a friendly, sympathetic approach may best yield that result. If you wish to pin down a deponent, a stern and controlled strategy may attain that goal. If you want to confront a deponent, an aggressive, distant approach may best achieve that purpose. If you want to preserve testimony for trial, a cooperative formal approach appropriate for trial may obtain such testimony. A generally formal and rigid line of questioning that produces limited responses to leading questions may produce a deposition that a court will restrict as to use.[1] A cooperative, informal approach that permits a deponent to tell a story in his or her own way spontaneously, coupled with a controlled and aggressive approach concerning selected topics, may produce a deposition for all seasons.

No amount of preparation will fully prepare you for everything, but the more preparation you do, the better you will be able to respond appropriately during a deposition, the more foresight you will have to anticipate problems, and the better you will be able to take advantage of later opportunities. On the other hand, over-preparation may have its drawbacks. You may establish your line of questioning and form your theories of the case and then proceed during the deposition to obtain specific answers and confirm specific theories. But the responses during a deposition may make your questions or theories inappropriate. You need to be flexible enough to adapt various lines of questions and explore new theories. The valuable part of the deposition is the opportunity you have both to prepare what you want to do and to remain open to unplanned things and to asking spontaneous questions. The answers obtained during a deposition may form a new approach to the case or create new issues, claims, and demands you could not anticipate, because the examination itself uncovers the requisite information. Rather than fit the deposition answers to your case, you may want to fit a theory, approach, claim, or demand to the deposition information.

§2.4.1 Outline Organization

The Boy Scouts and Girl Scouts are correct: Be prepared. If there is one absolute rule that should be followed it is: Prepare a complete and detailed outline for the deposition. The degree of detail depends

---

§2.4   [1]Stonsifer v. Courtney's Furniture Co., Inc., 474 F.2d 113, 115 n.2 (10th Cir. 1973).

upon several factors, one of which is your level of experience. The more experience you have, the less exhaustive the outline need be. Maybe.

A few attorneys are able to conduct an effective deposition without extensive written notes, relying upon an organization they have created in their minds. Some lawyers rationalize their lack of written preparation by thinking they can do this. Not many can. Most of us have too many things going on in our minds (or not enough mind for things to go on in) and need a written outline. It is difficult, if not impossible, for most of us to perform several skills at one time. You too may have found it difficult, for example, to stay awake, to think, and to respond in your law-school classes. Similarly, during a deposition, it may be difficult to talk, listen, observe the deponent, think, decide on a tactical maneuver, and formulate the next question, all in one brief moment. It is much more difficult to do all that when you experience the peer pressure and tensions that may accompany the deposition.

A thorough, planned and well-organized outline of what you want and need to cover during the deposition allows you the time to concentrate on your essential listening and observing skills. It also impresses the opposing attorney with your professional preparedness, prevents important topical areas from being omitted, allows you the flexibility to follow tangents spontaneously, prevents unintentional repetitious questioning, eliminates your having to guess what else you should cover during a deposition, reduces deposition time, and so saves your client money. Form books containing discovery lists for specific cases are sources for ideas about what to ask. After preparing a draft of an outline, you can review it and eliminate superfluous or unimportant areas.

The outline should be organized in some logical, chronological, or associational (organized by issues, claims, defenses, situations) sequence. Though as a strategic maneuver you may decide to skip around, and not to ask questions in a logical order during the deposition, your preparation of the outline should be orderly to avoid omitting topics. It is generally advisable not to write out all your questions, but only those important ones that need to be carefully phrased to elicit a certain response. Questions seeking vital admissions, leading questions that may confuse or trap the deponent, important foundation questions, and questions that will be asked at trial may need to be written out. Preparing too many questions may reduce your flexibility during the deposition, make you sound like a Double Jeopardy contestant, and take too long.

The rules of evidence should not unduly influence you in your preparation of the outline or in seeking information during the deposition. The evidentiary rules govern admissibility for trial purposes, not for discovery purposes. Unless the deposition is solely to preserve testimony for trial, you need not become preoccupied with what is or is not a proper question or an admissible answer. Sometimes it is best to forget the rules of evidence completely (easier for some of us than for others) and probe for triple and quadruple hearsay, for the worst evidence, for unauthentic documents, and for gossip and baseless opinions. All this may still not uncover the smoking paper, but it is certain to make things more fun.

The structure of your outline should also suit your personal and professional preferences. Its organization should be easy to read and easy to follow. Space should be allowed for you to make notes, record dandy responses by the deponent, or just to doodle, even if you are not a Yankee.

§2.4.2 Deposition to Preserve Testimony

Depositions are usually conducted in order to gather information from the deponent. But some depositions are taken for a more specific purpose: to preserve testimony. The strategies involved in taking this latter type of deposition differ dramatically from the strategies relating to discovery depositions. The decision to take a preservation deposition depends upon the availability of the deponent for trial. The deponent who will not or may not be able to testify at trial will have his or her testimony considered by the factfinder in five specific situations noted by Rule 32(a)(3):

1. The deponent dies before trial;
2. The witness is more than 100 miles from the trial site;
3. The deponent is imprisoned, ill, or infirm;
4. The witness cannot be subpoenaed for the trial;
5. Exceptional circumstances exist.

The examining attorney may anticipate one of these situations and decide to take a deposition to preserve testimony for trial.

Preservation depositions are taken of witnesses who have information supportive of the examining attorney's case; the deponents would testify at trial for the examining attorney. The deposition question-and-answer format parallels the direct examination format. The deposing attorney attempts to duplicate what would be the direct examination of this witness during trial. Witnesses can consist of deponents who are friendly or neutral and those who are unfriendly. In preserving the testimony of a friendly or neutral witness, consider:

1. Questions that elicit the reasons the deponent will be unavailable;
2. Using trial techniques to make the direct examination effective, such as simple, understandable questions structured to create and maintain interest;
3. Responsive answers detailing the necessary information, including sufficient foundation explanations;
4. Questions and answers designed to be read or summarized at trial;
5. Avoiding objectionable questions, such as leading questions, except to develop testimony.

Preservation depositions of unfriendly witnesses involve some different considerations since they usually seek admissions from an opposing party or expert or lay witnesses. The question-and-answer format parallels adverse direct examination with its use of leading questions to gain specific information and to control the witness. In all preservation depositions the examining attorney must be concerned that all questions and answers will be admissible at the trial.

These approaches differ markedly from discovery depositions, which are more free-wheeling and less concerned with trial matters. But depositions may not all be neatly divided into preservation or discovery classes. Because a deposition often serves several purposes, some of its parts may seek to elicit supportive admissions, while others attempt to discover information or reduce credibility and establish impeachment material. The examining attorney must be flexible enough to adapt the applicable strategies to the respective parts of a deposition.

The attorney representing the deponent must also be aware of the strategies involved in preserving testimony. That attorney must determine whether his or her deponent will be available at trial. If the witness will be unavailable, the attorney may want to schedule a deposition to preserve testimony, in addition to any discovery deposition noticed by the opposition. If this is not done, the only transcript available for trial will be the deposition transcript conducted as a cross-examination. It may not contain all the information necessary for trial and will certainly not be in a direct-examination format. So the deponent's attorney may have an interest in questioning the deponent to preserve information. If concise, this questioning could occur during the attorney's opportunity to "rehabilitate" the deponent.

§2.5 TAKING THE DEPOSITION

Taking the deposition involves a number of procedures and considerations, which are discussed in detail in the subsections that follow.

§2.5.1 Preliminary Procedural Matters

Rule 30(c) provides that the deposition officer shall put the witness under oath or affirmation (if the witness has valid objection to taking an oath) and shall personally, or by someone acting under his or her direction, record the testimony of the deponent. The more common oath and the occasional affirmation are usually routine matters. If the examination proceeds and the witness has not been sworn, the witness must either ratify the prior testimony or answer each question again. The officer must record certain information, including the caption of the case, the persons present, and the appearances of the attorneys. Most reporters obtain that information from the deposition notice and from one or more of the attorneys.

§2.5.2 The Demeanor of the Attorneys

Attorneys have an obligation to conduct themselves during a deposition as if they were at trial. Judges have so held, as passages from two opinions make clear:

> [T]he stenographic record of the examination before trial of Mr. Nimis clearly shows conduct on the part of counsel which would not have been indulged in were the testimony taken before a judge or in open court; nor would it have been indulged in, and certainly if indulged in, would not have been permitted, if it occurred in the trial of the action. There seems to be no reason why, therefore, counsel should conduct

themselves upon an examination before trial any differently than in the
trial of the case.[1]

> The federal rules envision that discovery will be conducted by skilled
> gentlemen [*sic*] of the bar, without wrangling and without the interven-
> tion of the court. The vision is an unreal dream. Regrettably, hostility
> and bitterness are more the rule than the exception in unsupervised
> discovery proceedings. Perhaps this is inevitable, for litigation at all
> stages and under the best of circumstances is fertile ground for conflict.
> The opposing self-interests of the parties, as each vies for advantage,
> often spawns not only bitterness but abuse of the discovery process.[2]

Depositions serve different functions from those of trial proceedings, and attorneys will have some liberty to do things differently.
Questions may be asked that would be inappropriate or inadmissible
at trial, and a hostile attitude, short of harassment, that would tactically
be bad form at the trial, can be taken toward a deponent.

Questionable attorney conduct can usually be controlled by peer
pressure, by noting such conduct on the record, by asking the offending attorney to stop, and if all else fails, by seeking a protective order
or Rule 37 sanctions. Rule 30(d) describes the situation and procedures available to seek relief from improper conduct by an attorney (or
a deponent):

> At any time during the taking of the deposition, on motion of a party
> or of the deponent and upon a showing that the examination is being
> conducted in bad faith or in such manner as unreasonably to annoy,
> embarrass, or oppress the deponent or party, the court in which the
> action is pending or the court in the district where the deposition is
> being taken may order the officer conducting the examination to cease
> forthwith from taking the deposition, or may limit the scope and manner
> of the taking of the deposition as provided in Rule 26(c). If the order
> made terminates the examination, it shall be suspended for the time
> necessary to make a motion for an order. The provisions of Rule 37(a)(4)
> apply to the award of expenses incurred in relation to the motion.

The demeanor of the attorneys during a deposition must be balanced by a number of considerations: appropriate trial decorum, aggressive and spirited advocacy, the purpose of the deposition conduct,

§2.5 [1]Detective Comics, Inc. v. Fawcett Publications, Inc., 4 F.R.D. 237, 239
(S.D.N.Y. 1944).
[2]Harlem River Consumer Coop., Inc. v. Associated Grocers of Harlem, Inc., 54
F.R.D. 551, 553 (S.D.N.Y. 1972).

the need for maintaining a cooperative approach, peer pressure, and the best interests of the client. Whatever the attorney does, he or she should have a reason for such conduct.

§2.5.3 Stipulations

"Usual stipulations, counsel?"

"Huh? Oh, sure, yes, indeed, certainly, by all means."

What stipulations? One of the attorneys may suggest, usually at the beginning or at the conclusion of the deposition, that the "standard" or "usual" stipulations apply to the deposition proceedings. The other attorney may mumble agreement without a consensus reached on what the stipulations are. The court reporter may specify in the transcript some version of the standard stipulations. Conversely, the other attorney may insist that some stipulations be specified and that others are unnecessary or undesirable. (Beginning stipulations that detail procedures governed by the rules are no longer necessary. A stipulation may state that the deposition is taken pursuant to the "Rules of Civil Procedure," but that statement serves no purpose, because the rules do indeed apply.) There are some legitimate reasons for a beginning procedural stipulation. For instance, in a deposition in a case involving many parties, a stipulation that an objection by one attorney will be deemed to have been made by all opposing attorneys can save time and prevent confusion. Stipulations can be agreed upon at any time during a deposition. Typical concluding stipulations will be reviewed in a later section (§2.8.1).

§2.5.4 Introductory Statements and Questions

Some customary introductory requests and explanations include the following:

1. An agreement from the opposing attorney that everything has proceeded properly and correctly up until that moment, to prevent him or her from later raising objections to the formalities, is usual. However, because Rule 32(d) provides that objections to the reporter's qualifications and to the taking of the deposition will be waived unless made prior to the beginning of the deposition or when the disqualification becomes known, such a request may invite an objection that would have been waived.

2. A statement, identifying who is present at the deposition,

should be made. The court reporter will usually note the appearances of counsel and the deponent at the beginning of the deposition transcript. Some attorneys prefer describing in the record who is there, so that the court reporter and the deponent know who is who. Most attorneys leave that matter to the court reporter, who obtains the necessary information from the notice of the deposition and case caption.

3. An explanation of whom the attorney represents may be helpful. This may not be necessary for a party deposition, but will be for a witness or multiparty deposition. An attorney who does not represent a witness, but represents the adverse party, cannot counsel that witness during the deposition and may not have standing to object to all questions. Some attorneys, however, will insist on objecting, and it is not clear what they can or cannot do. A request for an explanation will lay the ground rules for the remainder of that deposition.

4. Explanations and questions directed to the deponent will vary, depending upon the deposition approach and the relationship the deposing attorney wants to establish with the deponent. Traditional opening explanations, which help put the witness at ease and which serve as aids in preventing later inconsistent testimony, might go something like this:

Examining attorney: Mr. Witness, I am Jeffrey Haddock, and I represent the Cookie Monster in this lawsuit. Do you understand what a deposition is? (*Or,* Has your attorney explained to you what a deposition is?) (*If no, explain in detail. If yes, continue on:*)

I am going to ask you a series of questions about the incident involved here, and the reporter will take down your answers. If at any time you don't understand any question, please tell me and I will repeat or rephrase the question. If you answer a question, I will assume that you understood it. Is this understood and acceptable to you? (*The witness will invariably say yes.*)

This deposition will be transcribed by the reporter, and everything that is said here today will be recorded. At the trial, all the testimony you give will be available in booklet form, and if I ask you the same questions then that I will ask you today, and if your answers then differ from the answers given today, you may expect to be asked to account for the difference in your answers. Do you understand this? (*The witness again will usually answer yes, and some attorneys will continue with the following explanation:*)

Your testimony today is under oath, as if you were in a court of law. You have sworn to tell the truth, and if you fail to do so, adverse consequences may result. Do you understand this?

These explanations, which can be varied or modified, may establish some rapport with the witness. They will also effectively prevent witnesses from claiming at trial that they did not understand the questions asked, or understand that they would be asked the questions again, or that they were under oath. This portion of the deposition can be read at the trial for impeachment purposes. Other attorneys will not be this specific with the explanations or may omit the last explanation, because they do not want to suggest that the witness be cautious about answering questions.

Your opening explanations, statements, or questions will affect the atmosphere you want to create at the deposition. If you want to establish a friendly, informal relationship, your initial remarks should have a friendly, informal character to them. If you want to create a stern, formal atmosphere, your remarks should be stern and formal. Deponents will react to your opening. You can attempt to make them feel at ease or attempt to make them feel uneasy. You may not wish to employ any of the traditional openings and may prefer to begin immediately with the factual questioning. Whatever you decide, it must be planned.

§2.5.5 Handling Exhibits

Exhibits are best handled with the hands. A variety of exhibits may be available during the deposition. You may have had the deponent bring some materials and objects pursuant to Rule 34 or Rule 45. The deponent may voluntarily bring some documents or may use some materials to refresh his or her recollection. You may wish to question the deponent about things in your possession. Some attorneys read the exact nature of the document production request under Rule 34 or 45 into the record and then ask whether the documents brought to the deposition are responsive to such request, because there is no formal written response. The question and the answer make clear whether the disclosing side has fully or partially responded to the request. Attorneys also read into the record a description of the documents available at the deposition or have the deponent read part of the document being reviewed into the record. This makes clear what provision is being referred to, but it can be unnecessary and time-consuming. In these situations, the beginning and end of the provision can be noted on the record, or the deponent can mark the provision being reviewed.

Part of this identification process includes the marking of the deposition exhibits. The rules require that exhibits be marked for one reason: so that the record is clear regarding the identity of the exhibit and references made to it by the deponent and attorneys. The record would be confusing if an exhibit were not described in some fashion, to distinguish it from other exhibits. The record would also be lengthier than necessary if exhibits were referred to by some description including title, date, signatures, contents, or whatever. The process is simple. The court reporter marks an exhibit upon request of either attorney. Such a request may be made before the deposition starts, particularly if there are numerous exhibits, to save time later. Some attorneys merely hand the exhibit to the reporter and ask the reporter to mark it. Others describe the thing to be marked at least once on the record. For example:

Attorney: Reporter, please mark as Plaintiff's Exhibit 1 this three-page will, dated October 1, 1978, signed by Howard Hughes and witnessed by Saint Peter and Bugs Bunny.

Reporter, please mark as Defendant's Exhibit A this pale pink eraser, approximately two inches long and one inch wide, bearing the initials *R.N.*

All documents and objects should be marked before they are used, and all subsequent references to the exhibit should include the exhibit identification. For example:

Attorney: I hand you this letter, marked Plaintiff's Exhibit 2, and ask you whether that is your *X* on the bottom of page 3.

You may prefer showing the exhibits to the opposing attorney before you hand them to the deponent, particularly if the attorney is not familiar with the exhibit. It is professional courtesy to do so, and an experienced opposing attorney will insist on reviewing the exhibit before or with his or her client. Witnesses often discuss exhibits without identifying them, and you may need to clarify the record by designating the exhibit number or letter of the document or object they discuss. Further, you may want the exhibits marked by the witness with his or her initials or a specific mark, to designate significant portions of the exhibit the witness acknowledges or describes.

Part of the process of introducing exhibits in a deposition parallels the process of their introduction at trial, but there are some differences. There is no need to "offer" an exhibit at a deposition, because it automatically becomes part of the record, and any objections to the receipt of such an exhibit will be determined by the judge at trial. Likewise, while there is usually no need to lay a foundation before questioning the deponent about the exhibit, there may be reasons for doing so. The answers to foundation questions may produce sufficient information, helping you to compose later a Rule 36 admission request relating to the genuineness and authenticity of the document, or to frame a stipulation. The foundation questions may need to be asked at trial, and the answers to such questions at the deposition make trial preparation more effective and efficient. Lastly, a deposition transcript with exhibit foundation answers makes possible the introduction of such exhibits at trial, if the deponent is unavailable to testify.

Rule 30(b)(1) describes what happens to the exhibits after the deposition and what options the parties have regarding them:

> Documents and things produced for inspection during the examination of the witness, shall, upon the request of a party, be marked for identification and annexed to and returned with the deposition, and may be inspected and copied by any party, except that (a) the person producing the materials may substitute copies to be marked for identification, if he affords to all parties fair opportunity to verify the copies by comparison with the originals, and (b) if the person producing the materials requests their return, the officer shall mark them, give each party an opportunity to inspect and copy them, and return them to the person producing them, and the materials may then be used in the same manner as if annexed to and returned with the deposition. Any party may move for an order that the original be annexed to and returned with the deposition to the court, pending final disposition of the case.

The intent of Rule 30(b)(1)(a) is to permit an attorney to offer copies for marking and annexation to the deposition. These copies are the "substitute," and the originals used during the deposition would not be attached to the transcript, but would be returned to the party who provided them. These original documents must be retained and made available to the other party should the need arise. The deposition and the exhibits will be filed with the court in due course. Some clerk's offices will not accept the filing of non-paper exhibits like blueprints or x-rays, so other filing arrangements for the originals must be made by the attorneys involved.

§2.5.6   Discovery of Materials

Rule 34 is the appropriate discovery device to obtain copies of documents and things. But a deposition provides you with the opportunity to uncover the identity and location of materials and to request that you be allowed to inspect and copy such materials. Your request will not necessarily be complied with, but more often than not professional courtesy and the spirit of cooperation will prompt the other attorney to agree to your request.

You can ask questions concerning how thorough the search for the documents produced pursuant to Rule 34 was. A detailed inquiry into the mechanics of the search may indicate that some potential sources of documents were overlooked, and you can insist that such documents falling within the Rule 34 request be produced. Your questioning may also uncover documents the deponent used to refresh his or her recollection in preparing for the deposition. You have a right to review these documents. Courts require their disclosure, relying upon Rule 30(c) and Federal Rule of Evidence 612, which permit depositions to proceed in the same fashion that direct and cross-examination proceeds at trial.[3] Courts have required documents to be disclosed that were protected by the attorney-client privilege, because the use of documents to refresh recollection operated as an effective waiver of such privilege.[4]

You may insist that all documents discovered during a deposition be produced before the deposition terminates, during a break, or at a later date when the deposition has been continued. You may also uncover the existence and identity of documents not requested and not used to refresh recollection. You should seek an agreement from the other counsel during the deposition to allow you to review and copy these documents.

Any such agreement concerning the disclosure of documents and things should be reflected in the deposition record. If you are the attorney seeking the information, be certain the record reflects what the other attorney has agreed to provide and the date or deadline by which such things will be disclosed. For example:

[3]Prucha v. M. & N. Modern Hydraulic Press Co., 76 F.R.D. 207, 209 (W.D. Wis. 1977).
[4]Wheeling-Pittsburgh Steel Corp. v. Underwriters Labs., Inc., 81 F.R.D. 8, 10-11 (N.D. Ill. 1978).

Examining Counsel: The record will reflect that Mr. Smith has agreed to allow me to inspect and copy all correspondence exchanged between the plaintiff and defendant in September 1982, and that the records will be made available in defendant's office at 10:00 A.M., May 1, 1983. Would you further agree to provide me with a copy of the contract, dated November 1, 1982, signed by both parties?
Other Attorney: Yes.
Examining Counsel: Would you please mail me a copy within ten days?
Other Attorney: Yes.

These recitations should detail the contents of the agreement and the date. If the other attorney fails to provide such access or copies, the requesting attorney can still submit a Rule 34 request buttressed by the previous agreement.

If you are the attorney who has been asked for something, you may cooperate with the other attorney unless you have good reason not to. Do not give things away until you first have had the chance to review the items yourself. You do not want to disclose something without having reviewed its contents and appraised its discoverability.

An agreement on the deposition record to disclose documents raises the question of its enforceability. Does this commitment compel such disclosure without a formal Rule 34 request? May the attorney renege on the agreement and insist upon a Rule 34 request? The answer depends upon the circumstances. The attorney who changes his or her mind must have a good-faith, substantial reason for doing so, compelling enough to convince the other attorney not to initiate a Rule 37 motion, and sufficient to avoid the imposition of motion expenses and attorney's fees by a judge. The opposing lawyer must decide whether to serve a Rule 34 request before enforcing the deposition through Rule 37. Rule 34 does not appear to be the exclusive way to obtain access to documents. Stipulations can be enforced.

§2.5.7 Confidential Information

The deponent's attorney may refuse to disclose documents or reveal information, by claiming that the materials are confidential or privileged. These grounds may become the basis for an instruction not to answer a question. You must anticipate these situations and be prepared to counter such positions. Rule 26(c)(7) permits parties to obtain a court order preserving the confidentiality of information. This order can be obtained by a motion or a stipulated agreement between counsel. These agreements can be made upon the record at a deposition, later confirmed in writing and approved with a court order.

The significant terms of these agreements include the scope of the confidential materials (what is confidential and what is not) and who has access to the information. Usually the attorneys, a party or a representative of a party, and an expert will have access to the confidential information. Details, such as which attorneys and how many, which party representatives, and how many experts, will be negotiated by the attorneys. Problems relating to confidential matters can be anticipated and resolved prior to the deposition, so that the information or documents can be readily disclosed during the deposition itself.

§2.5.8   Reacting to Objections

Your opponent has a right to make objections during a deposition, though no one is authorized to rule on the objections at that time. Ordinarily, your reaction to an objection is to proceed and insist on an answer to the question. Rule 30(c) provides that "[e]vidence objected to shall be taken subject to the objection" and shall be "noted by the officer" upon the record. A later section will detail the place and extent for deposition objections. As the examining attorney, your primary concern with objections is to prevent them from interfering with your taking the deposition.

The opposing attorney may or may not specify the grounds for the objection. If you are uncertain why the attorney has objected, you may want to ask for specific or explanatory grounds for the objection. Sometimes you will ask a question that you know is poor, and if there is an objection, you will know why. You can then decide either to rephrase the question or withdraw it. At other times you will ask what you think is a perfectly proper question, and still receive an objection. If you are uncertain, you may want to ask the attorney the grounds, or you may want to proceed and insist upon an answer. Your reaction will largely depend upon the specific type of objection raised:

1.   If an objection to the form of the question is raised, then you should decide whether to rephrase the question. It may be improper, unclear, or not understandable. Rule 32(d)(3)(B) validates such objections. You may decide it is proper, and insist on an answer as originally stated.

2.   If an objection cites lack of foundation, you will probably want

to establish the foundation through additional questions. If the deposition is to preserve testimony, then most likely you will want to lay the proper foundation. But even if you have no intent to preserve testimony and do not care whether there is a sufficient foundation, you will nonetheless care about conducting a probing, intensive deposition, and so, again, you will ask questions to establish foundation. Rarely will there be situations in which you do not want to inquire about how a witness knows something.

3. If it is an objection based on relevancy or competency, you may be able to cure the objection by rephrasing the question or by asking a series of clearly relevant questions. If so, do it. If not, insist on an answer. Rule 32(d)(3)(A) authorizes such objections.

4. If the objection is based on any other grounds, ignore it and obtain your requested answer from the deponent. If the deponent is unsure of what to do, tell him or her to answer the question. You have a right to the answer regardless of the nature of the objection.

5. If the attorney objects and instructs the deponent not to answer, you will find it impossible to extract an answer. You should ask the witness to make his or her refusal clear, if he or she does refuse to answer. But the rules prohibit the use of bamboo shoots inserted in the fingernails. If there is an objection to your question, do not ask the other attorney if he or she is instructing the witness not to answer. There is no sense in putting ideas in his or her head, even though there may be room.

6. If the opposing attorney persists in an instruction, your recourse is to seek a court order under Rule 37, compelling an answer. To obtain such an order you must present to the judge the actual wording of the objectionable question, preferably in an excerpt from the transcript containing the objectionable question. It is possible to submit an affidavit describing what happened, but it is much better practice to have the court reporter mark the passage and prepare the excerpt from the deposition for the judge to read.

At the time the instruction not to answer is interposed, you should make certain that the transcript clearly and accurately details what happened. The transcript should reflect the following:

1. The question;
2. The objection;
3. The instruction not to answer;
4. The client's refusal to answer;
5. The reason supporting the refusal.

The sanctions available under Rule 37 need to be sought only occasionally, because the importance of the question diminishes as the time, effort, and expense in obtaining the answer mounts. Rarely is there an adjournment of the deposition to seek an immediate court ruling. Usually the deposition will continue and the order will be sought later. The deposing attorney may be able to avoid the problem, either by asking the same question later in a different form or by agreeing with the other attorney to obtain a partial answer to the question.

Reacting to objections should not include arguing with the other attorney about the correctness or appropriateness of the objection. There is no need to try to persuade the attorney that he or she is wrong; the question must be answered regardless. There may be a reason, however, to argue with an attorney over an instruction not to answer — if you do change the attorney's mind, it will save you a trip to the courthouse. Otherwise, arguing over objections wastes time, often tips the witness to the reason you asked the question in the first place, and allows the witness more time to conjure up a response.

If an attorney insists on interposing frequent objections to your questions, there are several ways you can handle the situation. You may suggest that the record reflect a continuing objection to all or certain of your questions, to avoid the other attorney's continually interrupting with objections. You may tactfully remind the other attorney that the rules provide that nearly all objections will be preserved for the trial and that there is no need for most objections. You may advise the other attorney that such unnecessary objections unduly interfere with the deposition and that you consider such conduct improper under the rules. Or you can, in egregious situations, seek a protective order or a Rule 37 sanction. If all else fails, you could ask the attorney for his or her home address.

§2.5.9 Controlling Interference

The primary concern of the deposing attorney is to maintain control over the deposition procedures. The preceding sections have described situations and suggested approaches allowing the attorney to prevent interference and maintain control. But interference may stem from the opposing attorney, the deponent, or strategy considerations.

The other attorney may engage in conduct that is designed to protect the deponent, but that interferes with the deposition. A later section will list tactics attorneys use to protect their witnesses. The deposing attorney should counter with the following safeguards:

1. Insist on doing things your way. If the rules do not resolve a matter and if your understanding of custom and practice differs from the other attorney's, insist on proceeding your way and argue that it is your deposition and you will do things your way. This suggestion holds true for all situations except those in which you are wrong.

2. Record everything that occurs. Especially record all non-verbal conduct by the opposing attorney, whether it involves passing a note to the witness, whispering something in the deponent's ear, signaling the witness, conferring with the client, or other conduct affecting the testimony.

The deponent may attempt to interrupt the deposition. A witness may ask to consult with his or her attorney about a response. There is nothing in the rules to prevent such a conference, but there are safeguards that can reduce the potential interference caused by this and other types of interruptions:

1. Include instructions in the beginning of the deposition, explaining to the deponent what you expect and what you will not tolerate.

2. Insist that the deponent respond to your question and only to your question. Insisting on complete answers, cutting off flippant and unnecessary remarks, interrupting rambling and self-serving responses, and not answering questions the deponent asks also establish control.

3. Ask the deponent whether the attorney conferred with him or her during a recess. The contents of any such conversation will, of course, be privileged, but the fact that it occurred is not. A direct question like that may forestall the deponent from changing or supplementing testimony.

You may decide to interrupt the deposition for reasons of strategy. Occasionally your preparation may not be complete, and you may need a break to obtain some more information or to rethink your approach to the deposition. Or the deponent may not be prepared to respond fully to a question, and you may want an adjournment to allow the witness to obtain some data or to review some materials. The deposition may uncover some documents, and you may want a recess to study them before continuing with the deposition. The other attorney may suggest a recess or lunch break during a deposition. Before acceding to such a request, you should be certain to complete a full segment of the deposition, in order to prevent a conference between the deponent and the attorney during the break that could lead to alterations or supplementations in the testimony later.

§2.5.10   Concluding Questions and Considerations

The examining attorney may wish to end the examination with several broad questions on the record to make clear that the witness has both understood everything and told all. Questions such as "Have you understood all the questions you answered?" or "Did you reveal all the facts you were asked about?" usually produce affirmative or "to the best of my recollection" responses and nothing further. They may bolster the impeachment value of the testimony. Other concluding questions have different purposes. "Do you wish to change any of your answers?" may produce a quick no or a statement from the deponent's attorney that the deponent has a right to read the transcript and to make any appropriate changes at that time. "Do you wish to say anything else?" is a stab-in-the-dark question, hoping that the witness will somehow say something damaging. This question may also prompt an objection that the question is too broad. Neither question will usually have any useful purpose.

Some examining attorneys advise deponents that they have an obligation to provide supplementary answers to the deposition questions if they recall any additional information after the deposition or if they need to update some answers. This supplementation commitment may or may not be mandatory under Rule 26(e). The opposing attorney may interrupt such an explanation and suggest that he or she will advise his or her client accordingly.

Rule 30(c) allows examination of the deponent by his or her counsel or attorneys representing other parties. This examination will occur after you have completed your questioning. You have an interest in making certain the other attorney receives that opportunity. If the opportunity has not been provided to an attorney, the deposition could be considered incomplete by a court and useless as evidentiary or even impeachment material. So it is good practice to ask on the record whether the other attorney has any questions of the deponent before ending a deposition.

Examining attorneys usually allow the other attorney to ask a reasonable number of questions for rehabilitation purposes. Questions that become excessive in number allow you to take the position that your deposition of the deponent has formally ended because the examination has become a deposition to preserve testimony. You can then advise the other attorney that you will no longer pay the court reporter. You could decide to be difficult (particularly if you have something else scheduled at that time) and leave. You probably should cooperate, however, and stay to listen to the answers and ask more questions after the examination. You can negotiate with the other attorney to have him or her assume the extra costs associated with the lengthened deposition.

§2.6 DEPOSITION QUESTIONING STRATEGIES

Some deposition questioning techniques are almost mandatory in application and will be used in every deposition. Techniques should not require any thinking; they should simply be implemented. Inexperienced or unsuccessful attorneys use a number of techniques that flag their inexperience or contribute to their losing percentages. They make interesting grist for analysis when formulated as precepts:

1. *Don't pay close attention to the deponent's responses.* It is hard enough to ask the questions, and if you must also listen closely to the answers, well, it might be too much for you. For example:

Deponent: All right, so I am not the real deponent. I didn't think you would ever find out. My name is. . . .
Counsel: Excuse me, let's take a short recess. I have to call and reserve a racquetball court for this afternoon.

2. *Don't observe the witness.* Witnesses may react in the most telling ways to certain questions. Their body posture and facial expressions may indicate their nervousness, or tension, or what seems to be an inconsistent answer. This all means nothing. For example:

Counsel: You were driving 105 miles per hour through the grade-school parking lot at the time you hit the milk carton, correct?
Deponent: Not really. *(Thud.)*
Counsel: Your client looks awfully uncomfortable. Must be the flu. How about a recess?

3. *React visibly to damaging information.* Experienced attorneys will impassively and neutrally respond to the most damaging information without indicating what surprises, bothers, disturbs, or pleases them. It may be better for your psyche (although not your law practice) to

release your primal instincts as your case disintegrates before your eyes. For instance:

Deponent: I remember the exact words your client spoke immediately after the accident. She said, "It was all my fault. I was 100 percent negligent, you were zero percent negligent." In fact, I wrote it down in this document in front of 38 impartial eyewitnesses, all of whom signed in the presence of three notaries.

Counsel: I got good grades in law school, I never complained about the bar exam, why should my career be tarnished?

4. *Ask complex, unclear questions, chock full of legalese.* Successful attorneys prefer using simple, clear questions, so that the deponent understands and that the questions will be appropriate for evidentiary or impeachment use later at trial. It may sound better to your blue-book ear if you ask discombobulated questions. For example:

Counsel: Allow me to recapitulate your previous testimony, which you have provided us with this day in immediate response to my direct question relating to the doctrine of incorporeal heraditaments, did you or did you not commit this act perpetrated on my client, the plaintiff in this civil action, file number. . . .

5. *Do not be curious.* If you are trying to find out what information the other side has or what the deponent knows, don't probe, don't ask follow-up questions, don't be inquisitive, and don't ask questions merely because you don't know or understand something. Keep your puzzlement to yourself. You have enough things to remember already and there is little use in becoming confused with the facts. But, above all, don't be curious or ask questions you suspect may reveal damaging information. What you don't know won't hurt you. For example:

Deponent: I told your client that it was probably going to be what we call a fornistan, but he insisted, and the next day. . . .

Counsel: Oh, a fornistan, sure. How long have you been a deponent?

6. *Assume everything is in your best interests.* Depositions can be significantly reduced in time, scope, and expense if you make assumptions about what happened, instead of asking question after question to discover what actually did happen. This guessing game also reduces the amount of actual information and evidence available for trial, mak-

ing your trial notebook lighter and making it easier on the law clerk who carries your briefcase to court. For example:

Counsel: State your name.
Deponent: Number 6746.
Counsel: Were you driving your car on the date this accident occurred?
Deponent: Yes.
Counsel: Thank you. No further questions. I'm bright enough to know what happened.

7. *Insist on generalizations and conclusions, not factual responses.* Experienced and successful attorneys insist on factual responses to factual questions. They know that most people tend to use generalized, conclusory words to describe things. They know that words have more than one meaning. They know that to prove a case at trial they need facts and admissible evidence, not generalizations and assumptions. They know they have to ask continually the key questions in depositions: "How do you know?" "What facts do you have to support that statement?" They know they may have to repeat or rephrase a question over and over again, until the witness answers with a factual description or retracts a prior response. They know there are many reasons a witness will reach a conclusion without having any data to support that position. They know that follow-up factual questioning often reduces a conclusion to a guess. But that process takes knowledge, patience, and persistence. It is much simpler to take what a witness says at face value and go on. After all, witnesses would not say anything unless they saw everything, remembered everything, and were able to recall at a later date everything that had happened, communicating it clearly in unequivocal words. Attorneys can all do that. But then, attorneys are supposed to be perfect. For example:

Counsel: Did Mr. Danforth sign the contract?
Deponent: Yes, of course.
Counsel: How do you know?
Deponent: Well, I saw his name on the bottom line. I assume he signed.
Counsel: You did not see him sign, did you?
Deponent: No.
Counsel: Then, you don't know if he signed the contract, do you?
Deponent: No.

Counsel: Did Mr. Danforth read the contract?
Deponent: Oh, yes.
Counsel: How do you know?
Deponent: He sat in the room with me for a while with the contract.
Counsel: Did he just glance over parts of the contract?
Deponent: I don't know.
Counsel: Did you observe his eyes as he looked at the contract?
Deponent: No.
Counsel: Did he say anything to indicate he read the contract?
Deponent: No. But he didn't say he didn't read it.
Counsel: You don't know whether he read it or not, do you?
Deponent: No. I thought so. I assumed he read it. I guess . . .all right, I confess. I read it. It took me about two minutes. The content was boring. So was your client.

It works every time.

There are a number of other strategic and tactical options that must be considered before and during the deposition and that affect its direction and success. The precise strategies to be employed will depend on the purposes of the deposition. The following subsections detail these tactical alternatives. Keep in mind that not all the strategies need to be considered in every deposition: each has its place and moment.

§2.6.1   Specific Techniques: How to Probe

1.   *Insist on responsive answers.* Attorneys should ordinarily insist that witnesses fully and accurately respond to the questions. But witnesses may respond in different fashions.

They may respond "I don't know," and they may not know. The best you can do is follow up and ask why they don't know, particularly if they should know something.

They may summarily respond "I don't know," but further questioning may be necessary to make certain they have no information. Follow-up questions may include: "Did you know something in the past?" "You don't know, or you don't presently remember?" "Is it your testimony today that you do not have any personal knowledge to answer that question?"

They may respond "I don't know for sure," but you are more interested in their estimate or even their guess about something. You can lead the deponent with "bracketing" questions to elicit some response:

Deponent: I don't know for sure.
Counsel: Wait until I ask a question. How far from the intersection was Mr. Haydock's motorcycle when you first saw the motorcycle?
Deponent: I don't know for sure.
Counsel: Was the distance less than 400 feet?
Deponent: Yes.
Counsel: Was the distance more than 200 feet?
Deponent: Yes.
Counsel: Was it more or less than 300 feet?
Deponent: I'm not sure. I really don't know.
Counsel: You are sure, though, that it was less than 400 feet and more than 200 feet, is that correct?
Deponent: Yes.

They may respond "I think so" or "probably" or "I'm not certain, but I believe so." You have to decide whether to follow up with further questions seeking a more definite answer, or a yes or no, or "I don't know." If the less-than-certain response is favorable, further inquiries may erode that favorable effect or may solidify that answer. If the response is unfavorable, further inquiries may erode or solidify that response. Your assessment of the situation and potential responses should be your guide.

They may respond "I don't recall" or "I don't remember." You have to decide whether you want to attempt refreshing their recollection or to leave the response as is. You may want to ask if there is anything that may refresh their recollection. It is usually important during a deposition to discover not only what the deponent knows but also what he or she does not know. If the deponent does not recall something, you can follow that response with "Then it is possible that. . . ."

They may respond with a selective memory, remembering only favorable information. It is the task of the examiner to refresh the deponent's recollection of other, perhaps damaging, information.

They may respond with an emerging pattern of ambiguous or evasive or incomplete answers. You then have to decide whether to ask questions that continue to elicit such responses. The deposition transcript will then show a witness who knew little, was evasive, and who will be worthless as a witness for the opposition.

2. *Decide upon a structured approach.* Some attorneys employ a standard questioning approach to obtain complete information about an event. One such technique includes: (1) asking general, open-ended questions to which the deponent provides narrative answers; (2) following up with specific, closed-ended questions that clarify and probe such answers; (3) concluding with questions that verify another version of the event to pinpoint similarities and differences between the accounts (without being obvious). This or other structured approaches assist the examining attorney in exhausting a particular area before moving on to another.

3. *Encourage the deponent to talk and ramble.* This, of course, depends on what he or she may say. The response may be self-serving and should be discouraged. It may be relevant or irrelevant. Loquacious witnesses sooner or later tend to disclose some damaging information or to say something inconsistent.

4. *Go from general to specific.* Often depositions seek information about both general and specific practices performed by the deponent. You must decide whether you want to have the deponent first explain the general, normal practices, then follow with questions delving into specific practices relevant to the litigation, or vice versa. The former approach may lock a witness into a particular version or force the witness later to explain inconsistencies between the normal practice and the practice questioned in the litigation.

5. *Proceed in a logical order or shift the subject matter of the questions frequently and suddenly.* A logical, orderly tactic should produce more and reliable information from the deponent. A haphazard, helter-skelter approach may cause difficulty for the deponent and result in confusing and inconsistent responses. Either tactic or a modified strategy requires organization and planning; they are discussed at length in §2.4.1.

6. *Explain what you want.* You can explain or instruct the deponent to answer in certain ways. You may tell the deponent exactly what it is you want. For example: "Tell me everything that you said and everything that he said." "Please explain, step by step, what happened, describing everything you saw." Or, "Answer the next questions either yes, no, or 'I cannot answer yes or no.' " These directions keep you and the deponent on the same track and establish a clearer record.

7. *Repeat questions.* You may repeat questions. Repeat questions. Not with the exact words each time. Sometimes answers to questions change if asked at different times during the deposition. This tactic also makes it difficult for a less-than-honest deponent, who may have

some difficulty remembering what was said previously. You may also have to repeat a lengthy line of questions relating to a series of separate events. This can become tedious and boring, but it may be your task to persevere.

8. *Short-circuit questions.* Depositions often involve inquiries into related documents or incidents and, rather than repeat an entire detailed line of questions for each document or incident, you may ask: "Would your answers pertaining to Exhibit 1 generally pertain to Exhibit 2 as well?" This shortened inquiry may be objected to as overly broad and may cause you to miss some detail.

9. *Lead the witness.* You may want to lead the witness with factual or leading questions because you want to obtain some responses that support your particular theories of the case. They can help you create a certain impression or perspective of a deponent, particularly regarding the deponent's memory. For example, if you want to establish that a deponent has a poor grasp of the circumstances of an auto accident, you should ask leading questions such as: "This accident happened very quickly. This was a frightening experience for you. You became tense anticipating the crash. You were moving at the time of the collision." If you want to establish that a deponent had a good grasp of what happened, you should ask leading questions such as: "You have a vivid memory of this event. You were especially alert because of the potential danger. You had a clear view of the scene. You were concentrating very intensely at the time of the collision." The more factual the leading questions are, the more likely an adverse deponent will have to agree with your question. For example, "You were wearing your sunglasses, you moved down before the impact." The more conclusory your leading question, the greater leeway the deponent has to disagree.

10. *Take notes.* You may want to take notes during a deposition, to record a response or to frame later questions on a topic. Notetaking may affect the deponent. Your writing causes you to lose eye contact with the deponent, who may naturally speak more slowly as you write or stop until you are done. Deponents may wonder why you are taking notes of some responses and not others, causing the deponents to expand or, more likely, limit their responses. Suspicious of your notetaking, and concluding that some of their responses are more important than others, they become more cautious and guarded.

11. *Pace the deposition.* Be aware of the time, rhythm, and pace of the deposition. A pace, or varying paces, that achieves your goals should be maintained. Fast-paced questioning tends to keep your

mind alert and quick, while forcing responsive answers and providing less time for the deponent to think about less-than-honest responses. But a quick pace may also discourage lengthy narratives by the deponent, interrupt responses, and make it difficult for you to keep track of what was asked and to remember what was said. Slower-paced questioning may eliminate these deficiencies by sacrificing the advantages. Whatever pace occurs, fast, slow, or moderate, you must be aware of it and what effect it has on the deposition.

§2.6.2 Specific Techniques: What to Ask

12. *Ask anything and everything.* Should you ask "why" questions, leading questions, potentially harmful questions, or questions inadmissible for trial? Most depositions seek factual information, so you ordinarily want to probe, explore, and press deponents for information until their memory is exhausted. All kinds of information should be elicited — the good, the bad, the neutral, and especially the harmful information, because discovery is the place and means for you to uncover the weaknesses as well as strengths in your case. Many depositions seek to know the reasons something happened or people have done something. They require "why" and opinion questions. Depositions with narrower purposes and scope do not call for such detailed and thorough questioning.

13. *Ask who, what, when, where, why and how questions.* These questions will usually produce detailed information, clarifying and supplementing a deponent's narrative response.

14. *Employ closing questions.* As the deposition progresses from topic to topic, you should consider whether you have taken enough precautions to prevent the deponent from legitimately modifying or adding to his or her testimony later. One such device is the use of wrap-up questions, such as "Have you told us absolutely everything that you remember happening at that time?" Or, "Did she say anything else to you on the telephone that you have not testified to?" Or, "Do you have any other information relating to the incident that you have not disclosed?"

15. *Probe the source of the information.* A deponent often provides information without clarifying whether that information is based upon personal observation or knowledge, hearsay, inference, or assumption. You are well advised to determine its exact source.

Questions about other sources of information also make the witness more accountable for his or her story. If the deponent thinks you have no corroborating or contrary source of information, he or she may be inclined to exaggerate. If the deponent realizes that you have access to another source, he or she usually attempts to formulate a story consistent with that source. Accountability reduces the chances of exaggeration and increases the likelihood of accuracy.

16. *Detail conversations.* Deponents usually provide a summary of a conversation when asked what was said. The examining attorney must then decide whether to seek clarifications through detailed questions and thus to determine whether the answer is (1) an impression of what was said, (2) a paraphrase of who said what, (3) a close approximation of what was said, (4) an exact quotation, or (5) some other recollection. Probing questions not only detail a deponent's story but also reflect on the deponent's credibility.

17. *Compare stories.* Your client or witness usually has a different version of what occurred from that of an adverse deponent. You must obtain sufficient information during the deposition to compare the conflicting versions. You may want the deponent to know that your questions are based upon information you have gained from another source, or you may want the deponent not to realize you are verifying another version. A deponent who senses that your questions are based upon contrary information may become more cautious in answering. The timing of such questions will also affect your use of this technique. In order not to influence the deponent's story, first ask narrative and neutral questions to obtain information. Or if you do hope to influence the response, ask suggestive, leading questions.

18. *Ask about feelings, emotions, opinions, thoughts, and attitudes.* Too often, examining attorneys limit their questions to what happened and what was said or observed. Other levels of questions may produce helpful information. "What were you thinking? What was your attitude? What judgment did you make about that person? What is your opinion? How were you feeling at that moment? What did that sound like? Did you notice any smell?" Questions dealing with thoughts, attitudes, judgments, opinions, feelings, emotions, impressions, and sense perceptions often explain the reason for some event and may lead to more information about it. Responses to these questions add another dimension to the typical, fact-oriented deposition.

19. *Inquire about witnesses and documents.* Whether a witness answers a question completely or incompletely, you should consider asking whether anyone else might have more information or whether there are any documents and things which might reveal more information.

Questions about witnesses, documents, material things, and persons with information should be routine and asked periodically during a deposition. The related technique of "working a document" during a deposition involves asking various sorts of questions designed to authenticate the document, to inquire into its creation or meaning, or to place the document in a favorable perspective.

20. *Have the deponent draw a diagram.* Drawing a diagram may make it easier for the deponent to testify accurately and for you to understand the testimony. It also commits the deponent to a specific diagram. Many cases involve visual aids and demonstrative evidence at the trial, and depositions of witnesses in these cases should include some visual diagram for the witness's testimony. Diagrams composed by a witness during a deposition cannot be changed for the trial, except that a deponent will ordinarily not be expected to draw a diagram to scale. Specially prepared trial diagrams are drafted by an attorney with an artist and are usually drawn to scale.

21. *Review pleadings and materials.* The deponent may be able to add to, explain, be surprised by, or become confused by legal materials. A party deponent may not be sufficiently familiar with his or her pleadings, answers to interrogatories, and other statements to deal with them directly. Deponents have a difficult time if not properly prepared to respond fully and persuasively to such broad questions as "Your complaint alleges that 'Plaintiff suffered actual damages amounting to $60,000.' What facts do you have to support that claim for damages?" Or, "Your answer denies a complaint allegation that 'defendant acted negligently.' Upon what facts do you base your denial?"

22. *Place the deponent at a specific time.* Questions causing the deponent to place himself or herself back in time at a particular event often help the deponent to recall more of the incident. These are called retrospective questions. You may wish to place the deponent at a time before he or she spoke to his or her attorney about the incident or about the deposition, in order to get at the witness's recollection before it may have been influenced by conversations with the attorney.

§2.6.3 Specific Techniques: How to React

23. *Use a gauge.* You usually have some means of determining whether the deponent has told everything and whether it is reasonable to believe the deponent's response. Time is one such gauge. The deponent may testify that a conversation occurred during a ten-minute

interval. This period of time can assist you in determining whether the witness has explained the complete event and conversation. You merely approximate the time it would take to do or say what the deponent testified to and match that with the time. You usually have to allow some additional time for events or conversation that the deponent testifies he or she does not remember. This total will help you determine whether the deponent has told you everything or whether you need to probe further. The deponent who tells you the conversation lasted ten minutes, and then only describes three minutes' worth, needs to be questioned further.

24. *Suggest a mistake.* Many depositions involve something that occurred as a result of someone's mistake, and deponents may refuse to admit their involvement in that mistake. The foil to such a position is simple: you ask the deponent whether it is inevitable that, on occasion, a mistake is made. After all, no one or no practice is perfect.

25. *Seek an admission.* Depositions produce information that can be phrased in the form of an admission. A deponent may be influenced by the examiner's specific or leading question, and agree with the question. But an examining attorney often proceeds to question a deponent, seeking to obtain an admission the deponent refuses to make. Though it is equally important to establish this contrary position, too often this questioning becomes repetitive and argumentative as the examining attorney attempts to force the deponent to agree with the admission. The examiner may fare better by probing into the basis for the deponent's reply rather than attempting to persuade by argument.

26. *Pursue an admission.* What should you do when the deponent makes an admission and you want to get the specifics? You must make a judgment: if you pursue the questioning, will the deponent attempt to retract or soften the admission, or will such detailed questioning firm up the admission? Proceeding and probing the grounds of the admission is probably best: it is better to uncover information in a deposition than not to explore the area.

27. *Summarize previous testimony.* The deponent may say something favorable, though not in the most favorable language. You can summarize what was said in more favorable words and ask the deponent if your statement is correct. Or a deponent may say one thing at one time, add another thing later, and, still later, make another modification. You can summarize everything said and ask the deponent if your summary is accurate. You cannot testify, but summarizing may be the next best thing.

28. *React to the deponent's disposition.* Witnesses display various dispositions in a deposition. They are friendly, confused, neutral, indifferent, partial, withdrawn, outgoing, aggressive, hostile, or some combination of these. You have to decide whether the deponent's disposition helps or hurts your approach and how to react to it. Should you respond in kind? Or to the contrary? Should you alert the deponent to his or her visible disposition? Should you attempt to control or change the disposition? Should you have it reflected in the record?

29. *Appear disbelieving.* Your disbelief may cause some deponents to second-guess their response. Questions such as "Are you sure?" affect an uncertain deponent. Some deponents become anxious and wonder whether they are indeed certain or sure. Your disbelief of their responses may cause them to change a "yes" to a "probably" or a "no" to a "possibly." Other deponents may become confused and believe that they made some mistake; still other witnesses may become paranoid and believe that you have proof supporting your disbelief, with which you can confront them.

30. *Undermine the deponent's credibility.* You must occasionally decide whether to attempt to impeach the deponent during a deposition. If you have some impeaching materials or indications that a deponent is wrong or is testifying to bizarre happenings, you have to decide whether to do anything in response. You can choose to ignore it and go on, or to doubt the information and intimate to the deponent that you have contrary information without disclosing it, or to challenge the testimony directly by disclosing impeaching material and not saving it for trial. This last tactic may backfire, giving the deponent an opportunity to prepare to counter such evidence at the trial; but with open discovery, the other side may discover such impeaching material in any event, without your voluntarily disclosing it. You should avoid arguing with the deponent, unless the tactic appears to succeed and the opposing attorney just sits there, ever so meek and humble.

31. *Ask about the deponent's memory.* You can ask factual questions to determine the extent of the deponent's memory. You can also ask directly: "Would you consider your memory a good or poor memory concerning that event?" This may produce a self-serving response, no good to you, but also may lock the deponent into a position which you can use for contrast later, particularly if a cautious witness with a selective or poor memory claims to have a good memory. The opinion question can extend to other areas, such as "Did you have an excellent view?" "Were you able to hear everything that was said?"

32. *Be persistent.* During a deposition you may become bored with

the tedious questioning, resigned to the damaging information, or put off by the opposing lawyer. These situations can affect your effectiveness as an examiner, and may require additional effort, patience, persistence, and time from you.

33. *Make assessments.* In most depositions one seeks to obtain information from a deponent and to assess that deponent as a witness. After each such deposition you should put yourself in the place of the opposing lawyer and ask "Will that deponent be an effective witness at trial?" One of your main purposes during a deposition is to have the opposing attorney leave the deposition answering that question in the negative.

What to do regarding these tactics during a deposition often requires a split-second judgment on your part. Experience will help you refine that judgment ability, but anticipating situations, rehearsing how you will react in certain circumstances, and preparing for the deposition will also assist in refining that decisionmaking process.

§2.6.4 Specific Techniques: Deposing the Expert

Despite specialization, each expert witness provides some common areas for examination. Rule 26 sets forth the various categories of experts and the discovery devices to be used to obtain information. Rule 33 interrogatories may reveal certain information regarding the background, opinions, and reasoning of an expert. Depositions can produce additional information. Each expert should be examined regarding the specific areas of his or her expertise, but a general list of topics can also be explored with most experts, including the following:

1. Their qualifications;
2. Their opinions;
3. The bases of their opinions;
4. The sources of information relied upon in forming their opinions and bases;
5. Their fees and whether they expect to testify for their party in the future;
6. The number of times they have testified for plaintiffs and defendants in previous cases;
7. Insufficient information, tests, or sources of information they have relied upon;
8. The degree of probability of their opinions;
9. Possible causes or explanations contrary to their opinion;

10.   Their familiarity with any treatises useful to the examining attorney's case.

Inquiry into these areas serves several of the purposes of deposing an expert: to explore the details of the expert's opinion, to prepare for cross-examination of that expert at trial, and to provide information necessary to counter or impeach the expert's testimony through the opinion of the deposing attorney's own expert at trial. These topics are not complete, but they should be considered, and their review may lead to additional areas of inquiry.

Deposition inquiries of an expert may be subject to some limitations, including: (1) The information sought must pertain to matters within the expert's knowledge and expertise; (2) hypothetical and opinion questions must be based on the facts in the case; (3) questions cannot be so broad as to require the expert to do research to provide an answer.

§2.7   REPRESENTING THE DEPONENT

The attorney representing the deponent serves a vital and important function in the deposition process. Some attorneys view the role as a passive one. They prefer to stay in the background. But lawyering functions require you to be as active and involved in the deposition as the examining attorney. You do not have many questions to ask, but there are many ways to participate actively in the proceedings.

The following subsections focus on the functions of deponent representation and also discuss the ancillary functions involved in attending depositions of non-client deponents.

§2.7.1   Selecting the Deponent

The notice of deposition usually designates the person to be deposed. Sometimes the other attorney may wish to depose someone you know does not have the information sought. You must decide whether to tell the other attorney, and perhaps suggest someone else to be deposed (and save everyone concerned wasted time and effort) or to appear at the deposition and snicker. Rule 30(b)(6) permits the deposing attorney merely to designate the subject matter of a deposition to be taken of a corporation, governmental agency, or other organizational party. The rule permits you to select the deponent or deponents and to designate or limit the matters on which they will testify. Whom do you and your client select? Obviously, you pick the person or persons who have information relating to the subject matter of the deposition. But what if there is more than one such know-everything witness? Then you should select:

Someone astute enough to understand the questions he is asked and to perceive what motivates opposing counsel to ask them;
Someone articulate enough to phrase answers that will read well when transcribed;
Someone resourceful enough to phrase what he says so as to make the best of the strengths of your case and to de-emphasize its weaknesses to the extent legitimately possible; and
Someone of character, a witness who will speak the truth and whose phraseology and tone of voice will manifest his candor and accuracy.[1]

Should you find such a witness, you should consider using that person for all your depositions regardless of the subject matter. If the deponent is that good, what he or she doesn't know won't matter.

§2.7.2   General Deponent Preparation

Your preparation of the deponent should include a complete and thorough preparation of the general elements of any deposition and of the specific elements of a particular case.

Preparing a deponent takes time and involves expense. You can reduce some of that effort by providing the deponent with written deposition instructions before meeting with him or her. A short set of general instructions appears on the following page, and a set of detailed deponent instructions appears in Appendix B.

The value of detailed written instructions is considerably enhanced by a preparation conference with your deponent. There you can emphasize or modify major points, provide additional instructions, and answer any remaining questions. You may even have your client observe a videotape of a simulated deposition designed to educate a prospective deponent.[2]

§2.7   [1]W. Barthold, Attorney's Guide to Effective Discovery Techniques 111 (1975).
[2] See R. Haydock & J. Sonsteng, National Institute for Trial Advocacy, Demonstration Videotape, Deponent Preparation (1980).

INSTRUCTIONS ON WHAT NOT TO DO
DURING A DEPOSITION
OR
IF YOU DO ANY OF THESE THINGS I WILL
IMMEDIATELY
WITHDRAW FROM THE CASE

1. Do not pretend that you do not know me.
2. Do not call me "doctor," "hey, you," or use my middle name in front of the other attorney.
3. Do not dress for the deposition like a zombie, look like a turkey, or wear two-tone leisure or pants suits.
4. Don't faint during the deposition. If you feel a faint coming on, lean away from me so you don't fall on me.
5. Do not respond "huh" when the other attorney asks you your name.
6. Do not eat during the deposition.
7. If the other attorney asks whether you are a party in the action, do not ask what time it starts.
8. If the other attorney asks about your major expenses, do not point to me.
9. If I ask you any questions during the deposition, do not laugh.
10. If I close my eyes during the deposition or slip out of my chair, don't poke me. It's all part of a strategic ploy on my part to make the other attorney think I'm a dolt.
11. Don't yelp when I tap your foot. If I tap once, it means you misunderstood the question. If I hit it twice, it means you made a mistake. If I stomp on it three times, it means you just lost the case.

§2.7.3 Specific Deponent Preparation

Your witness must understand the intricacies of depositions and all facets of your case. While the previous section dealt with general preparation, this section offers guidelines on specific preparation relating to the actual subject matter of the deposition.

1. *Explain what the case is all about to the witness.* You may have previously discussed the case with a client, but an updated explanation will aid the witness's understanding. You want to make certain he or she understands not only what is happening but why it is happening.

Use ordinary, everyday English, not law-school legalese, to outline the issues and theory, to detail what you have to prove, to explain the burden the other side has, and to indicate where that witness fits in the case. A witness will answer questions more knowledgeably, perceive the motives of the other attorney more easily, understand the impact of the answers more clearly, and be more at ease and confident during the deposition, if he or she knows as much as possible.

2. *Review the facts and file.* The deponent may have provided you with information earlier, but nonetheless you must review this information. It will help refresh the witness's recollection and may generate additional information. You should inform deponents about facts they may not know. You may have notes to refresh their recollection, documents and objects they should see, or other information in your file they should know about.

You should go over everything in the file that will be relevant to the deposition. Pleadings, discovery responses, statements, letters, materials, affidavits, you name it, the deponent should see it if it has any bearing on the subject matter of the deposition. Remember that documents a deponent reviews to refresh recollection may be discoverable, and this possibility may limit your disclosure.

3. *Explain conflicting stories.* You accept it as a fact of legal life that your witness's story will differ from the other side's and perhaps even differ from your other witnesses' stories, but the witness may not expect or understand this. You should explain that this is normal and that they should tell the truth using their best recollection, and not attempt to harmonize their story with someone else's version.

4. *Be the devil's advocate.* Tell your witness what you know about the examining attorney. It is essential that you explain the type and scope of questions the deposing attorney will probably ask. You may want to use practice questions and have yourself or another attorney from your law firm simulate the deposition by asking questions. You may want to use a tape recorder so the witness can listen to his or her responses and learn some strengths and weaknesses. You may want, in important cases, to use video equipment to provide witnesses with the opportunity to see themselves.

The preparation of a deponent who is a witness and not a client varies from the suggestions presented in these two sections. The attorney can still approach the witness and explain many of the previous instructions and all facets of the case if the witness does not have a lawyer. However, the attorney does not represent that witness and therefore cannot render legal advice or pursue matters that conflict with the client's best interests, nor instruct the witness about what to do during the deposition. Your preparatory explanation and instructions will then differ accordingly, to take into account the different relationship between you and the non-client deponent.

§2.7.4 Raising Objections during the Deposition

Rule 32(d) describes the situations requiring objections during depositions. Subsection (1) provides that all errors and irregularities in the deposition notice are waived unless a written objection is promptly served upon the party giving the notice. The requirement places the burden on the opposing party to raise any problem with the notice. This rule prevents a party who fails to appear at a deposition from relying on a technical defect. Not all errors or irregularities may give rise to this written objection requirement. Some may not be obvious in a notice. Even the listing of an incorrect date or location is not necessarily an error or irregularity, if the other party or deponent had otherwise been advised of a different time or place.

Subsection (2) provides that any objection based upon the disqualification of an officer who takes the deposition is waived, unless it is made before the taking of the deposition begins or as soon thereafter as the disqualification becomes known or could have been discovered with reasonable diligence. Disqualification situations are rare.

Subsection (d)(3)(B) details the objections that must be made concerning other errors. Any irregularities occurring at the deposition, regarding the taking of the examination, the oath or affirmation, the conduct of the parties, or "errors of any kind which might be obviated, removed, or cured if promptly presented," are waived unless seasonable objection is made at the deposition. For example, an opposing lawyer who is aware that a deponent has not been sworn will be unable to raise this objection later, because an objection made during the deposition would have provided timely notice and an opportunity to the party taking the deposition to cure the error.

The same subsection also applies this "seasonable objection" standard to the form of the questions and answers during the examination. Improper questions by an examining attorney that can be corrected at the deposition must be objected to in order to preserve the objection for trial. Examples of such form objections to inappropriate questions and responses include vague, confusing, ambiguous, misleading, complex, compound, argumentative, incomplete hypothetical questions;

misquoting the deponent; non-responsive answers. Most depositions allow leading questions because the deponent is an adverse party, an agent, or a hostile witness, and a leading objection in those depositions will be improper. The decision whether to object under the requirements of this rule is determined by whether the error produced by the objectionable question or answer can be obviated during the deposition by an objection to the form of the question.

Rule 32(d)(3)(A) delineates another situation requiring an objection to be made during a deposition: objections to the competency, relevancy, or materiality of testimony are not waived by a failure to make them before or during a deposition, unless the ground of the objection is one that might have been obviated or removed if presented at that time. The Federal Rules of Evidence have eliminated immateriality as an objection, and competency objections are not common. But relevancy objections are available and common. The official comments to this subsection offer no example of such situations nor any explanation for this subsection.

What situations require making a relevancy objection to avoid waiving such objection? Clearly, information discoverable during a deposition includes much evidence that will not be relevant for trial purposes. The scope of relevancy under Federal Rule of Civil Procedure 26 for deposition purposes far exceeds the scope of relevancy under Federal Rule of Evidence 401 for trial purposes. Since deposition questions seeking information that will be irrelevant for trial purposes are common and proper, the concern of the deponent's attorney is to object to those irrelevant questions which, if objected to, could somehow be cured by the examining attorney.

The failure to object to certain questions during depositions will result in the waiver of underlying rights. A client is also bound by an attorney's failure to raise a timely objection. For example, substantive Rule 26(b) makes privileged matter non-discoverable. A procedural lapse by a deponent's attorney in neglecting to object to inquiries into privileged matter during a deposition will operate as a waiver of the substantive protections. A later objection at trial to such inquiries will be overruled because of the waiver that occurred during the earlier deposition. Objections to privileged or other matters sought from a deponent will be necessary to preserve those objections and will also be preliminary to an instruction from the deponent's attorney not to answer the question.

Some attorneys, because of the uncertainty of the need to object to certain questions, prefer entering into a stipulation at the start of the deposition, stating, "It is stipulated that all objections to questions and answers shall be reserved by each party, except objections to the form of the question." Other attorneys perceive no need for this agreement and prefer having the rules control.

There are other reasons, based upon strategy, to make objections:

First, objections will sometimes actually work; an attorney will not pursue an answer after an objection to a question. An objection says, in effect, that the objecting attorney believes the question is improper or seeks non-discoverable information, and that belief has some effect on the thinking of the other attorney. This is particularly true in depositions involving both experienced and inexperienced attorneys. The experienced attorney may attempt through peer pressure and objections to limit the scope of the examination, and the inexperienced attorney may be convinced enough not to insist on answers. This is also true in situations in which the examining attorney has his or her own doubts about the legitimacy of the question or the hoped-for response. The objecting attorney may be right and the examining attorney may agree.

Second, objections will break the pace and rhythm of the examining attorney and may disrupt the rapport the attorney has with the deponent.

Third, objections are sometimes made to signal the deponent that something is wrong, as well as to indicate to the examining attorney that there is something objectionable.

You have a right to object to any questions posed to any deponent, including client and non-client deponents. If you make an objection, you should also state the ground for the objection. Whether your objection is correct or not, the examining attorney still has a right to insist on an answer, unless you instruct the client not to answer. Usually little purpose is served by a detailed explanation of the objection or an argument over the merits of the objection, unless you have legitimate strategic or procedural reasons for so doing.

Tactical ramifications will affect your judgment about whether you should object or not. For example, the examining attorney may inquire into the deponent's opinions on other matters without asking for foundation or establishing the witness's competency. Your objection to lack of foundation may prompt the examiner to consider the defect in the inquiry and to rectify it by asking foundation questions and obtaining more detailed responses and consequently more information. If you need or want that information detailed in the deposition, you should object. If you do not want the other attorney probing further, you should not object. You must decide during depositions not only whether you have a proper objection but also whether tactically it is wise to object.

Objecting merely for the sake of objecting and hoping to disrupt and interfere with the deposition is inappropriate deposition conduct. Many depositions are relatively objection-free, and you should not feel unfulfilled as an attorney if a deposition passes without your having to object to anything more substantial than the shape of the table.

§2.7.5 Instructing the Deponent Not to Answer

Sometimes an attorney presses an objection and instructs the deponent not to answer a question. Though it may not occur often, it may be necessary if the examining attorney delves into privileged areas ("And then what did your attorney tell you to say?"), asks totally irrelevant questions ("Did you graduate *cum laude* from kindergarten?"), or becomes argumentative or harassing ("How long have you been a compulsive liar?"). You must have justification for an instruction to refuse disclosure.

If you advise your deponent client not to answer, the other attorney may react in a number of ways. The attorney may turn to your client and ask whether he or she wishes to answer the question, regardless of your advice. The attorney may even go further and explain to the witness the dire effects that stem from a refusal to answer. You should prevent the other attorney from interfering with your representation of the client, by limiting the attorney merely to asking the deponent whether he or she will answer the question. Or you could enter into a stipulation during the deposition, such as "It is stipulated between the parties, through their respective attorneys, that if deponent should be instructed not to answer the questions propounded by examining counsel, deponent shall be considered to have refused to answer when so instructed."

The other attorney may later attempt to ask the same question in a different way (be alert), try to persuade you to change your mind, or seek a court order compelling a response. You must have a good-faith reason for instructing the deponent not to respond.

The most common, legitimate reasons relate to privilege and bad-faith questions. Rule 26(b)(1) clearly excludes privileged matter from the scope of discovery. Some courts have extended this protection to improper questions "unquestionably beyond the scope" of the issues of a case.[3] Rule 30(c) permits a party to seek a protective order from annoying, embarrassing, and harassing tactics; some courts prefer a deponent to seek such an order rather than unilaterally deciding not to respond. Though one court prohibited all parties from instructing their witnesses not to answer unless they claim a privilege objection,[4] courts have upheld refusals to answer on the grounds that the questions were unclear, imprecise, misleading, and argumentative.[5] Other courts have reviewed deposition transcripts and declared many questions duplicative and fully answered when the question is rephrased and the answer received.[6] An instruction not to answer, based on irrelevancy, has been declared to be inappropriate, because Rule 30(c) controls and permits such evidence to be taken subject to a later objection.[7]

One court reviewed the propriety of the following instructions:

Examining attorney: All right. Have you ever been convicted of a felony?

Deponent: Oh, no.

Examining Attorney: Have you ever been convicted of a lesser criminal offense?

Deponent's Attorney: I object. Instruct the witness not to answer the question.

Examining Attorney: Will you instruct the witness to answer the question?

Notary: I instruct you to answer the question.

Deponent's Attorney: And I instruct you not to answer it, Mr. Mellon.

Examining Attorney: Have you ever been convicted of operating a motor vehicle while under the influence of alcohol or drugs?

Deponent's Attorney: We will object to the question. Instruct the witness not to answer the question.

Examining Attorney: Instruct the witness to answer the question.

Notary: I instruct you to answer the question.

Deponent's Attorney: Do not answer it, Mr. Mellon, upon my advice.[8]

[3]Amco Engr. Co. v. Bud Radio Inc., 38 F.R.D. 51, 53 (N.D. Ohio 1965).
[4]Shapiro v. Freeman, 38 F.R.D. 308, 311-312 (S.D.N.Y. 1965).
[5]Mortensen v. Honduras Shipping Co., 18 F.R.D. 510, 512 (S.D.N.Y. 1955).
[6]In re Folding Carton Antitrust Litigation, 83 F.R.D. 132, 135 (N.D. Ill. 1979).
[7]Ralston Purina Co. v. McFarland, 550 F.2d 967, 973 (4th Cir. 1977).
[8]Mellon v. Cooper-Jarrett, Inc., 424 F.2d 499, 500 (6th Cir. 1970).

The court reversed a judgment for the deponent solely because the instruction not to answer was improper, because it denied the examining attorney relevant information likely to lead to admissible evidence regarding the deponent's credibility.

Courts that support the limited use of instructions not to answer reason that:

> [t]he harm caused by being required to take additional depositions of a witness who fails to answer a question based on an improperly asserted objection far exceeds the mere inconvenience of a witness having to answer a question which may not be admissible at the trial of the action.[9]

If you have no reason or a bad-faith reason supporting your decision not to respond, you have abused your role as an advocate, and you personally may have to pay attorney's fees and expenses incurred by the other side in procuring the necessary court order. This is not to suggest that you should refrain from using an instruction, but merely to emphasize the need for a legitimate reason.

An attorney cannot advise a non-client deponent not to answer. The attorney may suggest to the witness that the question need not be answered, but the witness must decide on his or her own. Further, the objecting attorney may not be able to advise a non-client deponent that he or she may be waiving a privilege, because such advice may violate the Code of Professional Responsibility.[10]

§2.7.6 Protecting the Deponent

Your primary role during the proceedings is to protect your client's best interests while conforming to generally accepted deposition customs, practices, and courtesies. You may want to protect your client during a deposition for a number of reasons: the examining attorney violated an accepted custom; your understanding of deposition practice differs from the other attorney's understanding; your client was not extended a common courtesy; the rules require you to say or do

[9]W.R. Grace & Co. v. Pullman, Inc. 74 F.R.D. 80, 84 (W.D. Okla. 1977).

[10]Code of Professional Responsibility, DR7-104 provides: "During the course of his representation of a client a lawyer shall not: . . . (2) Give advice to a person who is not represented by a lawyer, other than the advice to secure counsel, if the interests of such person are or have a reasonable possibility of being in conflict with the interests of his client."

something; it is your strategy in the deposition to be especially protective. Whatever your reason, it should be a legitimate one, not spurious or nefarious.

The previous sections, on objections and instructions, have indicated some ways you can protect your client. There are others. If you do not hear or understand a question, you can ask the court reporter to read the question back. If the examining attorney hands your client a document and begins to ask questions, you can interrupt, peruse the document, and ask your client to read the entire document before answering any questions. If your deponent appears fatigued, you can insist upon a recess. If your client asks for some assistance or appears to be having some difficulty, you can confer with him or her. If the deponent has made a misstatement, you may want to interrupt and ask the deponent whether he or she understood the question or even suggest that the witness may have misunderstood the question. If the deponent has difficulty remembering an exact name, date, time, distance, or some other precise fact, and the fact is a minor consideration in the case, you can volunteer the answer. If the deponent has difficulty with a response, and the answer appears in a document or writing, you can offer that document or writing to the deponent. If the deponent has answered a question and begins to ramble, you can interrupt and say "Thank you, you have answered the question." These and similar actions are all legitimate tactics.

Some attorneys protect clients in ways you may think are improper, inappropriate, or borderline. But it is difficult to characterize the propriety of some of these tactics: they may be highly improper in one situation, and fully appropriate in another. The following list of questionable practices is not offered to promote their use. Rather, the list is offered to acquaint you with them, so that you can decide which you will use and which you will discard, and to prepare you to counter an opponent's use of those you consider illegitimate. They usually surface when a deponent has made a misstatement, forgotten something, or made some other major mistake, and the deponent's attorney wants to correct the error or call the witness's attention to it. The attorney may

1. Whisper in the client's ear;
2. Signal the client with some objection or some gesture or facial expression;
3. Testify and correct the error;
4. Insist on going off the record or demand a recess or break.

A previous section on controlling interference (§2.5.9) outlined ways the examining attorney can respond to and handle such tactics. Using one of these tactics more than occasionally would be tantamount to abusive and bad-faith conduct on the part of the offending attorney.

§2.7.7 Questioning the Deponent

Rule 30(c) allows you to "cross-examine" the deponent. That term is actually a misnomer because usually the deponent is your client or a friendly witness, and you have no need or urge to cross-examine. You may want to ask him or her some questions at the end of a deposition, and you should proceed as if you were conducting a direct examination. If you did conduct a cross-examination and used leading questions, the other attorney would be able properly to object to these questions, and to move later to strike responses to your questions, which, when granted by a court, renders such deposition testimony inadmissible.

In what situations should you question your client deponent? Usually, the best question is no question — the sooner the deposition is over without the deponent putting his or her foot in his or her mouth, the better. Ordinarily, your preparation of the deponent does not include any preparation of questions. If you ask questions, you run the risk of the deponent's not understanding why you are asking a question or responding to it in a different fashion from what you expected. Further, the more questions you ask, the more information you provide the other side; the more questions you ask, the more time the other attorney has to think about what else to ask; and the more questions you ask, the more chance the other attorney has to ask still more questions.

Still, on some occasions you will need to ask questions. You must conduct a thorough direct examination to preserve the testimony of a deponent who either will not or may not be available at the trial. You must consider the possibility that your deponent will not be available for trial. Death, illness, being outside the jurisdiction of the court, or unforeseen circumstances may prevent the deponent from testifying. The only available testimony will appear in the deposition transcript, which will probably not contain all the information you need for trial and which will certainly not be in a format that will strengthen your case. Or, in other circumstances, if during the deposition the deponent did not have an opportunity to complete and answer or to explain a response, you may want to ask some questions, using that opportunity to clarify or supplement the record before the deposition ends.

Again, if the deponent made a misstatement or forgot to provide some known information, you may want to ask some questions to correct or complete the record. Or you may want to put on the record some testimony that you perceive bolsters your position for negotiations. You can then point to definite evidence in the transcript to support your position, rather than relying upon your paraphrasing of what your witness would say. You must remain alert for any areas that you may want to inquire into after the examining attorney has completed his or her questioning. Detailed rehabilitative questions may be necessary in light of these considerations.

Trouble may arise when the attorney representing the deponent begins to ask a lot of questions at the end of an informational deposition. The attorney who noticed the deposition is paying for the reporter's time, and if that attorney thinks the opposing lawyer is ranging far afield in such examination, he or she should advise the lawyer that the deposition will come to an end unless there is some agreement on sharing expenses. If you prolong the cross-questioning, you ordinarily become obligated to pay your fair share of the deposition costs.[11]

Rule 30(c) permits an attorney who cannot or chooses not to participate in the oral examination nevertheless to ask questions of the deponent. The attorney may serve written questions in a sealed envelope on the party taking the deposition, and that party shall give the envelope to the court reporter, who will ask the deponent the questions and record the answers. Obviously this is not the best way to proceed. However, if the deposition occurs in a distant location, if the deponent is not a party or a significant witness, or if you are only interested in objective information, it is an available device.

§2.8 CONCLUDING THE DEPOSITION

After all the questioning has been completed, there are some concluding matters relating to the transcription of the testimony to consider. Rules 30(e), 30(f)(1), 30(f)(3), and 32(d)(4) describe the concluding procedures:

[11]*See* Wheeler v. West India S.S. Co., 11 F.R.D. 396, 397-398 (S.D.N.Y. 1951); Baron v. Leo Feist, Inc. 7 F.R.D. 71, 72 (S.D.N.Y. 1946).

When the testimony is stenographically transcribed, the deposition shall be submitted to the witness for examination and shall be read to or by him, unless such examination and reading are waived by the witness and by the parties. Any changes in form or substance which the witness desires to make shall be entered upon the deposition by the officer with a statement of the reasons given by the witness for making them. The deposition shall then be signed by the witness, unless the parties by stipulation waive the signing or the witness is ill or cannot be found or refuses to sign. If the deposition is not signed by the witness within 30 days of its submission to him, the officer shall sign it and state on the record the fact of the waiver or of the illness or absence of the witness, the fact of the refusal to sign, together with the reason, if any, given therefor; and the deposition may then be used as fully as though signed, unless on a motion to suppress under Rule 32(d)(4) the court holds that the reasons given for the refusal to sign require rejection of the deposition in whole or in part.

The officer shall certify on the deposition that the witness was duly sworn by him and that the deposition is a true record of the testimony given by the witness. He shall then place the deposition in an envelope endorsed with the title of the action and marked "Deposition of (here insert the name of witness)" and shall promptly deliver or mail it to the clerk of the court in which the action is pending. . . .

The party taking the deposition shall give prompt notice of its filing to all other parties. . . .

Errors and irregularities in the name in which the testimony is transcribed or the deposition is prepared, signed, certified, sealed, endorsed, transmitted, filed, or otherwise dealt with by the officer under Rules 30 and 31 are waived unless a motion to suppress the deposition or some part thereof is made with reasonable promptness after such defect is, or with due diligence might have been, ascertained.

Implementation of the rules raises a number of questions, which we treat in the following subsections in a multiple-choice format.

§2.8.1 Stipulations

Typical stipulations at the end of a deposition include:

A. The waiving of the reading of the transcript by the deponent.
B. The waiving of the signing of the transcript by the deponent.
C. The waiving of the receipt of notice of the filing of the deposition.
D. All of the above.

If you choose either *A, B, C,* or *D*, at least you are not wrong. The common stipulations are the waiving of the reading, signing, and notice of filing of the deposition. Some attorneys routinely waive or demand waiver; others lump them all together under the rubric of "usual stipulations" and seek to have them waived. Examining attorneys sometimes expect and ask the attorney representing the deponent to explain to the deponent, on the record, the effect of waiving of the reading and signing of the deposition ("Counsel, please instruct your witness . . ."). What should you do? Whatever you do, you should have a reason for doing it.

§2.8.2 *Waiver of Reading and Signing by the Examining Attorney*

The examining attorney should request the waiver of the reading and signing:

A. Always.
B. Usually.
C. Only on alternate Tuesdays.

If you choose *A, B*, or *C*, you may want to rethink your career choice. Sometimes there is good reason to seek a waiver of the reading and signing, and sometimes there is not. If there is a waiver, and counsel later attempts to use the deposition for admission evidence or as impeachment materials, the deponent can say with some credibility that the response was not properly recorded or that the question was misunderstood. If, however, the transcript is read and signed by the deponent, no convincing, credible reason remains for the deponent to use to attempt to rebut the record later. On the other hand, reading the transcript provides the deponent with an opportunity to alter the testimony.

The waiver of the reading and signing does not *technically* affect the use of the deposition. That is, the rules permit the deposition to be used with the same force and effect as if it had been read and signed. Some attorneys prefer including such a statement in a stipulation to make that point clear.

§2.8.3   Waiver of Reading and Signing by the Deponent

The attorney representing the deponent should waive the reading and signing on behalf of the deponent:

A. If it reduces the impact of the transcript for evidentiary or impeachment purposes.
B. If the court reporter is competent and reliable in recording an accurate transcript.
C. If it saves time and money.
D. If there is no reason not to.

Reasons *A, B, C,* and *D* conform to the prevailing reasons in practice for waiving the reading and the signing, and if you choose them you are a conformist. A non-party deponent cannot individually make such waivers; the party who has noticed the deposition must consent to them. Regarding the reading of the transcript, both the non-party deponent and the party must waive that right jointly. Regarding the signing of the transcript, however, the party may individually waive that right without conferring with or receiving the approval of the non-party deponent. A party need not abide by the demands of a witness who insists on either waiving or signing the transcript, although a witness who physically refuses to sign will create a problem. The party may have to seek a court order, if the signing is a matter of importance to the case. Usually, because non-party deponents are friendly or neutral witnesses, there is no problem regarding such joint decisions. The reading and signing of a deposition make it more potent evidentiary or impeachment material. Court reporters are reliable and competent, and the waiver does save time and money.

Yet there are some reasons not to waive. The purposes behind reading and signing the transcript are to ensure the accuracy of the transcription by the reporter and to indicate that the deponent examined the deposition testimony and agreed with the transcription. The attorney can read the transcript, note any discrepancies or inaccuracies, and point them out to the deponent. You, as the deponent's attorney, may privately consult and confer with the deponent regarding making any changes. You should be cautious in pointing out corrections, and you should emphasize to the deponent that the transcript represents the deponent's account of the facts according to his or her best recollection. But the transcript may include incorrect statements, errors, or misspellings that can become the basis for an alleged admission or impeaching statement. Again, a court reporter may have had difficulties with the transcription of some names, figures, or technical data, and occasionally may even request that a transcript be read and signed. Any time or money saved by not reading and signing may be wasted later in trying to explain away the record. It is usually sound practice, therefore, not to waive the reading of the transcript and to have the client or the attorney read it. Waiving the signature does not have these consequences and can be waived through a letter sent to the reporter and opposing counsel, or by letting the 30 days run.

The rules provide that a party seeking to challenge the use of an unsigned deposition must bring a motion to suppress the deposition. Courts accordingly are inclined to allow the use of an unsigned deposition, unless a party brings a motion to suppress and claims prejudice as a result of this use.[1] They have denied such motions if failure to sign resulted from the deponent's death. The courts have considered several factors in making their decisions on the motion: (1) the relevance and importance of the testimony; (2) the degree to which the evidence may be impaired by the deponent's failure to review, correct, and sign the deposition; and (3) the prejudice that might result from its use.[2]

§2.8.4   Changes in the Record by the Deponent: Scope

A deponent can make the following changes in the record:

A. Whatever the deponent wants to change, as long as he or she has some reason.
B. Only those changes which correct a court reporter's error.
C. Only changes approved by the opposing counsel.
D. Only a change that decreases the speed from 45 r.p.m. to 33⅓ r.p.m.

The rules permit a deponent to do *A:* make any change in form and substance the deponent has reason to make.[3] The other answers are incorrect. If *B* or *C* were correct, there would have to be a court hearing to determine whose error it is and what constitutes a minor versus a major change. The rules do not permit a deponent to edit or

§2.8 [1]United States v. Garcia, 527 F.2d 473, 475 (9th Cir. 1975).
[2]Bernstein v. Brenner, 51 F.R.D. 9, 13 (D.D.C. 1970).
[3]*See* Rogers v. Roth, 477 F.2d 1154 (10th Cir. 1973).

rewrite a record: changes can be made, but only if the deponent has some reason to make them.

§2.8.5 Changes in the Record by the Deponent: Rationale

Reasons that would allow a deponent legitimately to make a change in the record include:

A. Any reason.
B. Any reason.
C. Any reason.

A, B, and *C* are correct. The reasons do not have to be substantial, significant, or persuasive; they may even be "inadequate."[4] As long as the deponent can express some reason, it suffices under the rules. Deponents have changed the record to (1) correct their substantive testimony, (2) make testimony in one place in the record conform with testimony at another place, (3) correct typographical errors, (4) correct transcription mistakes, and (5) change a yes response to a no response.[5] The deponent may consult privately with his or her attorney before and during the making of any changes.

Tactical reasons militate against making changes all over the transcript. Reasonable inferences that may be drawn from changes in the deponent's testimony will not be favorable to the deponent; the changes will appear to be alterations of harmful responses or inconsistent testimony. While the rules require no special reasons to make changes, strategy requires some substantial reason before toying with the record.

The rule requires that the officer, and not the deponent, enter any and all changes on the record. This is often disregarded in practice. The corrections may be made in a number of ways. The deponent can submit an affidavit listing the corrections. Then the officer can attach that affidavit to the transcript and note the changes appearing in the affidavit in the margins of the record, or, at the direction of the deponent, the officer can cross out the incorrect testimony and replace it with the correction. The original testimony should not be obliterated, because it is still part of the entire record. Additionally, the reporter

[4]De Seversky v. Republic Aviation Corp., 2 F.R.D. 113, 115 (E.D.N.Y. 1941).
[5]*See* Allen & Co. v. Occidental Petroleum Corp., 49 F.R.D. 337, 340 (S.D.N.Y. 1970).

can indicate in an addendum to the changes whether he or she agrees or disagrees with the changes, particularly those changes with reasons that contend an error was made by the reporter. Either attorney can, and may want to, ask the reporter to double check the accuracy of the recording and the transcription involving disputed changes. The one way changes cannot be legitimately made is by a deponent in his or her own handwriting with no statement or reasons provided.

Substantive changes in the record make the deposition incomplete and permit the examining attorney to reopen the deposition for further questioning. Typographical changes made by the reporter do not entitle the examining party to conduct a further deposition. Both versions, the original and the changes, constitute part of the case file and both are admissible in evidence.

Both attorneys have an interest in making sure the deposition is filed with the court, especially if they wish to use the transcript before, during, or after the trial. An unfiled deposition cannot be relied upon by the trial or appellate court, but a court does have discretion to supplement a record with an unfiled deposition if a party in good faith believed it to be filed.[6] If the originals of important documents have been attached to the deposition as exhibits, it will become virtually mandatory to file the deposition. The reporter has the obligation to file. The examining attorney has the responsibility to notify all the parties that the deposition has been filed, but this duty generally goes unperformed. Though the deponent's attorney often waives the notice of the filing, banking on a reliable court reporter, some attorneys will not waive. They want written assurance that the deposition has been filed. There have been occasions when, to the chagrin of the attorneys, a deposition was not properly filed.

§2.9 WRITTEN-QUESTION DEPOSITIONS

Rule 31 allows depositions to be taken by written questions, and Rules 31(a), (b), and (c) define the procedural and notice requirements, including the exchange of questions and cross-questions. Most likely a convention of all practicing attorneys who even occasionally use this

[6]Daiflon, Inc. v. Allied Chem. Corp., 534 F.2d 221, 226-227 (10th Cir. 1976); McDaniel v. Travelers Ins. Co., 494 F.2d 1189, 1190 (5th Cir. 1974).

discovery device could be held in a telephone booth. Though not widely used, written-question depositions do have a place in the overall discovery process and serve some vital purposes.

§2.9.1 Advantages

What can written-question depositions do for you?

1.   Written deposition questions can be particularly useful in obtaining information from a person who lives some distance away from the site of the lawsuit or who cannot attend an oral deposition because of poor health. It is a substitute for an oral deposition. Travel can be expensive and inconvenient; retaining local counsel can be costly and time-consuming.

2.   Written-question depositions can be less expensive than oral depositions. An attorney need not be present during the questioning.

3.   Written questions may be served upon a non-party as well as a party. Rule 33 interrogatories can be submitted only to a party.

4.   The discovering attorney can select the person he or she wants to respond to the written questions. Rule 33 allows the responding party to select the spokesperson for response to interrogatories.

5.   Written-question depositions can be used efficiently and economically to secure straightforward and non-controversial data; obtain objective information including names, dates and places; identify and authenticate documents by non-party witnesses; and discover otherwise selected information.

6.   A second or subsequent set of written questions can be used after the answers to the first set have been received and digested.

§2.9.2 Disadvantages

Part of the reason why written-question depositions are used so little is their awkwardness as a discovery device. Specifically:

1.   Rule 31 can be expensive. The attorney noticing the deposition must take the necessary time, effort, and care to draft precise questions. There is no flexibility for rewording the questions after they have been asked.

2.   Telephone depositions may better serve discovery needs in similar circumstances and may be more efficient, effective, and economical.

3.   Some cross-questions must usually be prepared and served before the answers to the prior questions are received.

4.   The format is not adaptable to depositions involving information that is subjective, complex, or dependent upon the demeanor and credibility of the deponent.

5.   The witness may be able to review questions circulated among all the parties before the deposition and prepare responses, eliminating spontaneity and perhaps the candor that accompanies unrehearsed answers.

6.   No attorney ever became famous using Rule 31 written-question depositions.

§2.10   USE OF THE DEPOSITION

The deposition is over. The testimony has been transcribed. The record is on file with the court. Now what? The deposition may have been an end in itself. It got you what you wanted and you will not need to refer to it again. In many cases, though, you may want it for negotiations, a motion hearing, or the trial. To use it properly you must know its contents, with which you are already familiar if you attended the deposition. But you must also be able to refer quickly to specific portions of the testimony. There are three steps you can use to help you recall its contents and use them quickly and efficiently. First, you can prepare a summary of the contents, including notes about the demeanor and credibility of the witness. Second, you can prepare a detailed index. Some court reporters will provide you with an index with the record, but it may not be sufficiently detailed. You can supplement it. Third, you can mark in the margins, on your summary or on the index, how you plan to use specific questions and answers. You may categorize these uses as (1) admissions, (2) cross-examination topics, (3) specific impeachment material, (4) objectionable questions and answers, or (5) other responses to be used or read into evidence at the trial.

§2.10.1   General Use of Depositions at Trial

Rules 32(a)(1) to (4) and court decisions have defined the use of depositions in court proceedings.

1. Any *deposition of anyone* may be used *by any party* to *impeach* that deponent. The most common use of depositions at trial involves comparing the deposition transcript with the trial testimony and impeaching the witness on cross-examination.

2. The *deposition of a party* or corporate, governmental, or other organizational party may be used *by the adverse party* for *any reason.* Depositions can be used as admissions, substantive evidence, impeachment and cross-examination,[1] and for any other reason, even if that deponent party or agent is available to testify[2] or has already testified.[3] Whether or not the deposition of an agent of a party may be used for any reason depends upon the status of that agent. Courts consider the following factors in determining that status: whether the interest of the individual agent is similar to that of the principal; whether the individual has functions, responsibilities, and authority regarding the subject matter of the litigation; whether the deponent could be relied upon to give testimony at the direction of the principal; and whether there is any person of higher authority than the deponent responsible for the particular matters testified to in the deposition.[4] This provision does not apply to non-party deponents.

3. The *deposition of anyone* may be used *by any party* for *any reason* if any one of five conditions is met:

(a) The deponent is dead;
(b) The deponent is more than 100 miles from the courthouse, unless such absence has been caused by the attorney offering the deposition;
(c) The deponent cannot testify because of age, sickness, infirmity or imprisonment;
(d) The deponent cannot be subpoenaed;
(e) Upon a showing of exceptional circumstances (i.e., if the jury would be confused by live testimony, if you can make the judge cry).

The availability of a witness will be determined at the time the deposition is offered at the trial.

4. A deposition *from another lawsuit* may be used in a common action if there was *a substitution of parties* or if the former action involved

§2.10 [1]Davis v. Freels, 583 F.2d 337, 342 (7th Cir. 1978).
[2]Coughlin v. Capitol Cement Co., 571 F.2d 290, 308 (5th Cir. 1978).
[3]Fey v. Walston & Co., 493 F.2d 1036, 1046 (7th Cir. 1974).
[4]Terry v. Modern Woodmen of Am., 57 F.R.D. 141, 143 (W.D. Mo. 1972).

the *same subject matter and parties.* Depositions may also be used in other cases if one or more of the adversaries had the same motivation to examine or cross-examine the deponent in the prior action.

Depositions serve as efficient, economical, and effective trial tactics. There are three primary uses of depositions during trial: (1) as substantive evidence in lieu of live testimony, (2) as materials to refresh the recollection of the witness during the trial, and (3) as impeachment for cross-examination purposes.[5] Deposition transcripts must be offered or used by an attorney during trial if they are to be considered by the factfinder. Nor can a judge base findings on a deposition that was filed but not introduced into evidence.[6] The following subsections employ a partial transcript to demonstrate these three uses of depositions during trial. Accompanying comments explain the reasons for the specific questions and answers.

§2.10.2   *Use of Depositions in Lieu of Testimony*

This subsection utilizes a transcript of a chambers discussion and courtroom proceeding to demonstrate the use of a deposition in lieu of live testimony.

Mr. Sonsteng: Your honor, as part of our case for the plaintiff, we plan to read portions of the deposition of Mr. Westby taken last May pursuant to the Rules of Civil Procedure. Mr. Westby will be unavailable for trial because he is ill at this time. We did not anticipate his becoming ill and we only wish to read to the jury some portions of his testimony relating to conversations he had with both the plaintiff and defendant in this case. We anticipate the introduction of the deposition and testimony will take about 15 minutes. We have advised opposing counsel of our intent to do this. She took the deposition of Mr. Westby and had full opportunity to cross-examine him.

Whether or not it is anticipated, if in fact the deponent is unavailable, a deposition may be used as substitute testimony. Ordinarily the entire deposition is not introduced; only portions are offered, although they may be lengthy. It is good practice to advise the opposing

[5]Depositions may also be considered as affidavits in a motion proceeding. Hopson v. Schilling, 418 F. Supp. 1223, 1242 (N.D. Ind. 1976).
[6]Processteel, Inc. v. Mosley Machinery Co., 421 F.2d 1074, 1076 (6th Cir. 1970).

attorneys that you intend to use the deposition as soon as you know of your need; it may even be required by pretrial order. This will save time and avoid a delay at trial while the opposition reviews the deposition for objections and for use in support of its own case.

Ms. McGrath: Counsel has advised us of his intent to read portions of the deposition appearing on pages 40 to 50 of the transcript. We have an objection to an answer by the deponent appearing on page 44:

> *Q:* What did the defendant, Ms. Dowlin, say in response to your question?
> *A:* She told me that she did not know, but thought that a Laura Broomell told her that the radio station had no written policy regarding promotions.

> Your Honor, we object and ask that the portion of the answer following "I don't know" not be admitted on the grounds that it is both speculative and hearsay.

Mr. Sonsteng: That answer is Mr. Westby's best memory of a conversation and that statement, while hearsay is a statement against the interest of Laura Broomell and should be admitted as evidence as an exception to hearsay.

Judge: The hearsay objection will be sustained. Counsel, any more objections?

Rule 32(b) provides that any objections to the receipt of deposition evidence may be made at trial. Admissibility of such evidence is determined by the Federal Rules of Evidence. The objections and rulings by the judge take place out of the hearing of the jury, often in chambers, usually on the record. These determinations may occur during a pretrial conference or during trial before the transcript is offered. The questions and answers that have sustained objections will be excised from the evidence presented to the factfinder.

Ms. McGrath: No, your honor. We do plan to offer other portions of the deposition transcript into evidence to clarify those portions introduced by Mr. Sonsteng. We want to introduce those segments immediately after Mr. Sonsteng has had his portion of the transcript read to the jurors.

Mr. Sonsteng: We have reviewed the transcript portions counsel has advised us she plans to introduce during the trial and object to the timing of their introduction during the presentation of our case. Many of the answers appearing on pages 80 and 81 constitute new information that has little bearing on the information that we will present to the jury.

Judge: Pages 80 and 81 appear related to the previous answers and seem to clarify rather than counter those other responses. It will not take much time to read this to the jury, and Ms. McGrath will be permitted to do so immediately after your reading.

Rule 32(a)(4) provides that if one attorney offers a part of a deposition in evidence, the opposing attorney may insist that the other parts be introduced "which ought in fairness to be considered." This prevents selective use of parts of the deposition, which may cause misinterpretations of the testimony. The trial judge has the discretion, upon the request of an attorney, to admit other portions of the testimony or any changes made in the transcript by the deponent along with the reasons. The rule does not specify when these additional portions should be introduced, but case law has rightly required that such introduction occur at a point close in time to the introduction of the first part, usually immediately thereafter.[7]

A discussion held with the judge before offering the deposition, about the propriety and timing of the additional segments, eliminates the need to interrupt the offering attorney (unless tactically you prefer to interrupt) and prevents an unnecessary delay in the trial (unless you want to attempt legitimately to delay the proceeding). A preliminary ruling by the judge also assists in developing the proper strategy in response to the introduction of the deposition. If the judge denies the attorney's request to offer the additional parts immediately, that attorney may decide to offer the segments in his or her case in chief or in rebuttal.

The decision regarding timing depends on the impact the additional portions have. If they clarify a segment of the deposition or if they put into perspective a question and answer taken out of context, the judge should grant the request to introduce the clarifying segments immediately. If these parts contradict the offered transcript or deal with unrelated information, the judge should delay the offering until a later time, after the offering party has completed introducing all of its segments of the deposition or during the presentation of the opposing lawyer's case.

[7]Westinghouse Elec. Corp. v. Wray Equip. Corp., 286 F.2d 491, 494 (1st Cir. 1961).

Mr. Sonsteng: We prefer introducing the transcript by my reading the questions, and my having a paralegal from our firm, a Charles Wojcik, read Mr. Westby's answers to the questions. We also prefer that your honor give the appropriate instructions to the jury concerning the reading of the deposition.

Ms. McGrath: We have no objection.

Judge: Let's begin the testimony.

Common practice has the offering attorney read the questions and the clerk or another employee of the court or someone from the attorney's office read the answers.[8] The advantage of having someone from your office read it is the opportunity you then have to prepare that person and improve the manner of delivery. Having transcripts read to them can quickly become boring for a jury. Someone who speaks in a monotone or who fails to emphasize the important questions and answers may reduce the value of the deposition evidence. Having the same person read both the questions and answers may also reduce the impact of the testimony. Opposing lawyers may object to the use of a reader employed by you. They may insist on a neutral person, and many judges will accede to such a demand because it seems reasonable.

Judge: Ladies and gentlemen of the jury, we are now going to have a deposition read to us. A deposition is a procedure that occurs before trial in which a witness is asked questions by the attorneys in the case and gives answers under oath. The witness, a Mr. Westby, is ill, and cannot testify during this trial. The transcript of his deposition allows the attorneys to present to you testimony that was taken during the deposition. You are to consider the testimony that you are now going to hear from this deposition as any other testimony in this case, and just as though Mr. Westby were here in person giving his testimony. Someone other than Mr. Westby will now sit at the witness stand and read to you the testimony. Will you please step forward. You may proceed, counsel.

Judges, either *sua sponte* or by request of counsel, usually explain to the jury what is about to happen with the deposition. Jurors may not understand what is happening and usually do not know what a deposition is. The more important part of the explanation details the consideration the jury is to give the answers. This testimony is not actually

[8]R. Haydock & J. Sonsteng, National Institute for Trial Advocacy, Deposition Manual for Demonstration Videotapes A-20 (Instructor's ed. 1980).

equivalent to other testimony in a case, since the jury has no opportunity to consider the witness's credibility, unless, of course, the deposition has been videotaped. Even videotaping deprives the jury of a three-dimensional view of the witness and the full atmosphere surrounding live testimony. Sometimes jurors transfer the credibility of the person who reads the answers to the deponent, which is another reason it is vitally important to have someone read the testimony who can do so effectively.

Such an explanation is usually repeated by the judge during his or her instructions to the jury following arguments. Some judges decline to give the jurors a preliminary explanation of the impact or effect of a deposition during the trial because they will do so later. Others may not even consider such an explanation part of their typical jury instructions, so the offering attorney must be certain to ask or submit such an instruction to the judge.

Mr. Sonsteng: The following questions were asked of Mr. Westby at his deposition taken on May 7th of last year.

Q: Would you please state your name and address?
A: William Westby, 103 East Chestnut, Chicago, Illinois.
Q: What is your occupation?
A: I am a division manager for the Elmhurst Corporation.
Q: Do you know an Alberta Dowlin?
A: Yes.

The reading proceeds in a question-and-answer format. The evidence begins at the start of the transcript but may jump to other segments. These jumps may be obvious if the transcript has not been edited and the attorney directs the reader to another page and line. If the transcript has been edited, some transition may be necessary so the jurors can follow the change of topics in the testimony, such as by the attorney who reads the question noting the change.

§2.10.3   Use of Depositions to Refresh Recollection

This subsection uses a transcript from a direct examination at trial to illustrate refreshing recollection by referring to a deposition.

Q: What was the date of your first conversation with the defendant regarding the sale of the tractor?

A: I believe it was November 15, 1980. Yes, that was the date.

Q: What was the date of your second conversation with the defendant concerning the sale of that tractor?

A: Ummm . . .the second conversation . . . I have a blank. . . .

Q: Do you recall having a second conversation with the defendant?

A: Yes.

Q: Do you recall the date of that second conversation?

A: Let me think. I want to be certain. I am not sure of the exact date.

Q: Do you recall several months ago opposing counsel asked you some questions during a procedure which we call a deposition?

A: Yes, certainly.

Q: Do you remember being asked then about the date of that second conversation?

A: I believe so.

Virtually anything, including depositions, can be used to refresh a witness's recollection. The foundation for refreshing recollection includes the showing of the lack of a present memory. A preliminary question may also briefly explain the deposition for the sake of the jury, who may be curious about where this transcript came from or is going.

Q: Would it help refresh your recollection now if you could review the transcript of that deposition?

A: Certainly.

Q: Mr. Hood, I'm handing you a transcript of your previous testimony. Please read on page 240 lines 20 to 28. *(Pause.)* Does that help your recollection?

A: Yes.

Q: I will take the transcript back. Do you now have a present memory of what happened when?

A: Yes.

Q: What was the date of the second conversation you had with the defendant concerning the sale of the tractor?

A: November 18, 1980.

The attorney may also want to establish the witness's need for something specific to help his or her memory. After the witness has reviewed the relevant portion of the transcript, he or she should hand it back or put it aside and testify independently of the transcript. The transcript is not evidence. It is only used as a refresher. The witness still testifies with a present memory.

§2.10.4   Use of Depositions for Impeachment

As the basis for a discussion of using depositions for impeachment purposes, this subsection examines a transcript of a cross-examination at trial.

Q: Ms. Mullen, you testified on direct examination that you were traveling in your car at 25 miles per hour just before you entered the intersection.

A: Yes.

Q: You further testified that you knew the speed to be 25 miles per hour because you had just looked at your speedometer immediately before driving through the intersection.

A: Yes.

Q: That is your testimony under oath today before this jury?

A: Yes, that is what I said.

You have to be intimately familiar with the deposition so that you can easily locate a prior inconsistent statement and have it available for your cross-examination. Proper indexing and thorough preparation will assist you in using a deposition for impeachment. It also helps to have a witness who changes his or her story on a significant fact or on several less significant matters.

The first step in impeaching a witness on cross-examination is affirming the witness's testimony on direct examination. You want to repeat, through leading questions, what the witness said on direct, so that you can lock the testimony, prevent the witness from later arguing that that was not said, reduce the witness's ability to explain away some ambiguity in the direct-examination testimony, and highlight the contrasting answers for the jury. It may be useful to phrase the question so that it is identical to the prior, direct question.

Q: Do you recall that you testified under oath regarding the facts of this case and later signed a transcript of your testimony?

A: Yes, I remember.

Q: You remember that we call that procedure a deposition?

A: Yes.

Q: There was a court reporter there taking down your statements just like there is a court reporter here today?

A: Yes.

Q: You took an oath and promised to give truthful answers?

A: Yes.

Q: You recall that your attorney was there with you?

A: Yes.

Q: And you recall that I was there?

A: Yes.

Q: During that deposition, questions were asked of you and answers were given by you just like today in court.

A: Yes.

Q: Those questions and answers related to what happened at the intersection of May Avenue and Ridge Boulevard?

A: Yes.

Q: You answered those questions at the deposition as best you could, correct?

A: Yes.

Q: You gave complete and honest answers?

A: I tried.

Q: You did not withhold any information, did you?

A: No.

Q: Before that deposition, you had an opportunity to talk with your attorney about the deposition.

A: Yes.

Q: You had an opportunity to prepare for the deposition and think about what happened at the intersection?

A: Yes.

Q: That deposition occurred just a few months after the accident?

A: Yes.

Q: The events of the accident were still fresh in your mind at the time of your deposition?

A: Yes.

A second step may involve the attorney's explaining the circumstances of the prior inconsistent statement. The Federal Rules of Evidence no longer require an attorney to call the witness's attention to such circumstances. But strategic considerations usually mandate the explanation: these questions explain the circumstances of the prior statement, which increases the jurors' understanding of what happened and increases the impact of the inconsistent statements on the jury. They reduce the witness's opportunity to explain away the background of the prior statement. They also increase the tension for the witness and prolong the ordeal, emphasizing for the jurors the importance of this line of cross-examination.

There is no required number of questions that should be asked to establish the circumstances. The questions recited here typify the variety of available areas to establish them. They need not all be asked. The case, the witness, the prior inconsistent statement, and the theory of your cross-examination determine how many and which questions you ask.

Q: Ms. Mullen, I'm handing you a document. Please look at it. Is this a transcript of your deposition?
A: It appears to be.
Q: Please turn to page 63 and look at line 10. You were asked this question then: "How fast were you driving when you first entered the intersection?" Do you see that?
A: Yes.

The attorney must call the witness's attention to the prior inconsistent statement, but there is no requirement that the witness be shown the deposition. More commonly, the attorney reads the witness the previous question and answer without showing the witness anything. Whatever the attorney does, the opposing lawyer will want to know the page and line numbers of the prior statement. The deposition need not be marked, because the transcript is not being offered as evidence. The reading itself of the prior testimony and the witness's affirmation of the answers is the evidence offered.

If the witness denies that the transcript is his or her deposition, the offering attorney can ask the judge to take judicial notice of the authenticity and accuracy of the filed deposition. Most judges will. If the opposing lawyer successfully objects to the judicial notice, the offering attorney may have to call the court reporter to testify. This is seldom necessary.

Q: And your answer to that question was: "About 25 miles an hour. I'm not real sure." Do you see that?
A: Yes.
Q: The next question you were asked was "Did you look at your speedometer any time before you entered the intersection?" And your answer was "No." Do you also see that "No" response?
A: Yes.
Q: Those were your answers a year ago, under oath.

It is advisable for the attorney to read both the deposition questions and the answers. This procedure maintains the constant control the lawyer has over this phase of cross-examination. A witness who reads an answer may be inaudible or lack the proper emphasis or voice inflection.

A: I may have misunderstood the questions.

Q: Ms. Mullen, you do recall that at the beginning of that deposition you were advised that if you did not understand a question to say so and it would be rephrased.

A: I'm not sure I remember that.

Q: The beginning of that transcript you hold includes that explanation and your response. Do you wish to read it?

A: That's not necessary.

Q: You did not at the time you were asked these specific questions say they were confusing, did you?

A: No.

Q: Do you recall several months after the deposition going to your attorney's office to read your deposition transcript?

A: Yes, I recall that.

Q: And you read over the answers that you gave?

A: Yes.

Q: And you understood at that time that you could make any changes if you had said anything incorrect or untrue?

A: I believe so.

Q: After reading your deposition, you signed the deposition.

A: Yes.

Q: Your signature appears on the last page of that transcript, correct?

A: Yes, that's my signature.

The attorney amplifies the circumstances of the prior statement by reminding the witness of the beginning of the deposition and the subsequent reading and signing of the transcript. You, as the attorney, do not want to drone on and on about surrounding circumstances. The excerpts here provide a variety of examples of questioning techniques.

The opposing lawyer has not interrupted and requested to have read additional parts of the deposition to clarify the prior responses. Rule 32(d)(4) permits such interruption and addition, but that rule specifies that additional segments may only be allowed when the deposition is being "offered in evidence." The rule is not triggered by impeachment or refreshing-recollection uses because the deposition itself is not submitted as evidence. The trial judge has general discretion to permit supplementation. Any interruption must be in good faith and must introduce some addition that clarifies the response and is not frivolous.

Q: And you signed that deposition, which contained your answer that you did not look at your speedometer before entering the intersection?
A: I didn't recall that then.
Q: You did sign and affirm your testimony in that deposition?
A: Yes.
Q: Ms. Mullen, a year ago you testified under oath that you did not look at your speedometer before entering the intersection and today you testified under oath that you did look at your speedometer before entering the intersection, didn't you?
A: Yes, it seems so.
Q: Thank you, Ms. Mullen. That concludes my questioning.

You should conclude the impeachment with an emphasis on the inconsistency. Some attorneys build and build on the circumstances and end with reading the prior inconsistent statement. This segment continues after the first mention of the inconsistency and attempts to use repetition for emphasis. You should be careful not to ask the one question too many, the question which allows the witness to explain the inconsistency. There is seldom, if ever, a need to ask the witness "why" the inconsistency. The other attorney may do so during redirect.

The witness's admission regarding the prior statement and deposition transcript not only is proof for impeachment purposes but also is evidence of the fact contained in the prior statement. It may be considered by the jury as substantive proof of that fact.

Judge: Redirect, counsel?
Q: Yes, your Honor. Ms. Mullen, please turn to page 116 of that same deposition, and look at line eight. That question was asked of you later in the deposition and it reads "Do you have any other basis for determining how fast you were going just before you entered the intersection?" Do you recall that question being asked of you that day?
A: Yes.
Q: Would you please read to the jury from your deposition the answer that you gave that day?

A: I said "My long years of driving experience. Other traffic was maintaining about my same speed. And it's possible, come to think of it, that I looked at my speedometer, which I often do."
Q: That was your testimony a year ago, under oath?
A: Yes.

The redirect examination begins with the attorney's introducing any segment of the deposition that helps bolster the accuracy of the direct examination testimony, reduces the impact of the prior statement, explains what the witness meant to say during the deposition and may show that cross-examining counsel attempted to use a response out of context. You have to be as familiar with your witness's deposition as you are with your opposing witnesses'.

§2.10.5 Effects of Use of Depositions at Trial

Rule 32(c) discusses the effect that taking or using the deposition has on its use by a party at trial. There are six basic rules:

1. A party who takes a person's deposition does not thereby make that person his or her witness for trial purposes.
2. A party does not make a deponent his or her witness at the trial if the deposition is used to impeach that witness.
3. A party does not make the adverse party his or her witness at the trial if the deposition of the adverse party is used for any reason.
4. Any other use by any party of a deposition of anyone else does make that deponent a witness of that party for purposes of trial.
5. Regardless of who is whose witness, any party may rebut any relevant evidence contained in any deposition, regardless of who introduces it for that purpose.
6. Any party at any time may continue reading this book and turn to Chapter 3.

§2.11 PROBLEMS

Deposition Planning

Planning a deposition requires consideration of several factors:

(a) When should the deposition be taken?
(b) What discovery should be completed before the deposition?
(c) Where should the deposition be held?
(d) Who should be present, if anyone, in addition to the deponent, attorneys, and court reporter?

Decide what you will do and explain your strategy decisions as counsel:

1. For the plaintiff in *American Campers v. Summers,* deposing Susan and John Summers.
2. For the defendants in *American Campers v. Summers,* deposing Carol Sexton.
3. For the plaintiff in *Bellow v. Norris,* deposing Fran Norris.
4. For the plaintiff in *Bellow v. Norris,* deposing Dale Oliver.
5. For the defendant in *Bellow v. Norris,* deposing Pat Bellow.
6. For the defendant in *Bellow v. Norris,* deposing Terry Warbler.
7. For the plaintiff in *Graham v. Turkel,* deposing Pat Kinney.
8. For the defendant in *Graham v. Turkel,* deposing Bert Latimer.

Deposition Preparation

Prepare a detailed outline of the topics and questions you will ask at the deposition the following persons.

9. Susan and John Summers by the plaintiff American Campers, in *American Campers v. Summers.*
10. Carol Sexton by the defendants Summers, in *American Campers v. Summers.*
11. Tom Arnold by the defendants Summers, in *American Campers v. Summers.*

12. Fran Norris by the plaintiff Pat Bellow, in *Bellow v. Norris.*
13. Dale Oliver by the plaintiff Pat Bellow, in *Bellow v. Norris.*
14. Pat Bellow by the defendant Fran Norris, in *Bellow v. Norris.*
15. Terry Warbler by the defendant Fran Norris, in *Bellow v. Norris.*
16. Pat Kinney by the plaintiff Andrew Graham, in *Graham v. Turkel.*
17. Bert Latimer by the defendant R. D. Turkel, in *Graham v. Turkel.*

Deponent Preparation

Prepare your deponent by:

(a) Reviewing the facts and file with the deponent;
(b) Discussing and describing deposition procedures;
(c) Having the deponent read the Client Deposition Instructions that appear in Appendix B;
(d) Supplementing those general instructions with specific instructions;
(e) Having the deponent answer questions that you anticipate will be asked during the deposition.

Your instructor may require other preparations. You may be asked to provide the deponent. The factual situations in the Hypothetical Case Files in Appendix A have been designed so that nearly anyone will be qualified and comfortable in assuming the role of a lay person deponent and so that a law student can assume the role of an expert witness. Your instructor may place some restrictions on who can be a deponent. It may be advisable in some situations to avoid having a friend of the deposing attorney be the deponent.

18. Prepare Pat Bellow to depose in *Bellow v. Norris.*
19. Prepare Fran Norris to depose in *Bellow v. Norris.*
20. Prepare Terry Warbler to depose in *Bellow v. Norris.*
21. Prepare Dale Oliver to depose in *Bellow v. Norris.*
22. Prepare Bert Latimer to depose in *Graham v. Turkel.*
23. Prepare Pat Kinney to depose in *Graham v. Turkel.*

Deposition Instructions

You will be assigned to take a deposition. Conduct the deposition by thoroughly examining the deponent, using probing questions. Your instructor may place a time limit on the deposition. If so, select a reasonable number of major areas to probe and avoid asking a few broad questions in many areas to fill the time.

There may not be a court reporter present during your deposition. The deposing attorney can assume the roles of the court reporter and administer the oath and mark documents. Your instructor may advise you to assume that the deponent has been sworn and that all documents have already been marked.

Be persistent; insist on responsive answers to questions relating to the subject matter of the case. Because of the hypothetical character of this skills exercise, some marginally relevant questions might unnecessarily confuse the deponent (for example, detailed questions about family, prior life experiences, graduation dates), so you should focus your questions on the facts and circumstances of the case and on relevant background questions.

Begin the deposition with some introductory remarks explaining the deposition. During the deposition have the deponent identify some documents. Conclude the deposition with any closing questions to the deponent and resolve with the other lawyer the matter of reading and signing the transcript and its filing.

24. Depose Fran Norris for the plaintiff in *Bellow v. Norris.*
25. Depose Pat Bellow for the defendant in *Bellow v. Norris.*
26. Depose Dale Oliver for the plaintiff in *Bellow v. Norris.*
27. Depose Terry Warbler for the defendant in *Bellow v. Norris.*
28. Depose Pat Kinney for the plaintiff in *Graham v. Turkel.*
29. Depose Bert Latimer for the defendant in *Graham v. Turkel.*

Written-Question Depositions

30. You represent the defendant in *American Campers v. Summers.* Carol Sexton has left the employment of the plaintiff and has moved to a distant state. You decide that Rule 31 provides the best opportunity to obtain the information you need. Draft a set of written-question interrogatories directed to Carol Sexton.

31. You represent the plaintiff in *American Campers v. Summers.* Re-

view the written questions you or a classmate has drafted for Carol Sexton in Problem 30 and draft a set of cross-questions on behalf of the plaintiff, directed to Carol Sexton.

Alternative Depositions

32.   You represent the defendant in *American Campers v. Summers.* Tom Arnold has left the employment of the plaintiff and has moved to a distant state. You are considering obtaining information from Arnold either by taking his deposition by telephone or by written questions. Make a list of the advantages and disadvantages of each of these two deposition methods. Decide which one you prefer to use in the case and explain your decision.

Depositions to Preserve Testimony

33.   Carol Sexton in *American Campers v. Summers* has left the employ of the plaintiff and plans to leave the United States and to live permanently in London. You represent the plaintiff. Would you take her deposition to preserve her testimony? Why or why not?

34.   Suppose that you represent the defendant. Would you take Carol Sexton's deposition before she left? State the reasons for your decision.

35.   John Summers in *American Campers v. Summers* has developed a debilitating case of bone cancer. His condition and treatment is such that by the end of October he will not be able to be deposed. His doctor predicts that John will die before the end of the year. John wants his testimony preserved. As his attorney, consider taking his videotaped deposition. Analyze the advantages and disadvantages of taking his videotaped deposition, indicate what type of deposition you would take, and explain your decision.

Chapter 3
INTERROGATORIES

What hath God wrought?

Numbers 23:23
quoted by Samuel F.B. Morse
on the discovery of the telegraph

§3.1 INTRODUCTION

You may never have the opportunity to submit interrogatories to a deity, but you can obtain discoverable information from another party through written interrogatories. This chapter analyzes and explains discovery rules, tactics, and strategies relating to interrogatories. Attorneys tend to have rather set, entrenched positions regarding the usefulness of this discovery device. Some find great success with selective use; others suffer through too many painful hours of composing responses; others have mixed reactions.

Explanations and suggestions in this chapter may help you discover and develop your own approach. The approaches discussed here reflect some of the more successful uses for interrogatories and responses. We now invite you to analyze interrogatory practice, beginning with the advantages and disadvantages of this discovery device.

§3.1.1 *Advantages*

As a discovery device, the interrogatory conveys several benefits:

1. It is an economical discovery method. If you have access to a typewriter, stationery, and stamps, you can inexpensively obtain information. Your time constitutes the major expense.

2. It is a simple method. If you are an employed attorney you can use it in any case.
3. It is a speedy method. You can serve interrogatories with pleadings.
4. It is a flexible method. You can ask different types of questions in different sets at different times during the pendency of a case.
5. It is an efficient system. You can play your scheduled backgammon game and need not (and cannot) be present during the research and preparation of the answers by the other side.
6. It is a homing device. It will find and locate the proper spokesperson, who must then reveal the correct and complete information.
7. It is the intended method to particularize the factual and legal bases for pleadings.
8. It considers nothing sacred. It draws on the collective knowledge of the other party and agents and will even discover information known to the other attorney.
9. It complements other methods of discovery. Answers received can be used to determine the best persons for later depositions or the best documents for a later request for production.
10. It reveals information that will put the parties in realistic and informed positions from which to negotiate a settlement or stipulate to agreed facts.

§3.1.2 Disadvantages

Of course, interrogatories have limitations, weaknesses, and risks. These include:

1. They may be directed only to parties to the action or inaction.
2. They permit less than satisfactory responses. The other party and its attorney may draft the answers to make that party look like a saint.
3. They can be gruesome to draft. You have to draft concise, precise questions that even a resurrected Clarence Darrow would have to answer fully and objectively.
4. They do not permit spontaneity. You cannot easily frame follow-up questions unless you can accurately anticipate the answers or unless you are Mandrake.

5. They may become uneconomical if your overzealous opponent responds with defensive tactics that include motions, briefs, and arguments. The additional expense imposed upon your client may eliminate the initial cost difference between interrogatories and depositions.
6. They permit attorneys to abuse the system and to play hide-and-seek with information.
7. They can make the opposing lawyer look like a cum laude graduate. A comprehensive set may require your opponent to research and prepare his or her case thoroughly in order to respond.

§3.1.3 Parties That Can Be Questioned

Interrogatories may be served only upon another party, not upon non-party witnesses.[1] The party need not be an adverse party but may be a third party, co-party, wild party, whatever. Likewise, interrogatories must be addressed to a party itself, not to an officer or employee agent or an attorney.[2] They may be addressed to a prospective party for purposes of perpetuating testimony under the auspices of Rule 27. Improperly addressed interrogatories may be stricken by opposing counsel.

Interrogatories call for the collective knowledge of the recipient. This requirement may compel a certain person's participation in the preparation of answers, whether that person is specifically addressed or not. In class actions, interrogatories may be served only upon named parties; unnamed members of the class cannot be served unless there is a very substantial reason, a strong showing of necessity, and the questions are limited in scope.[3] However, this requirement may be manipulated by class members who pick and choose which of their group shall be subject to discovery. Named plaintiffs are always subject to discovery, even if their actions are later consolidated, as in multidistrict litigation.

§3.1 [1]Fed. R. Civ. P. 33(a).
[2]Wirtz v. I.C. Harris & Co., 36 F.R.D. 116, 117 (E.D. Mich. 1964); Steelman v. United States Fidelity & Guar. Co., 35 F.R.D. 120 (W.D. Mo. 1964).
[3]In re Folding Carton Antitrust Litigation, 83 F.R.D. 260, 264 (N.D. Ill 1979).

§3.1.4   Timing of Interrogatory Submissions

Interrogatories may be served by a plaintiff with the summons and complaint, or they may be served by any party at any time after commencement of an action. The responding party has 30 days to respond to the interrogatories or 45 days if the questions are served with a summons and complaint. Rule 33(a) permits a court to shorten or lengthen these time limits. Rule 29(2) requires court approval for a stipulation between counsel that extends these times. The rationale, in part, for these court orders is to prevent the discovery process from dragging on mercilessly and prolonging the case on the court docket. In practice, many lawyers wink at these requirements and allow some flexibility in providing responses, and some jurisdictions permit attorneys to stipulate to extensions to avoid the need for court appearances.

Interrogatories may be submitted in one or more sets. A second set of questions is often required to clarify or detail answers received in the first set. It is sometimes wise to submit follow-up or revised questions after receiving objections or inadequate responses to a previous set. The number of sets can be limited if numerous sets become harassing and burdensome on the responding party.

A party who submits interrogatories within 30 days of a scheduled trial date has no automatic right under the rules to expect answers.[4] A motion must be brought upon good cause to seek a shorter response time. Examples of good cause include situations in which the interrogating party could not have been expected to ask such questions earlier, in which the responding party did not have the information earlier, or in which an attorney for the interrogating party has just been retained or just passed the bar exam.[5]

The timing provisions of interrogatories sometimes provide defendants with a tactical advantage: if the interrogatories are served with the summons and complaint, the defendant can serve interrogatories on the plaintiff and obtain answers before the defendant's own answers are due. In this situation, the defendants need not respond until 45 days after service, while the plaintiff must respond within 30 days. If the defendant serves such interrogatories personally within 14 days or by mail within eleven days of service of the summons, complaint, and plaintiff's interrogatories, the rules require the plaintiff to respond before the defendant is required to answer. While this tactic

---

[4]Brennan v. Sine, 495 F.2d 875 (10th Cir. 1974).

[5]See Geronymo v. Joseph Horne Co., 80 F.R.D. 86, 87 (W.D. Pa. 1978).

is neither available nor appropriate in many cases, it is there for what it is worth.

A second aspect of timing is that interrogatories are best used in the early stages of discovery to obtain general information. Interrogatories frequently precede depositions in the discovery process, and allow the discovery attorney to decide whom to depose, what areas merit inquiry, and whether documents might be available prior to the deposition (through a Rule 34 request) or at the deposition (by Rule 30 or 45).

§3.2 SUBJECT MATTER OF INTERROGATORIES

§3.2.1 *Primary Information*

Interrogatories may seek to discover any information discoverable under Rule 26. But interrogatories do have limitations, and certain kinds of information are not readily or satisfactorily discoverable with this device. Information based upon testimony, subjective and interpretive information, information dependent on the demeanor and credibility of the answering party, and complex or confusing types of information will all be better left to depositions. Some of the categories of information that interrogatories do disclose in a most efficient, effective, and economical way include the following:

1. The identities of persons who have provided a party with statements;[1]
2. The persons who have been interviewed in the course of trial preparation;[2]
3. The facts elicited from a witness who gave no written statement and who has become unavailable;[3]
4. The existence, description, nature, custody, condition, and location of documents, witness statements, and tangible things;

---

§3.2 [1]Chatman v. American Export Lines, Inc., 20 F.R.D. 76 (S.D.N.Y. 1956).
[2]Cannaday v. Cities Serv. Oil Co., 19 F.R.D. 261, 262 (S.D.N.Y. 1956).
[3]Arco Pipeline Co. v. S.S. *Trade Star*, 81 F.R.D. 416 (E.D. Pa. 1978).

5. Information concerning letters, memoranda, notes, and other materials that a party or witness has written, composed, signed, or read;

6. Summary explanations of technical data and statistics, manuals, reports, studies, and materials containing technical information;

7. Other contacts or transactions between or relating to the parties before or after the events of the case;[4]

8. Similar incidents, complaints, problems encountered by third persons and related to the subject matter of the case;[5]

9. Business and corporate information concerning the nature, extent, principal place of business, initial date of corporation, state of incorporation, and states that license the business;

10. Financial information, including reports, balance sheets, and financial status of a business and income, assets, and liabilities of parties;[6]

11. The financial status and net worth of a defendant who is defending a claim for punitive damages;[7]

12. Government licenses that authorize or regulate facets of a party's conduct;[8]

13. The names of expert witnesses who will testify at trial, who are employees of a party, or who have been retained, but not those only informally consulted;[9]

14. The opinions and bases for such opinions of the experts who will testify at trial or who are employees;[10]

15. The existence and coverage of liability or other insurance;[11]

16. Measurements, including accurate answers or best estimates of time, distance, speed, location, and other dimensions of occurrences;

17. Information relevant to a writ of execution under Rule 69;

[4]Renshaw v. Ravert, 82 F.R.D. 361, 363 (E.D. Pa. 1979).
[5]*But see* Wood v. McCullough, 45 F.R.D. 41, 42 (S.D.N.Y. 1968).
[6]Renshaw v. Ravert, 82 F.R.D. 361, 363 (E.D. Pa. 1979).
[7]Miller v. Doctor's Gen. Hosp., 76 F.R.D. 136, 140 (W.D. Okla. 1977).
[8]Cone Mills Corp. v. Joseph Bancroft & Sons, 33 F.R.D. 318 (D. Del. 1963).
[9]Baki v. B.F. Diamond Constr. Co., 71 F.R.D. 179, 182 (D. Md. 1976).
[10]In re Folding Carton Antitrust Litigation, 83 F.R.D. 256, 259 (N.D. Ill. 1979); Olmert v. Olson, 60 F.R.D. 369, 371 (D.D.C. 1973).
[11]Fed. R. Civ. P. 26(b)(2).

18. Facts going to the court's jurisdiction;[12]
19. Attorney work-product information, if good cause is shown, i.e., necessity.[13]

§3.2.2 Secondary Information

Other subject areas are ripe for interrogatories. We offer some explanation as to their efficacy and limitations.

1. The identity of all persons who have information about the subject matter of the case is routinely available, because Rule 26 explicitly uses the phrase "persons with knowledge." But what about the discovery of persons who *may* have knowledge? The more accepted view holds that this information is also discoverable, unless the responding party does not know it and would have to conduct an interrogation beyond the scope of Rule 26.[14]

2. Interrogatories may be used as an alternative means to obtain a more definite explanation of the allegations of pleadings and facts that support the pleadings' assertions.[15] Questions may be phrased to refer directly to the pleading paragraph numbers and subdivisions. They may ask a party to specify not only what happened and what the party knows, but also factual evidence relating to the amount and degree of damages or other relief demanded in the complaint, including the cost factors of reasonable attorney's fees. These questions force the disclosure of all the pertinent facts the opposition relies upon to prove its case. Such interrogatories are extremely useful and adaptable to almost every case.

3. The specific information that a party or witness knows about a case may be obtained, if the request is properly phrased.[16] But such requests may be broad or vague; the information sought may appear in a written statement; responses may be self-serving and unsatisfac-

[12]Wirtz v. Capitol Air Serv., Inc., 42 F.R.D. 641, 642 (D. Kan. 1967).

[13]Westhemeco Ltd. v. New Hampshire Ins. Co., 82 F.R.D. 702, 709 (S.D.N.Y. 1979); Duplan Corp. v. Deering Milliken, Inc., 61 F.R.D. 127, 130 (D.S.C.), *rev'd and remanded,* 487 F.2d 480 (4th Cir. 1973); United States v. 38 Cases, More or Less, 35 F.R.D. 357, 361 (W.D. Pa. 1964). *See also* Garner v. Wolfinbarger, 430 F.2d 1093, 1103 (5th Cir. 1970).

[14]4 Moore's Federal Practice ¶26.57[1], at 26-196 to 26-198 (2d ed. 1980).

[15]Lincoln Gateway Realty Co. v. Carri-Craft, Inc., 53 F.R.D. 303, 308 (W.D. Mo. 1971); B-H Transp. Co. v. Great Atl. & Pac. Tea Co., 44 F.R.D. 436, 438 (N.D.N.Y. 1968).

[16]In re Anthracite Coal Antitrust Litigation, 81 F.R.D. 516, 522 (M.D. Pa. 1979).

tory; and so depositions often provide a much better vehicle to obtain this information. A request for the summary of the "substance of subject matter" known by a witness may even be beyond the ken of a party and impossible to answer.[17] It may be more productive to limit such a request to what the responding party knows and what, if anything, a witness knows.

4.   Interrogatories may request that documents be provided in lieu of an answer to a specific question, but Rule 34 is a more appropriate vehicle for obtaining such information. Further, these questions can be phrased as an instruction statement and placed in the introduction, saving an interrogatory. Rule 34 is also more appropriate since no numerical limits on requests for documents are imposed by that rule or by local rules. It is a common practice among many lawyers to combine a Rule 34 request with Rule 33 interrogatories to obtain documents as well as answers.

5.   Interrogatories may be phrased as an admission, because often a question is both a proper interrogatory and an appropriate request for admission.[18] But why use an interrogatory if another discovery device will produce the same information? There are no limits to the requests that can be made under Rule 36. Interrogatories may be rephrased and asked under the auspices of those rules and not Rule 33. Not all questions can be rephrased, though. The interrogatory, "State all facts upon which you base your claim of failure to warn in Paragraph 3 of the Complaint," is preferable to the request for admission, "You know of no facts upon which you base your claim for failure to warn."[19]

6.   Interrogatories may ask whether the party will agree to supplement the answers to all or certain questions. These types of questions also may be phrased as statements and included in the preface, or even asked in a cover letter with the interrogatories. Rule 26(e) details which, if any, answers need to be supplemented. Some attorneys will supplement responses if asked regardless of the dictates of the rule.

7.   The names and identities of witnesses who will testify at the trial may be requested in an interrogatory. Rule 26(b) has no language either allowing or disallowing such information. The majority of

---

[17]*See* Lunn v. United Aircraft Corp., 25 F.R.D. 186, 188 (D. Del. 1960).

[18]Stonybrook Tenants Assn., Inc. v. Alpert, 29 F.R.D. 165, 167 (D. Conn. 1961).

[19]California Continuing Education of the Bar, California Civil Discovery Practice 333 (1975).

courts reviewing the propriety of lists of trial witnesses has ruled that the information need not be disclosed.[20]

A common response will be "Not known at this time."[21] There appears to be no continuing obligation to supplement that answer under the rules, unless the new answer contains the names of new expert witnesses. Some judges believe that the question is appropriate only as a pretrial request, either through a formal pretrial conference, a case readiness summary requested by local rule, or a letter to the other attorney asking for such names.

8.   Questions asking why a party did or did not do something, or could or could not have accomplished something, will be proper and appropriate. For example, the following interrogatories may be asked:

1.   What prompted you to drive the front of your car into the left rear of the 1956 Chevrolet on the occasion in question?
2.   In what way could you have avoided the collision?[22]

But responses to such questions may not be particularly revealing or helpful. The answer to the first question may be "nothing" if the assumption in the question (that something "prompted" the party) is incorrect. The answer to the second question may reveal more information. A later section (§3.6) discusses the propriety of responses.

9.   Interrogators may seek to identify persons who prepared or who were consulted with regard to the answers. This type of question is proper if it seeks the identity of any person who assisted with the response and who has knowledge of the information in the response. But questions may be improper if they seek the identity of all persons who participated in the mental processes and strategies involved in drafting responses, since this involves seeking information of non-discoverable mental impressions and work product, categories excluded by Rule 26.[23]

---

[20]*See* (for courts disallowing) Wirtz v. Continental Fin. & Loan Co., 326 F.2d 561 (5th Cir. 1964); Wirtz v. B.A.C. Steel Prods., Inc., 312 F.2d 14 (4th Cir. 1962). *See* (for courts allowing) United States Equal Employment Opportunity Commn. v. Metropolitan Museum of Art, 80 F.R.D. 317 (S.D.N.Y. 1978).

[21]*See generally* United States Equal Employment Opportunity Commn. v. Metropolitan Museum of Art, 80 F.R.D. 317, 318 (S.D.N.Y. 1978).

[22]Pressley v. Boehlke, 33 F.R.D. 316, 317 (W.D.N.C. 1963).

[23]Maritime Cinema Serv. Corp. v. Movies EN Route, 160 F.R.D. 587 (S.D.N.Y. 1973).

§3.2.3   Opinions and Contentions

Rule 33(b) explains the propriety of interrogatories that inquire into opinions and contentions:

> An interrogatory otherwise proper is not necessarily objectionable merely because an answer to the interrogatory involves an opinion or contention that relates to fact or the application of law to fact, but the court may order that such an interrogatory need not be answered until after designated discovery has been completed or until a pre-trial conference or other later time.

Interrogatories have long been used effectively to obtain information relating to a party's contentions, e.g., "Do you contend that plaintiff was contributorily negligent regarding the accident on August 6, 1980?" This question will usually be followed with a question seeking the basis for the contention: "State all facts upon which you base such contention."[24] Rule 33(b) has not altered the practice of asking this type of contention question. The rule explicitly permits interrogatories seeking opinions and contentions that relate the application of law to fact and resolves some, but not all, problems surrounding the scope of such permissible questions. Under Rule 33(b):

1. Interrogatories may seek factual opinions and conclusions;[25]
2. Interrogatories may obtain answers that relate to the application of law to facts;[26]
3. Valid objections may still be interposed to objectionable questions, but that implies that such questions can be objectionable;
4. Interrogatories seeking purely legal conclusions unrelated to the facts will be improper;[27]
5. A judge has the discretion to postpone compelling answers to questions in categories 1 and 2 if the circumstances warrant a postponement (e.g., it is too early in the progress of the case to expect the party to respond to such questions).

[24]California Continuing Education of the Bar, California Civil Discovery Practice 339 (1975).
[25]Leumi Financial Corp. v. Hartford Accident & Indem. Co., 295 F. Supp. 539, 542 (S.D.N.Y. 1969); Lincoln Gateway Realty Co. v. Carri-Craft, Inc., 53 F.R.D. 303 (W.D. Mo. 1971).
[26]O'Brien v. International Bhd. of Elec. Workers, 443 F. Supp. 1182, 1187 (N.D. Ga. 1977).
[27]Spector Freight Sys., Inc. v. Home Indem. Co., 58 F.R.D. 162, 164 (N.D. Ill. 1973).

Unresolved are two major questions. First, in what situations will questions falling into categories 1 and 2, above, be proper, and in what situations objectionable? Second, what is the difference between a question that relates the application of law to fact and one that seeks a pure legal conclusion?

The answers to these two questions are in the process of being resolved by the courts.

With regard to the first, it seems clear that interrogatories are proper and appropriate that seek opinions and conclusions that: (1) relate to an "essential element" of a case, like a prima facie element;[28] (2) seek an answer that would serve a substantial purpose in the litigation, like enabling the party to determine the extent of proof required[29] or narrowing the issues;[30] (3) seek disclosures about issues the responding party has raised as a claim or defense;[31] (4) constitute requests for the factual basis supporting the responding party's conclusory claims.[32]

Examples of such proper interrogatories include:

1. What acts of negligence were committed by defendant?
2. In addition to such alleged acts of negligence, upon what other grounds does plaintiff base the claim?[33]

It seems unclear why minor variations in language transform an improper conclusory question into a proper opinion interrogatory. The question "Why did the material fall from or above the defendant's property onto North St. on December 3, 1970" was held inappropriate; but the interrogatory "How, if you know, did the material fall . . .?" was considered to be proper.[34]

With regard to the second unresolved question, it is clear that an interrogatory that seeks a legal conclusion unrelated to the facts is

---

[28]Comment, Civil Procedure — Opinion Interrogatories after 1970 Amendment to Federal Rule 33(b), 53 N.C.L. Rev. 695, 699 (1975).

[29]Scoville Mfg. Co. v. Sunbeam Corp., 357 F. Supp. 943, 948 (D. Del. 1973).

[30]Union Carbide Corp. v. Travelers Indem. Co., 61 F.R.D. 411, 414 (W.D. Pa. 1973). *See* Schoone & Miner, The Effective Use of Written Interrogatories, 60 Marq. L. Rev. 29, 48 (1976).

[31]Diamond Crystal Salt Co. v. Package Masters, Inc., 319 F. Supp. 911, 912 (D. Del. 1970).

[32]Cornaglia v. Ricciardi, 63 F.R.D. 416, 419 (E.D. Pa. 1974) (fraud); Rogers v. Tri-State Materials Corp., 51 F.R.D. 234, 246 (N.D.W. Va. 1970) (negligence).

[33]Rogers v. Tri-State Materials Corp., 51 F.R.D. 234, 246 (N.D.W. Va. 1970).

[34]Goodman v. I.B.M. Corp., 59 F.R.D. 278, 279 (N.D. Ill. 1973).

improper.[35] An interrogatory that seeks a legal conclusion but that relates such contention to the facts is appropriate. It is proper, for instance, for a party to ask whether a defendant finance company was an "assignee" of plaintiff's promissory notes from a co-defendant.[36] It is also appropriate for a party to ask whether the opponent is relying upon some presumption of fact or law regarding a situation in a case and, if so, the nature of that presumption.[37] An interrogatory may properly ask whether a party contends that a certain claim or defense applies to the case, but may not ask whether such legal claim or defense is legally controlling or dispositive of the issues. It is proper for a plaintiff to ask whether the defendant contends anyone observed plaintiff commit an act believed criminal in nature, but not whether plaintiff committed a criminal act.[38] It appears inappropriate for one party to ask another party's opinion regarding the legal competency of a potential witness; a court held this to be strictly a question of evidence best left to the trial court.[39]

It is unclear how courts will distinguish between "pure" legal questions and "mixed" questions of law and fact. A pure legal question in "form" has been interpreted by one court as appropriately calling for a proper response in "substance"; the court believed that an interrogatory that asked "whether plaintiff contends a policy of not permitting retesting is racially discriminatory" (in a civil rights employment case) sought a purely legal conclusion in form, but was an appropriately mixed question in substance and so should be answered.[40] Another court held that the following question properly seeks an application of law to facts:

> In respect to each act and/or utterance listed in response to interrogatory 1, above, explain the manner in which each said act and/or utterance (a)violated plaintiff's responsibility toward [defendants] and (b)interfered with [defendants'] performance of their respective legal or contractual obligations.

[35]Fed. R. Civ. P. 33(b), Notes of Advisory Comm. — 1970 Amendments.
[36]Joseph v. Norman's Health Club, 336 F. Supp. 307, 319 (E.D. Mo. 1971), *judgment ordered*, 386 F. Supp. 780 (1975), *rev'd on other grounds*, 532 F.2d 86 (8th Cir. 1976).
[37]Rogers v. Tri-State Materials Corp., 51 F.R.D. 234 (N.D.W. Va. 1970).
[38]*See* Ballard v. Allegheny Airlines, Inc., 54 F.R.D. 67, 69 (E.D. Pa. 1972).
[39]Spector Freight Sys., Inc. v. Home Indem. Co., 58 F.R.D. 162, 164 (N.D. Ill. 1973).
[40]Roberson v. Great Am. Ins. Co. of N.Y., 48 F.R.D. 404, 415 (N.D. Ga. 1969).

The same court declared that the following, similar question improperly sought a pure legal conclusion unrelated to the facts:

> In respect to each and every constitutional provision listed in response to Interrogatory 2, state and explain the reason why each provision is not effected by operation of federal statute 29 U.S.C. §411(b). . . .[41]

Still another court required a party to specify the foreign law relied upon in its claims and defenses, by explaining the substance of the law and including citations of decisional authority.[42] It seems that interrogatories drafted to include some facts of the case and to seek some contention of the party will be proper and appropriate within the meaning of Rule 33(b). But it remains difficult to articulate specific criteria. Maybe, like another elusive standard, the courts know it when they read it.

§3.3   THE INTERROGATORY FORM

The document containing the interrogatories may well include more than just the questions. It is common for the document to include several parts: a preface, instructions, and definitions, followed by the questions themselves. Not all forms require the first three components, but there is usually good reason to include them. Some courts have set forth local rules regulating certain aspects of the proper interrogatory form.

§3.3.1   The Preface

The preface merely explains the request and the bases for that request. For example:

> Plaintiff requests that the defendant answer the following interrogatories in writing and under oath pursuant to Rule 33 of the

---

[41]O'Brien v. International Bhd. of Elec. Workers, 443 F. Supp. 1182, 1187 (N.D. Ga. 1977).

[42]Bernstein v. *N.V. Nederlandsche-Amerikaansche Stoomvaart-Maatschappij*, 11 F.R.D. 48, 49 (S.D.N.Y. 1951).

Rules of Civil Procedure and that the answers be served on the plaintiff within thirty (30) days after service of these interrogatories.

There is no requirement under the rules that this statement be included, but tradition and professional custom favor the use of some such preface. Some jurisdictions require that the first paragraph include certain information, such as the set number of interrogatories.

§3.3.2   Instructions

Instructions may be included in the introduction to inform the other party about certain conditions in answering the interrogatories. An instruction should clarify the nature and source of the information sought:

> In answering these interrogatories, furnish all information, however obtained, including hearsay that is available to you and information known by or in possession of yourself, your agents and your attorneys, or appearing in your records.

Rule 33(a) requires a corporate or government organization to furnish information through its officers and agents. This instruction paraphrases that rule. There is case law and expert commentary requiring a party to disclose such information even if not listed in an instruction.[1]

Another instruction can remind the recipient of the duty to conduct a reasonable investigation. Answers to interrogatories must contain all information possessed by the party.[2] This reminder may prod your opponent into greater diligence and may clarify your expectations.

An instruction may also explain what to do if the party does not have information:

> If you cannot answer the following interrogatories in full after exercising due diligence to secure the full information to do so, so state and answer to the extent possible, specifying your inability to answer the remainder, stating whatever information or knowledge you have concerning the unanswered portion and detailing what you did in attempting to secure the unknown information.

§3.3 [1] 8 C. Wright & A. Miller, Federal Practice and Procedure §2177 (1970).
[2] Budget Rent-a-Car of Missouri, Inc. v. Hertz Corp., 55 F.R.D. 354, 357 (W.D. Mo. 1972).

Again, there is case law requiring a party to include such an explanation in response to a question that cannot be fully answered, even if this instruction is omitted.[3]

Another instruction can suggest an alternative to detailed written answers:

> A question that seeks information contained in or information about or identification of any documents may be answered by providing a copy of such document for inspection and copying or by furnishing a copy of such document without a request for production.

Rule 33(c) expressly allows a responding party the option of supplying "business records" in answer to an interrogatory. This instruction reminds the other side that it may provide other types of records and documents as an alternative or supplementary response. Neither the rule nor this reminder permits the opposition to respond with a blizzard of incomprehensible documents. The Rule 33(c) option is not a procedural device with which to evade the duty to supply information. Rather, the interrogated party must state specifically and identify precisely those documents that will provide the information sought by the interrogatories.[4] Indeed, the rule explicitly states that the specification of documents must be detailed enough that the interrogating party can identify the records "as readily as can the party served." "Here is the room, here is the pile, open the drawers and see all the files" will no longer do.

Another instruction may require supplementary answers:

> These interrogatories shall be deemed to be continuing until and during the course of trial. Information sought by these interrogatories and that you obtain after you serve your answers must be disclosed to the plaintiff by supplementary answers.

This statement does not automatically make such questions continuing, unless the information must be supplemented pursuant to Rule 26(e) or unless the other party agrees to provide such information. However, the statement may encourage the updating of answers even if it does not compel such updating.

---

[3]*See, e.g.,* Harlem River Consumers Coop., Inc. v. Associated Grocers of Harlem, Inc., 64 F.R.D. 459, 463 (S.D.N.Y. 1974).

[4]*See, e.g.,* Steelman v. United States Fidelity & Guar. Co., 35 F.R.D. 120, 121 (W.D. Mo. 1964); Olmert v. Nelson, 60 F.R.D. 369 (D.D.C. 1973).

You may want to add another instruction specifying the time period relevant to the questions:

Unless otherwise indicated in an interrogatory, the questions shall refer to the time period from August 1, 1981, until August 15, 1981.

Additionally, an instruction can direct the party answering to provide some identifying information pursuant to Rule 33(a):

The person or persons who provide information in answer to the following interrogatories will each identify which answers have been provided and furnish his or her name, address, and title.

The practice in many areas ignores the separate identifications of all who provided information contained in an answer. Often, only the party named, an individual or one agent for a corporation, signs the answers. Sometimes the signature of the party's attorney appears on the answers. Rule 33(a) does require more specificity than that, however, and a requesting party needing such specificity can successfully enforce this rule.

Finally, other instructions may be added for other purposes, including the definition of certain terms.

§3.3.3 Definitions

Definitions may precede the interrogatories to define certain words or phrases used in the questions.[5] They serve several purposes.

First, definitions specify the exact meaning of a word that may mean different things to different attorneys:

Describe: This word means to specify in detail and to particularize the content of the answer to the question and not just to state the reply in summary or outline fashion.

Definitions also identify a word or phrase that is peculiar to or commonly used throughout the interrogatories:

August 15 Contract: This term refers to the contract signed by both the plaintiff and the defendant on August 15, 1980, and attached as Exhibit A to the Complaint.

[5]Harlem River Consumers Coop., Inc. v. Associated Grocers of Harlem, Inc., 64 F.R.D. 459, 465 (S.D.N.Y. 1974).

Third, definitions aid economy, by shortening the questions, avoiding the need to repeat the meaning of a much-used term, such as:

The word *document* means any written, recorded, or graphic matter, whether produced, reproduced, or stored on papers, cards, tapes, belts, computer devices, or any other medium in your possession, custody, or control or known by you to exist; and it includes originals, all copies of originals, and all prior drafts.

Finally, definitions can mask the exact number of questions asked by defining one term to include several subtopics. For example:

The word *identify* or *identity,* when used in reference to a natural person means to state his or her full name, present business and home addresses, present employer and position with employer, the relationship, business or otherwise, between such person and the person answering the interrogatory.

This technique does have its moments. Excessive use of such definitions may result in a seemingly reasonable number of interrogatories being rendered excessively burdensome and thereby subject to a successful motion to strike all or a portion of the interrogatories.[6] Some attorneys refrain from employing definitions, viewing their use as a substitute for well-drafted individual interrogatories.

§3.4 DRAFTING INTERROGATORIES

§3.4.1 General Techniques

Interrogatories should contain clear, precise, direct questions.[1] They should neither be vague,[2] nor too broad,[3] nor overly inclusive.[4] The questions should have the other attorney immediately thinking, "Yes, I understand what they want to know." Such thinking comes easier for some attorneys than others.

---

[6]*See* Diversified Prods. Corp. v. Sports Center Co., Inc., 42 F.R.D. 3, 4 (D. Md. 1967).
§3.4 [1]Jarosiewicz v. Conlisk, 60 F.R.D. 121, 127 (N.D. Ill. 1973).
[2]Heritage Furniture, Inc. v. American Heritage, Inc., 28 F.R.D. 319, 320 (D. Conn. 1961).
[3]Transmirra Prods. Corp. v. Monsanto Chem. Co., 26 F.R.D. 572, 575 (S.D.N.Y. 1960).
[4]Stovall v. Gulf & So. Am. S.S. Co., 30 F.R.D. 152, 154 (S.D. Tex. 1961).

Interrogatory drafting must take into consideration the myriad responses different attorneys may make to seemingly straightforward, innocent questions. There are the responders, the ramblers, the self-servers, the quibblers, the evaders, and the objectors. Their responses to a simple interrogatory vary:

State the name of your spouse.
Responders: Roger S. Haydock.
Ramblers: My spouse retained his original name after our marriage. Roger means wise and courageous in Teutonic. Haydock means calling for medical help in English.
Self-servers: Roger Haydock, but his income consists of law-school welfare benefits, which are exempt from execution on a judgment against me in this case.
Quibblers: By *name,* do you mean first, middle, maiden, birth, baptismal, confirmation, sur-, or nick-?
Objectors: The answer is readily known to his parents and is privileged under the Sixth Commandment.

The adversary system allows attorneys to take advantage of situations involving questions that are not reasonable, clear indications of the information sought. Poorly drafted interrogatories inevitably produce poor responses on the principle that if you ask a foolish question, you should expect, and will receive, a foolish answer.[5] Poorly drafted interrogatories may also allow your opponent to strike your interrogatories in their entirety.[6] You can avoid this situation by playing the devil's advocate after drafting your interrogatories:

1. Consider whether each question can be redrafted in a simpler, less complex fashion.
2. Ask yourself how the answer to each interrogatory will provide you with information helpful to the case.[7]
3. Decide whether some questions can be eliminated or consolidated.[8]

[5]Pressley v. Boehlke, 33 F.R.D. 316, 317 (W.D.N.C. 1963).
[6]*See* Boyden v. Troken, 60 F.R.D. 625, 626 (N.D. Ill. 1973).
[7]If you don't, the court will. Id.
[8]Again, if you don't, the court will. *See* In re U.S. Financial Securities Litigation, 74 F.R.D. 497 (S.D. Cal. 1975).

4. Consider ways the responses to your questions could be fudged and then attempt to redraft the questions to eliminate the fudge, but not the frosting.

Remember that properly drafted interrogatories seeking properly discoverable information must be answered in a responsive fashion. One of the rewards of careful draftsmanship is a successful motion for Rule 37 sanctions if your opponent has been improperly contentious or non-responsive.[9]

One effective drafting technique, particularly suitable for interrogatories, is the "ladder" or "branching" approach. A broad question is asked and then followed by specific questions relating to one or more of the possible responses. For example:

State whether defendant is a corporation or a partnership. If a corporation, identify the members of the board of directors. If a partnership, identify all the partners.

There are occasions when such drafting techniques may waste an interrogatory. A branching interrogatory may be phrased to receive a yes or no response followed by specific questions, but you may know, or be fairly certain, that the response will be yes, and be able to save an interrogatory. For example, a pleading may reveal that a defendant is a corporation. Rather than asking "State whether defendant is a corporation," and then asking follow-up questions, merely ask the follow-up question, "State the date and state of defendant's incorporation and its principal place of business."

§3.4.2 Number of Interrogatories

Drafting to conserve the number of interrogatories is necessary in many cases. Many district courts have adopted local rules or standing orders setting maximum numbers of interrogatories to be served on each party, unless the court increases the number for good cause or the other attorney agrees to answer more. Some rules limit the number that may be served by any party to no more than 20 or 30 or 50 interrogatories. Some judges, by standing orders, have adopted similar rules. Even if no strict numerical limit obtains, serving an excessive

---

[9]*See generally* Note, The Emerging Deterrence Orientation in the Imposition of Discovery Sanctions, 91 Harv. L. Rev. 1033 (1978).

number of interrogatories may create an undue demand on your opponent's resources and allow a successful objection on the basis of burdensomeness.[10]

The adoption of local rules and standing orders limiting the number of interrogatories may arguably be inconsistent with Rule 26(a), particularly in complex or complicated cases. Rule 83 limits district courts to creating rules that are "not inconsistent" with the civil rules.[11] One court has rejected this argument and upheld the propriety of local rules limiting interrogatories to 30 in number, declaring that such reasonable limitation is indeed consistent not only with Rule 83 but also with the purposes of discovery.[12] This decision appears correct, as long as the local rules permit parties reasonable access to the discovery methods provided under Rules 26 through 37. But local courts do not have unfettered discretion to impose restrictions. Some local rules may well have been proposals that were rejected by the committees, courts, and legislature that reviewed, analyzed, and adopted the current discovery rules. However, the rules and practice do allow local courts leeway to modify discovery procedures, if these modifications are reasonable and consistent with the purposes of discovery.

Limiting the number of interrogatories in a case may deprive one or both sides of sufficient opportunity to obtain relevant, necessary information from the opposition. This argument, or another good-cause argument, can be advanced before a court, which then usually grants leave to submit additional questions.[13] But not always.[14] The attorneys themselves can agree to respond to more interrogatories without court approval. So a court order or, more typically, a stipulation should permit a sufficient number of interrogatories in a case. The rationale supporting limitations is to coerce attorneys into drafting relevant and concise interrogatories and to prevent the misuse, burden, and abuse that the submission of 1,246½ interrogatories creates for the responding party.[15] This rationale justifies the limitations placed on the number of interrogatories in most cases. But why limits

---

[10]*See, e.g.*, Broyden v. Troken, 60 F.R.D. 625 (N.D. Ill. 1973) (209 interrogatories containing 432 separate questions held oppressive and burdensome).

[11]8 C. Wright & A. Miller, Federal Practice and Procedure §2168 (1970).

[12]Lykins v. Attorney General, 29 Fed. R. Serv. 2d 1232 (E.D. Va. 1980).

[13]*See* Crown Center Redevelopment Corp. v. Westinghouse Elec. Corp., 82 F.R.D. 108 (W.D. Mo. 1979).

[14]Lykins v. Attorney General, 29 Fed. R. Serv. 2d 1232 (E.D. Va. 1980).

[15]The number and detailed character of interrogatories is not a reason for disallowing them unless they are unduly burdensome and oppressive. Wirtz v. Capitol Air Service, Inc., 46 F.R.D. 484 (D. Md. 1969).

of 20, 30, or 50 in some states? Apparently these numbers seem reasonable, even with inflation. And although these numbers may seem firm on their face, there are conflicting opinions about what constitutes "one" interrogatory, even though we all learned in first grade that 1 + 1 = 2. Various local rules and interpretations provide assistance in answering the question "How many is one?"

Some rules, particularly those that limit interrogatories to a low number, such as 20, count as one interrogatory a question with subparts that relate directly to the subject matter of the question. The interpretation of this rule, of course, focuses on what is or is not related directly — no simple interpretation.

Some rules state that each subdivision or separate question will be counted as an interrogatory. The interpretation of this rule, of course, focuses on what is or is not a subdivision of what is or is not a separate question. Some commentators have interpreted "subdivisions":

> Separate subdivisions may be found either by multiple questions or questions which are subparts of other questions. For example, the following would consist of four questions: "State where the defendant's automobile was located at the time he first saw plaintiff's automobile, the location of plaintiff's automobile, the speed of defendant's automobile and the speed of plaintiff's automobile." The same question can be posed with subdivisions: "Did defendant see plaintiff's automobile prior to the accident? If so, state: (a) where the defendant's automobile was located at that time; (b) where plaintiff's automobile was located; (c) the speed of defendant's automobile; (d) the speed of plaintiff's automobile."[16]

The latter example contains five interrogatories. That sounds authoritative enough, but what if the questions were drafted to say "State the location and speed of both plaintiff's automobile and defendant's automobile when defendant first saw each one"? Does this example constitute only one question? Or two? Or four? Does a "subdivision" of a "separate" question include different topics? Distinct clauses? Does a subdivision include words separated by *and* or *or* or a comma, or a semicolon, or a number? For instance:

State whether the defendant is a human being. If yes, further state:
    (a)   His or her name, including
         (1)   His or her first name,

---

[16] J. Hetland & O. Adamson, Minnesota Practice 42 (1970).

          (2) His or her middle name, and
          (3) His or her last name; and
     (b) His or her home address, including
          (1) Street address,
          (2) City or town,
          (3) State,
          (4) Zip code,
          (5) Country,
          (6) Continent,
          (7) Hemisphere,
          (8) Longitude, and
          (9) Latitude.

Does that example constitute twelve questions? What if it were phrased "State the name and home address of the defendant"? Does it then contain one or two questions?

Careful drafting can alter the status of an interrogatory and reduce several questions to one. Suppose the defendant wishes to know whether or not A, B, C, and D were in plaintiff's car prior to the accident. If the question was "State whether A or B or C or D was in plaintiff's automobile," the question is multiple. The same question could be phrased "State the names of all persons in plaintiff's automobile." The question is then singular, even though it requires the disclosure of the four names.[17]

The example assumes that the first question, being multiple, equals four questions. Why? Because there is a possibility of four answers. Some multiple-phrased questions call for only one possible answer and will count as one question. For instance, "State whether the traffic light was red or green or yellow when plaintiff first saw the light."

Even some multiple-phrased questions that seek more than one alternative response may contain only one question. For example, the interrogatory, "Identify all office memoranda, letters, correspondence, or notes written by plaintiff to the defendant," may well equal four questions. But if the question were phrased, "Identify any and all office documents written by plaintiff to the defendant," it can be counted as one interrogatory. Does the use of a generic term to identify information sought, rather than listing the specific members of the class, solve the problem of multiple-phrased interrogatories? Or does

[17] *See* Crown Center Redevelopment Corp. v. Westinghouse Elec. Corp., 82 F.R.D. 108 (W.D. Mo. 1979).

it merely allow the responding party the leeway it needs to evade fully adequate answers?

§3.4.3 Specific Techniques

Those of you who enjoyed reading the previous section can create your own penumbras. Those of you who have not yet become paranoid about interrogatory limits should consider yourselves fortunate. There are ways to minimize the potential paranoia.

First, the current practice among many attorneys is to respond to interrogatories that may exceed the limitation, as long as they are not *numbered* over the limit and as long as they seem reasonable in length and scope.

Second, you can negotiate with the other attorney to obtain answers to questions above and beyond the limit. The other attorney may also want to submit more questions, or may want some information that you can provide in return. You should seldom need court approval for additional interrogatories, unless a court order so demands.

Third, perhaps you should have added additional parties to the case. The rules usually allow you to submit the maximum number of interrogatories to each party in a case, and a pleading consideration should involve the inclusion of appropriate parties, to take advantage of that allowance.

Fourth, you can try to convince a judge to permit more interrogatories, by employing such good-cause arguments as that the subject matter is complex, the case involves more discoverable information than a typical case, the other side has not cooperated in providing information, or you just can't count very well. Some judges routinely grant these orders, others require a showing of legitimate need for the information.

Fifth, you can plan to draft successive sets of interrogatories, reserving some questions until you review the answers to previous ones. Most of the rules permit this flexibility. You can submit all your questions to a party at one time, or half each time, or one-fifth each time, as long as the total number does not exceed the limit and as long as the number of different sets does not become harassing. Service of 50 different questions on 50 different days would be harassing, besides costing your client $10.00 in postage.

Sixth, you can draft your questions with the resolve and intent to package as much as possible in a single interrogatory and still compose a simple, direct and precise question.

The following drafting techniques may help you achieve the drafting goals explained above:

1. Avoid prefacing sublistings with letters or numbers. The use of (a), (b), (c), (d), and (1), (2), (3), (4) may create a subdivision when in fact there is no separate subdivision. Just list the subtopics seriatim.

2. Do not separate subtopics conspicuously, with conjunctive or disjunctive words or with unnecessary punctuation. Avoid using *and, or, the,* semicolons, and colons. Do not ask:

> Please state the name and address and the district number of the following educational institutions that plaintiff has attended: nursery school, kindergarten, grade school, high school, college, law school, and vocational school.

Rather, ask: "Please identify all schools that plaintiff has attended, beginning with nursery school."

3. Reduce a clause or lengthy phrase to one word or a concise phrase. Try to reduce all species of a thing to the basic genus. Do not ask:

> Please state the color, number of wheels, size of windows, and texture of the bumpers of defendant's self-propelled vehicular motor machine.

Rather, ask: "Please describe in detail defendant's car."

4. Include necessary specifications or exact details in the interrogatory by using related words and subtopics and by detailing the several species of a common genus. Ask:

> Please describe plaintiff's hair, including but not limited to the color, style, number of grey hairs, approximate length of sideburns, color of the roots, and the curvature in degrees of the cowlick.

5. Avoid multiple questions seeking multiple answers. Do not ask:

> State the names of the setter, swingperson, follower, chalker, and scorer of the Faculty Skittlepool Team.

Rather, ask singular questions that require multiple answers, such as "Identify all members of the Faculty Skittlepool Team by name and position."

6. Employ questions that seek only one possible response from a list of alternative suggested answers, unless you do not want to suggest any answers. Ask:

State whether plaintiff is a direct descendant of an Australopithecus robustus, a Dryopithecus africanus, or a homo habilis.

7.   Use instructions and definitions when introducing your interrogatories. A preceding section (§3.3) explains these uses.

These seven techniques apply to situations in which the interrogatory rule limits the number of questions and counts subdivisions as separate questions. Some rules that limit interrogatories do *not* count subparts as separate questions. Do you realize what this means? The reverse of the seven techniques suggested here then applies. Rather than eliminate subdivisions you may need to create them. Rest easy — we will not repeat any additional techniques. We trust you can reverse the techniques and employ other methods to draft appropriately phrased interrogatories.

§3.4.4   Form Interrogatories

Problems and concerns with the proper drafting of interrogatories and the appropriateness of the subject matter have been both reduced and exacerbated by the use of standardized interrogatories. The use of form books, photocopiers, and word processors results in frequent submission of large numbers of questionable interrogatories. Attorneys in specialized areas of practice, personal injury cases in particular, sometimes even exchange identical sets of interrogatories. Form books and standardized sets of interrogatories may not all be applicable to a case. Attorneys who indiscriminately use these form sets face objections, receive answers that will be limited in scope, and face the wrath of judges who, too politely, consider such practice "undesirable."[18] Some districts have therefore prohibited the use of standardized interrogatories, though others have adopted some set forms.

Correctly used form questions can assist an attorney in efficiently and economically drafting questions. Standardized questions should be selectively used and mixed and matched with custom-made interrogatories to achieve a proper and appropriate balance.[19]

It is often helpful in discovery practice to rely upon the ideas of others, particularly when such interrogatories have been drafted by

---

[18]See W. Glaser, Pre-Trial Discovery and the Adversary System 158 (1968).

[19]SCM Societa Commerciale S.P.A. v. Industrial & Commercial Research Corp., 72 F.R.D. 110, 113 n.5 (N.D. Tex. 1976).

experienced attorneys, have been accepted in the practice, and have been tested and approved by a bar committee or a court.[20] You should review such forms and decide, interrogatory by interrogatory, which will be appropriate for your cases, which can be modified, and which must be discarded.

§3.5 OBJECTIONS TO INTERROGATORIES

Rule 33(a) requires a party who has been served with interrogatories either to answer or to object to the questions. The first tactical consideration involved in responding concerns the availability of appropriate and strategic objections; the second consideration is composing the answers themselves. If a party fails to respond within 30 days after service of the interrogatories (45 days if served with the summons and complaint), objections to any interrogatories will be waived, and the party will have to answer all the questions.[1] Two holdings limit the impact of the waiver. A court still has the discretion to ignore an unintentional waiver and refuse to compel an answer to an interrogatory that is grossly improper.[2] And an objection based upon privileged information or work product or expert's opinion cannot be waived by failure to respond in a timely fashion.[3]

The tactical considerations involved in objections are discussed in this section. Those surrounding the answer are discussed in §3.6, below.

§3.5.1 Interposing Objections

Rule 33(a) provides that objections must be stated with particular grounds, may be served with the document containing answers to other interrogatories or separately, and must be signed by an attorney.

[20]*See* Pankola v. Texaco, 25 F.R.D. 184, 185 (E.D. Pa. 1960).
§3.5 [1]*See* Renshaw v. Ravert, 82 F.R.D. 361, 362 (E.D. Pa. 1979); 8 C. Wright & A. Miller, Federal Practice and Procedure §2174 (1970).
[2]Williams v. Krieger, 61 F.R.D. 142, 145 (S.D.N.Y. 1973).
[3]Bohlie v. Brass Rail, Inc., 20 F.R.D. 224 (S.D.N.Y. 1957).

Objections cannot be broad, blanket refusals to answer, but must be precise, valid reasons highlighting the deficiency of the question. One court permitted a party to object legitimately to an entire set of inappropriate interrogatories, although suggesting that a Rule 26 protective order is the preferred way of objecting.[4] Typical effective objections with specific grounds include:

1. Rule 26 objections (irrelevant, privileged).
2. Vague and ambiguous.[5]
3. Too broad, seeking identification of "all documents . . .which mention or pertain" to the issues.[6]
4. Excessive detail and number (2,736).[7]
5. Unduly burdensome, which the courts consider in the context of the following factors:
   (a) The amount of research and time required and costs incurred (eight interrogatories that require researching 10,000 answers held burdensome);[8]
   (b) The necessity for the information (compelling reasons in the case for burdensome answers);[9]
   (c) Whether the benefit gained by the requesting party outweighs the burden placed on the responding party (interrogatories requesting information about a span of 20 years reduced to questions covering eight years);[10]
   (d) The extent to which answers to the questions prepare the case of the requesting party (answers to questions about eyewitness observations could be obtained by the requesting party from the witnesses and by inspecting the accident site);[11]

---

[4]*See* Spector Freight Sys., Inc. v. Home Indem. Co., 58 F.R.D. 162 (N.D. Ill. 1973).

[5]Evans v. Local 2127, Intl. Bhd. of Elec. Workers, 313 F. Supp. 1354, 1361 (N.D. Ga. 1969).

[6]Deering Milliken Research Corp. v. Tex-Elastic Corp., 320 F. Supp. 806, 810-811 (D.S.C. 1970).

[7]In re U.S. Financial Securities Litigation, 22 Fed. R. Serv. 2d 710 (S.D. Cal. 1975); Jarosiewicz v. Conlisk, 60 F.R.D. 121, 126 (N.D. Ill. 1973).

[8]La Chemise Lacoste v. Alligator Co., 60 F.R.D. 164, 171 (D. Del. 1973); Spector Freight Sys., Inc. v. Home Indem. Co., 58 F.R.D. 162, 164 (N.D. Ill. 1973).

[9]*See* Alexander v. Rizzo, 50 F.R.D. 374, 376 (E.D. Pa. 1970).

[10]Professional Adjusting Sys. of Am., Inc. v. General Adjustment Bureau, Inc., 373 F. Supp. 1225, 1228 (S.D.N.Y. 1974).

[11]Reichert v. United States, 51 F.R.D. 500, 503 (N.D. Cal. 1970).

      (e)   Whether the information was sufficiently disclosed in responses to other discovery requests (testified about at a deposition).[12]
6.   Pure legal conclusions.
7.   Seeks documents or verbatim contents only available under Rule 34.

The availability of this last objection depends more on local practice than on the law. Rule 34 only requires a "written request" to obtain access to documents and things. One written discovery request may properly contain written interrogatories and a Rule 34 request. It is common practice in some areas to combine such requests in the same discovery submission. It is not acceptable practice in other areas, where two separate requests are expected.

§3.5.2 Ineffective Objections

Ineffective objections, usually not proper, include:

1.   The information is already known to the requesting party. It can still be sought,[13] though not all courts agree.[14]
2.   The information is equally available to the requesting party. If a party has the information, it should be disclosed regardless of its source and availability.[15] But the cases are split on the matter. If the responding party does not have custody of the information,[16] or if the answers are in public documents, the responding party need not provide the answers.
3.   The response would be inadmissible at trial.[17]
4.   The scope of discovery is limited to the responding party's interpretation of the issues and facts. The responding party

[12]Lincoln Gateway Realty Co. v. Carri-Craft, Inc., 53 F.R.D. 303, 307 (W.D. Mo. 1971).
[13]Rogers v. Tri-State Materials Corp., 51 F.R.D. 234, 245 (N.D.W. Va. 1970); Weiss v. Chrysler Motors Corp., 515 F.2d 449, 456 (2d Cir. 1975).
[14]See Reichert v. United States, 51 F.R.D. 500, 503 (N.D. Cal. 1970).
[15]United States v. 58.16 Acres of Land, 66 F.R.D. 570, 573 (E.D. Ill. 1975).
[16]See La Chemise Lacoste v. Alligator Co., 60 F.R.D. 164, 171 (D. Del. 1973).
[17]Greyhound Corp. v. Superior Ct., 56 Cal. 2d 355, 391, 364 P.2d 266, 273, 15 Cal. Rptr. 90, 108 (1961).

cannot limit discovery to its understanding of the facts or to its theory of a case.[18]

5. The interrogatory seeks an admission. Interrogatories, though they be identical to a request for an admission, must be answered.[19]

6. The information can be obtained through a deposition. If otherwise proper, an interrogatory must be answered, even though answers at an oral deposition may provide satisfactory or better responses.[20]

7. The question seeks factual opinions, conclusions, or legal contentions related to the facts.[21] These may be objected to if they are premature.

8. The interrogatory invades work product. Too often these general objections are made inappropriately.[22]

9. The answer "does not seem to be any business" of the questioning party. Flippant responses are usually held improper.[23]

§3.5.3 Objection Procedures

The party objecting to an interrogatory has the burden in any subsequent court proceedings to show the validity of the specific objection.[24] That burden will require the party initially to state specific and particular grounds for the objection.[25] A bare refusal to answer an interrogatory or an objection on the grounds that the interrogatory is "improper" may not be recognized as an objection, but rather as no

[18]United States v. 30 Jars of "Ahead Hair Restorer for New Hair Growth," 43 F.R.D. 181, 189 (D. Del. 1967); United States v. 216 Bottles of "Sudden Change," 36 F.R.D. 695, 700 (E.D.N.Y. 1965).

[19]Evans v. Local 2127, Intl. Bhd. of Elec. Workers, 313 F. Supp. 1354, 1361 (N.D. Ga. 1969).

[20]DiGregorio v. First Rediscount Corp., 506 F.2d 781, 787 (3d Cir. 1974).

[21]See Duplan Corp. v. Deering Milliken, Inc., 61 F.R.D. 127 (D.S.C.), rev'd and remanded, 487 F.2d 480 (4th Cir. 1973); and United States v. 38 Cases, More or Less, 35 F.R.D. 357, 361 (W.D. Pa. 1964).

[22]Lincoln Gateway Realty Co. v. Carri-Craft, Inc., 53 F.R.D. 303, 307 (W.D. Mo. 1971).

[23]DiGregorio v. First Rediscount Corp., 506 F.2d 781, 787 (3d Cir. 1974).

[24]See generally B-H Transp. Co. v. Great Atl. & Pac. Tea Co., 44 F.R.D. 436 (N.D.N.Y. 1968).

[25]In re Folding Carton Antitrust Litigation, 83 F.R.D. 260, 264 (N.D. Ill. 1979).

response and as a waiver of the objection.[26] Subsequently, at a court hearing, the objecting party has to show, by specific facts or by persuasive legal argument, the validity of the objection.[27] Broadly based generalizations of opinions about the nature of the objection are insufficient to sustain a burden. But the amount of detail necessary for a proper and complete showing depends on the nature of the objection. An objection based upon Rule 26 may require only a legal memorandum discussing the relevancy standards. An objection based on burdensomeness may require a detailed affidavit by a party, indicating the amount of work required to answer the question, including number of hours, number of employees, cost, extent of materials, and other factors.[28] An objection based upon privileged information or work product may require the judge to inspect the allegedly privileged documents in camera to determine their content and nature.

§3.5.4 Strategic Concerns

Questions that are objectionable on legitimate grounds should still be answered in some situations. If the answer will not prejudice or harm a client's case, it is usually advisable to answer the question, instead of wasting time and money objecting and facing the prospects of enforcement. This becomes even more important if disclosure of the information in an answer will strengthen a case for negotiation or other purposes. If a question can be modified or qualified to avoid the objectionable feature, it may well be advisable to prepare a limited or partial answer.[29] A broad, vague question may be interpreted narrowly and result in a limited answer. A question calling for mixed discoverable and non-discoverable information may be answered in part, by disclosing only the discoverable information. The responding attorney has discretion either to respond partially to improper questions or to interpret some questions in a reasonable manner that will result in some response. Occasionally, objecting to a question, with a subsequent Rule 37 proceeding, may require you to reveal more damaging

[26]Baxter v. Vick, 25 F.R.D. 229, 233 (E.D. Pa. 1960).

[27]*See generally* White v. Beloginis, 53 F.R.D. 480, 481 (S.D.N.Y. 1971).

[28]Wirtz v. D.A.C. Steel Prods., Inc., 312 F.2d 14 (4th Cir. 1962). *See* United States Equal Employment Opportunity Commn. v. Metropolitan Museum of Art, 80 F.R.D. 317, 318 (S.D.N.Y. 1978).

[29]Struthers Scientific & Intl. Corp. v. General Foods Corp., 45 F.R.D. 375, 379 (S.D. Tex. 1968).

information than a prompt answer. Strategically speaking, objections to borderline interrogatories may also cause the other side to object to borderline interrogatories you submit to them.

§3.6 ANSWERS TO INTERROGATORIES

Rule 33(a) requires that a party answer interrogatories in writing and under oath, and some local rules frequently require that the question be stated in full before each answer. The rules and strategic considerations should prompt you to consider several approaches to interrogatory responses:

1. Obtaining the information from knowledgeable sources;
2. Conducting a reasonable investigation for information;
3. Assisting in the preparation and drafting of the answers;
4. Interpreting the questions in a reasonable and rational manner;
5. Answering questions with accurate and complete information;
6. Qualifying responses with partial information;
7. Phrasing answers in the best possible way on behalf of your client;
8. Disclosing as little harmful information as possible, or perhaps disclosing as much favorable information as possible;
9. Seeking an extension of time;
10. Considering the ethical ramifications of answers;
11. Having a nightmare.

§3.6.1 Sources of Information

Whoever answers individual interrogatories must have the information or knowledge to provide. Interrogatories addressed to an individual party must be answered by that party. Interrogatories addressed to a corporate, governmental, or other organizational entity must be answered by any officer or agent or employee who has the requisite information. Identical sets of interrogatories submitted to several parties may be jointly answered by whoever has such information.

Rule 33(a) requires the answers to be signed by the "person making

them." This could include a party, an agent, or an attorney. There is
some doubt whether a corporation need disclose the identity of all the
persons assisting in the preparation of the answers[1] or the source of
particular information.[2] Someone must sign for the corporate party;
and it is usually sufficient that the officer, agent, or employee, or an
attorney who acted as an officer or agent and collated the information,
sign, rather than individuals who assisted in the preparation and contributed bits and pieces of the final response.[3] The disclosures of such
sources may well be unduly burdensome.[4] A corporation may wish to
disclose them, if the information is obtained from third persons and
the corporation does not want to vouch for, or be bound by, their
statements.

Parties must reveal whatever information they or their employees,
officers, subsidiaries and other agents:

1. Know;
2. Learned through hearsay;
3. Believe to be true;
4. Have in their records or documents;
5. Have in their possession; or
6. Have control over.[5]

A party must make a conscientious endeavor to make available all such
information that does not require undue labor or expense, although
a party need not engage in outside research. The party should also be
sure to inform the interrogating party of the effort expended, if the
responding party is unable to respond fully to the interrogatory. This
may eliminate the need for court intervention later, when the interrogating party alleges willful obfuscation of the issues.

---

§3.6 [1]United States v. National Steel Corp., 26 F.R.D. 599, 600 (S.D. Tex. 1960).
[2]See B. & S. Drilling Co. v. Halliburton Oil Well Cementing Co., 24 F.R.D. 1, 4 (S.D.
Tex. 1959).
[3]Wilson v. Volkswagen of Am., Inc., 561 F.2d 494, 514 (4th Cir. 1977).
[4]Evans v. Local 2127, Intl. Bhd. of Elec. Workers, 313 F. Supp. 1354, 1360 (N.D. Ga.
1969).
[5]See Riley v. United Air Lines, Inc., 32 F.R.D. 230 (S.D.N.Y. 1962).

§3.6.2 Duty to Investigate

A party has a duty to conduct a reasonable investigation to obtain information not readily available. This obligation does not prevent a responding party from answering "I don't know" to a question, but it does limit the situations in which such a negative response will be appropriate. A corporate or organizational party must search through its staff for answers. An interrogatory asked early in litigation may properly invoke an "I don't know yet" response because it is premature, although the preferred answer is that the "investigation has not yet been completed." The party who declines to answer a question because of little or no information needs to describe in the response the nature of the investigation, so that the requesting party can determine whether the investigation appears sufficient or whether additional investigation should be attempted.[6] The investigation need not be extensive to the point of being unreasonable.[7] An answer indicating a lack of knowledge and no means of obtaining knowledge is appropriate.[8] The responding party does need a good-faith basis for declining to conduct a reasonable investigation, however, and a party whose response indicates lack of knowledge must supplement that response if the party later acquires knowledge.[9]

§3.6.3 Reasonable Interpretation

Some questions permit more than one reasonable interpretation. The question may not be precisely drafted, the words or phrases may have more than one meaning, the questions may be objectionable in part. An attorney must interpret an interrogatory as a reasonable attorney in good faith would read and understand the interrogatory. Unreasonable extrapolations, petty quibbling, and stretched interpretations have no place in determining what information an interrogatory seeks. An attorney may rely upon any authoritative source for assistance in interpreting words and phrases, including statutes, case law, custom, practice, treatises, articles, dictionaries, and other reliable and recog-

[6]Digregorio v. First Rediscount Corp., 506 F.2d 781, 787 (3d Cir. 1974).
[7]La Chemise Lacoste v. Alligator Co., 60 F.R.D. 164, 171 (D. Del. 1973).
[8]Milner v. National School of Health Technology, 73 F.R.D. 628 (E.D. Pa. 1977).
[9]Brennan v. Glenns Falls Natl. Bank & Trust Co., 19 Fed. R. Serv. 2d 721 (N.D.N.Y. 1974).

nized sources — but not classical legal comics, picture books, or acrostics. Some attorneys are more prone to use these latter sources and apply uncommon sense in responding to interrogatories. The urge to answer some questions in an unreasonable way seems to strike a good number of them. Fortunately, all but a handful resist the temptation to act out their fantasies. Unfortunately, though, the handful is still practicing.

§3.6.4   Preparation of Answers

The attorney can and should take an active role in preparing and drafting the answers. Indeed, the attorney is expected to prepare the answers for the client's signature. A client or agent generally has to provide the requisite information, by letter or in person, but the attorney or paralegal can mold and shape the information into an appropriate response. It is the professional, and not the client, who best understands the tactics involved in answering interrogatories. Moreover, some questions require the attorney directly to provide the information. This is appropriate. The attorney's knowledge is part of the collective knowledge from which the client must supply answers. Such requests may be for information the attorney knows (e.g., information contained in the file that the client does not know) or information solely within the lawyer's expertise (the statutory citations, case law, or legal theory applicable to the facts).

§3.6.5   Phrasing Answers

An attorney can construct an answer by selecting words, phrases, clauses, and grammar that comprise a favorable yet honest response, a supportive yet responsive answer. One can promote the best interests of a client by phrasing answers in the best possible light leading to the best possible interpretation on behalf of a client, but such responses should not be rambling nor unnecessarily self-serving. An attorney can, with integrity and legitimacy, describe the same situations or circumstances in significantly different terms from those of the opposing attorney, without distorting the information.

All responses must be interpreted with the same degree of reasonableness used in interpreting interrogatories. Parties who interpret a response in an unreasonable or hypertechnical way cannot later claim prejudice because of their reliance on the unreasonable interpretation.[10]

§3.6.6 Qualifying Answers

Answers cannot be evasive, incomplete, or deceptive. Situations do arise, however, when a party cannot respond in whole or in part to a question, or may wish to qualify a response.

1. If a party is unable to answer a question because of lack of information or for other reasons, that party must indicate the reasons.[11]

2. If a party does not know any answer at the time the responses are due, the party may explain so in a response and provide the information later in a supplementary answer.[12]

3. If a party bases a response upon documents, records, or other sources of information,[13] that party can preface a response with an explanation, such as "according to records maintained by the defendant at its Chicago office. . . ."

4. If a corporate, governmental, or other organizational party has difficulty determining who knows what about its internal structure, the answering party may explain the scope of its inquiry, with language such as "All employees of the plaintiff involved in the August 16, 1980, gas test reviewed this interrogatory and had no (*or* the following) further information to reveal. . . ."

5. A party may prefer to answer one interrogatory by referring to a previous response. This is appropriate as long as that previous response does answer the later interrogatory. A related problem involves reference to information obtained through another source, such as a deposition transcript or a pleading. Neither of these sources may be sufficient, but that depends on the circumstances.

6. If a party discloses hearsay information, the nature of the information can be explained,[14] e.g., "I do not personally have any firsthand information concerning this question, however I have been informed by . . ." or "Upon information and belief. . . ."

---

[10]Pherson v. Goodyear Tire & Rubber Co., 590 F.2d 756, 759 (9th Cir. 1978).
[11]Pilling v. General Motors Corp., 45 F.R.D. 366, 369 (D. Utah 1968).
[12]Rogers v. Tri-State Materials Corp., 51 F.R.D. 234, 246 (N.D.W. Va. 1970).
[13]Coyne v. Monongahela Connecting R.R., 24 F.R.D. 357, 358 (W.D. Pa. 1959).
[14]Riley v. United Air Lines, Inc., 32 F.R.D. 230, 233 (S.D.N.Y. 1962).

7.   A party not wishing to vouch for the accuracy of some information or to be bound to a response as an admission can explain the source of the information or its uncertain status.[15] The response can be prefaced by wording such as "The following information in response to this question was obtained from . . ."or "We do not know the answer to this question, but we have received information that. . . ."

§3.6.7   Ensuring Complete Responses

Answers must be full and complete. All information known to the answering party must be disclosed, whether it is helpful, neutral, or harmful. An attorney compiling the information must be satisfied that it is accurate and complete. The following are examples of answers, in response to proper interrogatories, held to be insufficient by courts.[16]

Interrogatory: Please state in detail each action or omission the plaintiff claims constituted the negligence complained of in paragraph designated 4 of the complaint in the above-entitled action.
Answer: Plaintiff is not able to answer interrogatory *A* inasmuch as he was under anesthesia at all times during the operation complained of in his complaint.
Held: Plaintiff must disclose the specific acts of negligence relied upon in the case.[17]

Interrogatory: State to whom you announced your intention of running for the office of business representative.
Answer: The announcement was made to a group of the members of defendant's local gathered informally at the Sky-High Tavern *(address and date)*.
Held: Insufficient. Must disclose names of individuals present.[18]

---

[15]United States v. Lykes Bros. S.S. Co., 295 F. Supp. 53, 57 (E.D. La. 1968).
[16]For a case containing a lengthy discussion of various examples of proper and improper questions and answers, see Roberson v. Great Am. Ins. Co., 48 F.R.D. 404 (N.D. Ga. 1969).
[17]Bynum v. United States, 36 F.R.D. 14, 15 (E.D. La. 1964).
[18]Magelssen v. Local 518, Operative Plasterers' & Cement Masons' Intl. Assn., 32 F.R.D. 464, 466 (W.D. Mo. 1963).

Interrogatory: Requested identification of and location of documents.

Answer: Plaintiffs know the location of the documents referred to in interrogatory #3 and have same, except for such of said documents as may have been destroyed by fire, which occurred at the Annex Theatre Building in August of 1955.

Held: Incomplete. Must disclose identity of documents in existence and those destroyed.[19]

Interrogatory: State the date on which shipment was accepted by the respondent.

Answer: The bill of lading shows the goods were receipted for an October 31, 1950, date.

Interrogatory: Asked whether a dock receipt was issued at the time of the receipt of shipment.

Answer: A search is being made for any dock receipt given.

Held: Both answers incomplete and not responsive.[20]

Interrogatory: Requested whether plaintiff had any injuries, accidents, or illnesses within three years prior or subsequent to accident in issue and sought detailed description of injuries and dates.

Answer: Injured while at work. Injuries non-contributory to present claims.

Interrogatory: Asked whether party employed at time of accident, occupation, employer, and job description.

Answer: Contractor. The contractor's name I do not recall.

Held: Both responses totally insufficient.[21]

Interrogatory: Requested whether defendant received order from plaintiff for 25 pieces of cloth and terms of such order.

Answer: Yes. The terms were 6/10/60.

Held: Insufficient.[22]

Interrogatory: Requested date plaintiff returned to work after injuries.

Answer: Although I have worked since July 6, 1938, my work is of a

---

[19]Grand Opera Co. v. Twentieth-Century Fox Film Corp., 21 F.R.D. 39, 41 (E.D. Ill. 1957).

[20]International Fertilizer & Chem. Corp. v. Brasileiro, 21 F.R.D. 193, 194 (S.D.N.Y. 1957).

[21]Mangenelli v. Lahage, 27 F. Supp. 7, 8 (D. Mass. 1939).

[22]F. & M. Skirt Co. v. A. Wimpfheimer & Bro., Inc., 25 F. Supp. 898, 899 (D. Mass. 1939).

lighter nature than that which I had been doing previous to the accident. At times I have worked under great difficulty due to the effects of this accident on my health.

Held: Improper response. Must disclose exact or approximate date.[23]

Interrogatory: Asked over what period of time party performed contract and what he did.
Answer: He said he did everything required.
Held: Not an answer.[24]

Interrogatory: Requested details of claims in complaint.
Answer: Referred defendant to books and records of the plaintiff and of the defendant.
Held: Wholly insufficient. Must answer in detail.[25]

Interrogatory: Requested income information for one year.
Answer: Referred to testimony at previous deposition.
Held: Unsatisfactory answer. Must answer interrogatory.[26]

Interrogatory: Whether (a) defendant made any investigations and (b) if so, (1) names of persons interviewed; (2) dates thereof; and (3) existence of any memoranda relating thereto.
Answer: (a) None, except by counsel. (b) Not applicable.
Held: Both totally incomplete. Must explain.[27]

Interrogatory: Requested clearly relevant information.
Answer: Stated not applicable, available for physical inspection, and don't recall.
Held: Sham responses.[28]

Interrogatory: 3. Was plaintiff aware, prior to October 21, 1952, that a cartridge of the type now alleged to infringe the Hesson Patent No. 2,794,395 was being offered to the trade by:

[23]Baley v. General Sea Foods, Inc., 26 F. Supp. 391, 393 (D. Mass. 1939).
[24]Kieran v. Johnson-March Corp., 7 F.R.D. 128, 131 (E.D.N.Y. 1945).
[25]Nagler v. Admiral Corp., 167 F. Supp. 413, 416 (S.D.N.Y. 1958).
[26]Grimmett v. Atchison, Topeka & Santa Fe Ry. Co., 11 F.R.D. 335, 336 (N.D. Ohio 1951).
[27]In re Master Key Antitrust Litigation, 53 F.R.D. 87, 91 (D. Conn. 1971).
[28]Philadelphia Housing Auth. v. American Radiator & Standard Sanitary Corp., 50 F.R.D. 13, 18 (E.D. Pa. 1970), *aff'd,* 438 F.2d 1187 (3d Cir. 1971).

a. Armstrong Coalbreak Company, Benton Harbor, Michigan;

b. Covel Mfg. Co., Benton Harbor, Michigan;

c. Any other person, firm, or corporation.

4. If the answer to section c of Interrogatory 3 is other than a categorical negative, give the names and addresses of all such persons, firms and corporations.

Answer: 3a. No. Plaintiff had information prior to October 21, 1952, of a cartridge being used which it suspected might be of a construction embodying the invention of plaintiff's ownership as to which a patent application had been filed and upon which the Hesson et al. patent No. 2,794,395 was later granted. Plaintiff had no actual knowledge of the construction of such cartridge. Plaintiff was aware that the cartridge above referred to was called the 'Armstrong' cartridge but had no actual knowledge as to its manufacture or whether it was being offered to the trade.

3b. See Answer 3a.

3c. See Answer 3a.

4. See Answer 3a.

Held: Grossly inadequate, not a response. Does not answer question.[29]

Interrogatory: Sought to determine whether any illness or injury had affected a party permanently.

Answer: Inapplicable.

Held: Improper. Responding party interpreted "inapplicable" response as meaning no answer applied because there was no permanent illness or injury. Court declared such interpretation unreasonable.[30]

Interrogatory: Requested information concerning sales of bolted steel tanks made outside of the United States by Black, Sivalls & Bryson, Inc.

Answer: None, because there were no bolted steel tanks made outside of the United States by Black, Sivalls & Bryson, Inc.

Held: Deliberate misconstruction of the interrogatory. The interrogatory taken in the context of the other interrogatories referred

[29]Cardox Corp. v. Olin Mathieson Chem. Corp., 23 F.R.D. 27, 30 (S.D. Ill. 1958).
[30]Digregorio v. First Rediscount Corp., 506 F.2d 781, 787 (3d Cir. 1974).

to sales made outside of the United States, not the construction location of the tanks.[31]

§3.6.8   Disclosing Harmful and Helpful Information

An attorney needs to consider the effect a response has upon his or her client's case. Harmful information should be disclosed only to the extent reasonably necessary, given the nature and scope of the interrogatory. Helpful information may have to be added to clarify the meaning of an answer. For instance, responses that may also constitute an admission can result in damaging information, unless disarmed or tempered in the drafting. And interrogatories themselves that may constitute an admission can also result in damaging information unless carefully worded. Even interrogatories that merely request routine information can often yield distorted or unreasonably unfavorable answers unless some additional information is added.

§3.6.9   Amending Answers

Rule 26(e) controls whether answers need to be supplemented. But no rule resolves the issue of whether a responding party can later voluntarily submit another written response amending a previous answer. The situation rises when a party wants to change a response rather than supplement it. The rules seem to require a party to obtain a court order permitting such amendment, which then would require the party to present convincing reasons to the judge. The requirement of responding in 30 days also seems to preclude late or amended responses. It is the practice of many lawyers to submit amended answers unilaterally, and the practice of opposing lawyers is to accept these responses without objection, avoiding the need for a motion and order. Attorneys reason that the court would routinely grant such an order and, in any event, the party would testify to the change at trial.

---

[31]Hunter v. International Sys. & Controls Corp., 51 F.R.D. 251, 257 (W.D. Mo. 1970).

§3.6.10   Extension of Time

An attorney may and sometimes must seek an extension of time to respond to interrogatories. The interrogatories may have been served at an early stage in the litigation, and the formulation of some responses may not yet be possible, or the 30 days may not be sufficient time to collect, compile, and draft answers to the interrogatories. It is common practice both to request and to acquiesce in a reasonable extension of time. Rule 29 requires a court order to extend the time, but this provision is more often breached in practice than enforced. It is also a too-common practice among some attorneys to delay, sometimes negligently, sometimes intentionally, the service of answers until the other side serves a Rule 37 motion and notice of motion compelling answers. Such churlish delaying tactics have no place in the discovery process. If more time is needed, an extension should be agreed to and confirmed in writing, and that deadline should be met punctually.

§3.6.11   Ethical Concerns

An attorney cannot consider strategic drafting tactics in a vacuum. The highest standards of ethical conduct and integrity must guide the attorney in determining how to respond. The adversary system and the role of an advocate must be balanced with the Code of Professional Responsibility and a lawyer's sense of reasonableness and cooperative conduct.[32]

§3.6.12   The "Nightmare" Test

Practicalities and economics affect an attorney's decision whether to answer, object, or waffle. One test to determine whether your response meets the reasonableness standard of Rule 33 is the nightmare test. You can do this during one of your office committee meetings or, if you meet by yourself, in your car. Pretend that the opposing attorney has brought a Rule 37 motion before a judge whom you have recently skunked in racquetball and that the judge asks you, "How in the discovery world can you justify your response?" If you defend with a

---

[32]*See* Airtex Corp. v. Shelley Radiant Ceiling Co., 536 F.2d 145, 155 (7th Cir. 1976).

winning retort, your interrogatory response is reasonable. If you wake up in a sweat, you need to redraft your response.

§3.7   BUSINESS RECORDS

Rule 33(c) specifically provides one way to answer an interrogatory in lieu of a detailed factual response:

> Where the answer to an interrogatory may be derived or ascertained from the business records of the party upon whom the interrogatory has been served or from an examination, audit or inspection of such business records, or from a compilation, abstract or summary based thereon, and the burden of deriving or ascertaining the answer is substantially the same for the party serving the interrogatory as for the party served, it is sufficient answer to such interrogatory to specify the records from which the answer may be derived or ascertained and to afford to the party serving the interrogatory reasonable opportunity to examine, audit or inspect such records and to make copies, compilations, abstracts or summaries.[1]

A specification shall be in sufficient detail to permit the interrogating party to locate and to identify, as readily as can the party served, the records from which the answer may be ascertained.

The rule does not license a responding party to play hide-and-seek with discovery information. The burden on finding the exact answer in response to the interrogatory must be the same for both parties;[2] if the burden would be greater for the interrogating party, the responding party must collate the information and respond in writing.[3] The responding party must designate which specific documents answer what question. Once the responding party does specify the appropriate documents, the burden then shifts to the interrogating party to uncover the information.[4] The specification must be in sufficient detail

§3.7   [1]Fed. R. Civ. P. 33(c). For a discussion of the rule, see Daiflow, Inc. v. Allied Chem. Corp., 534 F.2d 221 (5th Cir.), *cert. denied,* 429 U.S. 886 (1976).

[2]In re Folding Carton Antitrust Litigation, 83 F.R.D. 260, 265 (N.D. Ill. 1979).

[3]United States Equal Employment Opportunity Commn. v. Metropolitan Museum of Art, 80 F.R.D. 317, 318 (S.D.N.Y. 1978); Foster v. Boise-Cascade, Inc., 20 Fed. R. Serv. 2d 466 (S.D. Tex. 1975).

[4]In re Master Key Antitrust Litigation, 53 F.R.D. 87, 90 (D. Conn. 1971).

for the requesting party to locate the answers readily from the provided documents. The responding party cannot merely refer to "a mass of records as to which research is feasible only for one familiar with the records."[5]

A responding party faced with a decision whether to use this option is also faced with some strategic decisions. Would sifting through such records and compiling the answers be valuable, helping you to understand the case better? Would the time saved in not compiling the information outweigh any advantage gained by sifting through the records? Do the records contain other information, which should not be disclosed to the other party? Would allowing the other party to explore the records produce more helpful information than the interrogatories seek? Are the records susceptible to varying interpretations, and so should the responding party seek to impose its interpretation through the answer, instead of allowing unfettered access to the records? May a compromise response be reached by having someone direct and observe the other party?

The responding party should also consider alternative ways to respond.[6] The party could read information from the records in the presence of the interrogating party. Or the responding party could have someone observe the interrogating party reviewing the records, to limit inquiry to certain records. The responding party could also draft an answer providing some information while allowing access to certain records for other information. Finally, the responding party could refer specifically to previously disclosed documents or other discovery information for such answers.

§3.8 PROOF STATUS OF INTERROGATORIES

§3.8.1 Effect of Answers

What effect do the answers to interrogatories have on the responding party? The Federal Advisory Committee Notes explain the general rule:

[5]Budget Rent-a-Car of Missouri, Inc. v. Hertz Corp., 55 F.R.D. 354, 357 (W.D. Mo. 1972); Fed. R. Civ. P. 33(c).
[6]See Concept Indus., Inc. v. Carpet Factory, Inc., 59 F.R.D. 546 (E.D. Wis. 1973).

The general rule governing the use of answers to interrogatories is that under ordinary circumstances they do not limit proof. Although in exceptional circumstances reliance on an answer may cause such prejudice that the court will hold the answering party bound to his answer, the interrogating party will ordinarily not be entitled to rely on the unchanging character of the answers he receives and cannot base prejudice on such reliance.[1]

Often interrogatories have to be answered before investigation has been completed in a case, before a party has firmly decided upon a particular legal theory, or before a party has planned an overall strategy. A party is not necessarily bound to an early response that subsequently becomes incomplete or inaccurate.[2] Nor does an interrogatory answer automatically bar a party from taking a different position at trial.[3] A party must respond as well as he, she, or it can in answering an interrogatory, giving whatever information is available or whatever judgment has been made.[4] The trial judge has the discretion at trial to resolve any conflicts between answers to interrogatories and proffered testimony.[5]

There are many occasions when a party must update answers and supplement information, or face the exclusion of such evidence at trial or some other restriction. The section on supplementary responses (§1.9) explains in detail the circumstances and rationales of such cases and the provisions of Rule 26. It is not a wise practice to refuse or neglect supplementing or updating answers, even if there is no specific rule or case requiring such disclosure. A conflict or inconsistency in factual matters, in legal opinions, or in available witnesses may very well adversely impress the factfinder, who has to resolve the conflict.[6] Whatever the changes from previous disclosures, you must have awfully persuasive and legitimate reasons to explain the inconsistency and to explain why you did not disclose such changes to the other party.

§3.8.2   Contesting Objections

Rule 33(a) provides that the requesting party challenge an objection or response by bringing a motion and seeking an order under Rule 37.

§3.8   [1]Fed. R. Civ. P. 33(b), Notes of Advisory Comm. — 1970 Amendments.
[2]See Marcoin, Inc. v. Edwin K. Williams & Co. Inc., 605 F.2d 1325 (4th Cir. 1979).
[3]McInerney v. Wm. F. McDonald Constr. Co., 35 F. Supp. 688, 689 (E.D.N.Y. 1940).
[4]See McElroy v. United Air Lines, Inc., 21 F.R.D. 100, 102 (W.D. Mo. 1957).
[5]Freed v. Erie Lackawanna Ry. Co., 445 F.2d 619 (6th Cir. 1971).
[6]See Victory Carriers, Inc. v. Stockton Stevedoring Co., 388 F.2d 955, 958 (9th Cir. 1968).

No time limit is specified within which such a motion must be brought. Some jurisdictions do include a time limit requiring a notice of motion, after which time the requesting party waives the right to obtain an answer or challenge an objection. The requesting party has the burden of scheduling the hearing and indicating the contested responses. The responding party has the burden of showing that the answer or objection was proper. The judge then decides the propriety of the question and the response.

Short of bringing a motion, the requesting attorney can discuss the objections with the opposing attorney, modify the question, and request an answer in response. Or the requesting attorney can seek the cooperation of the other attorney to reach some other compromise. Local rules may even require such an attempt. The judge also may attempt to settle the dispute by asking attorneys to resolve their differences or by suggesting changes in the question and answer. Practice encourages the attorneys to confer and negotiate in good faith to resolve disputes, thereby avoiding court hearings with their resulting waste of time and money.

§3.8.3 Use of Interrogatories and Responses at Trial

Rule 33(b) provides that answers to interrogatories may be used at trial "to the extent permitted by the rules of evidence." They can be used as admissions against interest and become admissible substantive evidence.[7] They can be used by the opposing party for impeachment purposes without being offered in evidence.[8] If introduced by the responding party as substantive evidence, however, interrogatory responses usually are not admissible, because they constitute self-serving statements and have not been subject to cross-examination.[9] Unusual circumstances, though, may permit their use as substantive evidence. For example, if an action cannot be maintained without having the factfinder consider the interrogatory answers, they may be received as evidence. One case involved the death of a party whose deposition had not been taken, but who had provided answers to interrogatories. The court declared that Rule 33 created an exception to the hearsay rule and so allowed such responses as evidence, with an

[7]Gridiron Steel Co. v. Jones & Laughlin Steel Corp., 361 F.2d 791 (6th Cir. 1966). *See* Stonybrook Tenants Assn., Inc. v. Alpert, 29 F.R.D. 165, 167 (D. Conn. 1961).

[8]Meadows v. Palmer, 33 F.R.D. 136, 137 (D. Md. 1963); Taylor v. Atchinson, Topeka & Santa Fe Ry., 33 F.R.D. 283, 285 (W.D. Mo. 1962).

[9]Rosenthal v. Poland, 337 F. Supp. 1161, 1170 (S.D.N.Y. 1972).

instruction to the jury that they should consider the lack of cross-examination in determining its probative weight.[10] Because it is not clear that the 1970 revisions of Rule 33 created a hearsay exception, not all would agree with this decision.[11] The Federal Advisory Committee Notes indicate that the use of answers to interrogatories at trial remains subject to the rules of evidence.[12]

Interrogatories and responses are not part of the pleadings. An attorney who wishes to use them in a trial must do something affirmative to them; they are not a proper subject for judicial notice.[13] Neither a judge nor a jury may consider answers in reaching a decision in a trial.[14] A judge, however, may rely upon interrogatory responses for some decisions.

Answers to interrogatories may serve these or other functions in addition to providing discovery information. The drafting of the questions and the composing of the responses need to take into account their potential use for negotiation, trial, and other litigation purposes.

§3.9 PROBLEMS

Drafting Interrogatories

Draft a variety of types of interrogatories in the following exercises, including questions directed toward discovery of fact, opinion, and application of law to fact, where appropriate. Form interrogatories may be useful as guides in composing questions but may not be copied. The local court rules in Summit limit the number of interrogatories to twenty (20). Your instructor may vary that number.

1. You represent the defendant in *American Campers v. Summers*. Draft interrogatories directed to the plaintiff.
2. You represent the plaintiff in *American Campers v. Summers*. Draft interrogatories directed to the defendant.

[10]Treharne v. Callahan, 426 F.2d 58 (3d Cir. 1970).
[11]4A Moore's Federal Practice ¶33.29[1.2] (2d ed. 1980).
[12]Fed. R. Civ. P. 33(b), Notes of Advisory Comm. — 1970 Amendments.
[13]Bracey v. Grenoble, 494 F.2d 566, 570 n.7, 572 (3d Cir. 1975) (concurring and dissenting opinions).
[14]Delaware Coca-Cola Bottling Co. v. General Teamsters Local Union 326, 474 F. Supp. 777, 787 n.17 (D. Del. 1979).

3. You represent the plaintiff in *Bellow v. Norris*. Draft interrogatories directed to the defendant.

4. You represent the defendant in *Bellow v. Norris*. Draft interrogatories directed to the plaintiff.

5. You represent the plaintiff in *Graham v. Turkel*. Draft interrogatories directed to the defendant.

6. You represent the defendant in *Graham v. Turkel*. Draft interrogatories directed to the plaintiff.

Responding to Interrogatories

7. You represent the plaintiff in *American Campers v. Summers*. The defendant has submitted the following interrogatories to you and your client. Draft responses to them on behalf of your client:

(a) Describe all oral representations made to defendants by plaintiff regarding the Voyageur Motor Home on May 25.

(b) Describe all facts that support plaintiff's statement, made by Carol Sexton to the defendants on May 25, that the Voyageur Motor Home would get 16 miles per gallon on the highway.

(c) Describe the facts and dates upon which you base your Complaint allegations that defendants have "defaulted" on the retail installment contract.

(d) Describe the defects with the Voyageur Motor Home that caused the problems with the electrical system, engine, transmission, and gas mileage that were allegedly repaired between June 13 and June 22 by American Camper.

(e) Why did you not charge the defendants for the repairs completed on July 11?

(f) What law supports plaintiff's refusal to accept defendants' revocation of acceptance of the Voyageur Motor Home? Why does the plaintiff continue to possess the camper in its service lot?

8. You represent the defendant in *American Campers v. Summers*. The plaintiff has submitted the following interrogatories to you and your clients. Draft responses to them on behalf of your clients.

(a) Describe all facts upon which you base your Answer, denying the statement in paragraph 2 of the Complaint that defendants "have defaulted on the contract."

(b)   Describe all "statements" and "representations" plaintiff made to you as alleged in paragraph 3 of the Answer.
(c)   Describe the specific amounts and types of actual, consequential, and incidental damages approximating the $15,000 alleged to have been incurred by defendants.
(d)   Describe the amount and type of damages for lost vacation and leisure time alleged to have been suffered by defendants.
(e)   Explain why you decided not to bring the Voyageur Camper to plaintiff for repairs on Monday, June 26, 19XX?
(f)   When and how did defendants revoke acceptance of the Voyageur Motor Home? What law supports defendants' alleged revocation of acceptance?

9.   You represent the plaintiff in *Bellow v. Norris*. Draft responses to the interrogatories prepared by the student attorney who represents the defendant.

10.   You represent the defendant in *Bellow v. Norris*. Draft responses to the interrogatories prepared by the student attorney who represents the plaintiff.

11.   You represent the plaintiff in *Graham v. Turkel*. Draft responses to the interrogatories prepared by the student attorney who represents the defendant.

12.   You represent the defendant in *Graham v. Turkel*. Draft responses to the interrogatories prepared by the student attorney who represents the plaintiff.

Chapter 4
REQUESTS FOR PRODUCTION AND PHYSICAL EXAMINATIONS

*The harpoon was darted; the stricken whale flew forward; with igniting velocity
the line ran through the groove — and ran afoul. Ahab stood to clear it; he did
clear it, but the flying turn caught him round the neck, and voicelessly as
Turkish mutes bowstring their victim he was shot out of the boat.*

— Herman Melville
Moby Dick

§4.1 INTRODUCTION

You will never have the discovery difficulty Captain Ahab had in inspecting and copying Moby Dick. All you need do is shout "Give Away"[1] and under Rule 34 you will have the document or thing from your opponent.

Nothing in life is quite that simple, but Rule 34 comes quite close. The rule permits any party to obtain from another party the production of documents, property, and tangible things merely by asking. Though it is not the exclusive discovery device for making available documents and objects, Rule 34 is the only discovery device that *requires* opponents to produce them. Rule 33(c) allows a responding party to produce business records in lieu of interrogatory answers; Rule 30(f)(1) authorizes documents and things to be produced during a deposition; and Rule 45 permits the discovery of tangible information from non-parties. A party can also request the production of objects and things informally, without relying upon a formal discovery

§4.1 [1] A whaling term meaning to begin the attack. Also the opposite of a children's game called "Keep Away."

request. But Rule 34 is the only device that has the enforcement capabilities to compel their disclosure.

Rule 35 allows physical, mental, or blood examinations of a party. Rule 35 permits such examinations under more restrictive conditions than apply to Rule 34 production. The party to be examined must place his or her physical condition in issue, and an examination is authorized only by court order. These examinations are, however, readily available in the appropriate case, and they can be a useful discovery tool. Physical examinations will be discussed in §4.21.

§4.2 SAYING *PLEASE*

If you can say *please* to the other attorney you can frequently obtain access to documents and things without reliance on Rule 34. Telephone and letter requests frequently result in unilateral or reciprocal exchange of documentary information. It is a common practice for attorneys to forward copies of documents to each other, with each side bearing the rather minimal copying costs. These informal agreements save time and money, but they also have some drawbacks. The disclosing party has the flexibility to define the scope of the request and to decide what relevant documents will be voluntarily turned over. You cannot be certain that all the documents you think you requested were produced. The discovery rules do not provide any specific sanction for the breach of an informal disclosure agreement, although such a breach may constitute an ethical violation.

Formalizing the agreements helps reduce these drawbacks. A letter can be sent after an informal oral agreement, confirming the scope of the request and the expected items. Likewise, a letter sent after production, listing all the things disclosed, can ask whether they comprise all the writings and things requested within certain designated categories. A stipulation can be drafted and executed, listing the terms of the disclosure exchange; the scope of the things requested; and the time, place, and manner of disclosure. The more formal these agreements become, the closer they approximate the time and money involved with a simple Rule 34 request and the less attractive they become as discovery alternatives.

§4.3 THE RULE

The rule *ipsa loquitur:*

> Any party may serve on any other party a request (1) to produce and permit the party making the request, or someone acting on his behalf, to inspect and copy, any designated documents (including writings, drawings, graphs, charts, photographs, phono-records, and other data compilations from which information can be obtained, translated, if necessary, by the respondent through detection devices into reasonably usable form), or to inspect and copy, test, or sample any tangible things which constitute or contain matters within the scope of Rule 26(b) and which are in the possession, custody or control of the party upon whom the request is served, or (2) to permit entry upon designated land or other property in the possession or control of the party upon whom the request is served for the purpose of inspection and measuring, surveying, photographing, testing, or sampling the property or any designated object or operation thereon, within the scope of Rule 26(b).[1]

§4.4 PARTIES

The rule permits production only from parties. Rule 45 allows obtaining documents and things from non-parties at depositions, hearings, and trials through a subpoena duces tecum. If materials are available from both party and a non-party, it is preferable for a requesting party to use Rule 34 rather than to impose the discovery burden on a non-party through a subpoena.[1] Rule 34 requests can be directed to representative parties in a class action and to absentee class members in certain situations. The request submitted to absent class members must seek documents that are unavailable from the representative parties and must be relevant to a decision of common issues.[2]

§4.3 [1]Fed. R. Civ. P. 34(a).
§4.4 [1]*See* Bada Co. v. Montgomery Ward & Co., 32 F.R.D. 208, 209-210 (D. Tenn. 1963).
[2]Dellums v. Powell, 566 F.2d 167 (D.C. Cir.), *cert. denied,* 423 U.S. 874 (1977).

§4.5 THE SCOPE

The scope of discovery under Rule 34 is identical with other discovery devices outlined in Rule 26 and explained in Chapter 1. "The rule authorizes the broadest sweep of access, inspection, examination, testing, copying, and photographing of documents or objects in possession or control of another party."[1] A showing of good cause is no longer a requirement for requested materials, and the mass of confusing and conflicting case law interpreting "good cause" is now left for legal historians. Instead, the Rule 26 standard of relevance establishes the scope of all types of discoverable information. Some courts require a more restrictive standard in some situations: a Rule 34 request that disrupts the opposition's routine, creates a hazard, or may produce only marginally reliable information may require the showing of necessity before a party can obtain access.[2]

The following categories of documents and things are discoverable:

1. *Documents defined as "writings, drawings, graphs, charts, photographs, phono-records, and other data compilations. . . ."* Anything that contains some written, printed, recorded information or images is discoverable. Such documents can be inspected and copied. A later section (§4.16) discusses the effect of the rule on computerized information.
2. *Tangible things that are discoverable under the aegis of Rule 26.* Any object can be inspected, copied, tested or sampled. Sections 4.14 and 4.15, below, discuss testing concerns and procedures.
3. *Land and other property.* Such real and personal property may be inspected, measured, surveyed, photographed, tested, and sampled.

Most, if not all, cases involve some sort of documents, and Rule 34 is the routine way of discovering them. A growing number of cases, such as product liability and environmental actions, involve tangible and real property. Increasingly, cases also involve access to property for innovative discovery purposes. Treatment facilities may need to be

---

§4.5 [1] 8 C. Wright & A. Miller, Federal Practice and Procedure §2206, at 607 (1970).
[2] *See* Belcher v. Bassett Furniture, 588 F.2d 904, 908-910 (4th Cir. 1978).

inspected, relative to their conditions and procedures, in a case seeking better treatment for the residents.[3] An inspection tour of a factory may be necessary to obtain evidence for a product liability or employment-discrimination case.[4] These situations may first require a discovering party to use less intrusive discovery devices, like a deposition, to establish a need for Rule 34 access.[5] Rule 34 may also be an appropriate device to create tangible things for discovery purposes. It may be possible to require a party, for example, to produce a voice exemplar by speaking into a tape recorder.[6]

§4.6 POSSESSION, CUSTODY, AND CONTROL

All these documents, things, and property must be in the possession, control, and custody of a party. Possession and custody include both actual and constructive possession and custody, while control means the party has a legal right to obtain the documents.[1] Case law has both clarified and confused the discoverability of various items:

1. Non-party witness statements are considered trial preparation materials, requiring a showing of substantial need and undue hardship before they may be obtained by a party.[2] Because a non-party witness may obtain his or her own statement without any special showing, the friendly witness may request a copy at the urging or on behalf of one of the parties.[3]
2. Documents and things in the possession, control, or custody of a party's attorney are discoverable, excluding trial preparation materials and written lawyer mental impressions.[4]

[3]*See* Hubbard v. Rubber Maid, Inc., 78 F.R.D. 631 (D. Md. 1978); Morales v. Turman, 59 F.R.D. 157 (E.D. Tex. 1972).
[4]Belcher v. Basset Furniture, Inc., 588 F.2d 904 (4th Cir. 1978); National Dairy Prods. Corp. v. L.D. Shreiber, 61 F.R.D. 581 (E.D. Wis. 1973).
[5]*See* J. Underwood, A Guide to Federal Discovery Rules 128 (1979).
[6]*See* Haff v. Grams, 355 F. Supp. 542 (D. Minn. 1973).
§4.6 [1]8 C. Wright & A. Miller, Federal Practice and Procedure §2210, at 621-625 (1970).
[2]Civil Trial Manual 184-185 (ALI-ABA 1974).
[3]Ossenfort v. Associated Milk Producers, Inc., 254 N.W.2d 672, 681 (Minn. 1977).
[4]In re Ruppert, 309 F.2d 97, 98 (6th Cir. 1962).

3. Documents of which a party does not have copies, but has a right or opportunity to copy, must be produced.[5]

4. Documents a party possesses, but which belong to a third person who is not a party, may have to be disclosed. A party need not "own" the documents; it is enough if the party possesses them.[6]

5. Documents prepared by or under the direction or supervision of an expert expected to be called at trial, including reports embodying preliminary conclusions,[7] excluding trial preparation materials and lawyers' written mental impressions, are discoverable.

6. Documents and objects that a party possesses, controls, or has custody of are discoverable, even though such records and things may be beyond the territorial jurisdiction of the court.[8]

7. Things and documents in possession of a party's liability insurer are discoverable in an action against its insured, on the basis that the insurer is a real party with an interest.[9]

8. A corporation is required to produce documents held by its subsidiaries.[10]

9. A party has control over income tax returns available from the IRS.[11]

10. Hospital and physician records of a party have been held to be both under the control[12] and not under the control[13] of a patient.

---

[5]Herbst v. Able, 63 F.R.D. 135, 137 (S.D.N.Y. 1972); Buckley v. Vidal, 50 F.R.D. 271, 274 (S.D.N.Y. 1970).

[6]Societe Internationale v. Rogers, 357 U.S. 197, 200, 204 (1958); United States v. National Broadcasting Co., 65 F.R.D. 415, 419 (C.D. Cal. 1974), *appeal dismissed,* 421 U.S. 940 (1975).

[7]Quadrini v. Sikorsky Aircraft Corp., 74 F.R.D. 594 (D. Conn. 1977).

[8]In re Harris, 27 F. Supp. 480, 481 (S.D.N.Y. 1939).

[9]Bingle v. Liggett Drug Co., 11 F.R.D. 593, 594 (D. Mass. 1951).

[10]Advance Labor Serv., Inc. v. Hartford Accident & Indem. Co., 60 F.R.D. 632, 634 (N.D. Ill. 1973).

[11]Reeves v. Pennsylvania R.R. Co., 80 F. Supp. 107, 109 (D. Del. 1968).

[12]Schwartz v. Travelers Ins. Co., 17 F.R.D. 330 (S.D.N.Y. 1954).

[13]Reeves v. Pennsylvania R.R. Co., 80 F. Supp. 107, 109 (D. Del. 1968); Greene v. Sears, Roebuck & Co., 40 F.R.D. 14, 16 (N.D. Ohio 1966).

§4.7   THE REQUEST PROCEDURE

A party wanting to inspect documents and things or to enter property needs merely to serve a request setting forth the what, when, where, and how of the examination. No longer are motions, affidavits, and court orders necessary to gain access to such objects and land. Rule 34(b) provides that "The request may, without leave of court, be served upon the plaintiff after commencement of an action and upon any other party with or after service of the summons and complaint upon that party." A request may accompany a deposition notice requiring the party deponent to bring certain documents to a deposition. Requests for production may be used in any sequence with other discovery devices to precede or supplement other information. The rule requires that a request (1) set forth with reasonable particularity a description of the items to be discovered; and (2) specify reasonable time, place, and manner for making the inspection and copying.

Official Form 24 of the Federal Rules of Civil Procedure suggests an illustration of a proper request:

Plaintiff *A.B.* requests defendant *D.C.* to respond within _____ days to the following requests:

(1)   That defendant produce and permit plaintiff to inspect and to copy each of the following documents: [*Here list the documents either individually or by category and describe each of them.*]

[*Here state the time, place, and manner of making the inspection and performance of any related acts.*]

(2)   That defendant produce and permit plaintiff to inspect and to copy, test, or sample each of the following objects: [*Here list the objects either individually or by category and describe each of them.*]

[*Here state the time, place, and manner of making the inspection and performance of any related acts.*]

(3)   That defendant permit plaintiff to enter [*here describe property to be entered*] and to inspect and to photograph, test, or sample [*here describe the portion of the real property and the objects to be inspected*].

[*Here state the time, place, and manner of making the inspection and performance of any related acts.*]

§4.8 REASONABLE PARTICULARITY

How do you know for certain whether the request you have drafted designates the items sought "with reasonable particularity"? You could ask the law-school classmate who stands one rank ahead of you in class standing. Or you could apply common sense. You can never be absolutely certain that your request meets the standard of reasonable particularity, because it is not a standard susceptible to an exact definition; it is, rather, a flexible standard that varies with the circumstances of a case.[1] Descriptions of materials by the subject matter they contain, by particular classification, or by definite time periods, is usually specific enough.[2] Moreover, there is a simple, two-prong test that, if met, reduces recurring nightmares about "reasonable particularity." The request should be sufficient to: (1) allow a person of ordinary intelligence to say "I know what they want;"[3] and (2) permit a judge to determine whether all the requested items have been produced.[4]

Rule 34 allows descriptions of the items sought to be stated with exactitude and precision ("I want the June 27, 2:00 P.M. to 2:45 P.M. tape") or with generally descriptive categorization ("I want all the files that contain the law school's bronzed bluebook exam answers"). However the request is phrased, it must meet the two-prong test described above and must occasionally comply with more stringent requirements imposed by case law. Most courts allow discovery of general categories of items if the description is "easily understood."[5] Some courts expect a party who has knowledge about the documents sought to be specific in designating the items requested.[6] And almost all courts disallow

§4.8 [1]*See, e.g.,* Mallinckrodt Chem. Works v. Goldman Sachs & Co., 58 F.R.D. 348, 353 (S.D.N.Y. 1973); Richland Wholesale Liquors, Inc. v. Joseph E. Seagram & Sons, Inc., 40 F.R.D. 480, 481 (D.S.C. 1966).

[2]SEC v. American Beryllium & Oil Corp., 47 F.R.D. 66 (S.D.N.Y. 1968).

[3]*See* Mallinckrodt Chem. Works v. Goldman Sachs & Co., 58 F.R.D. 348 (S.D.N.Y. 1973).

[4]8 C. Wright & A. Miller, Federal Practice and Procedure §2211, at 611 (1970). The cases do not indicate whether both the attorneys and judges involved must be of "ordinary intelligence."

[5]*See* Hillside Amusement Co. v. Warner Bros. Pictures, Inc., 7 F.R.D. 260, 262 (S.D.N.Y. 1944).

[6]"Any statements of witnesses" discoverable: Wilson v. David, 21 F.R.D. 217, 219 (W.D. Mich. 1957). "All photographs" of the accident scene discoverable: Simper v. Trimble, 9 F.R.D. 598, 600 (W.D. Mo. 1979). "Disbursement books, canceled checks, check stubs" discoverable: Michel v. Meier, 8 F.R.D. 464, 477 (W.D. Pa. 1948). "Receipts, settlements, compromises and releases" discoverable: Walling v. R.L. McGinley

general descriptions that are vague, ambiguous, or too broad. Afflicted with this malady are requests seeking, for example, "all diagrams or documents containing drawings,"[7] "written communications about financial transactions,"[8] "all data relating to certain" facts,[9] or simply "file pertaining to the defendants."[10]

There are better techniques, for example the "33-34 One-Two." You submit a Rule 33 interrogatory asking the other party to describe certain documents, and then after receiving the answer, you submit a Rule 34 request containing the document whose description appears in the interrogatory answer. There is also the "33-34 One." You combine in one document Rule 34 requests with Rule 33 interrogatories. Since Rule 34 merely requires a request to be "in writing," a request, in a set of interrogatories, that a party produce "all documents identified in the preceeding answers" is an appropriate Rule 34 request. You can also add a written snicker to your Rule 34 request.

§4.9 DRAFTING TECHNIQUES

The drafting suggestions described in the preceding chapter (§3.4) on interrogatories apply equally to requests for production. You want to draft with some specificity, to avoid allowing the other side to withhold some documents, while at the same time drafting with enough breadth to make certain that no existing documents escape your attention. Two drafting techniques that may be employed to make requests escape-proof and all-encompassing are: (1) draft requests seeking both specifically designated items and generally described items, and (2) use definitions. For example:

> Furnish all documents concerning any contractual breach by defendant alleged in paragraph 2 of the complaint including but not limited to:

Co., 4 F.R.D. 149, 150 (E.D. Tenn. 1943). "Documents, records and correspondence" discoverable: Quemos Theatre Co. v. Warner Bros. Pictures, Inc., 35 F. Supp. 949, 950 (D.N.J. 1940).

[7]Stark v. American Dredging Co., 3 F.R.D. 300, 302 (E.D. Pa. 1943).

[8]Wharton v. Lybrand, Ross Bros. & Montgomery, 41 F.R.D. 177, 180 (E.D.N.Y. 1966). *See also* Paiewonsky v. Paiewonsky, 50 F.R.D. 379, 381 (D.V.I. 1970).

[9]Dynatron Corp. v. U.S. Rubber Co., 27 F.R.D. 480, 481 (D. Conn. 1961).

[10]Balistrieri v. O'Farrell, 57 F.R.D. 567, 569 (E.D. Wis. 1972).

The original and all carbon or other copies of each letter or written communication between the plaintiff and defendant between May 1, 1981, and August 1, 1981;

All writings submitted by the plaintiff to the Banking Commissioner which contain any reference to the defendant;

All complaints plaintiff received relating to the conduct of defendant from May 1, 1981, to September 1, 1981. Complaints include any writings submitted by any person, corporation, organization, agency or other entity that in any way refer to the alleged conduct of the defendant described in the complaint.

The most important definition is usually the meaning of the word *document,* which can be expanded beyond the definition provided in Rule 34 to include the following, and then attached to a request:

The term *documents* means all writings of any kind, including the originals and all non-identical copies, whether different from the originals by reason of any notation made on such copies or otherwise, including without limitation, correspondence, memoranda, notes, diaries, statistics, letters, telegrams, minutes, contracts, reports, studies, checks, statements, receipts, returns, summaries, pamphlets, books, interoffice and intra-office communications, notations of any sort of conversations, telephone calls, meetings or other communications, bulletins, printed matter, computer printouts, teletypes, telefax, invoices, worksheets, all drafts, alterations, modifications, changes, and amendments of any of the foregoing, graphic or oral records or representations of any kind (including, without limitation, photographs, charts, graphs, microfiche, microfilm, videotapes, recordings, motion pictures), and any electronic, mechanical, or electric records or representations of any kind (including, without limitation, tapes, cassettes, discs, recordings, and computer memories).

Whew.

The request for production can include a preface and instructions similar to the introduction to interrogatories (see §3.3) and for the same reasons. A Rule 34 introduction can include one or more of the following or similar statements:

1. If your response is that the documents are not in your possession or custody, describe in detail the unsuccessful efforts you made to locate the records.

2. If your response is that the documents are not in your control, identify who has control and the location of the records.

3. If a request for production seeks a specific document or an itemized category that is not in your possession, control, or custody, provide any documents you have that contain all or part of the information contained in the requested document or category.

4. Identify the source of each of the documents you produce.

§4.10 TIME, PLACE, MANNER

Rule 34(b) requires that a stated time, place, and manner for inspection and copying be included in the request for production. The date must be scheduled at least 30 days after service of the request because the other party has at least 30 days to respond. The hour usually is during business hours. The place usually is the location of the documents[1] and occasionally the location of some copying equipment. The manner depends on the kind of items requested. The delineation in advance of a specific time, place, and manner can be difficult in some cases, and it is a common practice to use less definite statements in the request. It is sufficient if the requests include an alternative statement such as:

1. The time, place, and manner will be mutually agreed upon by the parties at a later date;
2. The time and place will be determined by the responding party;
3. The production and copying will occur at a specific time and specific place in a specific manner, but the responding party may contact the requesting party to arrange a more convenient time and place;
4. The responding party may make copies of the documents and forward such copies to the requesting party with a bill for the copying expenses.

§4.10   [1]Petruska v. Johns-Manville, 83 F.R.D. 32 (E.D. Pa. 1979).

§4.11 RESPONSE

Rule 34 requires the party receiving the request to serve a written response upon the requesting party (and all other parties) within 30 days after service of the request (or within 45 days if the request is served with the summons and complaint). A judge, upon a motion, may shorten or lengthen the time. The responding party may reply in one or more ways to the request.

1. Abracadabra! Produce the requested items according to the suggested time, place, and manner. Rule 34(b) specifically dictates how a party produces certain documents. It provides that "A party who produces documents for inspection shall produce them as they are kept in the usual course of business or shall organize them and label them to correspond with the categories in the request."

But not always. The requesting party and not the responding party may be required to organize documents if it would take a substantial amount of time to number a large number of documents.[1] A requesting party may also ask for too much. For example, a party may request written compilations of data that the responding party does not have. The responding party can then make available documents containing the data, which the requesting party can then use to make the compilations. This response comports with the duty to respond under Rule 34.[2]

2. Disclose the requested items but at another time, place, and manner agreeable to the requesting attorney.

3. Serve a written response upon the requesting party, stating that inspection and related activities will be permitted for the designated items or categories at the suggested or at another time, place, and manner.

4. Move for a protective order under Rule 26(c) to safeguard the disclosure of certain items.

5. Ignore the request (although this is not authorized by the rule).

6. Object to the production and state the reasons for the objection.

The first three responses comprise the typically cooperative response by an attorney. The party producing the documents must do so by organizing and labeling them, to correspond to the discovery

---

§4.11   [1]United States ex rel. Schneider, Inc. v. Rush Engr. Co., 72 F.R.D. 195 (W.D. Pa. 1977).
[2]Webb v. Westinghouse Corp., 81 F.R.D. 431 (E.D. Pa. 1978).

requests, or must allow the other party to inspect documents as the documents are kept in the ordinary course of business. This manner of production is clearly mandated by Rule 34. The current rule does not countenance the deliberate or negligent mixture of critical documents with irrelevant documents to obscure the location and importance of the critical ones. The responding party has the obligation to designate specific documents, and should not play games by disclosing edited information or truckloads of immaterial documents.

The fourth response has been discussed in Chapter 1 and may also be the subject of a stipulation between the attorneys.[3] The fifth response is deplorable and is dealt with in detail in Chapter 6 on enforcement of discovery requests. The sixth response has been discussed in the context of objections to interrogatories in Chapter 3, and many of the same considerations apply to objections to requests for production, discussed in the next subsection.

§4.12 OBJECTIONS

A responding party may object to part or all of an item or category requested for production. All objections must be bona fide and provide the responding party with substantial justification for the refusal to disclose. Even if there are valid technical or substantive objections, as a strategic matter you need first to determine whether the harm, if any, in disclosing an item justifies the effort required in opposing discovery, and second, to determine what impact your refusal to disclose may have upon the opposing lawyer's willingness to cooperate with you in your requests for production.

The more common objections[1] to Rule 34 requests state that the documents or items:

1. Are not in the possession, control, or custody of the responding party;[2]

---

[3]See §§1.10 and 1.11.1 for discussion of the use of protective orders and stipulations respectively. *See also* Thermorama, Inc. v. Shiller, 271 Minn. 79, 85, 135 N.W.2d 43, 47 (1965); Snyker v. Snyker, 245 Minn. 405, 408, 72 N.W.2d 357, 359 (1955).

§4.12 [1]An objection that is neither common nor well recognized, but is peculiar to a Rule 34 request by a government agency, is an objection based upon the Fourth Amendment's prohibition against unreasonable searches and seizures. *See* 8 C. Wright & A. Miller, Federal Practice and Procedure §2020, at 585 (1970).

[2]*See* Fed. R. Civ. P. 34(a)(1).

2. Are no longer in existence;[3]

3. Are not yet prepared;[4]

4. Contain words with fewer than eight syllables, simple sentences, and no Latin clauses, and thus will be undecipherable to an attorney;[5]

5. Are not discoverable under Rule 34;[6]

6. Are irrelevant beyond the scope of Rule 26;[7]

7. Are public records and available through requester's own efforts;[8]

8. Are trial preparation materials;[9]

9. Are mental impressions or opinions of a lawyer;[10]

10. Are materials from experts who will not testify at trial;[11]

11. Have an 18-minute gap;[12]

12. Impose undue burden or expense;[13]

13. Are sought through an overbroad request;[14]

14. Are sought through a vague and ambiguous request;[15]

15. The inspection of property is hazardous or extensively disrupts operations;[16]

16. The inspection of land invades the privacy of the property owner;[17]

17. The love letter in the sand blew away.[18]

---

[3]*See* William A. Meier Glass Co. v. Anchor Hocking Glass Corp., 11 F.R.D. 487, 491 (W.D. Pa. 1951).

[4]*See* Soetaert v. Kansas City Coca Cola Bottling Co., 16 F.R.D. 1, 2 (W.D. Mo. 1954).

[5]Legalese smorgasbord.

[6]*See* Haff v. Gram, 355 F. Supp. 542 (D. Minn. 1973).

[7]Fed. R. Civ. P. 26(b)(1).

[8]United Cigar-Whelen Stores Corp. v. Philip Morris, Inc., 21 F.R.D. 107 (S.D.N.Y. 1957).

[9]Fed. R. Civ. P. 26(b)(3).

[10]Fed. R. Civ. P. 26(b)(3).

[11]Fed. R. Civ. P. 26(b)(4).

[12]Remember Rosemary Woods.

[13]Fed. R. Civ. P. 26(c); Baskerville v. Baskerville, 246 Minn. 496, 507, 75 N.W.2d 762, 769 (1956).

[14]Biliske v. American Livestock Ins. Co., 73 F.R.D. 124 (W.D. Okla. 1977).

[15]Documents and things to be produced should be described with reasonable particularity, but the test is a relative one, depending on the degree of knowledge of the requesting party in each particular case. Roebling v. Anderson, 257 F.2d 615, 620, 621 (D.C. Cir. 1958); Flickinger v. Aetna Cas. & Sur. Co., 37 F.R.D. 533, 535 (W.D. Pa. 1965).

[16]Belcher v. Bassett Furniture Inc., 588 F.2d 904, 908 (4th Cir. 1978).

[17]*See* Hughes & Anderson, Discovery: A Competition between the Right of Privacy and the Right to Know, 23 U. Fla. L. Rev. 289 (1971).

[18]Sing along with Pat Boone.

The party who interposes the objection must show its validity and grounds.[19] This burden may be met by factual affidavits from a party or by legal memoranda from the attorney. In some cases the requesting party may also have a burden. Courts may require a requesting party to show necessity for the Rule 34 access if such a request creates a hazardous situation or produces minimally reliable information.[20]

Objections to Rule 34 requests, like objections to other discovery requests, must be made in good faith and with care. There exists a temptation, because of the difficulties inherent in complying with a Rule 34 request, to yell "It's impossible."

Objections based on undue burdens or overbroad requests are scrutinized by judges and often overruled, because the very nature of discovery renders such requests quite possible.[21] A responding party itself may have created part of the impossibility claimed, because of inadequate record management or poor filing systems or because the materials were maintained in a way that is undecipherable to the requesting party. Courts require responding parties to produce documents in an orderly and understandable way.[22]

The party who receives an objection response to part or all of the request may redraft the request to eliminate the objections or may attempt to negotiate with the responding attorney to reach a compromise on disclosure. Courts look very, very kindly on these good-faith efforts to resolve an objection and may mandate by local rule that these efforts be made. A party seeking materials that may place too heavy a burden on the responding party can reduce the burdens by offering assistance in collating or collecting documents or by paying the costs of their production.[23] Should these efforts fail, the requesting party may seek a Rule 37 order compelling production or may pout in a corner of his or her law office.

---

[19]*See* 8 C. Wright & A. Miller, Federal Practice and Procedure §§2206-2207, at 607-614 (1970).

[20]*See* J. Underwood, A Guide to Federal Discovery Rules 131 (1979).

[21]*See, e.g.*, Steinberg v. Elkins, 470 F. Supp. 1024 (D.C. Md. 1979); Kozlowski v. Sears, Roebuck & Co., 73 F.R.D. 73 (D. Mass. 1976).

[22]Alliance to End Repression v. Rockford, 75 F.R.D. 441 (N.D. Ill. 1977); Stapleton v. Kawasaki Heavy Indus., Ltd., 69 F.R.D. 489 (N.D. Ga. 1975).

[23]*See* Shang v. Hotel Waldorf-Astoria Corp., 77 F.R.D. 468 (S.D.N.Y. 1978).

§4.13 CONDUCTING THE EXAMINATION

The extent of your examination depends on the nature of the item. Rule 34(a) provides you with the right to inspect and copy documents; to inspect, copy, test, and sample tangible things; to enter and to inspect, measure, survey, photograph, test, or sample land and property; to observe machinery or manufacturing, production, distribution, and other business processes.

Your inspection and perusal of the requested documents and things should proceed with two primary considerations: (1) Has everything you requested been turned over to you? Or too little? Or too much? (2) Do the records indicate that other relevant documents are still outstanding?

You should maintain some means of listing and identifying the exact documents and things examined. A good record can later quell any questions about what was produced when. You can create such a record with some distinctive mark or initials. Although you need the permission of your adversary if you plan somehow to mark the items, your adversary usually has a similar interest and will cooperate in maintaining an accurate and complete record.

Copying of the items is usually at your own expense. You can arrange to use the adversary's copying equipment and reimburse your opponent or arrange for your own copying facilities. You may wish to photograph or tag some items as physical evidence. The manner of copying or recording is usually one of accommodation and cooperation between the attorneys.

§4.14 TESTING

You have a right to test certain items. The decision to test, according to one commentator, turns on a consideration of five questions:

1. Is the test I am considering likely to do more harm than good, by destroying or materially altering evidence which, in its present condition, provides vivid proof of the point I am urging?
2. Is it feasible to consider deferring the testing until the trial, and conducting it as a courtroom experiment?

3. Will the disadvantages of my proposed testing outweigh whatever I may gain from it?
4. Am I confident enough of the results of the tests to stake my case on them?
5. Even if my proposed tests are permissible under the rules of discovery, will the court receive them in evidence at the trial?[1]

Whatever testing you do must be done with the full knowledge of the opponent. Your request for production should spell out in detail what and how you intend to test. It is wise to seek a written stipulation or a court order detailing the testing procedure. This is mandatory if testing destroys or alters material evidence.[2] Testing may then proceed along the lines dictated by the stipulation or order, with an exhaustive or videotaped record made of everything that occurs during the testing.

It is also wise to obtain a test report in the form of a letter, so that you may later claim a privilege or work-product protection for such information. It is not wise, however, to request two reports, one a slanted report to disclose to the opposing side, and the other a "confidential and candid report" for your purposes only. The contents of both reports may be discoverable. The existence of both reports is certainly discoverable and a proper subject for cross-examination at the trial. If a report appears to be incomplete or inadequate, merely request a supplementary report. Their discoverability depends on the status of the expert.[3]

§4.15 DESTRUCTIVE TESTING

Although most testing under Rule 34 consists of examination and tests that can be repeatedly performed, it is sometimes advantageous or necessary to conduct destructive examinations or tests. Although attorneys have found need for such testing for years, the recent surge

§4.14 [1]Quoted from W. Barthold, Attorney's Guide to Effective Discovery Techniques 187-188 (1975) (footnotes omitted).

[2]See City of Kingsport v. SCM Corp., 352 F. Supp. 287 (E.D. Pa. 1971).

[3]Experts are discussed in §1.8 of this text. See also Leininger v. Swadner, 279 Minn. 251, 156 N.W.2d 254, 259-260 (1968).

in product liability litigation has dramatically increased the number of requests for destructive testing.

Courts require a specific court order prior to the conducting of destructive tests.[1] Even as a practical matter, however, a party desiring to conduct destructive testing of any evidence should want to obtain an order approving such testing. If an order is not procured, a compelling argument exists at the time of trial to exclude the evidence obtained from the testing on the basis of unfairness, since opposing parties have not had an opportunity to conduct such tests. The destruction itself of the evidence may give rise to an even stronger argument at trial against the party destroying the evidence.[2]

The trial court has discretion in deciding whether to issue an order allowing destructive testing.[3] The court's discretion is normally guided by two factors: the usefulness or need of the discovery to the party requesting it and the prejudice or handicap that will occur to the party or parties opposing destructive testing.[4] The court becomes involved in the destructive testing dispute upon either the motion of the parties seeking testing to compel production of the article to be tested or upon the motion for protective order from the party holding the article to be tested. Most frequently the motion to compel production of the article is met by a motion for a protective order, and both motions are heard at once.

Courts, in attempting to balance the need of the party to obtain information regarding the article with an underlying concern for fairness, generally either deny the right of any party to conduct destructive testing,[5] postpone such testing until shortly before trial, or most frequently, permit the testing under the provisions of a protective order.[6] The terms of such a protective order frequently include:

§4.15　[1]Cameron v. District Court, 565 P.2d 925, 931 (Colo. 1977); Sarver v. Barrett Ace Hardware, Inc., 63 Ill. 2d 454, 349 N.E.2d 28, 30 (1976).

[2]In a criminal case the introduction of destructive testing results was held to be reversible error. People v. Dodsworth, 60 Ill. App. 3d 207, 376 N.E.2d 449 (1978).

[3]"Destructive testing is not a matter of right, but lies in the sound discretion of the trial court." Cameron v. District Court, 565 P.2d 925, 929 (Colo. 1977).

[4]See Sarver v. Barrett Ace Hardware, Inc., 63 Ill. 2d 454, 349 N.E.2d 28, 30 (1976).

[5]Home Ins. Co. v. Cleveland Elec. Illuminating Co., 7 Fed. R. Serv. 2d 731 (N.D. Ohio 1959); State ex rel. Crawford v. Moody, 477 S.W.2d 438 (Mo. App. 1972).

[6]Cameron v. District Court, 565 P.2d 925, 931 (Colo. 1977); Sarver v. Barrett Ace Hardware, Inc., 63 Ill. 2d 454, 349 N.E.2d 28, 31 (1976); Foster-Lipkins Corp. v. Suburban Propane Gas Corp., 72 Misc. 2d 457, 339 N.Y.S.2d 581 (1973); Edwardes v. Southampton Hosp. Assn., 53 Misc. 2d 187, 278 N.Y.S.2d 283 (1967); Martin v. Reynolds Metals Corp., 297 F.2d 49 (9th Cir. 1961); Petruk v. South Ferry Realty Co., 2 App. Div. 2d 533, 157 N.Y.S.2d 249, 255 (1956).

1. A testing plan;
2. An opportunity prior to testing for all other parties to examine and photograph the article to be tested;
3. A notice to all parties of the testing;
4. The right of any party to be present at the testing, with consultants or experts if necessary;
5. Careful and thorough recording of test activities and test results;
6. The availability of test results to all parties;
7. The availability of reports by persons conducting the testing to all parties;
8. The right of other parties to take additional samples for similar testing, if material is available.

Although the concern of courts in destructive-testing cases is generally toward preventing a party from being prejudiced in the pending litigation by the destruction of crucial evidence, testing is sometimes also sought that threatens to cause monetary damage to the item being tested. If this situation occurs, the party conducting the testing should be held liable for damages.[7] A practical solution to this problem, perhaps, is for the court to require the parties seeking the tests to post an appropriate bond to protect against any damage that might be done to the article being tested.[8] An attorney should not be misled, however, into thinking that a surety bond will prevent hardship to the party opposing discovery in all respects. If evidence is destroyed by testing in which the party opposing destructive testing is not allowed to participate, the difficulty of proving recovery under the surety bond is no less than the difficulty of proving the underlying action. Thus the surety bond may be an illusory protection to parties opposing destructive testing.[9]

---

[7]Fisher v. United States Fidelity & Guar. Co., 246 F.2d 344, 350 (7th Cir. 1957).

[8]*See* Williams v. Continental Oil Co., 215 F.2d 4 (10th Cir. 1954), *cert. denied,* 348 U.S. 928 (1955); Arkansas State Highway Commn. v. Stanley, 234 Ark. 428, 353 S.W.2d 173, 177 (1962).

[9]*See* People v. Dodsworth, 60 Ill. App. 3d 207, 376 N.E.2d 449 (1978) (reversible error to introduce destructive testing results in criminal case).

§4.16   COMPUTERIZED INFORMATION

Rule 34(a) permits the discovery of any "data compilations from which information can be obtained, translated, if necessary, by the respondent through detection devices into reasonably usable form." In other words, documentary information stored on punched data cards, electronic disks, recording tapes, and computer banks is discoverable. What's more, the responding party must furnish it in a manner understandable to the requesting party and must bear the cost and expense of compiling the data and translating them into a readable printout or some other machine-readable format.[1]

Courts draw a distinction between producing computer information and designing new computer programs to extract data; they require the former and deny the latter unless the requesting party bears all such programming costs.[2] A party can seek an order protecting it from excessive expenses, and parties can negotiate to share the costs. In some cases a party may prefer to obtain programs or raw data in a format that can be used on that party's computer. In this fashion, by analysis and review, facts may be uncovered that might otherwise remain hidden in a computer printout.[3]

Rule 34 is deliberately broad to accommodate disclosures of all types of information and provides safeguards through Rule 26 and Rule 37 to balance proper disclosures. The courts will need to develop case law guidelines on the manner and means for disclosure of such discoverable information. Complicated questions will arise involving the disclosure of information that can be digested and understood only by another computer and not by people, disclosure of confidential programming systems and non-discoverable material in the computer stores, and disclosure of work-product and trial preparation materials and privileged information contained or generated by computers. These problems will also affect other discovery rules besides Rule 34.[4]

---

§4.16   [1]Adams v. Dan River Mills, Inc., 15 Fed. R. Serv. 2d 1275 (W.D. Va. 1972).
[2]Sanders v. Levy, 21 Fed. R. Serv. 2d 1213 (2d Cir. 1976).
[3]Morris, Hospital Computers in Court, 1963 Modern Uses of Logic in Law (now Juris. J.) 61, at 64.
[4]For more information about discovery and the computer age, see 8 C. Wright & A. Miller, Federal Practice and Procedure §2218, at 174, 175 (1970, Supp. 1980).

§4.17   INDEPENDENT ACTIONS

Rule 34 and Rule 45 are not the exclusive ways to obtain documents and property from a party or a person not a party. Rule 34(c) makes clear that the rules do not preclude an independent action against a non-party person for the production of documents and things and for permission to enter lands. Federal courts have also recognized the availability of such an action.[1] Some state advisory committee notes indicate that an action in the nature of a bill in equity is available.[2]

§4.18   PRODUCTION FROM NON-PARTIES

While Rule 34 discovery is available only against parties, unless an independent action is filed, Rule 45 allows for the use of a subpoena duces tecum to compel the production of documents and things from non-party witnesses at depositions, trials, and hearings, but not at other times or places.[1] The scope of discovery under this subpoena is the same as that applicable to Rule 34. This rule protects non-parties from indiscriminate use of discovery procedures, from improper searches and seizures, and from intrusive fishing expeditions.[2] A party should resort to a Rule 45 subpoena only if the documents are unavailable from an adversary or not otherwise available through the requester's own efforts.[3] Although there is no separate "discovery" rule, similar to Rule 34, directed at non-parties and allowing for the inspection and copying of items, the subpoena may command the person to

§4.17 [1]United States v. 25.02 Acres of Land, 495 F.2d 1398 (10th Cir. 1974).
  [2]*See* Minn. R. Civ. P. 34, Notes of Advisory Comm. *See also* McGuire v. Caledonia, 140 Minn. 151, 167 N.W. 425 (1918).
  §4.18 [1]Ghandi v. Police Dept. of City of Detroit, 74 F.R.D. 115 (E.D. Mich. 1977). A subpoena duces tecum, where there was no notice to take a deposition, nor a hearing, trial, or conference set to be heard by the court, was quashed because of noncompliance with Rule 45.
  [2]Premium Serv. Corp. v. Sperry & Hutchinson Co., 511 F.2d 225 (9th Cir. 1975). Plaintiff's request for documents was sweeping and would have placed a tremendous burden on the defendant employees, who would have had to sift and analyze the documents. The court held that the plaintiff's offer to do the sifting itself was unrealistic and constituted an impermissible fishing expedition. *See also* 8 C. Wright & A. Miller, Federal Practice and Procedure §§2208 & 2209, at 2457 (1970).
  [3]In re Penn Central Commercial Paper Litigation, 61 F.R.D. 453 (D.C.N.Y. 1973).

whom it is directed to produce materials, thus allowing for inspection and copying.[4]

There are three methods for obtaining desired documentary materials from non-parties. (1) A deposition of a non-party witness can be scheduled and a subpoena served upon that person, ordering him or her to bring designated documents and things. (2) A motion hearing can be scheduled and a subpoena served upon a person, ordering him or her to bring designated items. Or (3) a court may issue an order requiring a party to produce documents and things at other times and places.[5] The failure to schedule a deposition or motion hearing or to obtain a court order renders a Rule 45 subpoena ineffective.[6]

The rules specifically detail the scope of such discovery and the protections afforded the non-party who wishes to object to disclosures of such data. Rule 45(d) details the procedures applicable to depositions:

> Proof of service of notice to take a deposition as provided in Rules 30(b) and 31(a) or in a state where the action is pending constitutes a sufficient authorization for the issuance of subpoenas for the persons named or described therein. The subpoena may command the person to whom it is directed to produce and permit inspection and copying of designated books, papers, documents or tangible things which constitute or contain matters within the scope of the examination permitted by Rule 26(b), but in that event the subpoena will be subject to the provisions of Rule 26(c) and subdivision (b) of this rule.
>
> The person to whom the subpoena is directed may, within 10 days after the service thereof or on or before the time specified in the subpoena for compliance if such time is less than 10 days after service, serve upon the attorney designated in the subpoena written objection to inspection or copying of any or all of the designated materials. If objection is made, the party serving the subpoena shall not be entitled to inspect and copy the materials except pursuant to an order of the court from which the subpoena was issued. The party serving the subpoena may, if objection has been made, move upon notice to the deponent for an order at any time before or during the taking of the deposition.

[4]*See* 8 C. Wright & A. Miller, Federal Practice and Procedure §2452 (1970). *See also* J. Underwood, A Guide to Federal Discovery Rules 136 (1980).

[5]*See* Eastern States Petroleum Co. v. Asiatic Petroleum Corp., 27 F. Supp. 121, 122 (S.D.N.Y. 1938).

[6]Ghandi v. Police Dept. of City of Detroit, 74 F.R.D. 115 (E.D. Mich. 1977).

The rule goes on to describe the location of the deposition, which is indeed geographically limited.[7] The designated documents can be discovered only during the deposition, and the subpoena duces tecum that accompanies a deposition will be quashed if there is no thought by the subpoenaing party to take the deposition of the person served.[8] Rule 45(b) details further procedures:

> A subpoena may also command the person to whom it is directed to produce the books, papers, documents or tangible things designated therein; but the court, upon motion made promptly, and in any event at or before the time specified in the subpoena for compliance therewith, may (1) quash or modify the subpoena if it is unreasonable or oppressive, or (2) condition denial of the motion upon the advancement by the person in whose behalf the subpoena is issued of the reasonable cost of producing the books, papers, documents or tangible things.

The subpoena describes the documents to be produced. The drafting practices followed or involved with Rule 34 apply as well to subpoenas. You should mix general and specific descriptions of documents with "reasonable particularity," even though this term is nowhere found in Rule 45. Thus, like a Rule 34 request, you can specify documents you want or you can command production of all documentary information relating to a specific matter or issue. You can also combine Rule 45 and Rule 34 in sequence: after reviewing the Rule 45 documents at the deposition, you can submit a Rule 34 request to a party for additional documents.

The grounds for obtaining an order quashing the subpoena duces tecum or limiting its scope mimic the objections available to a Rule 34 request for production. Additional objections may also include the possible ground (1) that the discovering party can obtain such documents and things from a party to the case and should first use a Rule 34 request before employing a Rule 45 request against a non-party,[9] and (2) that a non-party's privacy outweighs a party's need for the information.[10]

[7]"A resident of the district in which the deposition is to be taken may be required to attend an examination only in the county wherein he resides or is employed or transacts his business in person, or at such other convenient place as is fixed by an order of court. A nonresident of the district may be required to attend only in the county wherein he is served with a subpoena, or within 40 miles from the place of service, or at such other convenient place as is fixed by an order of court." Fed. R. Civ. P. 45(d)(2).
[8]McLean v. Prudential S.S. Co., 36 F.R.D. 421, 426 (E.D. Va. 1965).
[9]Bada Co. v. Montgomery Ward & Co., 32 F.R.D. 208, 210 (E.D. Tenn. 1963).
[10]Premium Serv. Corp. v. Sperry & Hutchinson Co., 511 F.2d 225 (9th Cir. 1975).

The burden to establish that the subpoena should be quashed or modified is on the person seeking the order. The non-party witness served with a subpoena duces tecum clearly has standing to quash or limit it. But in addition to the subpoenaed non-party witness, a party to the action may also have standing to quash or limit it if that party has some personal right or privilege in the subject matter of the subpoena.[11] Rule 45(j) provides that the failure of a party "without adequate excuse" to comply with a subpoena may be deemed contempt of court.

§4.19 PRODUCTION FROM THE GOVERNMENT

Parties involved in litigation with the federal government, and frequently with state governments, have the same discovery obstacles they would encounter with non-governmental litigants. The federal Freedom of Information Act (FOIA),[1] however, provides an additional means of obtaining access to governmental records not available in most lawsuits. Statutes similar to the FOIA have been passed in a number of states, giving litigants and potential litigants access to documents in the hands of state governmental agencies.[2]

The Freedom of Information Act was enacted in 1966 as a means of bringing government activity into the public eye, thus creating an informed electorate and a responsive, open government. Subsequent amendments and the Federal Privacy Act have modified the initial FOIA.

The FOIA allows broad disclosure of documents held by the government, and states that the governmental agencies must release any identifiable agency records in the agency's possession to "any person." No reason need be given for a request under the FOIA. Access to records is provided either by publication in the Federal Register, access at the agency's headquarters, or by making copies available upon

---

[11]Shepherd v. Castle, 20 F.R.D. 184, 188 (W.D. Mo. 1957).

§4.19   [1]5 U.S.C. §552 (1976).

[2]For a compilation of state acts relating to access to governmental information, see Guidebook to the Freedom of Information and Privacy Acts 265–435 (Appendix C) (R. Bouchard & J. Franklin eds. 1980).

request. Most information is disclosed by an agency's designated information officer, who makes copies available upon request.

The act contains nine specific exemptions to disclosure, and these exemptions are given narrow interpretations by the court in order to effectuate the broad purposes of the FOIA. The exemptions are:

1. Classified defense or national security documents;
2. Agency internal personnel-rule documents;
3. Documents specifically exempted by other statutes;
4. Confidential or privileged trade-secret, commercial or financial information;
5. Interagency or intra-agency memoranda not otherwise discoverable;
6. Personnel and medical files;
7. Law enforcement investigatory records;
8. Documents pertaining to examination and supervision of financial institutions;
9. Geological and geophysical information concerning wells.

The FOIA contemplates a simple procedure for obtaining agency documents and requires the agency to respond within ten days. An appeal is permitted from an adverse decision on disclosure, and the agency must determine the administrative appeal within 20 working days. A party may thereafter commence an action in the court to enjoin the withholding of agency records.[3]

Perhaps the biggest advantage of using FOIA for discovery is that the government may put together a vast *collection* of information for you. For example, the Consumer Products Safety Commission (CPSC) amasses information on injuries involving many types of products, regardless of their manufacturer. Although a product liability action may be commenced against a single manufacturer, the information contained in CPSC files relating to all manufacturers may be very useful. Presumably the information about the particular defendant in your action or intended action will be directly discoverable from that party, while the government records may provide a large collection of cases involving parties from whom discovery would be difficult or expensive. The FOIA is also useful in that it permits "discovery" to take place even prior to the commencement of an action. For a party

[3]5 U.S.C. §552(a)(3) (1976).

contemplating litigation with the government, the use of a request for documents under FOIA may be a very useful tool for investigation.

§4.20 USE AT TRIAL

The production, examination, inspection, copying, testing, sampling, or whatever, done under Rule 34, does not automatically make the documents and property admissible evidence for the trial. Interrogatories, deposition questions, and Rule 36 requests can be employed to determine the existence of originals, the authenticity of documents, and their author or custodian for hearsay exception purposes and as background information for foundation purposes. The trial lawyer must do something affirmatively with the information through a Rule 34 request to make it admissible at trial. Admissions made through the discovery devices or through stipulations can be used to render the documents and things admissible without having to establish the best evidence, authenticity, hearsay exceptions, or foundation.

§4.21 PHYSICAL EXAMINATIONS

Rule 35 governs medical, physical, and blood examinations. The rule requires a motion and order for these "adverse" examinations, and courts grant the orders after due consideration of a motion brought by an adverse party. Rule 35(b)(3) and Rule 29 permit examinations to be held by agreement of the parties; the provisions and procedures of Rule 35 apply to stipulated examinations unless the agreement expressly provides otherwise. In practice, most examinations occur as a result of an agreement between attorneys. The courts are eager to give effect to stipulations and ratify their use with respect to any physical, mental, or blood examination.[1] The courts recognize that Rule 35 is a device that should be used only if the parties fail to agree on an examination.

§4.21 [1] *See* Liechty v. Terrill Trucking Co., 53 F.R.D. 590 (E.D. Tenn. 1971). *See also* discussion in §1.11.1 of this text.

Rule 35 applies broadly to any case in which there is controversy about the physical, mental, or blood condition of the person to be examined; it is commonly applied to the examination of an injured plaintiff and sought by the defendant or defendants in a personal-injury action. Other types of litigation that may involve Rule 35 examinations include paternity, citizenship, incompetence, and undue influence.[2] These cases typically involve physical, mental, or blood condition questions. And while the condition of a dead body may be ascertained through a Rule 34 procedure for the production of tangibles,[3] conceivably Rule 35 also stands as an additional authority allowing a medical examination of a dead person.

Is a particular party subject to examination? Is his or her physical or mental condition in controversy? Can a significant showing of good cause be made in support of the motion to compel examination? These are all questions that the moving party must answer affirmatively in order to prevail. The Supreme Court has stated that the rule prohibits "sweeping examinations . . . automatically ordered merely because the person has been involved in an accident . . . and a general charge of negligence is lodged."[4] The Court does not sanction the "routine" ordering of such examinations but instead requires the trial judge to apply the rule "discriminately." Rule 35 practice, however, does not always appear to follow the dictates of this holding. Personal-injury actions involving an auto accident and allegations of negligence routinely prompt a Rule 35 examination. When this occurs, the Rule 35 criteria usually have been strictly met by a claim of serious or permanent physical injury.

The rule creates three standards to be met in obtaining an adverse examination: the physical, mental, or blood condition of an *examinee* must be *in controversy* and *good cause* must be shown for the examination. The trial court has broad discretion in considering and acting upon a Rule 35 request.[5]

---

[2]*See* 4A Moore's Federal Practice ¶35.03[1] (2d ed. 1980); Szet Foo v. Dulles, 18 F.R.D. 237 (S.D.N.Y. 1955).

[3]*See* Zalatuka v. Metropolitan Life Ins. Co., 108 F.2d 405 (7th Cir. 1939).

[4]Schlagenhauf v. Holder, 379 U.S. at 121 (1964).

[5]Coca-Cola Bottling Co. of Puerto Rico v. Torres, 255 F.2d 149 (1st Cir. 1958); Bucher v. Krause, 200 F.2d 576 (7th Cir. 1952). *See also* 4A Moore's Federal Practice ¶35.04, at 35-21 (2d ed. 1980).

§4.21.1   The Examinee

The rule applies to all parties, defendants as well as plaintiffs, and extends examinations to include *agents* as well as *persons under control of the party.* An agent of a party is an agent of the party — even a cursory review of your notes on agency will provide that definition. A person under the legal control of the party is a person under legal control of the party — a cursory review of the word "control" will not provide a workable definition here, though. Nonetheless, some situations are clear. The Federal Advisory Committee states that the rule settles "beyond doubt that a parent or guardian suing to recover for injuries to a minor may be ordered to produce the minor for examination."[6] The committee clearly intended the rule to cover a required blood examination of minors in cases involving their paternity.[7] Other situations remain unresolved. Professors Wright and Miller state:

> It is not quite so clear, but it would seem that when a husband has a substantive right to recover for injuries to his wife, the wife is under his legal control for this purpose and he can be ordered to produce her for physical examination.[8]

Control does have its limits. The Federal Advisory Committee Notes state that "an order to 'produce' the third person imposes only an obligation to use good faith efforts to produce the person."[9]

§4.21.2   The Controversy

Personal injury cases almost automatically include some condition in controversy. Other cases may also raise the question of whether the plaintiff or defendant voluntarily has placed physical, mental, or blood condition in issue. One party may attempt to place an opponent's condition in controversy. A more pronounced showing of actual "controversy" will be required of a party who initiates the dispute concerning the condition of another. Mere conclusory allegations that a

---

[6]Fed. R. Civ. P. 35(a), Note of Advisory Comm.
[7]Fed. R. Civ. P. 35(a), Note of Advisory Comm. The rule conforms to the holding in Beach v. Beach, 114 F.2d 479 (D.C. Cir. 1940).
[8]8 C. Wright & A. Miller, Federal Practice and Procedure §2233, at 669 (1970).
[9] Fed. R. Civ. P. 35(a), Note of Advisory Comm.

condition is in controversy will not provide the basis for a Rule 35 order.

The party seeking an examination must make a showing beyond a mere allegation that the evidence itself places the condition in dispute. For example, the plaintiff in one personal-injury case clearly placed her physical condition in controversy by asserting physical injuries to her head and body in the complaint. Defendant argued that plaintiff's mental condition was also in controversy, contending that the real question was whether plaintiff's physical condition was affected by her mental condition. This argument was supported by an expert's adverse medical examination report, which found plaintiff to be minimally injured and predicted that plaintiff's residual symptoms would disappear when the litigation settled.[10]

In another illustrative case, the plaintiff in a negligence action, which involved the collision of a bus with a tractor-trailer, sought a Rule 35 examination of the defendant and the bus driver.[11] The plaintiff contended that the bus driver was "not mentally or physically capable" of driving the bus and sought examinations in internal medicine, ophthalmology, neurology, and psychiatry. The plaintiff supported its motion with affidavits alleging that the rear lights of the trailer were visible for one-half mile and that the driver had been involved in a previous accident. The United States Supreme Court found sufficient controversy for the ophthalmological examination on the basis of one affidavit, but not for the other three examinations.[12] Two Justices dissented, noting that the record supported a finding that the physical and mental condition of the driver were in controversy and the three examinations would produce highly relevant evidence. The dissenters remarked in a practical and telling observation that such an accident prompts a reasonable person to inquire "What is the matter with that driver? Is he blind or crazy?"[13]

A creative attorney may be able to formulate a persuasive argument that physical, mental, or blood condition is in controversy in a type of lawsuit not ordinarily involving Rule 35 examinations. A defamation action involving alleged defamatory remarks concerning the plaintiff's physical, mental, or blood condition may justify a Rule 35 examination

[10]Haynes v. Anderson, 39 Minn. 185, 232 N.W.2d 196 (1975).
[11]Schlagenhauf v. Holder, 379 U.S. 104 (1964).
[12]379 U.S. at 120-121.
[13]379 U.S. at 123.

to allow the defendant to establish the defense of truth. The "in controversy" requirement may also be met by a dispute over the right or competence of a party to maintain an action or defense. One court has authorized a mental examination to determine if the plaintiff was capable of understanding the nature and effect of the lawsuit involved.[14] The court issued the order on the authority of both Rule 35 and Rule 17(c), the rule providing for prosecution of actions by representatives of incompetent persons. The court stated that this type of examination would not be permitted as a routine practice and issued the order subject to certain protective provisions.[15] This precedent is not uniform, however. Another court has denied a Rule 35 motion based on similar allegations of controversy.[16]

§4.21.3   The Good Cause

Rule 34 may no longer require a showing of good cause for the production of documents, but Rule 35 continues this requirement for compulsory examinations. This good-cause requirement frequently creates difficulty in obtaining a Rule 35 order. The standard for determining the question of good cause goes beyond a mere formality, requiring (1) that the moving party establish that the prospective information meets the relevancy standard of Rule 26 and (2) that the moving party need such information. Courts impose varying burdens upon parties seeking Rule 35 orders, but they routinely grant such motions in personal-injury actions, where physical or mental condition is usually in controversy and "good cause" is self-evident. Courts also grant Rule 35 requests in cases not ordinarily involving questions of mental, physical, or blood conditions, but they impose a higher burden on the party seeking the examination if the proposed examination will be either painful or of dubious probative value. One court declined to order a bone-scan examination because of its questionable value and the potential pain to the party to be examined.[17]

Although higher standards may be imposed in such cases, courts

---

[14] Bodnar v. Bodnar, 441 F.2d 1103 (5th Cir. 1971), *cert. denied,* 404 U.S. 913 (1972). *See also* Buck v. Board of Educ., 17 Fed. R. Serv. 2d 165 (E.D.N.Y. 1973).

[15] Bodnar v. Bodnar, 441 F.2d 1103, 1104 (5th Cir. 1971), *cert. denied,* 404 U.S. 913 (1972). *See also* Swift v. Swift, 64 F.R.D. 440 (E.D.N.Y. 1973).

[16]*See* Raymond v. Raymond, 105 R.I. 380, 252 A.2d 345, 348-349 (1969).

[17]Hernandez v. Gulf Oil Corp., 21 Fed. R. Serv. 2d 1378, 1379 (E.D. Pa. 1976).

nonetheless order a painful examination or dangerous procedure if appropriate.[18] The determination of good cause involves a balancing approach: weighing the pain, danger, or intrusiveness of the examination against the need for, or usefulness of, the information to be gained. One court suggested that if a party complains about the difficulty and pain involved in an examination, that party could avoid examination by stipulating that no evidence would be introduced at the trial based upon the same or similar type of examination.[19]

Judges wish to avoid the indiscriminate use of Rule 35 examinations and are open to considering rational and deliberative factors before granting an order for one. An attorney who opposes such an examination may be successful in restricting the scope of an otherwise inevitable court order permitting it.

§4.22 PROBLEMS

Requests for Production

Draft Rule 34 requests for production of whatever documents or things you deem appropriate for the following situations. Form requests may be useful as guides in composing requests but cannot be copied. The Summit Discovery Rules place no specific limit on production requests but do require that requests be reasonable in number. Your instructor may specify limits.

1. You represent the defendants in *American Campers v. Summers*. Draft requests for production directed to the plaintiff.
2. You represent the plaintiff in *American Campers v. Summers*. Draft requests for production directed to the defendants.
3. You represent the plaintiff in *Bellow v. Norris*. Draft requests for production directed to the defendant.
4. You represent the defendant in *Bellow v. Norris*. Draft requests for production directed to the plaintiff.
5. You represent the plaintiff in *Graham v. Turkel*. Draft requests for production directed to the defendant.

[18]*See, e.g.,* Klein v. Yellow Cab Co., 7 F.R.D. 169 (N.D. Ohio 1945).
[19]*See* Klein v. Yellow Cab Co., 7 F.R.D. 169 (N.D. Ohio 1945).

6. You represent the defendant in *Graham v. Turkel.* Draft requests for production directed to the plaintiff.

7. You represent the plaintiff in *Bellow v. Norris.* Respond to the requests for production prepared by the student attorney representing the defendant by:

(a) Indicating which documents or things or other requests you would provide.

(b) Noting your objections to other requests and explaining the basis for the objections.

8. You represent the defendant in *Bellow v. Norris.* Respond to the requests for production prepared by the student attorney representing the plaintiff by:

(a) Indicating which documents or things or other requests you would provide.

(b) Noting your objections to other requests and explaining the basis for the objections.

9. You represent the plaintiff in *Graham v. Turkel.* Respond to the requests for production prepared by the student attorney representing the defendant by:

(a) Indicating which documents or things or other requests you would provide.

(b) Noting your objections to other requests and explaining the basis for the objections.

10. You represent the defendant in *Graham v. Turkel.* Respond to the requests for production prepared by the student attorney representing the plaintiff by:

(a) Indicating which documents or things or other requests you would provide.

(b) Noting your objections to other requests and explaining the basis for the objections.

11. You represent the plaintiff in *Bellow v. Norris.* Draft a request for production and inspection of the Dodge Omni owned by the defendant.

12. You represent the defendant in *Bellow v. Norris.*

(a) Through an interrogatory answer you discover that the manufacturer of the helmet (Stirling Helmets) failed to have that
model helmet certified to meet the Department of Transportation's safety standards. You want to inspect the helmet's post-
accident condition to judge its conformity with DOT
impact-resistance standards. The plaintiff's lawyer has told
you that they also wish the helmet to be inspected by an expert.
Your expert advises that the only accurate test is a procedure
that impacts the helmet into a flat anvil, which might crush and
destroy the helmet.

    (1) Draft a request for production and destructive testing
of the helmet.

    (2) Draft a proposed court order anticipating plaintiff's
objection to a destructive testing procedure.

(b) You want to substantiate the evidence that the motorcycle
headlight might not have been working while the plaintiff was
riding north on Oak Avenue. Your expert advises you that
inspection and testing of the filament in the headlight could
determine if the light was on at the time it shattered on impact.
Draft a request for production, inspection, and testing of that
part of the motorcycle.

13. Draft a combined set of interrogatories and requests for production in *American Campers v. Summers:*

(a) For the plaintiff, directed to the defendants.
(b) For the defendants, directed to the plaintiff.

Rule 45 Subpoena

14. You represent the defendants in *American Campers v. Summers.*

(a) Draft a Rule 45 subpoena directed to the Mitchell National
Bank to obtain documents from the bank.
(b) What discovery advantages do you gain if you were to make
the Mitchell National Bank a party to the lawsuit with American Campers?

Physical Examinations

15.   Draft a motion for an adverse physical examination of the opposing party in *Bellow v. Norris* by a physician of your choice:

(a)   You represent the plaintiff.
(b)   You represent the defendant.

16.   Draft a proposed order for an adverse physical examination in *Bellow v. Norris.*

(a)   You represent the plaintiff.
(b)   You represent the defendant.

17.   You believe that the opposing party in *Bellow v. Norris* is a malingerer and is claiming illusory physical injuries because of psychological disorders. Draft a motion for an adverse psychological evaluation of the opposing party.

(a)   You represent the plaintiff.
(b)   You represent the defendant.

Chapter 5
REQUESTS FOR ADMISSIONS

*Your request for admission to our law school
has been received and we are pleased to inform you. . . .*

Your First Admission

§5.1 INTRODUCTION

Few attorneys specialize in Rule 36 practice. In fact, requests for admissions are the least used of the discovery devices.[1] Though most trial lawyers have at one time or another drafted requests and responses, few devote their professional lives to a study of requests for admissions.

This chapter contains a transcript of an exclusive interview the authors obtained from the only full-time "admitter" using Rule 36 in the United States. The "admitter" consented to an anonymous interview so the identity, gender, and law school colors of this interviewee will not be revealed.

Q: What is an admitter?
A: It is someone who employs Rule 36 to obtain admissions from a litigant regarding the truth of facts, the authenticity of documents, some opinions, and some legal propositions related to the facts.

---

§5.1   [1]*See* F. Connolly, F. Holleman, & M. Kuhlman, Judicial Controls and the Civil Litigative Process: Discovery 28 (1978).

§5.2   PURPOSES

Q: Why are you an "admitter" and not a "discoverer"?

A: Because Rule 36 is not a true discovery device. It does not require a party to disclose any information, but is limited to coercing concessions from a party by way of admissions, denials, or simple statements.

Q: Can't requests for admissions be phrased like interrogatories or deposition questions?

A: Yes, but Rule 36 requests serve different purposes and are more effective in certain situations. An interrogatory answer or a deposition response may be phrased in a self-serving and equivocal manner, while responses to admission requests do not permit that flexibility. Interrogatories and depositions usually seek information, whereas admission requests seek simple commitments. Responses to other discovery devices are not conclusive proof and may be contradicted at trial, whereas responses to Rule 36 constitute conclusive evidence, unless withdrawn, and cannot be contradicted at the trial.[1]

Q: Is Rule 36 more of a trial practice rule than a discovery procedure?

A: You could say that. In fact, you just did. Rule 36 was designed in part as a device to establish some facts and legal propositions in a case without having to prove them formally at trial. Admissions expedite trials and relieve the parties of expenses involved in proving facts.

Q: What is the scope of Rule 36?

A: Rule 36 explicitly incorporates the scope of Rule 26(b): requests can seek any matter or thing relevant to the subject matter of a case and information "reasonably calculated to lead to the discovery of admissible evidence." The scope is as broad as any other discovery device.

Q: Does this scope have any limits?

A: It might. Earlier editions of Rule 36 (pre-1970 versions) equated the relevancy scope of Rule 36 with the relevancy of evidence at trial. Judicial interpretations have broadened this scope.[2] Of course, Rule 36 presupposes that some information has been discovered

§5.2   [1]4A Moore's Federal Practice ¶36.08 (2d ed. 1980).
[2]*See* 3 H. Kooman, Federal Civil Practice §36.07 (1970).

and is known. The request for admission shapes the information into statements designed primarily for evidentiary purposes for trial.

Q: Are you saying that most requests for admissions focus on matters that are relevant and admissible at trial?

A: Yes, it is fair to say that, though many requests are submitted during pre-trial stages to determine which facts and issues will be relevant and admissible at trial.

Q: What similarities, in addition to the Rule 26(b) scope, does Rule 36 have to other discovery devices?

A: There are several. Rule 36 is one major device under the discovery rules to obtain information, views, positions, and admissions from a party. The considerations involved in drafting requests for admissions are quite similar to those involved in drafting interrogatories or phrasing deposition questions that seek similar responses. Alternative responses to Rule 36 requests, including protective orders, objections, and extensions, are identical to other discovery devices.

Q: Well then, which is it — a discovery device or something else?

A: That depends. It is a discovery device when it pins an adversary to a definite position and avoids surprises. It is something else when it narrows and clarifies the disputed issues of a case and reduces the time and expense of introducing evidence at trial. Rule 36 admissions are both a discovery device and a trial expedient.

Q: Does the use of another discovery device, say an interrogatory, preclude a request for an admission on the same topic?

A: No. The discovery procedures are cumulative and complementary.

§5.3 REQUESTS

Q: Who can be required to respond to a request for admission?

A: Only a party.

Q: When can requests be served upon a party?

A: Anytime, even with the pleadings, but usually not later than 30 days before a certain trial date; otherwise a responding party will not be compelled under the rules to respond or can claim that the requests may delay the trial date.

Q: Who has to be served with Rule 36 requests?

A: The party who has to respond, naturally, and all other parties to the lawsuit.

Q: Does Rule 36 prescribe any format for, or limitations on, requests?

A: "Each matter of which an admission is requested shall be separately set forth." Period. However, at least three jurisdictions have local rules that limit the number of requests.[1]

Q: That's it? What are some examples of requests?

A: Few cases list the actual requests submitted. The 1939 *Walsh* case[2] does detail a number of early American, though still appropriate, requests:

The defendant, The Connecticut Mutual Life Insurance Company, requests the plaintiff, Mabelle Walsh, to make the following admissions for the purpose of this action only, and subject to all pertinent objections to admissibility, which may be interposed at trial:

That each of the following statements is true:

1a. In October, 1922, Samuel A. Walsh (plaintiff's deceased husband) sustained a personal injury, to-wit, a fracture of his jaw.

1b. Said fracture was on the right side of lower jaw.

1c. Said Samuel A. Walsh consulted Dr. Henry S. Dunning of New York, in October, 1922.

1d. Said Samuel A. Walsh consulted said Dr. Dunning in October, 1922, for said fracture of the jaw.

1e. Exhibit A, annexed hereto, is a correct copy of said Dr. Dunning's record of his treatments of said Samuel A. Walsh in October and November, 1922.

1f. The facts stated in Exhibit A, annexed hereto, are correct.

1g. In or about October, 1922, or thereafter, said Samuel A. Walsh informed the plaintiff that he had received an injury to the jaw. . . .

1i. Said Samuel A. Walsh informed the plaintiff that he sustained said injury to his jaw by being struck by a person's fist.

1j. Said Samuel A. Walsh informed the plaintiff that he sustained said injury to his jaw while he was intoxicated by the use of alcoholic stimulants.

§5.3 [1]*See* S.D. Cal. P. 230-1 (25 requests); D.S.C. Order Re Requests for Admission (20 requests); W.D. Tex. R. 26(d)(1) (10 requests).
[2]Walsh v. Connecticut Mut. Life Ins. Co., 26 F. Supp. 566, 569-570 (E.D.N.Y. 1939).

1k. Said Samuel A. Walsh informed the plaintiff that he sustained said injury while engaged in a fight or brawl.
1l. Said Samuel A. Walsh informed the plaintiff that he had been treated by Dr. Dunning for said injury.

Q: Is there any preferred request form?
A: Form 20 appended to the Rules of Civil Procedure provides an official illustration:

> Plaintiff *A.B.* requests defendant *C.D.* within _____ days after service of this request to make the following admissions for the purpose of this action only and subject to all pertinent objections to admissibility which may be interposed at the trial:
>
> (1) That each of the following documents, exhibited with this request, is genuine. [*Here list the documents and describe each document.*]
>
> (2) That each of the following statements is true. [*Here list the statements.*]

Q: Why does the form have a blank for the number of days allowed for the response?
A: The time could vary but usually does not. The rule allows a party a minimum of 30 days to respond (45 days if served with the summons and complaint). Consequently, the number 30 or 45 would usually appear on that blank line. Rule 29 prohibits the attorneys from extending the time, but Rule 36(a) allows a court to increase or decrease the responding time and, interestingly enough, such allowance may be made upon an *ex parte* application by the requesting party.[3] Such requests are unusual, however, and it would be even more unusual for a judge to grant an order without allowing the responding party an opportunity to oppose any such application.
Q: As a matter of strategy, when is it best to submit Rule 36 requests?
A: That depends. The use of requests early in a case may avoid the efforts and expenses of further discovery and trial preparation, but it is not possible in many cases to frame Rule 36 requests intelligently until after thorough discovery or during trial preparation.
Q: The request form seems so short; there is no legalese, surplusage or redundancy.

---

[3] 8 C. Wright & A. Miller, Federal Practice and Procedure §2257 (1970). *See also* Minn. R. Civ. P. 36.01.

A: Exactly. The form is one and one-half inches in length, shorter than many law firm letterheads.

Q: There must be more to Rule 36 requests than just that.

A: Frequently there is. Strategy and drafting tactics may require the inclusion of:

1.   A preface regarding alternative responses to admissions;
2.   Definitions describing the meaning of certain words or phrases;
3.   References to the time periods of the requests;
4.   Other appropriate instructions.

Q: How should the request be drafted?

A: With a typewriter or word processor and according to the following guidelines:

1.   Draft a precise and direct request, not an interrogatory.

Ask: Do you admit that: You said "The sky is falling" when you first saw the sky falling?

Not: Describe in detail what you said about the sky falling when you observed the sky falling from the sky.

2.   Phrase a request for which a yes or no answer provides you with the admission or denial you seek.

Ask: Do you admit that: The color of the sky you saw falling was blue?

Not: Do you admit that: The color of the sky you saw was blue, green, yellow, orange or some other color?

3.   Eliminate unnecessary adjectives, adverbs, and other characterizations.

Ask: Do you admit that: A one-foot square piece of sky hit your school desk?

Not: Do you admit that: A large, segmented portion of the upper, thinner atmosphere landed with a shattering thud upon the relatively small location you occupied in the school room?

4.   Draft requests as simple, singular requests in separately-numbered paragraphs.

Do not ask: Do you admit that: The sky that fell from the sky, which you observed fall on August 20, 1980, hit the top of your head on

August 21, 1980, causing you hospital emergency-room expenses of three bushels of corn?

Rather ask: Do you admit that: (1) you saw a piece of the sky fall on August 20, 1978? (2) a piece of the sky fell on August 21, 1978, and hit the top of your head? (3) you were treated at the Roost Hospital Emergency Room on August 21, 1978? (4) you paid a Roost Hospital bill of three bushels of corn on August 21, 1978?

5. Avoid incorporations by reference.[4] Compose each request as a complete admission by itself.

Do not ask: Do you admit: Paragraph 3 of the cross-complaint?

Rather, ask: Do you admit: Plaintiff hit Robert Fall on his jaw with her fist on June 1?

Some complex cases involving wholesale information and documents may require the use of admissions incorporating some of the information or documents by reference. If so, indicate what is incorporated by reference as precisely as possible. Incorporation by reference is especially practical if the documents, such as attachments to the pleadings or numbered deposition exhibits, are formally identified.

Q: Is there any limit to the requests that can be served?

A: There is no numerical limit on the number of requests or the number of sets of requests, but requests cannot be harassing, unduly burdensome, or excessive in number. The Federal Advisory Committee recognizes that "requests to admit may be so voluminous and so framed that the answering party [will find] the task of identifying what is in dispute and what is not unduly burdensome," and the committee suggests that the responding party do something in these situations.[5]

Q: Like what?

A: Like seeking a protective order under Rule 26(c).

---

[4]The court in SEC v. Micro-Moisture Controls Inc. articulated a rationale: "Such incorporation by reference is improper since it unjustly casts upon the defendants the burden of determining at their peril what portions of the incorporated material contain relevant matters of fact which must be either admitted or denied." 21 F.R.D. 164, 166 (S.D.N.Y. 1957).

[5]Fed. R. Civ. P. 36(a), Notes of Advisory Comm. — 1970 Amendments.

§5.4 OPINIONS AND CONCLUSIONS

Q: You mentioned earlier that requests may seek factual opinions and legal conclusions. Can you explain what you meant?

A: Of course. Before 1970 there was some doubt whether admission requests could seek responses to opinions and conclusions. But Rule 36(a) now provides that requests may "relate to statements or opinions of fact or the application of law to fact." It is now clear that one party can demand that another party respond to factual statements, opinions, and conclusions and to legal statements, opinions, and conclusions. The Federal Advisory Committee Notes supply an explanation and illustration:

> [T]he subdivision provides that a request may be made to admit any matters within the scope of Rule 26(b) that relate to statements or opinions of fact or of the application of law to fact. It thereby eliminates the requirement that the matters be "of fact." This change resolves conflicts in the court decisions as to whether a request to admit matters of "opinion" and matters involving "mixed law and fact" is proper under the rule. . . .
>
> Not only is it difficult as a practical matter to separate 'fact' from "opinion," . . . but an admission of a matter of opinion may facilitate proof or narrow the issues or both. An admission of a matter involving the application of law to fact may, in a given case, even more clearly narrow the issues. For example, an admission that an employee acted in the scope of his employment may remove a major issue from the trial. In *McSparran v. Hanigan,* plaintiff admitted that "the premises on which said accident occurred, were occupied under the control" of one of the defendants.[1] This admission, involving law as well as fact, removed one of the issues from the lawsuit and thereby reduced the proof required at trial. The amended provision does not authorize requests for admissions of law unrelated to the facts of the case.[2]

Q: Can you provide us with examples of comparative fact, opinion, and concluding requests?

A: A factual request would be: "Do you admit that: A piece of the sky, which fell on August 21, 1980, hit your head?" An opinion or conclusion would be: "Do you admit that: The individual who first

§5.4 [1]225 F. Supp. 628, 636 (E.D. Pa. 1963).
[2]Fed. R. Civ. P. 36(a), Notes of Advisory Comm. — 1970 Amendments.

advised you that the sky was falling on August 21, 1980, appeared to be upset?" An application of law to fact response would be: "Do you admit that: The corporation who manufactured the sky was licensed to do business in Minnesota?"

Q: Did the sky fall at all that day?

A: No, but law-school classes began.

§5.5 DOCUMENTS

Q: You also mentioned earlier that requests may be made regarding documents. Can you explain further?

A: The rule specifically allows requests regarding the genuineness of documents, and it requires that copies of documents be served with the request, unless the documents have been otherwise made available or furnished to the responding party. However, many other sorts of admission requests can be made concerning documents: their authenticity, their status as originals or copies, the identity of the author who drafted them, or any Rule 26 relevant matter.

Q: Must the original of the document be attached to a request?

A: No, a copy will suffice. The responding party seldom wants to admit something about a copy without first having reviewed the original. But the responding party who has the original or who copied the original during a Rule 34 inspection can conveniently compare the Rule 36 copy with the original copy.

Q: What if the Rule 36 request seeks the admission of a document unfamiliar to the respondent?

A: Your "what if" should seldom occur, because a request usually seeks the admission of some familiar matter. Should it happen, however, the respondent will either deny the sought-for admission because of the lack of familiarity or demand that the requesting party make the original available for review.

Q: How detailed should a Rule 36 document description be?

A: The description need only be detailed enough to identify the document sufficiently for the respondent. A description such as "Exhibit 1 is a copy of the original August 1, 1980, Employment Agreement between the plaintiff and defendant" is more than sufficient to apprise the respondent of the identity of an attached exhibit.[1] In many cases, the circumstances make it clear that the attached is a copy of an original and such a notation may not be necessary.

Q: When would a more detailed description be necessary?

A: Not often. A more detailed description might be necessary if the respondent did not have the original access to the document.

Q: Does Rule 36 permit the admission of other things besides documents?

A: Absolutely. The rule specifically allows a request to be submitted regarding the truth of "any matter." That includes statements and documents, tangible things and property, and anything admissible at trial.

Q: Does this last "anything" include demonstrative trial exhibits, like a diagram or other visual aid, as well as real evidence?

A: Yes. Anything means any thing.

§5.6 RESPONSES

Q: What about the party receiving the requests; what must he, she, or it do?

A: Respond in one or more ways appropriate to the particular requests.

Q: Does the party have any options in responding to requests?

A: Yes, some seven alternatives.

Q: Seven?

A: Count them. A responding party may:

1. Do nothing,
2. Admit;
3. Deny;
4. Qualify the answer;
5. Object to the request;
6. Move for a protective order; or
7. Request or seek an extension of time.

§5.5 [1]4A Moore's Federal Practice ¶36.03[4] (2d ed. 1980).

A party must respond to each individual request by specifying which of these alternative responses apply.

Q: Can a party respond in the alternative to a singular request?

A: No.[1] A party must choose one and only one of the seven responses for each request and cannot respond alternatively as in a pleading.

Q: What is the proper form for a response?

A: The response should be a single writing, listing the various requests, followed by the corresponding responses in order, and signed by the party or his or her attorney.

Q: Upon whom must the response be served?

A: All parties to the action.

Q: What is the effect of doing nothing?

A: Rule 36 is self-executing and quite clear: if you say nothing and send nothing, you have admitted the requests.

Q: What is a timely response?

A: One that is made in time: 45 days if the admission requests are served with the summons and complaint. Otherwise, 30 days, unless a court orders a different time.

Q: How strictly do courts enforce these time limits?

A: That depends in part upon the reaction of the opposition. If the opposing party accepts a late response, the response is effective. If the opposing party refuses to accept the late response, the court, in its discretion, determines whether to waive the rule's automatic deadline effect. The court's discretion turns on the degree of prejudice suffered by the party relying upon the automatic-effect rule.[2] One court has refused to permit a late reply when the discovering party relied upon the rule and dismissed some witnesses whose relocation would seriously inconvenience and prejudice that party.[3]

Q: When else does no response or a late response not result in an admission?

A: An admission seeking something beyond the scope of Rules 26 or 36 will probably be ineffective. For example, a request seeking an admission of a law not applicable to the facts exceeds the scope of Rule 36, so failure to respond to such a request does not consti-

---

§5.6 [1]Havenfield Corp. v. H. & R. Block, Inc., 67 F.R.D. 93, 97 (W.D. Mo. 1973).
[2]Pleasant Hill Bank v. United States, 60 F.R.D. 1, 3 (W.D. Mo. 1973).
[3]Brennan v. Varrasso Bros., Inc., 17 Fed. R. Serv. 2d 718, 718 (D. Mass. 1973).

tute an automatic admission.[4] However, one court did establish jurisdiction by an unanswered admission.[5]

Q: What should a responding party do if 30 days have passed and no response has been submitted to requests for admissions?

A: File responses and argue that the late responses constitute "amendments,"[6] or seek a court order, arguing that the delinquent responses have not prejudiced the opposition.

Q: What if a party properly serves a set of admissions through the mail and the opposing party never receives them?

A: You should prepare law-school final exams. A party who has not in fact received the requests must persuade a judge of that fact. The persuaded judge would most correctly conclude that the request was never served and thus there has been no failure to respond. This type of reasoning is called common sense.

Q: What if a party goes into hiding to avoid admitting something?

A. You must have prepared law-school final exam questions. Interestingly, a court considered such a situation, found that the respondent had not taken adequate steps to inform the other party of its address, reasoned that the non-receipt excuse may encourage parties to hide rather than respond, and held that the failure to respond constituted an admission even though the respondent claimed it never received the requests.[7]

Q: How does one go about deciding whether to admit, deny, or qualify a response?

A: A party must respond to the request in a truthful, specific, straightforward, and unconditional manner.[8] Honesty determines how to respond.

Q: How does a party admit something?

A: By responding yes or in some other specific affirmative or appropriate fashion.

Q. On what does a party base an admission?

A: On whatever knowledge and information has been obtained during discovery.

Q: What if a party has no personal knowledge of a fact but only information obtained from a third person?

[4]Williams v. Krieger, 61 F.R.D. 142, 144 (S.D.N.Y. 1973).
[5]Oroco Marine, Inc. v. National Marine Service, Inc., 71 F.R.D. 220 (S.D. Tex. 1976).
[6]United States v. Cannon, 363 F. Supp. 1045, 1049 (D. Del. 1973).
[7]Freed v. Plastic Packaging Materials, Inc., 66 F.R.D. 550, 552 (E.D. Pa. 1975).
[8]See Dulansky v. Iowa-Illinois Gas & Elec. Co., 92 F. Supp. 118, 124 (S.D. Iowa 1950).

A: If the party believes the information to be accurate, the party must admit it, regardless of the source of the information.[9]

Q: What if a party has some doubt about the information?

A: If a party has a reasonable doubt, the party need not admit the fact.[10] For example, supposing a witness to an accident told a party that she thought the traffic light was red, a party need not admit requests querying whether the light was red, if that party has a reasonable doubt about the accuracy of the statement or the credibility of that witness.

Q: The decision to admit a fact provided by a witness may depend, then, on the assessment a party makes of that witness's credibility?

A: Sure. Requests for admission may delve into the attorney's mental impressions of a witness made during investigation and so they need not be admitted if they fall under the protections provided such lawyer's mental process under Rule 26.[11]

§5.7 DENIALS

Q: Under what circumstances can a party deny something?

A: The rule states that a denial must be specific about what is being denied and must "fairly meet the substance of the requested admission." This means that a party must review and ask: "Can I specifically, in good faith, honestly, and unconditionally deny all or part of this request?" The rule also requires a party to specify which part of a request is true and which untrue.

Q: What must the denial deny?

A: The truth of the matter.

Q: How specific must the denial be?

A: An absolute denial, that is, the use of the word *denied,* unqualified by any other statement, constitutes a sufficient denial.[1] Parties who state that they "refuse" to admit something have not properly de-

---

[9]*See* Finman, The Request for Admissions in Federal Civil Procedure, 71 Yale L.J. 371, 406 (1962).

[10]*See* Shapiro, Some Problems of Discovery in an Adversary System, 63 Minn. L. Rev. 1055, 1087 (1979).

[11]These provisions are discussed in §1.7.3 of this text.

§5.7 [1]*See generally* Annot., 36 A.L.R.2d 1192 (1954).

nied the request.[2] And parties who deny the "accuracy" of a request have likewise not properly denied a statement.[3]

Q: Can a party admit and deny something at the same time?

A: Your question presupposes the impossible. So the answer is no, but that does not mean lawyers have not tried. For example, one request for admission asked the plaintiff to admit that the plaintiff had released the defendant's corporation from responsibility "for all indebtedness." The response was "Admitted, except that it is denied that the said corporation was released of all indebtedness."[4]

Q: What did the court do?

A: It held, apparently with a straight face, that the reply constituted an admission.

Q: Is a denial based upon information and belief effective?

A: That depends on how the denial is phrased. Some authorities construe Rule 36 to require an explanation of the sources for the information and belief for it to be an effective denial.[5] An information-and-belief denial without some explanatory sources may well be ineffective.

§5.8   QUALIFYING RESPONSES

Q: What about qualifying responses?

A: A party has to respond in whatever direction the facts, opinions, and conclusions lead. The rule requires a party to "set forth in detail the reasons why the answering party cannot truthfully admit or deny the matter." A general statement that does not include detailed reasons is insufficient.[1]

Q: Can a party attempt to be evasive or to avoid direct responses by using qualifying answers?

---

[2]Fuhr v. Newfoundland-St. Lawrence Shipping Ltd., Panama, 24 F.R.D. 9, 13 (S.D.N.Y. 1959).

[3]Southern Ry. Co. v. Crosby, 201 F.2d 878, 880 (4th Cir. 1953).

[4]Riordan v. Ferguson, 147 F.2d 983, 986 n.1 (2d Cir. 1945).

[5]*See* 23 Am. Jur. 2d, Depositions and Discovery §304 (1965).

§5.8   [1]Villarosa v. Massachusetts Trustees of Eastern Gas & Fuel Assocs., 39 F.R.D. 337, 338-339 (E.D. Pa. 1966). Stating that defendant can "neither admit nor deny the truthfulness of the statements" is insufficient as a response.

A: Absolutely not. The courts do not countenance such conduct.[2] Someone once said, very perceptively, "It is the genius of Rule 36 that responses that do not advance the cause of clarifying and simplifying the issues must be explained."[3]

Q: Are there any limits to qualifying responses?

A: Yes. The rule provides that "an answering party may not give lack of information or knowledge as a reason for failure to admit or deny unless he states that he has made reasonable inquiry and that the information known or readily obtainable by him is insufficient to enable him to admit or deny."

Q: What is a reasonable inquiry?

A: That usually depends upon the nature of the request and the extent of the potential inquiry. The Federal Advisory Committee Notes explain that the rule imposes upon the responding party a "reasonable burden" to obtain the information. The notes say that the extent of such investigation should mimic the investigation necessary to the preparation of a case or should include an investigation of all information "close enough at hand to be 'readily obtainable.' "[4] Cases have held that a party must make a reasonable effort to discover a date, short of undue hardship[5] or of any substantial reason to the contrary.[6]

Q: That does not seem adequately to define the limits of what is a reasonable inquiry.

A: Little in life is certain. The guidelines all reduce to one standard: what inquiry would a reasonable attorney advise his or her client to make?

Q: There are such things as "reasonable attorneys"?

A: As I said, little in life is certain.

Q: Are there any other ways a party can qualify a response?

A: The rule allows a party to plead an inability to respond fully, by claiming that the requested admission involves a contested issue in the case: "A party who considers that the matter of which an admission has been requested presents a genuine issue for trial may not, on that ground alone, object to the request; he may, subject to the

---

[2]Dulansky v. Iowa-Illinois Gas & Elec. Co., 92 F. Supp. 118, 124 (S.D. Iowa 1950).

[3]J. Underwood, A Guide to Federal Discovery Rules 164 (1979).

[4]Fed. R. Civ. P. 36(a), Notes of Advisory Comm. — 1970 Amendments.

[5]E.H. Tate Co. v. Jiffy Enterprises, Inc., 16 F.R.D. 571, 574 (E.D. Pa. 1954).

[6]*See* Lumpkin v. Meskill, 64 F.R.D. 673, 678 (D. Conn. 1974).

provisions of Rule 37(c), deny the matter or set forth reasons why he cannot admit or deny it."

Q: Are there more rules after 36? What does Rule 37(c) do?

A: That rule concerns the expenses that a party who fails to make an admission may have to bear if that party has no good reason for declining to admit.

Q: If a request contains correct information except for a date or a last name, can a party deny the statement, or must the answer be qualified?

A: The general rule and the intent of Rule 36 are to admit any request that is substantially correct by admitting what is correct and denying the part that is incorrect. However, in some requests, one piece of information renders the entire request deniable in good faith. It can often be a difficult and close decision.

Q: Can a party ever add more information to a response than the request seeks?

A: It is an appropriate tactic for an attorney to include helpful information in some responses. The legitimacy of the tactic depends on the precise request and response, but some requests may require a qualified response that includes some narrative information. Usually such a tactic can be used if a request has not been carefully and precisely drafted, leaving room for an interpretive or narrative response.

§5.9 OBJECTIONS

Q: What are proper objections to a request?

A: Any objection that pinpoints the defects of a request is proper. The types of objections appropriate to requests for admission are the same types applicable to interrogatories and requests for production.[1] Whatever objection is interposed, specific reasons explaining the grounds must be included. Objections based on inaccurate, immaterial, or incompetent grounds may be insufficient.[2]

---

§5.9 [1]*See* 4A Moore's Federal Practice ¶36.06 (2d ed. 1980); and §§3.5 and 4.12 above.

[2]*See* United States v. Schine Chain Theatres, Inc., 4 F.R.D. 109, 112 (W.D.N.Y. 1944).

Q: Are some objections to requests used more than others?

A: It may be that objections based upon Rule 26(b) irrelevancy and upon claims of privilege are more common than others, but it is difficult to estimate.

Q: You mentioned earlier that Rule 26(a) determines the scope of Rule 36 requests. What effect does an irrelevancy objection based upon the more restrictive Federal Rule of Evidence 401 have upon a request?

A: It seems that it should have no effect, but it might. The remnants of previous decisions and past rules affect current practice. Some practitioners, judges, and commentators continue to recognize as a legitimate objection a response that the request seeks an admission useful only for informational purposes and not for trial purposes.[3]

Q: But this practice runs counter to the clear intent of Rules 26 and 36.

A: Yes and no. The split personality of Rule 36 supports such practice. Remember it is both a discovery device and a trial expedient.

Q: Is an objection based upon privilege defined by the discovery rules?

A: No. The law of evidence exclusively determines the propriety of a privilege-based objection to a request. A legitimate privilege objection can arise in a number of settings. My good friend, the "discoverer," could discuss that subject for hours on end.

Q: What about an objection based on "defective drafting"?

A: That objection may be more properly phrased as "vague" or "ambiguous" or "compound" or with some other word specifying the nature of the defect. These may also be fairly common objections.

Q: What about an objection based on a ground sufficient to obtain a protective order, like a confidential trade secret?

A: It is conceivable and realistic.[4] Consider its advantage: such an objection relieves you of the need to seek a Rule 26 protective order and places the burden on the opposition to obtain a Rule 37 order. The objection must contain the specific grounds on which it is based.

Q: Are there any improper objections that would be inappropriate responses?

A: Yes. Rule 36 has eliminated a number of formerly valid objec-

---

[3]4A Moore's Federal Practice ¶36.04[2] (2d ed. 1980).
[4]K. Sinclair, Federal Civil Practice 739 (1980).

tions, including: the request presents an issue for trial; the request includes disputable matter; the request seeks a factual opinion or a mixed question of law and fact. Case law also has declared a number of objections improper, including: the requesting party already knows the answer,[5] or the request relates to matters on which the requesting party has the burden of proof.[6]

Q: I recall reading about an objection that the request seeks an admission on a matter "in dispute."

A: You have an excellent memory — for history. That old objection is no longer recognized. Remember, "The very purpose of the request is to ascertain [what] . . . is a genuine issue for trial."[7] Matters in dispute are usually fair game for the requesting party.

§5.10 RESPONSE STRATEGIES

Q: What strategies need to be considered in responding to requests?

A: An attorney must consider the impact of the responses upon the case. The more harmful the impact an admission may have upon a case, the more scrutiny an attorney should devote to uncovering objections or drafting good-faith qualifying answers or denials. This scrutiny must also weigh the risk that the responding party may challenge the sufficiency of a response that is not an admission. A non-admission may increase costs, expenses, and time disproportionately to its impact on a case. Moreover, admissions usually foreclose an area to discovery, whereas denials may prompt the other attorney to use discovery devices to ferret out information.

Q: Why may discovery be precluded?

A: An admission constitutes proof of a matter and eliminates any need for discoverable information to support or rebut the admission — any subsequent request is irrelevant.

Q: How does a party obtain more time to respond to requests?

A: By court order. Rule 29 makes it clear that "stipulations extending the time provided in Rule . . . 36 may be made only with the

---

[5]Electric Furnace Co. v. Fire Assn. of Philadelphia, 9 F.R.D. 741, 743 (N.D. Ohio 1949).

[6]Adventures in Good Eating, Inc. v. Best Places to Eat, Inc., 131 F.2d 809, 812 (7th Cir. 1942) (burp).

[7]Fed. R. Civ. P. 36(a), Notes of Advisory Comm. — 1970 Amendments.

approval of the court." You can't get much clearer than that. However, some attorneys overlook the technical enforcement of this rule and accept a response after more than 30 days.

Q: What is the effect of an untimely response served upon the requesting party?

A: Requests to which response is not timely become admitted. However, a court has the power to convert an untimely response into a timely response by retroactively extending the time limit.[1] Rule 36 also allows untimely answers as "amendments" to admissions: Rule 36(b) allows a party to "withdraw" admissions and "amend" answers. A party who files an untimely response could seek to withdraw the admissions and substitute the late responses as amendments. The rule allows this unless it adversely affects the presentation of a case or otherwise prejudices the requesting party.[2]

Q: How does a requesting party question the legitimacy of an objection?

A: Rule 36 allows a requesting party to dispute an objection through a motion and court hearing. If the court determines that the objection is justified, it will stand. If not, the court must order an answer.

Q: Who has the burden of showing the validity of the objection?

A: The objecting party.[3] That makes sense. If the objection does not make sense, the court may order the objecting party to pay cents to the requesting party who had to seek the hearing.

§5.11 CHALLENGING RESPONSES

Q: How does the requesting party challenge the sufficiency of a response?

A: Rule 36 allows a requesting party to challenge the sufficiency of any response through a motion and court hearing. If the court determines that a response did not comply with Rule 36, the court has three options: (1) to declare the request admitted,[1] (2) to order

---

§5.10 [1]French v. United States, 416 F.2d 1149, 1152 (9th Cir. 1968).
[2]Pleasant Hill Bank v. United States, 60 F.R.D. 1, 3 (W.D. Mo. 1973).
[3]*See* K. Sinclair, Federal Civil Practice 741 (1980).
    §5.11 [1]Weva Oil Corp. v. Belco Petroleum Corp., 68 F.R.D. 663 (N.D.W. Va. 1975); Jackson v. Riley Stoker Corp., 57 F.R.D.120 (E.D. Pa. 1972); United States v. Heichman, 45 F.R.D. 122 (N.D. Ill. 1968).

an amended answer,[2] or (3) to postpone the "final disposition" of the request until a pretrial conference.

Q: When would a court choose the third alternative?

A: Most likely when the request either seeks a factual response that requires detailed investigation or seeks a mixed question of law and fact. The judge may recognize that the responding party simply needs more time to formulate a response.

Q: Then what is the effect of an improper response to a request?

A: A non-response to a request automatically becomes an admission after the appropriate time passes. An improper response must be challenged by the requesting party and may lead to an admission if the judge so orders.

Q: Delaying a decision may cause a problem in some cases?

A: Yes. Not to decide is to decide.[3] The Advisory Committee Notes explain that it is usually more effective and fair to decide the fate of a response within a reasonable time before trial. This avoids an untimely or an unfair surprise at trial for one of the parties.

Q: What discovery device can be employed to supplement requests for admissions?

A: Any and all. For instance, an attorney can submit interrogatories to the responding party asking that the party explain the "whys" of or facts supporting the denial or qualification of a response.

§5.12   CHANGING ADMISSIONS

Q: What if the responding party wants to retract or change an admission? Can that be done?

A: Yes, Rule 36 permits a party to seek a court order allowing the withdrawal of the previous admission and substitution of an amended response.

Q: What factors does the court consider in permitting withdrawals or amendments?

A: The rule spells out the considerations the court must employ:

---

[2]Alexander v. Rizzo, 52 F.R.D. 235, 236 (E.D. Pa. 1971).
[3]Harvey Cox Poster. College Placement Office. Circa 1967.

Subject to the provisions of Rule 16 governing amendment of a pre-trial order, the court may permit withdrawal or amendment when the presentation of the merits of the action will be subserved thereby and the party who obtained the admission fails to satisfy the court that withdrawal or amendment will prejudice him in maintaining his action or defense on the merits.

Q: What reasons must a respondent advance to persuade a court that a case will be "subserved thereby"?

A: One reason might be that the admission was a genuine mistake, should not have been made, and distorts the merits. Another reason might be that the circumstances have changed, so the admission is no longer true.[1]

Q: How do requesting parties persuade a court that a withdrawal or amendment will "prejudice" a case?

A: By indicating that they relied upon the admission to their detriment. They may be able to show that some investigation was deferred, some discovery curtailed, or some bit of evidence deteriorated as a result of reliance on the admission.

Q: How can the requesting party counter these prejudice claims?

A: With great difficulty. A factor significantly influencing the degree of prejudice is the timing of the request for the withdrawal or amendment. The sooner the change is sought after submission of the admissions, the more likely the court will grant it. The closer in time to trial the change is sought, the more likely the court will deny it.

Q: Does this provision of the rule include amendments to other responses besides admissions, like denials, objections, or qualifications?

A: No. Why would a responding party want to amend a favorable response like a denial or an objection? A party might want to amend a qualification, but the provision specifically limits the procedure to "admissions." Only the portion of a qualified response that was an admission would be included within the provisions.

Q: How do the provisions of Rule 26(e) on supplementation of responses affect amendments to admission responses?

A: A party has an obligation under Rule 26(e) to supplement responses to admission. Those provisions do not square with the Rule 36 provisions regarding amendments. Rule 26 requires a party uni-

§5.12   [1]J. Underwood, A Guide to Federal Discovery Rules 156 (1979).

laterally to amend an admission. A reconciling interpretation of the two rules would seem to be that a party has a duty to supplement admissions under Rule 26, but that the supplementation cannot be done unilaterally. It requires a court order under Rule 36.[2]

§5.13 EFFECTS OF ADMISSIONS

Q: What is the effect of an admission?

A: Rule 36(b) declares admissions to be conclusive proof of the matter asserted for purposes of the pending action only, unless a court allows a withdrawal or an amendment. The Federal Advisory Committee explains that an admission has the same effect as a pleading admission or as a stipulation of facts executed by the attorneys.[1] The factfinder (the judge or jury) must accept the admissions as accurate and proven and cannot disbelieve them. The party that made the admissions cannot contradict or rebut the admissions at trial.

Q: Are admissions automatically admissible at the trial?

A: Admissions have a ticket for the trial. A party need only offer them to the court.

Q: Can another party object to their being offered?

A: Yes. Admissions may not have a reserved ticket for the trial. They remain subject to any appropriate evidentiary objections brought by any party. For example, even though a party has admitted a request, the court could sustain that party's irrelevancy objection to that request and thereby exclude an admission from the trial.

Q: What is the effect of an admission that has been withdrawn and amended?

A: The courts have apparently not resolved the question. A requesting party could introduce a withdrawn admission as a prior inconsistent statement at the trial and the responding party could explain or rebut it.[2]

Q: Does a denial of an admission have any effect at trial?

A: Yes. A denial can be used for impeachment purposes or to pre-

---

[2] 8 C. Wright & A. Miller, Federal Practice and Procedure §2264 (1970).
§5.13 [1] 4A Moore's Federal Practice ¶36.08 (2d ed. 1980).
[2] 8 C. Wright & A. Miller, Federal Practice and Procedure §2264 (1970).

clude the denying party from introducing contrary evidence. An unjustified denial, which causes the requesting party to prove the matter at trial, results in the responding party's paying for the costs of proof.[3]

Q: What are the other sanctions applicable to Rule 36?

A: I defer to my cousin, the "enforcer," who wrote the following chapter.

§5.14 PROBLEMS

Draft a variety of Rule 36 requests for admissions in the following problems, including statements involving facts, opinion, genuineness of documents, and application of law to fact. Form requests may be useful as guides in composing requests but may not be copied. The Summit Discovery Rules place no limit on the specific number of requests but do require the requests to be reasonable in number. Your instructor may specify limits.

1. You represent the plaintiff in *American Campers v. Summers.* Draft requests for admissions directed to the defendants.

2. You represent the defendants in *American Campers v. Summers.* Draft requests for admissions directed to the plaintiff.

3. You represent the plaintiff in *Bellow v. Norris.* Draft requests for admissions directed to the defendant.

4. You represent the defendant in *Bellow v. Norris.* Draft requests for admissions directed to the plaintiff.

5. You represent the plaintiff in *Graham v. Turkel.* Draft requests for admissions directed to the defendant.

6. You represent the defendant in *Graham v. Turkel.* Draft requests for admissions directed to the plaintiff.

7. You represent the plaintiff in *American Campers v. Summers.* The defendants have submitted the following requests for admissions to you. Draft responses to these requests.

---

[3]Fed. R. Civ. P. 37(c). *See* Popeil Bros., Inc. v. Schick Elec., Inc., 516 F.2d 772, 777 (7th Cir. 1975); Leas v. General Motors Corp., 50 F.R.D. 366, 368 (E.D. Wis. 1970).

Do you admit that each of the following statements is true?

(a) Carol Sexton was an agent and employee of Plaintiff and was at all times acting within the scope of her employment in dealing with Defendants on May 25 and 26, 19XX.

(b) Plaintiff provided Defendants with a "Limited Warranty," an exact copy of which appears as Exhibit A in the Answer.

(c) Between June 11 and June 22, Plaintiff did not check nor test the gas mileage of the Voyageur Camper.

(d) On June 25, 19XX, Susan Summers telephoned and talked to Tom Arnold.

(e) The Voyageur Motor Home was in the possession of Plaintiff for repairs from July 1 through July 8.

(f) The law of the State of Summit permits Defendants to revoke acceptance in this case if defects in Voyageur Motor Home substantially impair its value to Defendants.

8. You represent the defendants in *American Campers v. Summers*. The plaintiff has submitted the following requests for admissions to you. Draft responses to these requests.

Do you admit that each of the following statements is true?

(a) Susan and John Summers failed to pay the July 24, 19XX installment of $229.02.

(b) Susan and John Summers signed a Retail Installment Contract, an exact copy of which appears as Exhibit A in the Complaint.

(c) Susan and John Summers accepted the Voyageur Camper on May 26, 19XX.

(d) Susan and John Summers drove and used the Voyageur Camper from May 28 to July 30, 19XX.

(e) The failure to pay the July 24, 19XX, installment payment of $229.02 constituted a default of the retail installment contract.

(f) Paragraph 4 of the Retail Installment Contract permits American Campers to accelerate all payments if a default occurs.

9. You represent the plaintiff in *Bellow v. Norris*. Respond to the requests for admissions prepared by the student attorney representing the defendant.

10. You represent the defendant in *Bellow v. Norris*. Respond to the

requests for admissions prepared by the student attorney representing the plaintiff.

11. You represent the plaintiff in *Graham v. Turkel.* Respond to the requests for admissions prepared by the student attorney representing the defendant.

12. You represent the defendant in *Graham v. Turkel.* Respond to the requests for admissions prepared by the student attorney representing the plaintiff.

Chapter 6
ENFORCEMENT OF DISCOVERY RIGHTS

> *I can't get no satisfaction.*
> *I can't get no satisfaction!*
> *Cause I try and I try . . .*
> *I can't get no, I can't get no satisfaction, no satisfaction.*
>   Mick Jagger and Keith Richard

§6.1 INTRODUCTION

Discovery is designed to take place primarily with satisfaction and without court involvement. Interrogatories, depositions, document production, and requests for admissions are all normally used without a judge's ever ordering or barring them. Of course, medical examinations are available only after a showing of need to the court, but they are routinely ordered when appropriate.

Discovery does not always follow this design. Legitimate attempts to discover information may be met not with satisfactory responses, but rather with silence, objections, insults, threats, or worse. Rule 37 provides a judicial remedy; other devices provide informal approaches to obtain information from your opponent. You can increase your chances of discovery success by exhausting informal methods of enforcing your discovery rights. Local rules or practice may even require you to employ these informal cooperative devices before seeking judicial relief.

§6.2 INFORMAL ENFORCEMENT

If your initial discovery request is ignored, receives inadequate response, or is met by objection, a Rule 37 motion is frequently not the best first step. A telephone call or a letter reminding opposing counsel of the discovery obligation and asking for a definite response will occasionally bring an adequate response, especially if noncompliance is due to simple inadvertence by opposing counsel. A letter is probably preferable to a telephone call since it documents the request for voluntary compliance should a motion to compel discovery become necessary. Even if noncompliance is not inadvertent, however, such a letter can bring results. And if the letter is met only with objections or inadequate response, you are in a better position to obtain judicial assistance because your opponent will have told you the basis for the non-response. If the letter does not bring a response, your case for a court order compelling discovery or penalizing your opponent for noncompliance is strengthened.

Negotiation is another important tool for enforcing your discovery rights. Documenting your negotiation offers also bolsters your position if you should have to seek an order from a judge. If you can demonstrate that, despite your willingness to accommodate the reasonable objections of your opponent, discovery has still not been forthcoming, a court will be more inclined to order discovery and to award you the expenses incurred in having to seek the order. For example, demands for interrogatory answers and production of documents may be objected to on the grounds that the information sought constitutes trade secrets and other confidential information. Rule 26(c)(7) specifically provides that this is a proper subject for a protective order to limit the use of this information. Offering to stipulate to only limited use may obviate having to bring a motion to achieve the same result. The broad provisions of Rule 29 would support stipulations to overcome objections to discovery even if there is no specific ground for objecting or for obtaining a protective order.

In addition to being informal and efficient, an attempt to resolve discovery disputes between counsel may be required by local court rule. Many federal district courts have adopted local rules that require counsel to meet and confer in an attempt to resolve a discovery dispute without the necessity of court involvement. These "meet and confer" rules generally require an attorney to discuss the discovery dispute with opposing counsel and to certify to the court that such a conference has been held prior to the filing of any motion to compel discovery. Obviously, if you are practicing in a district that requires such a conference, it is a very good idea to hold one. Although the Federal Rules of Civil Procedure do not specifically require a meeting with opposing counsel prior to a motion to compel discovery, the 1980 amendments to the rules do require such a meeting before an attorney may request a discovery conference. This recent amendment reflects the increasing judicial preference for informal resolution of discovery disputes.

Throughout attempts to resolve discovery disputes informally, remember the ultimate goal: obtaining the discovery to which you are entitled. It is frequently possible to use the informal procedures to set up the discovery motion and to place your case in a most favorable light.

§6.3 THE DISCOVERY CONFERENCE

The discovery conference envisioned in Rule 26(f) is a useful tool to facilitate the resolution of discovery disputes. This rule has been declared the most important recent amendment to the discovery rules.[1] The 1980 amendments to the federal discovery rules provide that the court may call a discovery conference at any time. The rule gives no guidance as to what is a "reasonable effort," prior to moving for a discovery conference, to resolve the discovery dispute with opposing counsel. At a minimum, it would appear that a proposal to resolve the dispute be made to opposing counsel and some discussion or correspondence be held on that proposal.

Just as the procedures suggested by the Manual for Complex Litigation may provide a useful framework for organizing discovery in a civil action,[2] so the Rule 26(f) discovery conference may provide a valuable tool to an attorney desiring to move forward with discovery in an action. A party faced with repeated objections to discovery may have numerous issues resolved in one conference. The Advisory Committee makes it clear that the discovery conference is intended to be used in

§6.3 [1]*See* McKinistry, Civil Discovery Reform, 14 Forum 790 (1979).
[2]*See* Manual for Complex Litigation with Amendments to June, 1977 (1978).

relatively few cases, not when a single dispute exists. It is available, however, for use when several problems exist. The discovery conference envisioned by Rule 26(f) is a new device; it is not a pretrial conference, like those held under Rule 16. It is a device that may provide valuable assistance in a case involving difficult discovery problems. Presumably judges will welcome its use in such cases, and it will serve its intended purpose of resolving discovery disputes quickly and inexpensively.

§6.4   FORMAL ENFORCEMENT

Rule 37 provides methods for obtaining judicial assistance in enforcing discovery rights. It is also the *exclusive* source of authority under the rules for the imposition of discovery sanctions.[1] The rule foresees a two-step process: first, an order compelling discovery must be obtained, if needed, under Rule 37(a); then sanctions may be imposed if the order is not obeyed. This two-step process is not required in every instance (what is?), but it is the usual procedure.

§6.4.1   The Order Compelling Discovery

A court order is a condition precedent[2] to imposing sanctions.[3] An order compelling discovery is required only in those types of discovery normally made without any order. For example, a second order for a physical examination is not required before sanctions can be imposed for failure to comply with an initial Rule 35 order; Rule 37(b)(2) allows

---

§6.4 [1]Courts occasionally rely on Rule 41, governing dismissals, or on some consideration of "inherent power," in imposing discovery sanctions. The United States Supreme Court has rejected this practice, stating that use of these devices "can only obscure analysis of the problem before us." Societe Internationale Pour Participations Industrielles et Commerciales, S.A. v. Rogers, 357 U.S. 197, 207 (1958). The Supreme Court relied heavily upon the analysis of this problem by Professor Rosenberg. *See* Rosenberg, Sanctions to Effectuate Pretrial Discovery, 58 Colum. L. Rev. 480, 484 (1958).

[2]Consult your contracts course notes.

[3]*See, e.g.,* National Hockey League v. Metropolitan Hockey Club, Inc., 427 U.S. 639, 643 (1976); Schleper v. Ford Motor Co., 585 F.2d 1367, 1371 (8th Cir. 1978); Wembley, Inc. v. Diplomat Tie Co., 216 F. Supp. 565, 573 (D. Md. 1963).

imposition of sanctions directly in this case. Neither is an order compelling discovery needed under Rule 37(d) for complete failure to appear for a deposition, to serve answers or objections to interrogatories, or to provide a written response to a request for production or inspection under Rule 34.[4] In order for this subdivision to be applicable, however, there must be a total failure to make discovery. Rule 37(d) does not provide relief for partial response or arguably inadequate responses.[5] Willfulness may be of importance in determining which, if any, sanction should be imposed for failure to comply with the order, but it is not intended to be of significance in determining whether the order itself should be granted.

If a motion to compel discovery is granted, the rules encourage the award of attorney's fees and other expenses to the party seeking the order. The Federal Advisory Committee Note specifically explains the 1970 amendment that encourages the award of fees and expenses. The Advisory Committee stated:

> At present, an award of expenses is made only if the losing party or person is found to have acted without substantial justification. The change requires that expenses be awarded unless the conduct of the losing party or person is found to have been substantially justified. The test of "substantial justification" remains, but the change in language is intended to encourage judges to be more alert to abuses occurring in the discovery process. . . .
>
> The proposed change provides in effect that expenses should ordinarily be awarded unless a court finds that the losing party acted justifiably in carrying his point to court.[7]

[4]*See* Danforth, The 1975 Amendments to the Minnesota Rules of Discovery, 3 Wm. Mitchell L. Rev. 39 (1977). *See generally,* Note, The Emerging Deterrence Orientation in the Imposition of Discovery Sanctions, 91 Harv. L. Rev. 1033 (1978). See §6.7 of this text for a more detailed discussion of sanctions on these cases.

[5]*See, e.g.,* Israel Aircraft Indus., Ltd. v. Standard Precision, 559 F.2d 203, 208 (2d Cir. 1977).

An order compelling discovery is available for a failure to answer. Rule 37(a)(3) states that "an evasive or incomplete answer is to be treated as a failure to answer." The rule was most recently amended to remove any requirement of showing the failure to be willful.[6]

[6]Fed. R. Civ. P. 37(a)(4), and Notes of Advisory Comm. — 1970 Amendments. *See, e.g.,* Societe Internationale Pour Participation Industrielles et Commerciales, S.A. v. Rogers, 357 U.S. 197, 212 (1958); Fox v. Studebaker-Worthington, Inc., 516 F.2d 989, 993 (8th Cir. 1975).

[7]Fed. R. Civ. P. 37(a)(4), Notes of Advisory Comm. — 1970 Amendments.

The committee makes clear the intent of the rule: to make the award of expenses presumptively appropriate without limiting the power of the court to exercise its discretion in this area.[8]

By presenting an accommodating, reasonable posture to a discovery request, you can greatly enhance your chances of convincing the court that expenses should be awarded in your case. (You might also, for added effect, hold a plastic Bic instead of a Cross pen during the hearing.) If you are opposing a portion of a discovery request, the prompt and complete response to those portions not meriting objection helps establish your good faith in objecting to the other portion. The award of attorney's fees is sometimes, by terms of the order, expressly made the obligation of the attorney and not of the client.[9] This is a variation of the "deep-pocket" theory, but also reflects the extreme reluctance of courts to allow a case to suffer on the merits at the expense of inappropriate or unethical practice on the part of a party's attorneys.[10]

A request for an order compelling discovery is made upon motion, with notice to all parties and to any other affected persons (e.g., a non-party deponent).[11] Local rules may place a time limit on filing this motion in certain instances. The motion may be brought in either of two courts: the court where the action is pending or the court where a deposition is being taken. The latter court is appropriate only when a deponent fails to answer questions at either an oral or a written-question deposition. The party then has the option to bring the motion in either court, unless the deponent is a non-party. (In the latter event, the motion may be brought only in the court where the deposition is being taken.) The provision is designed to minimize the burden on a deponent who is not otherwise involved in the litigation. Any motion for an order compelling discovery other than for failure to answer deposition questions may be brought only in the court where the action is pending. Even if there is a choice of courts, one court may deter-

---

[8]Fed. R. Civ. P. 37 & 37(d), Notes of Advisory Comm. — 1970 Amendments.

[9]For the circumstances justifying imposition of sanctions against attorneys, see §6.5.8 of this text. Fees and costs are the sanctions most frequently imposed against attorneys, although contempt is also available.

[10]For a discussion of the reluctance of courts to impose sanctions that penalize a party's case on the merits for the actions of that party's attorneys, see Renfrew, Discovery Sanctions: A Judicial Perspective, 6 Litigation 5 (Winter 1980).

[11]Notice is required to these parties and non-parties by Fed. R. Civ. P. 6(d). The procedural requirements of discovery motion practice are discussed in §6.8.2 of this text.

mine that the other is a more appropriate court, and have the motion heard there.[12]

§6.4.2 Imposition of Sanctions

Rule 37(b) offers the court a wide range of sanctions that may be imposed for failure to comply with an order for discovery. The rule allows the imposition of contempt only for violation of an order in the court where a deposition is being taken. But in all other cases the court is granted authority to enter "such orders in regard to the failure as are just." Rule 37(b)(2) lists the major sanctions that are specifically authorized:

1. Facts may be deemed established;
2. Evidence may be barred;
3. Pleadings may be stricken or a dismissal or default judgment entered;
4. A party may be found in contempt; or
5. The six-way power seat may be removed from the attorney's Mercedes.

Local rules may provide supplementary sanctions for noncompliance and may also provide sanctions for misuse or abuse of the discovery process.

An order compelling discovery results in immediate compliance in the vast majority of cases. The objecting party may feel that the information sought is not discoverable, or that producing it will be unduly burdensome, or may have some other good-faith objection, but in virtually all cases a decision by a court on the merits of the objection will end the dispute — and the party will comply with the court's order. Various local rules set forth a 7- to 15-day time limit for compliance with the order.

If the order does not result in compliance, a second motion for an order imposing sanctions must be made, with notice and hearing given. The choice of sanction to be imposed is left to the discretion of the court, however, so the party seeking a severe sanction must literally move the court to impose it. Courts traditionally stated that

[12]*See* Fed. R. Civ. P. 37(a)(1), Notes of Advisory Comm. — 1970 Amendments.

the more severe sanctions of contempt, default, and dismissal would be imposed only as last-ditch efforts to punish a party who willfully abuses the discovery process or who flagrantly flouts the court's authority.[13] Until recently, the imposition of severe sanctions was frequently reversed by appellate courts, which found that the severe sanctions amounted to an abuse of discretion.[14] Now, however, courts have recognized that the more severe sanctions of contempt, default, and dismissal may be imposed as a deterrent to disobedience of discovery orders as well as to provide a penalty to the party who has disobeyed such an order.[15] The United States Supreme Court gave its clear approval to the use of discovery sanctions to deter abuse of the discovery process in *National Hockey League v. Metropolitan Hockey Club, Inc.*[16] The trial court had, as a discovery sanction, dismissed the plaintiffs' antitrust suit. The court of appeals reversed the dismissal, finding that "extenuating factors" existed, including a lack of bad faith on the part of the plaintiffs' attorneys. The Supreme Court reversed the court of appeals and reinstated the dismissal, stating:

> [T]he most severe in the spectrum of sanctions provided by statute or rule must be available to the district court in appropriate cases, not merely to penalize those whose conduct may be deemed to warrant such a sanction, but to deter those who might be tempted to such conduct in the absence of such a deterrent.[17]

The more drastic sanctions still are not imposed by most courts unless the noncompliance with the order is flagrant.[18] If you feel that dismissal or default is warranted, you must make a strong showing of

---

[13]*See, e.g.,* Wilson v. Volkswagen of Am., Inc., 561 F.2d 494, 503 (4th Cir. 1977); Kropp v. Ziebarth, 557 F.2d 142, 146 (8th Cir. 1977); In re Professional Hockey Antitrust Litigation, 531 F.2d 1188, 1193-1195 (3d Cir. 1976).

[14]*See, e.g.,* Sapiro v. Hartford Fire Ins. Co., 452 F.2d 215, 217 (7th Cir. 1971) (per curiam); B.F. Goodrich Tire Co. v. Lyster, 328 F.2d 411, 415 (5th Cir. 1964); Gill v. Stolow, 240 F.2d 669, 670 (2d Cir. 1957).

[15]*See, e.g.,* Robison v. Transamerica Ins. Co., 368 F.2d 37, 39 (10th Cir. 1966) ("The office of 37(d) is to secure compliance with the discovery rules, not to punish erring parties.").

[16]427 U.S. 639 (1976) (per curiam).

[17]427 U.S. at 643.

[18]*See, e.g.,* Societe Internationale Pour Participations Industrielles et Commerciales, S.A. v. Rogers, 357 U.S. 197, 212 (1958); Fox v. Studebaker-Worthington, Inc., 516 F.2d 989, 993 (8th Cir. 1975). The sanctions actually imposed vary widely. Recent decisions on the imposition of various sanctions are discussed in §6.5 of this text.

the opponent's notice of the order, understanding of what was required, repeated violations, any expressions of intent not to comply, and the degree to which your position has been prejudiced. The presence of prejudice may be a key factor, on appeal, in determining whether dismissal or default is properly within the discretion of the trial court.[19]

If less severe sanctions are possibly adequate, you should expect that they will be relied on by the court. The exclusion of evidence on a certain claim or defense or the establishment of facts supporting your claim or defense are powerful sanctions and may adequately remedy the noncompliance with the court's order. The recalcitrant party is denied a trial only to the extent that he or she has been uncooperative. These orders are seldom reversed on appeal (what is?) and may therefore be even more desirable if otherwise adequate.

§6.5   SELECTION OF A SANCTION

§6.5.1   Sanctions after National Hockey League

Since the range of sanctions available is great, and substantial policy reasons support the imposition of either severe or mild sanctions, it is frequently difficult to determine which sanctions a court might reasonably be expected to impose in a particular case. The United States Supreme Court decision in *National Hockey League* constituted a major change in the purpose of discovery sanctions. A review of the trial-court and appellate-court decisions after *National Hockey League* is useful for learning the major rationales currently expressed by courts in evaluating the imposition of sanctions. The following discussion analyzes some of the major factors.

---

[19]Wilson v. Volkswagen of Am., Inc., 561 F.2d 494, 504-505 (4th Cir. 1977). *See also* Thomas v. United States, 531 F.2d 746, 749 (5th Cir. 1976) ("Consideration must be given to such factors as good faith, willful disobedience, gross indifference to the rights of the adverse party, deliberate callousness or gross negligence.").

§6.5.2   Default and Dismissal

Courts are willing to impose the severe sanctions of default or dismissal when the conduct giving rise to the sanction is repeated and clearly taken with knowledge of the court's order compelling discovery. In one case, a default judgment for $142,500 was entered against a defendant for failure to respond to interrogatories and produce documents after repeated requests and an order of the court.[1] Another court ordered a default judgment of $285,000, with interest and expenses, for willful failure to appear for a deposition and to produce documents pursuant to request.[2] The courts have held that attempts to comply with discovery orders after a history of noncompliance do not necessarily exonerate a party. Courts have continued the imposition of the most extreme sanctions of default and dismissal notwithstanding such eleventh-hour actions.[3]

Making inaccurate or misleading statements to the court regarding discovery may also be the basis for imposition of severe sanctions. In *Independent Investor Protective League v. Touche Ross & Co.*,[4] the court noted the district court's conclusion that appellants acted "pursuant to an evolving plan to first deceive counsel and later the court" regarding discovery matters. Based upon this finding, the court ordered dismissal of the complaint.[5]

§6.5.3   Contempt

A contempt sanction is a severe sanction available against both a party and an attorney,[6] but it is not favored by the courts. If the factual circumstances surrounding the discovery conduct justify the finding of contempt, the dismissal or default sanction would probably also be available. Since a contempt sanction may require an additional eviden-

§6.5 [1]*See* Affanato v. Merrill Bros., 547 F.2d 138, 141 (1st Cir. 1977).

[2]*See* Paine, Webber, Jackson & Curtis, Inc. v. Inmobiliaria Melia de Puerto Rico, Inc., 543 F.2d 3 (2d Cir. 1976), *cert. denied*, 430 U.S. 907 (1977). *See also* Brown v. McCormick, 608 F.2d 410, 414 (10th Cir. 1979).

[3]*See* Factory Air Conditioning Corp. v. Westside Toyota, Inc., 579 F.2d 334, 337-337 (5th Cir. 1978) (per curiam); State of Ohio v. Arthur Andersen & Co., 570 F.2d 1370, 1374 (10th Cir.), *cert. denied*, 439 U.S. 833 (1978).

[4]607 F.2d 530 (2d Cir. 1978).

[5]607 F.2d at 533. *See also* G-K Properties v. Redevelopment Agency of the City of San Jose, 577 F.2d 645, 647 (9th Cir. 1978).

[6]*See* Schleper v. Ford Motor Co., 585 F.2d 1367, 1372 (8th Cir. 1978).

tiary hearing, while default or dismissal requires no further hearing and actually removes a case from the court's calendar, these latter sanctions tend to be preferred in situations involving a party's non-compliance.[7]

The contempt sanction takes two forms: civil contempt and criminal contempt. The distinction between them has been the subject of much discussion. Generally, however, civil contempt is imposed to compel compliance with a court order, while criminal contempt is imposed to punish an affront to the court's authority.[8] Civil contempt is thus resorted to when other sanctions would be either less effective or more difficult for the court to impose or administer. Civil contempt is an appropriate sanction for use to compel a non-party's compliance with a discovery order since other sanctions, such as default, dismissal, and preclusion of evidence, may have little, if any, impact on the non-party.

Litigants have sometimes taken the position that contempt is inappropriate when the litigant acted upon the advice of counsel. But it is generally held that reliance upon counsel's advice is not a *defense* to the contempt sanction, although it may properly be considered by a trial court in determining whether or not to find contempt.[9]

§6.5.4 Preclusion Orders

Since a preclusion order is generally considered a less severe sanction than dismissal or default, the *National Hockey League* opinion, presumably, has had little effect upon its availability. Courts have been willing to enter preclusion orders for simple failure to identify documents or witnesses, regardless of whether that conduct constitutes flagrant or repeated violation of court orders.[10]

---

[7]An evidentiary hearing is required by the courts, to determine if a factual issue exists, in determining whether or not a valid order had been violated. No such hearing is required if the party found in contempt opposes contempt merely on legal grounds. *See* I.B.M. Corp. v. United States, 493 F.2d 112, 119-120 (2d Cir. 1973), *cert. denied,* 416 U.S. 995 (1974).

[8]*See, e.g.,* Ramos Colon v. United States Attorney for the District of Puerto Rico, 576 F.2d 1, 4-5 (1st Cir. 1978).

[9]*Compare* United States v. I.B.M. Corp., 60 F.R.D. 658, 666 (S.D.N.Y.), *appeal dismissed,* 493 F.2d 112 (2d. Cir. 1973), *cert. denied,* 416 U.S. 995, *direct appeal dismissed,* 416 U.S. 976 (1974), *with* Colorado Milling & Elevator Co. v. American Cyanamid Co., 11 F.R.D. 306, 307 (W.D. Mo. 1951).

[10]*See, e.g.,* Admiral Theatre Corp. v. Douglas Theater Co., 585 F.2d 877, 897 (8th Cir. 1978).

A preclusion order may be a serious sanction, however. If the evidence or witness precluded (or issue determined) is of crucial importance, and if no other evidence exists on that issue, it is possible for the preclusion order to be determinative. In one case, summary judgment was issued after the entry of a preclusion order.[11]

§6.5.5 Restriction of Further Discovery

Another sanction frequently imposed by courts, whether deliberately or not, is the restriction of the recalcitrant party's discovery rights. Experienced litigation attorneys have long known that failure of a party to comply with valid discovery requests essentially negates any rights that party may have to enforce its own discovery requests. Thus, at least during the period of a party's noncompliance, discovery may be delayed or unavailable. Rule 37(d) specifically permits the court to stay further proceedings. This is a sanction that, though not frequently used in the form of an absolute stay, is occasionally relied upon by courts to enforce discovery.[12]

§6.5.6 Imposition of Costs

The rule favors the award of expenses, including attorney's fees, to the party bringing a meritorious motion for imposition of sanctions, and courts have been willing to enter appropriate orders compelling payment of substantial costs.[13] Attorneys frequently forget that the award of expenses is primarily compensatory and not punitive and that eleventh-hour compliance with the motion or prior order does not erase the liability for expenses of bringing the motion. Courts are increasingly willing to award expenses, even if the underlying motion has been "mooted" by an eleventh-hour disgorging of information. The seeking of such an award may be wise tactically, since it may

---

[11]Riverside Memorial Mausoleum, Inc. v. Sonneblick-Goldman Corp., 80 F.R.D. 433, 437 (E.D. Pa. 1978). *See also* State of Ohio v. Arthur Andersen & Co., 570 F.2d 1370 (10th Cir.), *cert. denied,* 439 U.S. 833 (1978).

[12]*See, e.g.,* Griffin v. Aluminum Co. of Am., 564 F.2d 1171, 1173 (5th Cir. 1977) (the court suggested that barring further proceedings by recalcitrant *pro se* plaintiff would be an appropriate means of sanctioning his refusal to appear for a deposition).

[13]Marquis v. Chrysler Corp., 577 F.2d 624, 641-642 (9th Cir. 1978); Goodsons & Co., Inc. v. National Am. Corp., 78 F.R.D. 721, 723 (S.D.N.Y. 1978).

prompt a more timely response to future discovery requests. This holds equally true for motions for orders compelling discovery and for motions to impose sanctions.

§6.5.7   Failure to Make Admissions

Failure to make admissions under Rule 36 may result in an order requiring the party failing to admit to bear the cost of proving items not admitted. This order is to be granted under Rule 37(c) unless the court finds that:

> (1) The request was held objectionable pursuant to Rule 36(a), or (2) the admission sought was of no substantial importance, or (3) the party failing to admit had reasonable grounds to believe that he might prevail on the matter, or (4) there was other good reason for the failure to admit.

The Federal Advisory Committee Notes indicate that the award of expenses is "intended to provide post-trial relief," and the courts generally follow the clear indication of the rule.[14] The courts have generally given narrow interpretation to the four exceptions to imposition of costs under Rule 37(c). Having reasonable ground to believe that a party might prevail is probably the most likely basis for defeating a claim for costs.[15] A party generally has a difficult time establishing that the admission sought was of no substantial importance[16] or that there was other good reason for failure to admit.[17] As with every other discovery request, poor drafting may make the request objectionable even if a properly drawn request might not be so.

§6.5.8   Sanctions against Attorneys

It is important to remember that sanctions may be imposed against parties and also against their attorneys. Now do we have your full attention? Rule 37(b) of the Federal Rules of Civil Procedure specifically provides that the award of expenses may be made against "the

---

[14]Ogletree v. Keebler Co., Inc., 78 F.R.D. 661, 662 (N.D. Ga. 1978).

[15]See, e.g., Security-First Natl. Bank of Los Angeles v. Lutz, 297 F.2d 159, 166 (9th Cir. 1961).

[16]See 8 C. Wright & A. Miller, Federal Practice and Procedure §2290, at 804 (1970).

[17]See, e.g., David v. Hooker, Ltd., 560 F.2d 412, 419 (9th Cir. 1977).

party failing to obey the order *or the attorney advising him or both.* " Courts have been willing to impose sanctions directly against the attorney if the record clearly establishes that the attorney's conduct is responsible for the discovery violation.[18] The imposition of costs against the attorney, and not against the client, is more likely if the circumstances make it appear that the client was reasonably diligent in responding to the discovery request.[19] In one case, the court exonerated both parties to an action but found that counsel for both sides had so frustrated the discovery process that it ordered each attorney to pay the attorney's fees of the other party, with an express provision that the parties were not to reimburse the attorneys for these expenses.[20] The award of attorney's fees under Rule 37 is for the benefit of the party injured by the conduct of the dilatory party or attorney, not for the benefit of that party's attorneys.[21] Monetary sanctions against attorneys have also recently been imposed under the authority of an obscure federal statute which provides that:

> Any attorney or other person admitted to conduct cases in any court of the United States or any Territory thereof who so multiplies the proceedings in any case as to increase costs unreasonably and vexatiously may be required by the court to satisfy personally such excess costs.[22]

This statute was adopted early in this century, but it has been used only rarely.

---

[18]*See* Edgar v. Slaughter, 548 F.2d 770, 773 (8th Cir. 1977). *See also* Comment, Sanctions Imposed by Courts on Attorneys Who Abuse the Judicial Process, 44 U. Chi. L. Rev. 619 (1977). In Roadway Express, Inc. v. Piper, 447 U.S. 752, 766-767 (1980), the Supreme Court affirmed the imposition of sanctions on attorneys who unreasonably extend court proceedings.

[19]*See* Independent Investor Protective League v. Touche Ross & Co. 607 F.2d 530, 534 (2d Cir. 1978); Stanziale v. First Natl. City Bank, 74 F.R.D. 557, 560 (S.D.N.Y. 1977) (ignorance of the date upon which the interrogatory answers were due); Szilvassy v. United States, 71 F.R.D. 589 (S.D.N.Y. 1976) (it was not clear to what extent, if any, plaintiff was at fault).

[20]Associated Radio Serv. Co. v. Page Airways, Inc., 73 F.R.D. 633, 636-637 (D. Tex. 1977).

[21]Hamilton v. Econo-Car Intl., 636 F.2d 745 (D.C. Cir. 1980), *rev'g,* Hamilton v. Motorola, Inc., 85 F.R.D. 549, 551-552 (D.D.C. 1979).

[22]28 U.S.C. §1927 (1976). Sanctions may be imposed under this statute only against attorneys, not against parties or clients. Chrysler Corp. v. Lakeshore Commercial Fin. Corp., 389 F. Supp. 1216, 1224 (E.D. Wis. 1975).

§6.5.9   Sanctions against Pro Se Parties

Appellate courts have been willing to establish more lenient standards for imposition of sanctions against parties appearing without trained lawyers. Although the *pro se* party is not excused from compliance with the discovery rules, the party is generally not subjected to severe sanctions unless it appears affirmatively that the party was aware of the obligations imposed by the rules and willfully disregarded them. One court reversed the dismissal of a complaint by a *pro se* plaintiff, who had failed to appear at his deposition and failed to produce documents upon request. The court found that the party did not adequately understand his obligations under the discovery rules and concluded that dismissal was inappropriate. The court also found the imposition of monetary sanctions inappropriate and concluded that an order staying further proceedings would have been appropriate under the circumstances. Finally, the court noted that, although an order compelling attendance at a deposition is not required prior to the imposition of sanctions, it would be appropriate in a case involving a *pro se* litigant.[23]

The courts do not, however, permit the *pro se* plaintiff to take advantage of a lack of representation. In one case in which the *pro se* plaintiff made misrepresentations to the court, the court permitted dismissal of the action for failure to appear for a deposition.[24] It is thus prudent for counsel involved in litigation with unrepresented parties to ensure that the parties are specifically aware of the obligations under the rules, that they are provided copies of all pertinent documents, and that they are advised of dates, deadlines, and the nature of their obligations. It is probably prudent to obtain an order compelling discovery against any *pro se* party, even if the discovery involved is one of those types that does not require an order compelling discovery as a condition precedent to the imposition of sanctions.

[23]Griffin v. Aluminum Co. of Am., 564 F.2d 1172, 1173 (5th Cir. 1977). *See also* United Artists Corp. v. Freeman, 605 F.2d 854, 856 (5th Cir. 1979).

[24]Roberts v. Norden Div., United Aircraft Corp., 76 F.R.D. 75, 81 (E.D.N.Y. 1977). *See also* Hines v. S.J. Enterprises, Inc., 25 Fed. R. Serv. 2d 227, 228-229 (E.D. Mo. 1978).

§6.6   STREAMLINING THE TWO-STEP PROCESS

Rather than holding two hearings on two separate motions, as discussed previously, courts frequently indicate in the order compelling discovery what sanction will be imposed for failure to comply with the order. The court may specifically order that no further hearing will be necessary or available in the event of noncompliance. The sanction may then be imposed upon motion and affidavits demonstrating noncompliance with the order. A second hearing may not be required. The use of this streamlined procedure has been upheld,[1] and there are tactical advantages to attaining a sanction within the order to compel discovery. In addition to saving time and expense, an order that specifically outlines what will happen if it is not followed may result in a stronger likelihood of compliance. Judges may be more inclined to impose harsh sanctions conditionally, in the hope of obtaining compliance, and less inclined to impose a harsh sanction after the fact.

In a different situation the two-step process does not function meaningfully. If a party provides answers that appear to be complete, but that do not disclose claims, defenses, witnesses, or documents upon which the answering party plans to rely at trial, there is clear potential prejudice. But a motion compelling discovery is of no use; the party seeking discovery has no means either of knowing that the answers are incomplete or of convincing a court to enter an order compelling discovery. Rule 37(d) allows the imposition of certain Rule 37(b) sanctions without any preceding order compelling discovery. It provides the strongest tool to combat the undisclosed claim, defense, witness, or piece of evidence: barring the use of that witness or evidence or the introduction of proof on a claim or defense that is not timely disclosed.[2]

---

§6.6   [1]Johann Maria Farina v. Roger & Gallet, 296 F.2d 119, 120 (2d Cir. 1961) (court found conditional order not appealable); O'Neil v. Corrick, 307 Minn. 497, 239 N.W.2d 230 (1976) (per curiam).

[2]Rule 37(d) is especially useful to prevent the testimony of an undisclosed expert witness.

§6.7 NARROWER ENFORCEMENT PROVISIONS

Rule 37(d) applies to three types of failure to make discovery: failure to appear for a properly noticed deposition, failure to serve any answers or objections to interrogatories, and failure to serve a written response to a request for a Rule 34 inspection. This rule, like Rule 37(b), authorizes the court to impose sanctions as it deems appropriate and lists specific sanctions. The only sanction not repeated from Rule 37(b) is the contempt sanction. Since no court order is in force in a situation calling for Rule 37(d) sanctions, contempt is considered to be an inappropriate sanction.[1]

The rule does give a trial judge the power to remove any tactical advantage gained by playing a fast and loose game of discovery and allows this conduct to be penalized. Striking pleadings, entering judgment by default or dismissal, barring evidence, and deeming facts established are all available. The most frequently imposed sanctions are to bar testimony from the undisclosed witness, to bar receipt in evidence of the unproduced document, or to deem facts established when the recalcitrant party has control of the proof.[2] Monetary sanctions, also available under Rule 37(d), may apply in addition to or in lieu of any other sanctions. The award of attorney's fees and expenses is presumptively appropriate under this rule.[3]

§6.8 MOTION PRACTICE

§6.8.1 Reasons for a Motion

The most obvious reason for bringing a motion is to compel certain relief. To have an order compelling discovery entered, you must serve a motion on all opposing or otherwise interested parties. As mentioned above, a motion may be unnecessary to obtain discovery. A

§6.7 [1]Schleper v. Ford Motor Co., 585 F.2d 1367, 1371 (8th Cir. 1978).

[2]Renfrew, Discovery Sanctions: A Judicial Perspective, 67 Calif. L. Rev. 264 (1979).

[3]Fed. R. Civ. P. 37(d), Notes of Advisory Comm. — 1970 Amendments, reprinted in 28 U.S.C.A. 66 (West Supp. 1980).

formal motion is an expensive way to achieve what a phone call will sometimes accomplish.

But if your opponent is being particularly stubborn, you may feel it simpler to convince a judge, rather than your hard-headed opponent, of your right to the information sought. There may be an advantage to bringing a motion: it will reveal to the court, and establish in the record, your opponent's attitude. Depending on you and your opponent, it may also make the motion docket more interesting for the other attorneys present.

A discovery motion can also give you an opportunity to see and evaluate your opponent: to learn how well prepared, how familiar with court procedures, and how convincing opposing counsel is. Motions may also serve the less laudable, not to mention potentially unethical, purpose of delaying the process or increasing the burdens of litigation for a financially weaker opponent.

Discovery motions have disadvantages as well. If you are asserting any objections to your opponent's discovery requests, a court is quite likely to treat both parties the same way, by granting discovery to both or denying it to both.[1] A motion taken under advisement, even if followed by a favorable order, may not yield discovery for months, while less favorable terms arrived at by agreement may result in immediate discovery. Although the rules clearly favor the award of expenses, including attorney's fees, to the prevailing party in a discovery motion, judges have often not shown the same enthusiasm in awarding them.[2] Except in flagrant cases of obstreperousness, courts frequently follow the general American rule and require each party to bear the costs incurred by that party.

§6.8.2   *Motion Procedures*

Assuming you decide a motion compelling discovery or a motion for some form of protective relief is either necessary or desirable, how do you bring such a motion?

Rule 6(d) sets out some of the mechanics of all motion practice. A notice of motion and the motion must be served on *all* parties. If other persons are affected by the relief sought, they too must be served. The

---

§6.8 [1]Although not truly an equitable maxim, trial judges have apparently followed on frequent occasion the rule that "what's sauce for the goose is sauce for the gander."
[2]*See* Fed. R. Civ. P. 37, Notes of Advisory Comm. — 1970 Amendment.

motion must specify the relief sought, state the grounds upon which the relief is sought, and generally set forth the portions of the record which support the motion. A well-drafted motion sets forth the relief sought in a fashion that could be incorporated into a court order upon the moving party's prevailing.

Many courts have imposed an additional condition precedent to holding a hearing on any discovery motion: local "meet and confer" rules. As mentioned above, these rules generally require the party seeking the discovery to make a good-faith attempt to resolve the discovery dispute informally with opposing counsel and to certify to the court that such a good-faith attempt has been made prior to the filing of any motion to compel discovery. The purpose of these rules is obvious — to minimize the number of discovery motions the court must decide. Even if it is certain that a particular dispute may not be resolved informally, it is necessary that you make the attempt. And even if your position is ultimately correct, you may not obtain a hearing on your motion unless you comply with the provisions of any local "meet and confer" rules.

The motion should be supported by affidavits, a memorandum of law, and a proposed order. Some courts require these to be filed before the matter will be set on a calendar for hearing. The better practice is to file these documents in advance, regardless of whether a local rule requires them or not. The practice of plopping a memorandum or affidavit in front of opposing counsel at the time of the hearing detracts significantly from your presentation, makes it look like surprise is your strongest weapon, and may make you the brunt of luncheon conversation. It may also engender sympathy for your surprised opponent in the judge's eyes.

The subject matter of affidavits varies, of course, with the subject matter of the motion. Most affidavits are adequate if they establish: (1) your compliance with the rules and (2) your opponent's noncompliance. If you can also establish prejudice to your position, it will clearly be to your advantage.

Ideally, the hearing on the motion will be short. The judge will already be familiar, for example, with what interrogatories are and with the fact that the rules require answers or objections. Most judges do not permit reiterating or expounding upon these basic things. Even if a judge is patient enough to allow such exposition, it is hardly inspiring. Rather, a more persuasive approach would be to explain the facts, why you need (or cannot give up) the information, what prejudice granting (or denying) the motion will have on your client, and why expenses should or should not be awarded.

Some districts have eliminated oral motion arguments; they decide these matters on the basis of the written submissions. Other districts have recently been employing conference calls, with the judge listening to and asking questions of counsel. These alternatives to court hearings will increase in use and frequency as ways to reduce discovery costs.

If the motion is one for imposition of sanctions, it is appropriate to assist the court in deciding which sanction should be used. Two experienced trial judges have stated with respect to the question of selection of sanctions:

> [I]t is well for counsel bringing a motion to enforce discovery or to enforce an order made for discovery to determine which sanction he would particularly prefer and to be able to advise sound reasons for his choice. While the court's duty is to sanction an offending party and not to reward the other party, it is often possible, and sometimes beneficial to rule enforcement, to do both.[3]

Help the court to rule in your favor by presenting the facts and arguments that support the sanction you desire. It should be obvious that this does not mean you should make the strongest pitch for contempt, dismissal, or default in every case. Some cases do not require or justify the imposition of such severe sanctions. Your client may better be served by seeking a less severe sanction, with its greater likelihood of actually being imposed, than attempting to obtain a sanction so severe as to be unreasonable.

§6.8.3 Strategy and Tactics

You want to look as "good" as possible and make your opponent look as "bad" as possible. For this precept,

"good"= cooperative, accommodating, and reasonable, while
"bad" = unreasonable, demanding, or tardy.

Present the court with legal authority for your position. Since the federal rules provide a large body of case law on discovery practice,

[3]Amdahl & Winton, Tell Me What You Want, Counsel! in Minnesota Continuing Legal Education, Everything You Wanted to Know about the Rules of Civil Procedure but Were Afraid to Ask 75, at 92 (1976).

federal trial court decisions on discovery are persuasive, if not precedential, in many state court proceedings. Few states publish their trial court opinions; the trial court opinions on discovery contained in Federal Rules Decisions, Federal Rules Service, and Federal Supplement, as well as various loose-leaf services, may be the only authority available on discovery questions.

Two important factors affect the reliance on case authority: trial courts are given a wide discretion upon review, and the discovery decisions themselves are not appealable in most cases. These two factors tend to make the trial judge free to rule in any reasonable manner, even if a strong body of case law suggests that a different ruling would be appropriate. The non-appealability of discovery usually presents no problem. If discovery is absolutely crucial to a case, a discretionary appeal[4] may be sought or an extraordinary writ may be obtained. Although these forms of appellate relief are rarely granted, they are available in unusual circumstances.

The discretion of the trial judge is exercised in view of the facts and the procedural history of the case. The most important strategic policy to prompt discovery is to:

1. Establish need for the information (if not in the strict sense of *need,* at least in the relevance sense);
2. Convince the court that no excessive burden is imposed;
3. Demonstrate that you are willing to comply with any reasonable discovery requests of your opponent; and
4. Provide the judge with a citation to this book.

§6.9 APPELLATE REVIEW OF DISCOVERY ORDERS

Probably the single most important thing to remember about appellate practice and review of discovery orders is that discovery orders are rarely appealable. Discovery orders are always subject to appellate *review,* but that review is generally available only in an appeal from the final judgment in a lawsuit or from a judgment entered pursuant to Rule 54(b). Generally interlocutory in nature, discovery orders are

---

[4]A discretionary appeal may be available under the authority of 28 U.S.C. §1292(b) (1976).

immediately appealable only permissively under 28 U.S.C. §1292(b). Only occasionally have courts permitted interlocutory appeals under this statute.[1] Since the discretionary appeal statute requires that a controlling question of law be present and that an immediate appeal should "materially advance the termination of the litigation," discretionary review is rarely appropriate.[2]

The non-appealability of discovery orders is universal in the sense that it makes little difference what particular kind of order is involved. Although a default judgment or judgment of dismissal is appealable, the order granting default is not appealable until judgment is entered.[3] An order that imposes dismissal as a conditional sanction (i.e., one to be imposed at a future date if discovery is not made) is similarly not appealable until the judgment is finally entered.[4] Again, orders establishing facts, precluding evidence of an issue, or staying further proceedings are not appealable;[5] nor is an order imposing a civil contempt sanction appealable. An order imposing a criminal contempt sanction, however, is immediately appealable because it punishes a violation of law and is itself a final judgment.[6] Thus, it matters little what sanction has been imposed against your client: you cannot obtain immediate judicial review of an order requiring discovery, refusing to order discovery, or imposing sanctions (other than criminal contempt) for failure to comply with a discovery order.

In view of the probable non-appealability of a discovery order and in view of your representation, it is obviously most desirable to win your discovery motion at the trial court level. If you do lose the first round at the trial court, it is possible that you may avail yourself of the interlocutory nature of the discovery order, i.e., that it is subject to revision by the trial court. Perhaps subsequent discovery, pleadings, obtaining of admissions, or developing case law may prompt the trial

---

§6.9   [1] *See, e.g.,* Groover, Christie & Meritt v. LoBianco, 336 F.2d 969, 970 (D.C. Cir. 1964).

[2] *See, e.g.,* United States v. Woodbury, 263 F.2d 784, 786 (9th Cir. 1959).

[3] *See, e.g.,* Bache & Co. v. Taylor, 458 F.2d 395, 395-396 (5th Cir. 1972).

[4] Johann Maria Farina v. Roger & Gallet, 296 F.2d 119, 120 (2d Cir. 1961).

[5] *See* Cromaglass Corp. v. Ferm, 500 F.2d 601, 609 (3d Cir. 1974) (preclusion order not appealable); Hartley Pen Co. v. United States District Court, 287 F.2d 324, 329 (9th Cir. 1961) (order staying further proceedings not appealable); United States v. Richardson, 204 F.2d 552, 556 (5th Cir. 1953) (order staying further proceedings not appealable).

[6] Cromaglass Corp. v. Ferm, 500 F.2d 601, 604 (3d Cir. 1974); I.B.M. Corp. v. United States, 493 F.2d 112, 114 (2d Cir. 1973), *cert. denied,* 416 U.S. 995 (1975); Hodgson v. Mahoney, 460 F.2d 326, 328 (1st Cir. 1972).

court to modify its initial decision. A discovery order entered early in a case may seem inappropriate to the trial judge at the time of trial, due to these changes. The renewal of a motion previously denied, or a motion for reconsideration of an opponent's motion that was granted, may also improve the chances of successful appellate review of that trial court decision.

A difficult problem arises, however, when a non-appealable discovery order that requires the disclosure of information by a party is entered. Even if the order is manifestly unfair and improper, judicial review upon the entry of a final judgment may be meaningless. Once privileged information has been disclosed pursuant to an order violating the privilege, little meaningful redress is available to the party forced to disclose the information. Trial courts may recognize this problem and attempt to facilitate interlocutory appeal. This may be done directly by stating that the order is appealable and encouraging the appellate court to take jurisdiction of the appeal. An attorney faced with this dilemma may also decide to disregard the court's order. This tactic, obviously a risky one, may result in the imposition of a criminal contempt sanction against the attorney or the party. An order finding a party in criminal contempt of court is immediately appealable since it punishes a violation of law and is a final judgment.[7] A civil contempt order, however, is designed to coerce compliance with the order, and is not appealable.[8] The obvious problem that arises, aside from the substantial risk which intentional disregard of a court order may entail, is the difficulty in distinguishing between criminal and civil contempt. If the contempt order is determined to be merely civil, appellate review will not be achieved, and the contempt order will not be reviewed until a final judgment is rendered.

There are certain circumstances in which a discovery order may be held not to be interlocutory. First, if discovery is sought in a district other than that where the action is pending and is sought from a non-party, quashing a subpoena for a deposition is immediately appealable.[9] If the district court denies a motion to quash such a subpoena, it is possible that disregard of the discovery order and review of the resulting contempt citation would be the only effective review.

---

[7]*See* I.B.M. Corp. v. United States, 493 F.2d 112, 114 (2d Cir. 1973), *cert. denied,* 416 U.S. 995 (1975).

[8]*See* I.B.M. Corp. v. United States, 493 F.2d 112, 114-115 (2d Cir. 1973), *cert. denied,* 416 U.S. 995 (1975).

[9]*See* Premium Serv. Corp. v. Sperry & Hutchinson Co., 511 F.2d 225, 228 (9th Cir. 1975).

Obviously, if the subpoena were quashed by the court in which the action was pending, it would not differ from any other discovery order and would be non-appealable. Second, any order imposing sanctions on a non-party for failure to comply with a discovery order may also be appealable.[10] This holding is necessary to permit the non-party to have effective review since the non-party would not, for example, have any standing to appeal from the final judgment. The sanction order itself is final as to the non-party.

The other possible means of obtaining appellate review is by use of extraordinary writs. The federal courts have been extremely reluctant to use extraordinary writs to review lower court discovery orders.[11] Nonetheless, in extraordinary situations involving unjustified usurpation of power by the district court or grave miscarriages of justice, appellate courts have ruled upon extraordinary writs. In one case, the trial court required a plaintiff to disclose trade secrets. Because the "cat would be out of the bag" by the time any final judgment would be entered, mandamus was issued to prevent a grave injustice.[12] If the discovery ruling you feel should be appealed involves a question of the trial court's discretion or questions such as relevance, an extraordinary writ will not be available. But fundamental questions of attorney-client privilege or work product may be the subject for interlocutory review.[13]

§6.10 DISCOVERY MALPRACTICE

The increased willingness of courts to impose severe discovery sanctions may give rise to increased claims of malpractice against attorneys. The orders entered by courts, directing attorneys and not their clients to bear the costs of discovery motions, clearly impose a penalty upon counsel who abuse the discovery process. The findings of the court

---

[10]*See* David v. Hooker, Ltd., 560 F.2d 412, 415-416 (9th Cir. 1977).

[11]*See, e.g.,* Guerra v. Board of Trustees of the California State Univs. & Colleges, 567 F.2d 352, 355 (9th Cir. 1977); Kerr v. United States Dist. Court, 511 F.2d 192, 197 (9th Cir. 1975), *aff'd,* 426 U.S. 394 (1976).

[12]Hartley Pen Co. v. United States Dist. Court, 287 F.2d 324, 331 (9th Cir. 1961).

[13]*Compare* Heathman v. United States Dist. Court for the Cent. Dist. of California, 503 F.2d 1032, 1035 (9th Cir. 1974) *with* Harper & Row Publishers, Inc. v. Decker, 423 F.2d 487, 492 (7th Cir. 1970), *aff'd,* 400 U.S. 348 (1971).

may be pertinent in subsequent claims brought by a party against the attorney. Courts frequently impose monetary sanctions directly against the attorneys, when they perceive the attorney to be at fault in obstructing discovery, although they are increasingly willing to visit the attorney's negligence or willfulness upon the client. It is clear, then, that the possibility of imposition of severe sanctions exists and should cause attorneys to be especially careful to ensure compliance by their client, as well as by themselves, with any court orders regarding discovery. Recognizing this problem, some have even suggested that counsel should seriously consider withdrawing from representation of clients who refuse to fulfill their discovery obligations.[1]

A leading case exhibiting the willingness of the courts to punish a party for the failure by its attorney to act is *Affanto v. Merrill Bros.,*[2] in which the court affirmed an award of default judgment for $142,500 upon defendant's failure to answer interrogatories despite repeated orders that they be answered. The court, saying the sanction was being imposed for the acts of defendant's attorney, stated:

> What is important is that the conduct of counsel with which defendant is chargeable consisted of a series of episodes of nonfeasance which amounted, in sum, to a near total dereliction of professional responsibility by the associate in the law firm defendant had obtained. Granting that isolated oversights should not be penalized by a default judgment, the court was entitled to conclude that the conduct here went well beyond ordinary negligence, and that the final default was appropriate.[3]

Obviously, this judicial finding of conduct "well beyond ordinary negligence" will be of substantial value to the defendant in pursuing contribution or indemnity from the law firm or the individual attorney involved.

A more novel claim of malpractice might be grounded upon a client's complaint that his or her own attorney conducted inadequate discovery. Economic factors impinge upon every decision either to conduct or refrain from additional discovery. If the attorney and client consider these factors and together decide not to pursue further discovery, it appears unlikely that a malpractice claim could be perfected.

---

§6.10 [1]*See, e.g.,* Epstein, Corcoran, Krieger & Carr, An Up-Date on Rule 37 Sanctions after *National Hockey League v. Metropolitan Hockey Clubs, Inc.,* 84 F.R.D. 145, 172-173 (1980).

[2]547 F.2d 138 (1st Cir. 1977).

[3]547 F.2d at 141.

But such a decision should be documented in writing to eliminate any future disputes surrounding it. Whether to conduct additional discovery is most often a discretionary decision within the attorney's judgment.[4] Failure to prepare a party for deposition testimony may similarly provide the basis for malpractice liability.[5]

It has been pointed out that one of the pressures to refrain from discovery might be especially hard to document in a subsequent malpractice action: pressure from a weary trial judge who suggests that discovery has proceeded far enough.[6] As is true of all malpractice claims, it is impossible for an attorney to avoid all possibility of a claim's being asserted. Nonetheless, discovery provides a field in which malpractice considerations should be considered. The prudent attorney can minimize exposure to malpractice by maintaining good communication with the client, by involving the client in decisionmaking, and by documenting decisions made and advice given regarding those decisions.

§6.11 CONCLUSION

The discovery rules are not self-enforcing. Although attorneys frequently modify discovery rights and attempt to resolve discovery disputes without court involvement, it is important that the discovery sanctions available under the Rules of Civil Procedure be understood. It is also important to recognize the fundamental purpose of discovery, because courts impose sanctions in order to secure that very purpose: the just, speedy, and inexpensive determination of litigation.[1] Courts exercise wide discretion in determining how this end may best be achieved. It is therefore important for attorneys to approach discovery disputes from both a practical and legal standpoint.

[4]*See, e.g.,* Identiseal Corp. of Wisconsin v. Positive Identification Sys., Inc., 560 F.2d 298, 302 (7th Cir. 1977).

[5]*Cf.* Bevevino v. Saydjari, 76 F.R.D. 88, 96 (S.D.N.Y. 1977), *aff'd,* 478 F.2d 676 (2d Cir. 1978). Although not a legal malpractice case, the court suggested that legal malpractice would be available (at 93 n.9, 94 & n.11). This case involved substantial damages since the judgment ultimately entered for plaintiff amounted to $550,000.

[6]*See* Barthold, "Negligence" in Discovery: No Paper Tiger, 6 Litigation 39 (Fall 1979).

§6.11 [1]Fed. R. Civ. P. 1.

§6.12 PROBLEMS

1. You represent the defendants in *American Campers v. Summers.* In October Susan Summers developed respiratory problems. A medical expert who examined her has advised you that inhalation of fumes from the propane stove (the fumes were released because of the fire on June 29) may have caused damage to her lungs. The court has allowed you to amend the counterclaim by adding a product liability claim.

You have submitted a request for production, Number 17, for documents that contain the names and addresses of all customers of the plaintiff who have purchased Voyageur Motor Homes with propane stoves. You intend to contact these individuals and discover whether they have had any problems with the stove. The plaintiff has refused to disclose these names, contending that: (1) such information is confidential; (2) the documents that contain such names also contain private business data that is irrelevant to the claim; and (3) the privilege of these customers will be unnecessarily breached by the defendants.

Your investigation has revealed that the plaintiff designed and manufactured the propane stove installed in the Voyageur. You have submitted a request for production, Number 18, seeking documents detailing the design and manufacturing processes involved in the production of the propane stove. The plaintiff has refused to comply with this request, explaining that (1) American Campers has a patent on the Saf-T-Lok valve on the stove; (2) such documents contain trade secrets; and (3) the disclosure of the information would put American Campers at a significant disadvantage with its competitors.

(a) Draft a motion seeking a protective order to obtain the information sought in request Numbers 17 and 18.
(b) Draft a protective order that provides you with the information you need and which meets the legitimate concerns of the plaintiff.

2. You represent the plaintiff in *American Campers v. Summers.* The defendant has failed to respond within 30 days to the interrogatories that you drafted (see §3.9, Problem 8). You subsequently wrote a letter to the defendant's attorney demanding answers. You never received a response to that letter. Draft a Rule 37 motion and proposed order

seeking appropriate sanctions for the defendant's failure to respond.

3. You represent the defendants in *American Campers v. Summers.* The plaintiff has failed to respond within 30 days to the interrogatories that you drafted (see §3.9, Problem 7). You subsequently wrote a letter to the plaintiff's attorney demanding answers. You never received a response to that letter. Draft a Rule 37 motion and proposed order compelling answers and seeking appropriate sanctions for the plaintiff's failure to respond.

4. You represent the plaintiff in *American Campers v. Summers.* The defendants have responded to your interrogatories (see §3.9, Problem 8) by completely and satisfactorily responding to interrogatories (a) and (c) and by answering the remaining questions as follows:

(b) The plaintiff was present and knows this information.
(d) It would be difficult and burdensome to respond. Ask this question during the defendants' depositions.
(e) Improperly drafted question.
(f) We object on the grounds that this question seeks legal information.

Draft a Rule 37 motion and proposed order compelling answers and seeking appropriate sanctions.

5. You represent the defendants in *American Campers v. Summers.* The plaintiff has responded to your interrogatories (see §3.9, Problem 7) by providing complete and satisfactory answers to interrogatories (c) and (d) and by answering the remaining questions as follows:

(a) This information is available from the defendants.
(b) Burdensome. A deposition is a more appropriate discovery device to use to obtain these facts.
(e) Objection. Requires a legal conclusion.

Draft a Rule 37 motion and proposed court order compelling answers and seeking appropriate sanctions.

Appendix A
HYPOTHETICAL CASE FILES

CASE FILE: AMERICAN CAMPERS v. SUMMERS

CASE SUMMARY

American Campers, the plaintiff, sold a motor home to John and Mary Summers, the defendants. The Summers purchased the camper on a retail installment contract and received a written warranty from American covering the motor home.

The defendants subsequently experienced problems with the camper and failed to make their installment payments. The plaintiff declared default, accelerated the payments, and brought this action for breach of contract. The Summers counterclaimed, alleging breach of warranty. The complaint seeks $9,510 and attorney's fees; the counterclaim seeks $15,000 plus additional damages.

The case file includes:

1. Factual Summary
2. Complaint
3. Retail Installment Contract
4. Answer and Counterclaim
5. Exhibit A, Limited Warranty
6. Reply to Counterclaim
7. Legal Memorandum

FACTUAL SUMMARY

Susan and John Summers had long wanted to own a camper motor home. On May 24, 19XX, they read an advertisement in the Mitchell Sunday Press by American Campers advertising a new 20-foot motor home on sale for $17,300. They drove the ten miles from their home to American Campers on the next day with their two young children. Carol Sexton, a salesperson, showed them the Voyageur camper and gave them a descriptive brochure. The Summers looked over the camper and brochure and then asked to take a test drive. During the ten-minute drive, they recall that Sexton explained that the motor home would get "16 miles a gallon on the highway," that financing could be readily arranged, and that American Campers had an "experienced" service department and an "extensive" parts department. Sexton recalls explaining that the camper would get "6 to 8 miles per gallon on the average," that financing was available, and that American had an "experienced" service and parts department.

The Summers agreed to buy the motor home, paying $8,000 down and financing the balance. Sexton obtained approval of the financial terms from Mitchell National Bank, and the contract was executed on May 25. Sexton told the Summers that the camper would be checked, serviced, and ready the next day. On May 26, the Summers picked up their new camper and drove home. A written limited warranty and an owner's manual were provided, but the Summers received no oral instructions on how to operate the motor home.

On the way home, the Summers noticed that the automatic transmission slipped a bit when shifted, but because of their unfamiliarity with the camper, they did not become concerned. On the weekend of June 1–3, they took a 240-mile camping trip. They checked their gas mileage and found they only got 8 miles to the gallon. They paid an average of $1.20 a gallon. They also noticed that the transmission continued to skip and developed a jerk. Susan called Sexton, who explained that the gas mileage was always lower during the initial break-in period and that as long as the transmission was not leaking oil it could be checked at the 1000-mile maintenance inspection.

The next Friday, June 8, they drove 100 miles to a campground. That night, all the interior lights and electrical outlets in the camper went dead. The Summers stayed at a $41 motel that night and drove home on Saturday. The transmission problems persisted, and the gas mileage did not improve. About 20 miles from home, the engine temperature gauge indicated "hot" and the camper stalled. John turned off the engine and checked the coolant level, which appeared to be sufficient. John then tried to restart the engine but failed, and after several minutes the battery gradually lost its power. It cost the Summers $30 to have the motor home towed to American Campers. They had a friend drive them home. Tom Arnold, the service manager, called the Summers on June 13 and told Susan that the electrical parts needed to repair the camper were not available, so it would not be ready until June 22. On June 15, the Summers received a letter and payment book from Mitchell National Bank.

John picked the camper up on June 22 with no charge for repairs. Arnold had not determined the cause of the electrical problem, but he thought that the Summers overloaded the electrical circuits. Arnold discovered that the temperature light was defective and supposed that John had flooded the engine while trying to restart it and so had drained the battery. When Arnold test-drove the camper, he did not notice any transmission problems. Arnold does not recall the Summers mentioning any gas-mileage problems. The cost of the warranty repairs was $376.

The Summers left on June 22 for a weekend camping trip 150 miles away. The engine and electrical system worked, but the transmission still slipped and jerked, and the gas mileage did not improve. While camping on Saturday, the water system failed to drain completely. While driving home Sunday, the front brakes developed a squeal. That Monday, June 25, Susan telephoned Arnold, who said the service department was very busy until after the July 4th holiday, but they could bring the camper in for repairs if they wanted. Arnold recalls that the service department was busy, but he does not recall that telephone conversation with Susan. The Summers, who wanted to use the camper for another planned weekend camping trip, decided to wait until the 1000-mile inspection and reluctantly sent their June $229.02 payment to the bank.

On June 29, they began a 130-mile camping trip. On that Friday drive, the windshield wipers broke. On Saturday while preparing dinner, the propane stove burst into flames. Susan used a fire extinguisher to douse the fire, but not before the stove and refrigerator units were extensively damaged. No one was injured. The Summers stayed in a $43 motel that night and returned home Sunday. They took the camper in Monday and complained to Arnold.

Arnold called the Summers on July 10. He informed them that the camper had been repaired and inspected at no charge. It was his opinion that John's and Susan's unfamiliarity with the camper had caused the problems. He considered charging them for these repairs ($743), which he believed were not covered by the warranty, but, to preserve good customer relations, he decided against doing so. He did advise them to read carefully and follow the owner's manual. The Summers told him that their vacation began on July 20, that they planned to drive through rough country roads, and that the camper must be working properly for this one-week trip.

They picked the camper up on July 10 and drove it 90 miles around town for ten days; everything seemed to operate well, though the gas mileage was still low. On July 20 they left for their vacation campgrounds 150 miles away. After driving 70 miles on paved roads and another 40 miles on unpaved roads, the transmission problems reappeared. On Saturday morning, John started the engine, but the oil warning light remained on. Susan checked the oil level and found none measured on the dipstick. They refilled the engine with six quarts of oil at $1.30 a quart. By adding another four quarts, they managed to drive the camper back home. On Monday, they had it towed to American Campers and called Sexton to cancel the contract and to complain about their lost vacation. They spent the remainder of their vacation at home.

One week later, on July 30, they received a letter from American Campers refusing to cancel the contract, asserting that the oil leak was due to their misuse of the camper on rough roads that had damaged the crankcase, and offering to make the needed engine repairs for an estimated $620 at their expense. The Summers wrote back, demanding the return of their down payment, their June payment, and reimbursement for $340 of camping accessories usable only with that camper. Two weeks later, on August 13, they received a letter from Mitchell National Bank demanding the July payment. Susan wrote to the bank explaining their refusal to pay. On August 25, she received a telephone call from Sexton, who said the bank had returned the contract to American, and she demanded the July and August payments. The Summers refused to pay and were served with a summons and complaint on August 31.

Case File: American Campers v. Summers

American Campers sued for the balance of the retail installment contract and did not repossess the motor home. The camper remains unrepaired in the American service lot. American Campers claims the Summers own the camper; the Summers claim they have revoked acceptance.

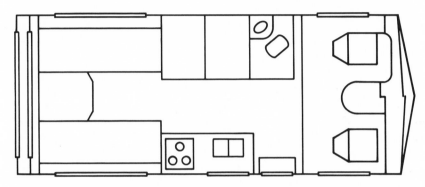

Voyageur 20' Camper Motor Home

COMPLAINT

State of Summit
County of Little

District Court
First Judicial District

American Campers, Incorporated,
    Plaintiff,

vs.

Susan and John Summers,
    Defendants.

COMPLAINT

File No. 338217

Plaintiff for its Complaint states and alleges that:

1. On May 25, 19XX, Plaintiff and Defendants entered into a retail installment contract for the purchase of a new 19XX Voyageur camper, a copy of which contract is attached to this Complaint.

2. Defendants failed to make the July and subsequent installment payments and have defaulted on the contract.

WHEREFORE, Plaintiff requests that this Court enter judgment against Defendants in the amount of $9,510.33 plus reasonable attorney's fees, interest, and costs and disbursements.

Dated: August 29, 19XX

ROGERS AND WESTBY

By: _____

Fran Westby
Attorneys for Plaintiff
1000 First State Bank
Mitchell, Summit
789-1234

Case File: American Campers v. Summers

RETAIL INSTALLMENT CONTRACT

RETAIL INSTALLMENT CONTRACT   Date   May 25, 19XX
Number   JC505

BUYER:	SELLER:
Susan and John Summers 1479 Laurel Mitchell, Summit	American Campers, Inc. 875 Grand Avenue Mitchell, Summit

Subject to the terms on the adjacent page, the Seller sells and the Buyer(s) buy the following property:

New?	Year	Make	Model	Motor Home	Vehicle No.
	19XX	Voyageur	20 foot	Camper	BN 481BB569

1.	Cash Price		$17,300.00
2.	Down Payment		
	A. Cash	$8,000.00	
	B. Trade-in	$	
	C. Sub-Total		$ 8,000.00
3.	Unpaid Balance of Cash Price		$ 9,300.00
4.	Other Charges:		
	A. Tax	$ 418.50	
	B. License & Title Fees	$ 80.30	
	C. Credit Life	$	
	D. Credit Disability	$	
	E. Credit Life & Disability	$	
	F. Property Insurance	$	
	G. Document Filing Fees	$ 16.50	
	H. Sub-Total		$ 515.30
5.	Unpaid Balance (3 + 4H) AMOUNT FINANCED		$ 9,815.30
6.	Finance Charge		$ 3,925.90
7.	Total of Payments (5 + 6)		$13,741.20
8.	Total Sale Price (1 + 4H + 6)		$21,741.20
9.	ANNUAL PERCENTAGE RATE		14.13 %

REPAYMENT SCHEDULE: Buyer promises to pay the Total of Payments to Seller in 60 installments of $299.02 each, commencing on June 25, 19XX and continuing on the same day of each following month until paid.

Seller: *Buyer(s):*

_____   _____

_____   _____

CONTRACT TERMS

1.   DELINQUENCY CHARGES: Seller may collect from the Buyer in the event any installment shall not have been paid within 10 days after it becomes due, delinquency charges in the amount of 5% of the delinquent installment or $5, whichever is less.

2.   SECURITY INTEREST: Seller shall have a Security Interest, as the term is defined in the Uniform Commercial Code of the state in which this contract is executed, in the property until all amounts due under this contract are paid in full.

3.   REBATE: Upon default or prepayment by Buyer, a refund credit will be computed in accordance with the Rule of 78's and the laws of the State of Summit.

4.   DEFAULT AND ACCELERATION: If Buyer defaults in any payment, or fails to comply with the terms of this contract, or if Seller deems Buyer insecure, Seller shall have the right, at its election, to declare the unpaid portion of the Total of Payments of this contract to be immediately due and payable.

5.   ATTORNEY'S FEES: Seller shall be entitled to reasonable attorney's fees from Buyer in an amount equal to the fees and costs incurred by Seller in collecting from Buyer under this contract.

6.   ASSIGNMENT: This contract may be assigned by Seller at its option without the approval or consent of Buyer. The assignee assumes all rights and obligations under this contract pursuant to the laws of the state of Summit. After notification of an assignment, Buyer shall make all payments directly to the assignee.

ANSWER AND COUNTERCLAIM

State of Summit   District Court
County of Little   First Judicial District

American Campers, Incorporated,
    Plaintiff,

vs.

**ANSWER AND
COUNTERCLAIM**

Susan and John Summers,
    Defendants.

File No. 338217

Defendants for an Answer to Plaintiff's Complaint state and allege:

1. Defendants admit paragraph 1.
2. Defendants deny paragraph 2 and all other claims of the Complaint.

AFFIRMATIVE DEFENSE AND COUNTERCLAIM

3. Plaintiff by statements, representations, conduct, advertisements, brochures, descriptions, and a written warranty provided Defendants with express and implied warranties covering the 19XX Voyageur Motor Home. A copy of the written warranty is attached as Exhibit A.

4. Plaintiff breached such warranties.

5. Defendants subsequently revoked acceptance of the Voyageur.

6. The remedies provided by Plaintiff have failed in their essential purposes.

7. Defendants have incurred actual, incidental, and consequential damages approximating $15,000 and have suffered additional damages for lost vacation and leisure time in an amount to be determined at trial.

WHEREFORE, Defendants demand that Plaintiff's Complaint be dismissed and that Defendants be awarded a judgment in an amount to be determined at the trial of this case plus reasonable attorney's fees, interest, and costs and disbursements.

Dated: September 22, 19XX

DAVID AND BOWER

Dale Bower
2000 Federal Bank Building
Mitchell, Summit
345-9876

EXHIBIT A, LIMITED WARRANTY

Limited Warranty   Voyageur Motor Home
American Campers, 875 Grand Avenue, Mitchell, Summit, warrants
each new camper according to the following terms:

1. TIME. This warranty extends for 12 months from the date of purchase or 12,000 miles, whichever occurs first.
2. SERVICE. American Campers will repair or replace, at its option, any part defective in material or workmanship.
3. NO CHARGE. Warranty repairs will be made without charge for parts or labor.
4. LOCATION. Warranty service will be provided by American Campers at any authorized American Campers dealer during normal business hours.
5. EXCLUSIONS. This warranty does not cover:

   (a) Normal maintenance, services, and parts used in connection with such services.
   (b) Repairs necessitated by accident, misuse, negligence, unsuitable alterations, or use not intended for the camper.

AMERICAN CAMPERS DISCLAIMS ANY RESPONSIBILITY FOR ANY INCIDENTAL OR CONSEQUENTIAL OR OTHER DAMAGES OR REMEDIES EXCEPT THOSE PROVIDED FOR IN THIS WARRANTY. ANY IMPLIED WARRANTIES ARE LIMITED TO THE DURATION OF THIS WARRANTY.

Some states do not allow limitations on how long an implied warranty lasts or do not permit exclusion of limitations of incidental or consequential damages, so the above limitations or exclusions may not apply to you.

This warranty gives you specific legal rights, and you may also have other rights which vary from state to state.

AMERICAN CAMPERS, INCORPORATED
APRIL 19XX

REPLY TO COUNTERCLAIM

State of Summit   District Court
County of Little   First Judicial District

American Campers, Incorporated,
    Plaintiff,
                                            REPLY TO COUNTERCLAIM
vs.
                                            File No. 338217
Susan and John Summers,
    Defendants.

    Plaintiff for its Reply to Defendant's Answer and Counterclaim
states and alleges that:
    1. Plaintiff admits that it provided Defendants with the written
limited warranty attached as Exhibit A to the Answer but denies providing any other warranties.
    2. Plaintiff denies all allegations contained in paragraphs 3, 4, 5,
6, and 7 of the Counterclaim.
    WHEREFORE, Plaintiff requests that the Counterclaim be dis-
missed.

Dated: October 2, 19XX

                    ROGERS AND WESTBY

By: _____

          Fran Westby
          Attorneys for Plaintiff
          1000 First State Bank
          Mitchell, Summit
          789-1234

LEGAL MEMORANDUM

This memo summarizes some of the case law, statutes, and consumer-transaction practice in the State of Summit relevant to the litigation in *American Campers v. Summers.* Your instructor may prefer to have the law of another state apply and will advise you accordingly.

1. The State of Summit does not have a statutory retail installment sales contract act. The state does have an interest-rate statute that permits the assessment of the 14.3% annual rate contained in the Summers contract.

2. Summit has adopted the 1962 version of the Uniform Commercial Code.

(a) Article 2 involving warranties and remedies was adopted verbatim. Implied warranties may be limited to the duration of an express written warranty. Remedies for incidental and consequential damages may be limited if they do not fail in their essential purpose.

(b) Article 9 involving security interests was modified to require a secured party (American Campers) to elect a remedy: either the party must repossess the secured property (the camper) or sue for the unpaid balance. The statutory amendment eliminated deficiency judgments.

(c) Summit statutory law prohibits the use of waiver-of-defense clauses in retail installment contracts. An assignee assumes the identical rights and obligations of the assignor, except that the assignee becomes liable to the Buyer only in an amount equal to the contract balance at the time of the agreement.

3. The agreement between American Campers and Mitchell National Bank allowed the bank to cancel the assignment and return the contract to American if the consumer defaulted on contract payments.

4. The $9,510.33 amount included in the complaint is the unpaid balance of the contract plus delinquency charges, less a refund credit computed as explained in Contract Term 3.

5. The attorney for Summers has determined that:

(a) The Limited Warranty conforms to the federal Warranty Act.
(b) The credit disclosures comply with the provisions of the federal Truth in Lending Act.

CASE FILE: BELLOW v. NORRIS

CASE SUMMARY

Pat Bellow, the plaintiff, was riding a motorcycle on Oak Avenue and collided with a car driven by the defendant, Fran Norris, at the intersection with Elm Street. The plaintiff, a law student, suffered head and shoulder injuries. The defendant, a security officer, suffered facial and back injuries. There were two witnesses to the accident. The plaintiff sued the defendant based on negligence, and the defendant counterclaimed on the same basis. Both the complaint and the counterclaim seek damages in excess of $50,000.

This case file includes:

1. Complaint
2. Answer and Counterclaim
3. Reply to Counterclaim
4. Traffic Accident Report
5. Medical Records of Pat Bellow from Midway Hospital
6. Medical records of Pat Bellow from Samaritan Clinic
7. Medical Records of Fran Norris from Mitchell Clinic
8. Legal Memorandum

The lawyers for Bellow and for Norris obtained a copy of the Traffic Accident Report from the police and voluntarily exchanged medical reports without resort to any formal discovery device.

The Supplement contains additional, confidential facts for each party.

COMPLAINT

State of Summit   District Court
County of Little   First Judicial District

Pat Bellow,
      Plaintiff,
                                                COMPLAINT
vs.
                                                File No. 338417
Fran Norris,
      Defendant.

---

1. On March 31, 19XX, at the intersection of Elm and Oak in Mitchell, Summit, Defendant, while driving an automobile negligently collided with Plaintiff, who was riding a motorcycle.

2. As a result, Plaintiff was injured, was unable to attend law school, suffered severe and continuing pain, was unable to lead a normal life, and incurred expenses for medical attention and the damaged motorcycle.

WHEREFORE, Plaintiff demands judgment against Defendant in an amount in excess of $50,000 plus costs and interest.

Dated: June 1, 19XX

WILLIAM & PARKER

Chris Parker
100 First State Bank
Mitchell, Summit
789-4321

ANSWER AND COUNTERCLAIM

State of Summit   District Court
County of Little   First Judicial District

Pat Bellow,
        Plaintiff,
                            ANSWER AND COUNTERCLAIM
vs.
                            File No. 338417
Fran Norris,
        Defendant.

---

1.   Defendant denies the allegations of paragraphs 1 and 2 of the Complaint and all other claims of the Plaintiff.

AFFIRMATIVE DEFENSE AND COUNTERCLAIM

2.   On March 31, 19XX, at the intersection of Oak Avenue and Elm Street in Mitchell, Summit, Plaintiff, while riding a motorcycle, negligently collided with Defendant, who was driving an automobile.

3.   Defendant suffered physical injuries and continuing pain, was unable to work and perform normal activities, and incurred damages for medical and automobile expenses.

WHEREFORE, Defendant requests that Plaintiff receive nothing and that judgment be entered against Plaintiff in an amount in excess of $50,000 plus costs and interest.

Dated: June 20, 19XX

                            BROWN AND WILLOW

                            Bert Willow
                            200 Federal Bank Building
                            Mitchell, Summit
                            340-6789

REPLY TO COUNTERCLAIM

State of Summit   District Court
County of Little   First Judicial District

Pat Bellow,
     Plaintiff,
                   REPLY TO COUNTERCLAIM
vs.
                   File No. 338417
Fran Norris,
     Defendant.

---

1. Plaintiff denies all allegations of Defendant's Counterclaim.

Dated: June 26, 19XX

                   WILLIAM & PARKER

                   Chris Parker
                   100 First State Bank
                   Mitchell, Summit
                   789-4321

TRAFFIC ACCIDENT REPORT

Date of Accident:	Month 3	Day 31	Year XX	Day of Week WEDNESDAY	Time 12:45 am pm	County	city -twp.	LITTLE of MITCHELL
Route System on: ELM STREET & OAK AVENUE					No.Vehs. 2	No.Killed 0		No.Injured 2

UNIT NO.1 - VEHICLE 1		UNIT NO.2 - VEHICLE 2	
Driver Lic. No. N-461-744-431-610	State SUMMIT	Driver Lic. No. B-454-621-082-943	State SUMMIT
First Name FRAN Middle A. Last NORRIS		First Name PAT Middle S Last BELLOW	
Number and Street 1212 MARSHALL		Number and Street 435 CENTER	
City MITCHELL State SUMMIT Zip Code		City MITCHELL State SUMMIT Zip Code	
Date of Birth 3 / 29/ XX Lic. Class A		Date of Birth 12 / 28/ XX Lic. Class C	
Vehicle #1 4-DR COMPACT	Year&Make 19XX OMNI Color BLUE	Vehicle #2 MOTORCYCLE	Year&Make 19XX HONDA Color SILVER
Lic. Plate No. DCN-051 Year 19XX State SUM No.Occ. 2		Lic. Plate No. 50-451 Year 19XX State SUM No.Occ. 1	

DESCRIPTION:
#1 HEADING WEST ON ELM--STOPPED AT INTER-SECTION. #2 PROCEEDING NORTH ON OAK AT 35 mph. #1 STARTED TO MAKE LEFT TURN AND PULLED OUT IN FRONT OF #2. COLLISION OCCURRED IN MIDDLE OF RIGHT-HAND INTER-SECTION LANE. NO SKID MARKS. NO CARS IN PARKING LANE. NEITHER DRIVER DRINKING, ILL, OR ON DRUGS. UNABLE TO DETERMINE WHO RESPONSIBLE FOR ACCIDENT.

NAMES OF INJURED PERSONS	VEHICLE	POSITION	SAFETY EQUIP.	LOCATION	INJURY
1. FRAN NORRIS	CAR	DRIVER	NONE	CAR	FACIAL CUT
2. PAT BELLOW	CYCLE	DRIVER	HELMET	PAVEMENT	HEAD/SHOULDER
3.					

CONDITIONS	
Weather: CLEAR	Obstructions: NONE
Road Surface: DRY ASPHALT	Road Character: STRAIGHT & LEVEL
Traffic Controls: STOP SIGNS ON ELM	Road Work: NONE
Posted Speed Limit: 30 mph ON OAK	Road Design: 1 LANE N WITH PARKING LANE 1 LANE S; 2 LANES EAST & WEST

MEDICAL RECORDS OF PAT BELLOW
FROM MIDWAY HOSPITAL

| MIDWAY HOSPITAL | Pt. Name: Pat Bellow
Pt. No.: 251125 |

Date	Narrative
3-31-XX	*Chief Complaint:* Shoulder abrasion and "neck pain."

History: Patient is a 25-year-old who was just admitted thru receiving with injuries from motorcycle accident. Patient was riding cycle, which struck a car and impacted the pavement with enough force to split open cloth jacket, injuring the shoulder. In addition, the head and neck were "bent back." Current complaint is "my head's throbbing." No loss of consciousness. Patient was wearing a helmet.

Past Medical History: Usual childhood diseases; no allergies; on no medications.

Physical examination: Pulse 96; blood pressure 118/66; respiration: 16; temp. 98.4° (oral).

Head: Neck appears normal with full range of motion; no masses. Head free of lesions. Eyes, nose & throat normal.
Chest: Normal
Heart: Regular at 96. No murmurs.
Abdomen: Normal

Extremities: Deep red weeping 10×10 cm. excoriation of right acromion. Lesion is literally packed with sand and asphalt and clothing particles. Full range of motion only with extreme difficulty. Other assorted superficial epidermal abrasions.

Neurologic: Cranial nerves normal. Reflexes moderate and symmetrical. Mental status: alert & oriented to time, place, & person.

Impression: Deep dermal abrasion to right shoulder.

X-rays: (1) right shoulder — negative; no fracture or separation.
(2) head and cervical spine — normal; no fractures.

Plan: Admit for irrigation and dressing of right shoulder abrasion. Observe for possible central nervous system effects. Meds: Codeine 10 mg. every 4 hrs. as needed for pain.

Took patient to treatment room. Irrigated wound and debrided away (nearly) all of the particulate debris. Patient somewhat uncooperative because of significant discomfort.

| | Pt. Name: Pat Bellow |
| MIDWAY HOSPITAL | Pt. No.: 251125 |

Date	Narrative
4/1 9:00 AM	Redressed patient's wound. Moderate continued serous weeping of the surface with early crust formation. No sign of infection.
	Patient complains of acute headaches and severe neck stiffness and pain. Physical exam confirms this. There is tenderness in the neck area; markedly decreased range of motion as noted yesterday. Cervical musculature very firm to palpation; consistent with spasm and/or ligamentous damage.
	Plan: Discharge home. Codeine 10 mg. every 4-6 hrs. for pain. Robaxin 1 gram 4 times/day for muscle relaxation. Bedrest. Patient to see me in clinic in 3 days.
4/5	Physical therapy to relieve complaints of cramps in neck. Exam revealed firmness in muscles and limited motion. Treatment consisted of 10 min. massage, 20 min. of hot pads, 10 min. of ultrasound. *P.T.*
4/7	Treatment repeated. Patient still having cramps and spasm. Marked decrease in muscle firmness after therapy. *P.T.*
4/9	Treatment repeated. Patient's cramps and spasm receding. Continued decrease of firmness after therapy. *P.T.*
4/11	Treatment repeated. Patient comfortable. Significant decrease in muscle firmness. *P.T.*
4/13	Final treatment. Patient had no cramps and spasms since last treatment. Exam revealed full motion without pain and no muscle binding. Patient discharged. *P.T.*

MEDICAL RECORDS OF PAT BELLOW
FROM SAMARITAN CLINIC

SAMARITAN CLINIC

Pt. Name: Pat Bellow   Office File: B13-117

Date	Narrative
4/4/XX	Patient returns four days after motorcycle accident with continuing complaint of headache, shoulder abrasion, and neck stiffness. *Physical Exam:* Shoulder injury healing well with good crusting. No evidence of infection. Re-dressed. *Neck:* Fair range of motion; residual but decreased tenderness and firmness. *Plan:* (1) Physical therapy with heat/massage and ultrasound every other day for 5-7 days. (2) Continue Codeine and Robaxin. (3) Return in 14 days.
4/18/XX	Shoulder healing well. Continues to complain of head and neck pain. Will discontinue meds. Patient to take aspirin 5 grains up to 8/day. Patient discharged from care. Return as needed.
5/1/XX	Patient continues to complain of occasional neck and head pain. Cannot read or watch TV for over 30 minutes without symptoms (unrelieved by aspirin). *Shoulder:* Looks good. A few particles of debris "tattooing" injury area. Slight loss of pigmentation.
5/15/XX	Still complaining of head and neck ache. Physical exam of area negative. Patient will use heat for muscle spasm. Advised to sleep without a pillow.

MEDICAL RECORDS OF FRAN NORRIS
FROM MITCHELL CLINIC

Patient: Fran Norris
Clinic File: N31F37
MITCHELL CLINIC   Doctor: Chambers

Date	Explanation	Initials
3/31/XX	26-year-old involved in minor car accident with motorcycle. Patient driver had 2.5 cm. laceration over the left zygomatic arch and complained of lower-back discomfort. *Exam:* Pulse 98, blood pressure 122/70; no allergies; on no medication. (1) Laceration as above caused by impact with car door. (2) Low back pain without radiation to lower extremities. Reflexes normal. *Diagnosis:* (1) moderate laceration. (2) low back pain *Plan:* (1) Close with 1% Xglocaine anesthesia and steri-strips. (2) Tetanus toxoid i.m. (3) Bed rest for back strain (4) Return in seven days for suture removal or earlier if back pain persists.	*S.C.*
4/2	Patient returns. Back pain has increased. Unable to sleep or find comfortable position. *Exam:* Low back tenderness. Reflexes normal. No indication of any organic cause of pain. Patient had no history of back pain. Straight leg raising test indicates decreased range of movement and low back pain. Sore musculature in lumbar region consistent with accident damage to low back. Laceration healing well. *Impression:* Marked increase in back pain. *Plan:* (1) Darvon compound 65 for pain. (2) Back exercises. Instructed in low back exercise plan to be done every day. (3) Return for suture removal or as needed.	*S.C.*

Date	Explanation	Initials
4/6	Patient back for suture removal. Scar prominent but should improve in appearance over time. Patient continues to complain about low back pain. Unable to comply with exercise regimen. Exam reveals continued soreness in lumbar region.	
	Recommend attempting ten-day traction-stretching program with R. Lucas in Physical Therapy.	*S.C.*
4/7	Patient begins traction program. Hung by upper body in harness for 30 min. at 50° angle. Complained of low back discomfort.	*P.T.*
4/8	Patient hung for 30 minutes at 60° angle. Low back pain continues.	*P.T.*
4/9	Patient hung for 30 min. at 70° angle followed by five min. of low back stretching exercises. Discomfort present.	*P.T.*
4/10	Patient hung for 30 min. at 80° followed by ten min. of stretching exercises. Pain decreasing.	*P.T.*
4/11	Patient hung for 30 min. at 90° followed by 15 min. of stretching exercises. Periodic low back pain remains.	
4/11	Program appears to be working. Soreness and tenderness in low back receding. Back pain subjectively diminishing. Analgesics ended.	*S.C.*
4/12	Patient hung for 45 min. at 90° followed by 15 minutes of exercises. Pain reducing in intensity.	*P.T.*

Page 3
MITCHELL CLINIC

Patient: Fran Norris
Clinic File: N31F37
Doctor: Chambers

Date	Explanation	Initials
4/13	Patient hung for 45 minutes at 90° and for two one-minute periods at 135° upside down on traction unit. 15 minute exercises continued. Limited pain persists.	*P.T.*
4/14	Patient hung for 45 min. at 90° and for two 90-second periods upside down at 180°. Exercises continued. Pain gradually lessening.	*P.T.*
4/15	Patient free of pain since yesterday. Hung 45 min. at 90° and for three 90-second periods at 180°. Exercises completed without pain.	*P.T.*
4/16	No complaints of pain. 45 minutes of 90° hanging and 5 minutes 180°. Exercises completed without pain.	*P.T.*
4/17	Exam revealed normal musculature in lumbar region. Reflexes normal. Leg raising tests revealed full motion and only slight pain. Advised patient to continue 15-minute daily exercises for two months. To return at that time.	*S.C.*
6/25	Patient complains of some low back discomfort and inability to perform strenuous activity. Exam revealed no apparent soreness or tenderness. Musculature, reflexes, and movement normal. Patient will probably continue to suffer subjective pain. Aspirin will relieve discomfort. Recommend continuing exercise program for three more months and return only if condition regresses. Patient discharged.	*S.C.*

LEGAL MEMORANDUM

This memo summarizes some of the case law and statutes of the State of Summit and other information relevant to the litigation of *Bellow v. Norris*. Your instructor may prefer to have the law of another state apply and will advise you accordingly.

1 The State of Summit has a modified Comparative Fault Act, which bars a claimant from recovery if the fault of the claimant is greater than the fault of the person against whom recovery is sought. Therefore, contributory negligence is not an absolute bar to recovery.

2. Summit case law has recognized the doctrine of last clear chance. It is not clear whether that doctrine continues to be recognized after enactment of the Comparative Fault Act.

3. Summit does not place any limits on the type or amount of damages sought by the parties.

4. Summit does not have a "no-fault" act.

5. The Summit Safety Code:

(a) Requires that motorcycle headlights be on whenever a motorcycle is driven on the street.

(b) Does not require motorcyclists to wear helmets.

(c) Does not require automobile drivers or passengers to wear seatbelts.

(d) Provides that the person driving on a through street has the right of way.

6. Evidence of any breach of a safety-code statute, including a speeding violation, is admissible as evidence of negligence but does not constitute negligence per se.

7. Summit law does not require the drivers involved in an accident to file accident reports if the police have done so.

8. The federal Department of Transportation requires all motorcycle helmets manufactured or sold in the United States to comply with published safety standards. The Department does not certify helmets, but it does randomly check helmets to determine if they meet the standards. Failure to comply with the DOT regulations renders the manufacturer subject to a civil lawsuit by the government seeking injunctive relief and a monetary penalty.

9. The stopping distance for a Honda Silverwing from 30 m.p.h. is 33 feet; and from 60 m.p.h. it is 140 feet.

CASE FILE: GRAHAM v. TURKEL

CASE SUMMARY

Andrew Graham, the plaintiff, had retained R.D. Turkel, an attorney who is the defendant in this case, to represent him in a real estate lease, which subsequently evolved into a lawsuit, *Graham v. Staples*. The defendant in that action, Jean Staples, owned a shopping center and allegedly leased some retail space to Andrew Graham for his sports equipment store. Graham claimed she later breached the lease, and he had R.D. Turkel sue her. She answered, and her attorney submitted interrogatories to Turkel, who in turn asked Graham for information to respond to the interrogatories. Problems encountered by both Graham and Turkel delayed preparation of the interrogatory answers. The time for responding elapsed, and the attorney for Staples obtained an order dismissing the cause of action because the plaintiff had failed to submit answers. Graham subsequently brought this malpractice action against Turkel, claiming that Turkel's negligence had caused the case to be dismissed with prejudice. The malpractice complaint seeks $76,-000 in damages. Turkel has denied the allegations and claims that Graham's negligence prevented the interrogatories from being answered on time.

The case file is organized in reverse-chronological order, with documents from the present action, *Graham v. Turkel*, followed by relevant documents from the prior lawsuit, *Graham v. Staples*. The file includes:

1. Deposition Testimony of Andrew Graham (October 12)
2. Deposition Testimony of Jean Staples (October 11)
3. Deposition Testimony of R.D. Turkel (October 10)
4. *Graham v. Turkel* Answer (July 30)
5. *Graham v. Turkel* Complaint (July 13)
6. *Graham v. Staples* Case Activity Log (by R.D. Turkel)
7. *Graham v. Staples* Order of Dismissal (June 17)
8. *Graham v. Staples* Memorandum (June 17)
9. *Graham v. Staples* Application for Dismissal (June 17)
10. *Graham v. Staples* Order Compelling Discovery (June 6)
11. Letter from Graham to Turkel (June 5)
12. *Graham v. Staples* Notice of Motion and Motion (May 30)
13. Letter from Turkel to Graham (May 11)
14. *Graham v. Staples* Defendant's Interrogatories (April 18)

Case File: Graham v. Turkel

15. *Graham v. Staples* Answer (April 18)
16. *Graham v. Staples* Complaint (April 1)
17. Letter from Turkel to Staples (March 7)
18. *Graham v. Turkel* Legal Memorandum

The Supplement contains additional, confidential facts for each party; they will be supplied by your teacher.

DEPOSITION TESTIMONY OF ANDREW GRAHAM

Present were Andrew Graham; Chris Vernon, his attorney; Dale Conroy, attorney for R.D. Turkel; and June McGee, court reporter. This testimony is a portion of testimony taken and recorded on October 12, 19XX, during the deposition of Andrew Graham conducted by Dale Conroy.

I have owned a sports equipment store in Boston, Massachusetts, for the past two and a half years. The store, Marathon Sports, specializes in shoes, clothes, and equipment for runners. The business has been a financial success, netting profits of $72,000 for the first year and $84,000 for the second. A fire during the second quarter of the third year reduced sales, but business appears to be prospering again.

Last year, I began thinking about expanding and opening a second store in another city where running was popular. I considered several locations and decided on Mitchell because of its high population of runners and because the prestigious Summit Races are held there every year during the first week in June. These week-long races feature numerous runs of varying distances for runners of different abilities and attract over 50,000 runners a year to Mitchell.

On February 24 of this year, I flew to Mitchell, toured the metropolitan area, and met with a sales marketing consultant at Marketing Associates. The consultant recommended as the best possible and most suitable location the corner, street-level, 6,000-square-foot retail space at Park Plaza, a new shopping center. This prime location was adjacent to the starting and finishing lines for the Summit Races, was near the densely populated University area, was within walking distance of downtown offices, and was on a high-traffic, main thoroughfare. The location was almost too good to be true.

The consultant gave me the name of the owner and manager, Jean Staples. I telephoned her on February 25. After she told me the space was still available, I immediately met with her at Park Plaza. I toured the space and just knew it would be ideal for my store. She told me she was offering a standard one-year lease for $8 a square foot and that those terms were firm. I told her I wanted the property beginning April 1 and only needed some time to arrange financing. Staples then told me that there was another prospective tenant who was seriously considering leasing the space effective March 1. I then decided to lease the premises and gave her a check for $4,000 "to close the deal for April 1." This amount represented rent for March. There was an under-

standing that a twelve-month lease would begin April 1. Staples gave
me a written lease with her signature on it. I told her I would sign it
after my attorney reviewed it and would have it returned to her "by
March 15."

That evening I celebrated, and the next morning I visited a few
banks in Mitchell to seek financing. Their interest rates were higher
than I anticipated, so I decided to seek financing in Boston. That
afternoon, before my plane left, I decided to drive around Mitchell and
inspect a few other locations the marketing consultant had suggested.
I drove by Town Center and Market Mall; they merely confirmed my
decision to lease the space at Park Plaza. I left Mitchell to visit my
family in Montreal for several days before returning to Boston.

I returned to Boston on March 4 and spent two days arranging
financing for the new store, with my Boston bank agreeing to lend me
the money. On March 7 I contacted my Boston lawyer, Jane Romero,
and explained what happened and that somehow I had accidently lost
the lease agreement Staples gave me. She immediately telephoned an
attorney, R.D. Turkel, in Mitchell. I talked to him over the phone and
explained everything.

On March 10, my mother died suddenly in Montreal. I called Jane
Romero and told her that I did not want to be bothered for any reason
until I returned to Boston in several days. I just forgot about the March
15 deadline with Staples. I arrived home in Boston on March 16 and
checked for telephone messages on my home telephone recorder.
There was one message from Jean Staples on March 11, asking me to
return her call. Turkel called me on that day, March 16, and told me
Staples had leased the Park Plaza space to another retailer, Sports
Unlimited, and advised me that I had an excellent claim against Staples
and could sue for damages. I told Turkel that I didn't care what it cost
but to sue for as much as possible. I explained to Turkel the income
I projected from a store in Park Plaza and sent him a $500 retainer.

I heard nothing further from Turkel until May 13, when I received
a complaint, answer, and a set of interrogatories along with a letter
from Turkel. I decided to postpone responding to the questions until
I returned from my four-day business trip to Calgary and Vancouver.
I left May 14. I did not realize the importance of providing the information to Turkel at that time. The four-day business trip unexpectedly
took me to Edmonton, Winnipeg, and Toronto. I did not return until
May 24. I received Turkel's May 17 and 20 messages on May 25 and
telephoned Turkel that day. I promised to send Turkel the information, and he told me that that would be all right.

That night, May 25, a fire destroyed part of the Marathon Sports store in Boston. I spent more than one week working morning and night to clean up and re-open the store. I just plain forgot all about answering the interrogatories. By the end of that long week I was exhausted and did not check my telephone messages at home until June 3. I returned Turkel's May 30 call on June 3. I did what he told me; I found the interrogatories and sent the answers on June 4. I worked a few more days in the store, until everything was operating smoothly, and decided to take a short and well-deserved vacation. I left June 12 for a five-day camping and canoe trip in Ontario. I went by myself. I didn't tell anyone where I was going so I couldn't be bothered. On June 20 Turkel telephoned me in Boston and told me that my lawsuit against Staples had been dismissed because of my failure to answer the interrogatories in time. I asked why he had not explained such consequences to me. Turkel said nothing in reply, but he did ask if I wanted to pursue the matter and obtain some kind of order re-opening something. I got mad and fired him. I later received a bill from him. I paid it, thinking the matter was ended and I had no other choice.

On July 1, I flew to Mitchell and again toured the city, looking for another location for my store. The consultant at Marketing Associates advised me that in addition to Sports Unlimited, a similar sports store had opened in Market Mall on June 1 and that Town Center had no retail space available. He said that opening Marathon Sports would be a very risky venture at this time and that it would be wiser to wait until next spring to review the situation. I became bitter at this turn of events and thought about all the money I lost because Turkel had bungled my lawsuit. I then decided to sue him for malpractice.

DEPOSITION TESTIMONY OF JEAN STAPLES

Present were Jean Staples; Leo Olsheski, her attorney; Dale Conroy, attorney for R.D. Turkel; Chris Vernon, attorney for A. Graham; and Alan Anderson, court reporter. This testimony is a portion of testimony taken and recorded on October 11, 19XX, during the deposition of Jean Staples conducted by Chris Vernon.

I own and manage Park Plaza, a small shopping center in Mitchell. This new mall and eleven of its twelve retail stores opened on March 1 of this year. I leased the remaining space, a corner retail location consisting of 6,000 square feet, on March 16 to Sports Unlimited. Sports Unlimited sells various sorts of sports equipment, including shoes, clothing, and related accessories for runners.

Mel and Diane Apsberg, the owners of Sports Unlimited, first contacted me around February 19 and expressed their interest in leasing the space beginning March 1. They currently leased space at another location in Mitchell and hoped to move by March 1. On February 25 Andrew Graham telephoned me to ask about the corner location at Park Plaza. I mentioned it was still available. He wanted to see it immediately. I met him there that afternoon and told him my lease terms were $8 a square foot for one year, with additional rent and years negotiable. He told me that he needed the space beginning on April 1 and still had to arrange for financing. He described his plans for the Marathon Sports store and told me he wanted the space beginning April 1, assuming, he added, he could arrange financing by that time. I told him that another retailer had expressed some interest in the space for March 1. He then gave me a check for $4,000 to "hold the deal open for April 1" until his attorney contacted me "by March 15." I accepted the check as payment for an option to lease through March 15 and gave him a copy of the standard Park Plaza lease agreement. I did not sign any lease agreement. I thought $4,000 was a bit high for such a short option, but he seemed extremely interested in the space and it was his money. We shook hands and he left.

On February 26, the Apsbergs from Sports Unlimited called me to lease the space for two years beginning March 1. I told them about the option I gave Andrew Graham. They were disappointed, but I told them to call on March 16 to check on the Marathon Sports lease. I never heard from Graham again. I telephoned him twice, on March 8 and 11 at the Boston phone number he gave me, and left a recorded message each time to return my call. He never did. I assumed he no longer had any interest in the property.

On March 16, the Apsbergs called me and we negotiated a two-year lease at $8.75 a square foot for the first year and $9.25 for the second year. An attorney, R.D. Turkel, also called me that day, asking me about the lease with Graham. I explained what happened. Turkel also asked me about a March 7 letter; I replied that I never received such a letter.

That was the last I heard until Graham sued me.

DEPOSITION TESTIMONY OF R.D. TURKEL

Present were R.D. Turkel; Dale Conroy, his attorney; Chris Vernon, attorney for A. Graham; James Kirkwood, court reporter. This testimony is a portion of testimony taken and recorded on October 10, 19XX, during the deposition of R.D. Turkel conducted by Chris Vernon.

I am a lawyer practicing in Mitchell, Summit. I graduated from law school ten years ago, spent two years as a public defender, and worked for the last eight years in private practice as a solo practitioner. I am admitted to practice in the State of Summit and before the Federal District Court in Summit. I am a member of the American, the Summit, and the Little County Bar Associations. I have a general practice. I spend about 40 percent of my time in personal injury work, another 20 percent in workers' compensation matters, probably 20 percent in family law cases, and the remaining 20 percent in real estate and miscellaneous matters. Over the past several years my practice has been good. My average active caseload is about 120 files.

On March 7, I received a telephone call from Jane Romero, from Boston. I worked on a real estate matter with Jane about five years ago. She asked me to represent Andrew Graham and prepare a retail lease agreement for him regarding rental property in Mitchell. I agreed. Andrew Graham explained the situation to me over the phone. He never told me about any March 15 deadline; all I knew was that Graham needed a written lease before April 1. I immediately wrote to Jean Staples confirming the lease arrangements and requesting a copy of the agreement. I heard nothing from Staples or Graham. I telephoned Jane Romero on March 11, and she told me about the death of Graham's mother. I decided to do nothing until he returned. On March 16, before I tried to contact Graham, I thought it would be wise to contact Staples to obtain a copy of the lease agreement. Staples told me that she had leased the space to another retailer and explained her position. I asked her if she had received my March 7 letter. She said she had not.

I immediately telephoned Graham and advised him of what happened. I suggested that I research the validity of any claim he might have against Staples to determine if he should sue. Graham was terribly upset at the news and insisted that I sue. I told him I thought he had a valid claim against Staples but that it was weak because there was nothing in writing. I further explained that it was possible to seek a court order enjoining enforcement of the lease between Staples and

Sports Unlimited but that such an action probably would be unsuccessful. Graham said that he only wanted damages and that I should sue Staples immediately. I tried to explain the costs and my fees, but he said he didn't care what it cost as long as Staples got hers. I asked him some questions about projected lost profits and requested a $500 retainer, which Graham paid.

I completed work on two workers' compensation cases and a few family law matters for other clients. Then I prepared a summons and complaint and had them served on Staples on April 1. On April 20, my office received an answer and a set of five interrogatories from F. James Shyer, attorney for Staples. I was involved in a two-week personal injury trial that ended just as my 10-day vacation began on April 30. I thought there would be more than enough time to answer the interrogatories by May 20. I reread the interrogatories when I returned on May 11 and realized that I needed some information from Graham to answer. I immediately sent him a cover letter and a copy of the complaint, answer, and interrogatories. Graham didn't call me. I tried to call him at home on May 17 and at his store in Boston. I left a message at the store in case he called during his business trip. I wasn't overly concerned when May 20 passed because it isn't uncommon for attorneys to send interrogatories late. On May 20 I again called Graham and left a message. On May 24 I received a telephone call from F. James Shyer insisting on the answers. On May 25 Graham finally called me. I told him I needed the information immediately.

After the Memorial Day weekend (May 27–29), I became concerned. On May 30 I received a motion and notice of motion from James Shyer scheduling a hearing on June 6 to seek an order compelling answers. I immediately telephoned Boston, only to discover that the telephone at Marathon Sports had been disconnected. I then called Graham's home and left a recorded message. I didn't know what else to do. On June 3, Graham finally called me, told me about the fire in his store, apologized for his forgetfulness, and promised to send me the answers the next day. That same day I called James Shyer to explain that the answers would be coming in a day or two and that there was no apparent need for the hearing. Shyer disagreed. He said he planned to obtain a court order with sanctions for noncompliance. I suggested that I would not appear and oppose the motion if any sanctions would be deferred until June 16 and if Shyer did not seek attorney's fees at the hearing. Shyer agreed and obtained a court order on June 6, a copy of which I received on June 7.

On June 7, when the information from Graham was received at my office, I was in trial in Elmhurst, Summit, 135 miles from Mitchell. My secretary told me by telephone that the answers had arrived. I assumed they were complete. When I returned to my office on June 13 and read Graham's letter, I first realized the information was incomplete. I immediately tried to reach Graham in Boston but he was not available. I obtained his family's telephone number in Montreal and called but did not reach anyone until June 14. They did not know where he was. I called James Shyer on June 14 and left an urgent message. Shyer called back on June 15. I suggested that I contact Judge Wall, who signed the order, and have him extend the pre-sanction period for ten more days. Shyer seemed willing to agree but needed the approval of his client. The next afternoon, Shyer called back and told me Staples wanted the order enforced and would not agree to an extension. I called Judge Wall but she refused to take any action *ex parte* without a motion and hearing.

After June 17, I researched Summit law to determine what could be done. It was possible to bring a motion seeking to re-open the judgment. I called Graham on June 20 at his store to tell him that his case had been dismissed because of his failure to answer the interrogatories on time. He got mad and blamed me. I told him it was possible to re-open the case, but he replied that he had had enough. He did not ask me then or at any time why I did not explain the consequences of failing to answer interrogatories. I know I explained those consequences to him during one of our telephone conversations, but I can't remember which one. I sent him a final bill for my services, which he paid within a week. I never heard from him again until I received the summons and complaint in this case.

GRAHAM v. TURKEL ANSWER

State of Summit   District Court
County of Little   First Judicial District

Andrew Graham,
    Plaintiff,

                             ANSWER
vs.
                           File No. 338820
R. D. Turkel,
    Defendant.

---

1. Defendant admits paragraph 1 of the Complaint.
2. Defendant denies all other allegations of the Complaint.

AFFIRMATIVE DEFENSES

3. Plaintiff's claimed damages were caused by Plaintiff's own negligence and failure to act.

4. Plaintiff's claimed damages were caused by the conduct and negligence of third persons over whom Plaintiff has no control.

WHEREFORE, Defendant requests this Court to dismiss the Complaint and to enter judgment for Defendant, including the costs and disbursements of this action.

Dated: July 30, 19XX

Dale Conroy
Peters, Conroy, and Goldberg
1130 City Center
Mitchell, Summit
346-1620

GRAHAM v. TURKEL COMPLAINT

State of Summit   District Court
County of Little   First Judicial District

Andrew Graham,
    Plaintiff,

                                     COMPLAINT

vs.

                                 File No. 338820

R.D. Turkel,
    Defendant.

---

1.   On or about March 7, 19XX, Plaintiff Andrew Graham, doing business as Marathon Sports Enterprises, retained Defendant R.D. Turkel, an attorney at law, to represent Plaintiff with respect to a claim against Park Plaza Associates and Jean Staples (collectively "Park Plaza").

2.   Defendant advised Plaintiff that Plaintiff had an excellent cause of action against Park Plaza, and Plaintiff directed Defendant to commence a lawsuit to enforce Plaintiff's rights.

3.   Defendant commenced a lawsuit against Park Plaza ("Park Plaza Action"), but negligently and in breach of Plaintiff's agreement with Defendant, Defendant permitted such lawsuit to be dismissed with prejudice.

4.   Plaintiff's causes of action against Park Plaza have been permanently barred by Defendant's negligence and breach of contract.

5.   Plaintiff has sustained damages in the amount of $76,000.00 as direct and proximate results of Defendant's negligence and breach of contract.

6.   Plaintiff is entitled to recover attorney's fees incurred in this action.

WHEREFORE, Plaintiff prays for judgment against Defendant R.D. Turkel in the amount of $76,000.00, for a jury trial, for costs and disbursements including attorney's fees, and for such further relief as this Court may deem appropriate.

Dated this 13th day of July, 19XX.

BRODER AND VERNON

By: _____

Chris Vernon
800 Mitchell Place
Mitchell, Summit
346-2162

GRAHAM v. STAPLES
CASE ACTIVITY LOG

CLIENT: Andrew Graham   CASE: Graham v. Staples
ATTORNEY: R.D. TURKEL   FILE NO: 338820

Date	Activity	Time in hours
3/7/XX Monday	Opened file. Interviewed Graham. Wrote letter to Staples.	1.25
3/11 Friday	Telephoned Romero in Boston. Advised of death of Graham's mother. Will return March 15.	.15
3/16 Wednesday	Telephoned Staples. Advised of lease with Sports Unlimited.	.20
3/16	Telephoned Graham. Advised him of situation. He insists I sue Staples. Requested $500 retainer.	.25
3/18 Friday	$500 retainer received from Graham.	.20
4/1 Friday	Completed summons and complaint and had them served on Staples.	1.0
4/20 Wednesday	Received answer and interrogatories from F. James Shyer, lawyer for Staples.	.50
5/11 Wednesday	Reread interrogatories. Sent Graham pleadings and request for information.	.25
5/17 Tuesday	Telephoned Graham and left message.	.50
5/20 Friday	Telephoned Graham and left message.	.50
5/24 Tuesday	Received telephone call from James Shyer, requesting answers to the interrogatories. Advised Shyer that answers would be provided by 5/31.	.20
5/25 Wednesday	Graham returned my calls and told me information will be sent immediately.	.20
5/30 Monday	Received Notice of Motion and Motion from Shyer seeking order compelling answers.	.15
5/30 Monday	Telephoned Graham in Boston. Phone at Marathon Sports disconnected. Left message at home recorder.	.25

GRAHAM v. STAPLES
CASE ACTIVITY LOG

CLIENT: Andrew Graham   CASE: Graham v. Staples
ATTORNEY: R.D. TURKEL   FILE NO: 338820

Date	Activity	Time in hours
6/3 Friday	Graham returned call, apologized for his mistakes, and promised information immediately.	.20
6/3 Friday	Telephoned Shyer and explained situation. Shyer will seek order on own with no attorney's fees and ten days until enforcement.	.25
6/7 Tuesday	Served with court order. Case to be dismissed if interrogatories not answered by June 19.	.20
6/7 Tuesday	Received information from Graham.	.50
6/13 Monday	Reviewed information from Graham. Insufficient. Telephoned Graham in Boston. Not at home. Tracked down his family in Montreal; telephoned and left message.	1.25
6/14 Tuesday	Montreal family called me. No idea where Graham is. Telephoned Shyer and left urgent message.	.20
6/15 Wednesday	Shyer returned call. Was agreeable to postpone dismissal date. Will contact Staples and confirm.	.30
6/16 Thursday	Shyer called and told me Staples insists on enforcing order. Realized date was June 16, not 19. Telephoned Judge Wall, who refused to do anything.	.30
6/17 Friday	Received court order. Researched law on alternative remedies. Decided best remedy was to bring motion to re-open case.	1.50
6/20 Monday	Telephoned Graham in Boston. Advised him of dismissal. He told me to do nothing further.	.50
6/20 Monday	Sent Graham final bill for services. 11.10 hrs. + $60 an hour = $666 − $500 retainer = $166 bal.	.20
6/27 Monday	Graham paid bill in full. File closed.	.10

GRAHAM v. STAPLES ORDER OF DISMISSAL

State of Summit   District Court
County of Little   First Judicial District

Andrew Graham, *doing business*
as Marathon Sports Enterprises,
    Plaintiff,

                         ORDER OF DISMISSAL AND
vs.   **MEMORANDUM**

Jean Staples, *doing business*   **File No. 338617**
as Park Plaza Associates,
    Defendant.

This matter again came on for consideration of Defendant's motion to compel discovery, pursuant to the sworn application of F. James Shyer, attorney for Defendant.

It appearing that Plaintiff has willfully failed to comply with Defendant's valid discovery requests and has willfully failed to comply with this Court's June 6, 19XX, Order Compelling Discovery,

IT IS HEREBY ORDERED that Plaintiff's action shall be, and hereby is, dismissed with prejudice and on the merits pursuant to Fed. R. Civ. P. 37(b) and 37(d), and that each party shall bear its own costs and disbursements.

The attached Memorandum is made a part hereof.

LET JUDGMENT BE ENTERED IMMEDIATELY.

                                   Judge R. Wall

Dated: June 17 19XX

359

GRAHAM v. STAPLES
MEMORANDUM

This action has been before the Court upon a motion to compel discovery and now upon an application for imposition of sanctions. Inasmuch as discovery responses are now seriously overdue, and this Court's June 6, 19XX, Order Compelling Discovery has been ignored, dismissal of Plaintiff's action appears the only appropriate remedy. Fed. R. Civ. P. 37(a) would permit the imposition of this sanction even without the second chance provided Plaintiff by this Court's June 6 Order. Dismissal is now authorized by Fed. R. Civ. P. 37(d) and 37(b).

R.W.
6-18-XX

Case File: Graham v. Turkel

GRAHAM v. STAPLES APPLICATION FOR DISMISSAL

State of Summit   District Court
County of Little   First Judicial District

Andrew Graham, *doing business*
as Marathon Sports Enterprises,
     Plaintiff,

vs.   **APPLICATION FOR DISMISSAL**

Jean Staples, *doing business*   **File No. 338617**
as Park Plaza Associates,
     Defendant.

    F. James Shyer, being first duly on oath sworn, deposes and states that:

    1. Affiant is an attorney at law, and one of the attorneys for Defendant in this action.

    2. Affiant caused this Court's June 6, 19XX, Order Compelling Discovery to be mailed to counsel for Plaintiff.

    3. Plaintiff has not complied with this Court's June 6, 19XX, Order, and Defendant's Interrogatories have not been answered.

    4. Defendant respectfully requests this Court to dismiss Plaintiff's action pursuant to this Court's June 6, 19XX, Order.

_____

F. James Shyer

Subscribed and sworn to before me
this 17th day of June, 19XX.

_____
    Notary Public

GRAHAM v. STAPLES ORDER COMPELLING DISCOVERY

State of Summit   District Court
County of Little   First Judicial District

Andrew Graham, *doing business*
as Marathon Sports Enterprises,
    Plaintiff,   **ORDER COMPELLING DISCOVERY**

vs.   **File No. 338617**

Jean Staples, *doing business*
as Park Plaza Associates,
    Defendant.

This matter came on before the undersigned upon the motion of Defendant for an order compelling discovery. F. James Shyer appeared for Defendant. There was no appearance by or on behalf of Plaintiff, although due notice was given.

The Court being fully advised in the premises,

IT IS HEREBY ORDERED that:

1. Plaintiff shall provide full and complete answers to interrogatories served by Defendant by June 16, 19XX.

2. Defendant's request for attorney's fees, being withdrawn at the hearing hereby shall be, and is, denied.

3. If Plaintiff shall fail to comply with this Order by June 16, 19XX, this Court will dismiss Plaintiff's action with prejudice upon sworn application of Defendant's counsel, but without further notice or hearing.

SO ORDERED.

Judge R. Wall

Dated: June 6, 19XX

LETTER FROM GRAHAM TO TURKEL

MARATHON SPORTS
1680 Randolph
Boston, Massachusetts

June 5, 19XX

R.D. Turkel
1200 Summit National Plaza
Mitchell, Summit

Dear R.D.:

I apologize for the delay in responding to you. Cleaning and re-opening my store after the fire took all my time and attention. In any event, the answers:

1. You know who I am.
2. The $72,000 was and is based on a rough estimate of the net profits I think I would have made in the store in Mitchell. This figure is based on my profits from the first year of operation of the Boston store.
3. (a) Marathon Sports, 1680 Randolph, Boston, Mass.
    (b) Sports equipment.
    (c) Me.
    (d) Opened in January, two years ago.
    (e) Confidential. I don't feel we should disclose this.
    (f) Why do they want to know this? Twelve people work for me, who need not be involved in this case.
4. I don't know of any. Unless they mean my accountant.
5. Jean Staples. I think that is all? Good luck. I am off for a much-needed rest.

Very truly yours,

Andrew Graham

GRAHAM v. STAPLES NOTICE OF MOTION AND MOTION

State of Summit
County of Little

District Court
First Judicial District

Andrew Graham, *doing business as* Marathon Sports Enterprises,
    Plaintiff,

vs.

Jean Staples, *doing business as* Park Plaza Associates,
    Defendant.

NOTICE OF MOTION AND MOTION

File No. 338617

TO: Plaintiff Andrew Graham, and his attorney of record, R.D. Turkel

PLEASE TAKE NOTICE that Defendant Park Plaza will bring the following motion on for hearing before the Honorable R. Wall on the 6th day of June, 19XX, at Courtroom 3, Summit District Courthouse, at 9:30 A.M., or as soon thereafter as counsel may be heard.

MOTION TO COMPEL DISCOVERY

Defendant respectfully moves this Court for its Order, pursuant to Rules 33 and 37 of the Federal Rules of Civil Procedure, compelling Plaintiff to serve full and complete answers to Interrogatories, awarding him his costs of obtaining relief, including a reasonable attorney's fee, and providing that Plaintiff's action be dismissed if discovery is not made as ordered.

Dated: May 30, 19XX

BARBERO, WILKSTAD &
SHYER

F. James Shyer
1550 Mitchell Towers
Mitchell, Summit
346-6584

LETTER FROM TURKEL TO GRAHAM

R.D. Turkel
Attorney at Law
1200 Summit National Plaza
Mitchell, Summit
346–7809

May 11, 19XX

Andrew Graham
Marathon Sports
1680 Randolph
Boston, Massachusetts

Dear Mr. Graham:

Enclosed is a copy of our complaint, as well as the answer and set of interrogatories served upon us by the attorney for Staples. We have until May 20 to respond. Please read the interrogatories and provide me with the information I need to answer the questions.

If you have any questions about the lawsuit or its progress, please contact me. My evaluation remains positive; we have a strong case based on the facts developed to date. I hope to conclude promptly.

Yours very truly,

R.D. Turkel

RDT:ad

GRAHAM v. STAPLES DEFENDANT'S
INTERROGATORIES

State of Summit   District Court
County of Little   First Judicial District

Andrew Graham, *doing business*
as Marathon Sports Enterprises,
      Plaintiff,   **DEFENDANT'S**
                                                  INTERROGATORIES
vs.

                                               File No. 338617
Jean Staples, *doing business*
as Park Plaza Associates,
      Defendant.

TO: Plaintiff Andrew Graham

Defendant requests answers to the following interrogatories, under oath, within thirty (30) days, pursuant to Fed. R. Civ. P. 33.

1.   State the name, address, Social Security number, date of birth, and residence address of the person answering these interrogatories.
2.   State all facts upon which you base the estimate, contained in paragraph 3 of your Complaint, that Plaintiff sustained $72,000.00 for lost income, identifying the dates and amounts, and all witnesses having knowledge thereof.
3.   If Plaintiff has any experience in operating a business such as that intended to be operated at Park Plaza, please identify all locations of such experience, and for each location state

    (a)   the street address, city and state;
    (b)   nature of business;
    (c)   identity of owner of premises;
    (d)   dates of operation;
    (e)   monthly sales, cost and profit data; and
    (f)   identify and state present location of all employees.

4.   Identify any accountants, economists, or other experts consulted by you during the operation of your business or in this lawsuit, and provide the opinions of any such experts you intend to call to testify at trial.

5. Identify all individuals having any information about or concerning the facts of this action, the transaction of the parties, or Plaintiff's claimed damages.

Dated: April 18, 19XX

BARBERO, WILKSTAD &
SHYER

_____

F. James Shyer
1550 Mitchell Towers
Mitchell, Summit
346-6584

GRAHAM v. STAPLES ANSWER

State of Summit

County of Little

District Court

First Judicial District

Andrew Graham, *doing business
as* Marathon Sports Enterprises,
    Plaintiff,

vs.

Jean Staples, *doing business
as* Park Plaza Associates,
    Defendant.

ANSWER

File No. 338617

---

    1. Defendant admits that on March 16, 19XX, Defendant leased the retail premises at 101 Park Plaza to Sports Unlimited and not to Plaintiff.

    2. Defendant denies all other allegations of the Complaint.

    3. Defendant asserts that Plaintiff failed to exercise its option to rent the premises by March 15, 19XX.

Dated: April 18, 19XX

                        BARBERO, WILKSTAD &
                        SHYER

By: _____

              F. James Shyer
              1550 Mitchell Towers
              Mitchell, Summit
              346-6584

GRAHAM v. STAPLES COMPLAINT

State of Summit   District Court
County of Little   First Judicial District

Andrew Graham, *doing business*
as Marathon Sports Enterprises,
    Plaintiff,
                                                        COMPLAINT
vs.
                                                        File No. 338617
Jean Staples, *doing business*
as Park Plaza Associates,
    Defendant.

Plaintiff for his cause of action against Defendant alleges that:

1.   On February 25, 19XX, Plaintiff Andrew Graham, who planned to open a Marathon Sports store, and Defendant Jean Staples, who owns and manages Park Plaza, entered into a lease agreement for the rental of the premises at 101 Park Plaza for a term of one year at a rate of $8 per square foot, occupancy to begin April 1, 19XX.

2.   On March 15, 19XX, Defendant breached this lease agreement by renting the premises to another retailer not the Plaintiff.

3.   As a result, Plaintiff has incurred damages, including a $4,000 rental payment and lost income from store profits estimated to be $72,000.

WHEREFORE, Plaintiff requests that this Court award Plaintiff a judgment against Defendant in the amount of $76,000 plus interest and costs.

Dated: April 1, 19XX

R.D. Turkel
Attorney for Plaintiff
1200 Summit National Plaza
Mitchell, Summit
346-7809

LETTER FROM TURKEL TO STAPLES

R. D. Turkel
Attorney at Law
1200 Summit National Plaza
Mitchell, Summit
346-7809

March 7, 19XX

Jean Staples
Management Office
Park Plaza
Mitchell, Summit

Re: Lease for Retail Space at 101 Park Place.

Dear Ms. Staples:

Andrew Graham has retained me to represent him regarding his leasing of retail premises at Park Plaza. He has informed me that an agreement has been reached with you for the 6,000 square feet at 101 Park Plaza for a term of one year at $8 a square foot. He has also advised me that you provided him with the written lease bearing your signature. Unfortunately, Mr. Graham has misplaced this lease, and I am writing to ask that you send me a copy of the agreement for my review. I understand the lease is to begin April 1, and I would appreciate receiving a copy from you as soon as possible.

Yours very truly,

_____

R.D. Turkel

RDT:ad

GRAHAM v. TURKEL LEGAL MEMORANDUM

This memo summarizes some of the case law and statutes of the State of Summit and provides additional information relevant to the litigation. Your instructor may prefer to have the law of another state apply and will advise you accordingly.

1. Summit Statute 342.36(a) requires that a contract or lease be written to be enforced if such an obligation "cannot be completed within one year from the date of its inception." The Summit Supreme Court has never reviewed or interpreted this provision.

2. The Summit Supreme Court has established precedent in several contract cases that substantial part performance will render an unwritten contract enforceable. The court has not established any guidelines for what "substantial part performance" includes.

3. The Summit Supreme Court, the State Advisory Committee to the Rules of Civil Procedure for Summit District Courts, and the District Court Judicial Conference, which is composed of District Court judges, have all recently urged judges to enforce strictly the discovery rules and time limits in order to reduce discovery abuses. Two years ago, the Summit Supreme Court in *Holland v. National Freezer Co.,* 346 Sum. 678, upheld the lower court's dismissal with prejudice of a case because the plaintiff had failed to respond to requests for documents on time.

4. The elements of a cause of action for a legal malpractice case in Summit are:

   (a)   Existence of an attorney-client relationship;
   (b)   Negligence by the defendant;
   (c)   Acts by the defendant that proximately caused plaintiff's damages;
   (d)   But for the defendant's conduct, plaintiff would have been successful in the underlying action.

The test of negligence is whether the attorney acted reasonably in applying the standards maintained by lawyers in the community. Contributory negligence is not an absolute bar to such an action.

5. *Graham v. Turkel,* if appealed, would be a case of first impression for the Summit Supreme Court.

6. The plaintiff has retained, as an expert he plans to call at trial, Bert Latimer, presently a law professor at Summit University College of Law. Latimer teaches professional responsibility and trial advocacy

and supervises law students in a civil-practice clinic. Latimer has been a professor for six years and has authored a casebook, Cases and Materials on Professional Responsibility, for Little, Brown and Company. Latimer has also published various trial and practice articles in legal magazines and law reviews and has been a trainer and consultant with the American Trial Lawyers' Institute (ATLI) for the past four years. Latimer practiced for several years as a solo practitioner in Summit before becoming a law professor.

7. The defendant has retained Pat Kinney as an expert witness who will testify at trial. Kinney is currently the Director of the Summit State Bar Association and has held that position for the past four years, administering a staff of six people. Kinney previously served for four years as Director of the Summit State Board of Professional Responsibility, which board had the responsibility to investigate, determine, and recommend to the Supreme Court sanctions for attorneys who violated the Code of Professional Responsibility. Kinney previously practiced for 8 years as a civil litigator and partner with a large law firm in Mitchell. Kinney has published several articles on professional responsibility over the past five years in various legal magazines and law reviews. Kinney graduated from Summit University Law School 28 years ago.

8. Neither party plans to call any other expert at trial.

9. The Supplement contains confidential information, consisting of a resume and opinion letter from each of the experts. The opinion letters are general in nature and do not contain the detail of and bases for the expert opinions. In preparing your expert, you will need to add such details consistent with the facts and law.

Appendix B*
CLIENT DEPOSITION INSTRUCTIONS

Your deposition will soon be taken. It is a normal, regular procedure in a case such as yours. These instructions are meant to explain to you what a deposition is, acquaint you with procedures, answer most of your questions about depositions, and advise you how to conduct yourself during the deposition. Please read these guidelines thoroughly and carefully. We have already met or will meet before the deposition to review the facts and to prepare you fully for the depositions.

This booklet will assist you with that preparation by presenting general guidelines applicable to all depositions. However, individual depositions vary because of different people, different lawyers, and different facts. There may well be some differences between depositions, as discussed here, and what we have already discussed or will later discuss about your deposition. You should always follow my specific advice. Should you have any questions after you read these guidelines, ask me them the next time we meet or before the deposition.

Your deposition has been scheduled for ____*time*____, at _____*place*_____. Please meet me before the deposition at ____*time*____, at _____*place*_____. Please meet me at my office to prepare for the deposition at ____*time*____. Should the above dates and time conflict with your schedule, please telephone _____ immediately at _____.

---

*Some ideas appearing in this appendix are adapted with permission from the copyrighted publication, About Your Deposition: 95 Questions and Answers. The booklet contains an excellent explanation of personal injury depositions, and it may be obtained from The Lawyers and Judges Publishing Co., P.O. Box 42050, Tucson, AZ., 85733.

Contents

I. GENERAL INFORMATION

A. Definitions and Background Information

Q: What is a deposition?

A: A deposition is one of a number of procedural "discovery" methods used by an opposing attorney to "discover" information about your case. It is part of the other side's investigation of the case. The opposing attorney will ask you a series of questions. You will take an oath to tell the truth in answering all questions.

Q: What is a deponent?

A: A deponent is a person who gives information to the lawyer in a conference-type setting. This whole process in which the lawyer questions the deponent and the deponent gives information is called a deposition. The "depondent" is the same as the "witness."

Q: Why is my deposition being taken?

A: So that the opposing lawyer can determine what you know about the facts and details of the case. A deposition enables a lawyer to form an impression and to make an appraisal about you, about what you know, and about how you say it.

Q: What rules govern the deposition?

A: The rules that regulate what happens during a lawsuit. These rules allow the lawyers to obtain information through discovery before the trial to better prepare for the trial. These rules also increase the chances of settling the case so that you may not have to testify again at trial.

Q: How is this information going to be used?

General Information

A: The information tells the other side what you know. Your deposition gives the other lawyer an opportunity to determine how good a witness you are going to be. The information also helps settle cases because both sides know the various versions of what happened and they can more easily agree on a settlement before trial.

Q: What if this case goes to trial? How is the deposition transcript used in court?

A: Statements that you make during a deposition may be evidence for court. If you admit or deny certain things or give certain information, this information may be used as evidence in court. It may also be used as "impeachment" evidence; that is, evidence that will be used to show that you have said something inconsistent. If your testimony differs at trial from your testimony during the deposition, the other attorney may be able to read from, or have you read from, the deposition transcript, and point out the inconsistency to the judge and jury. The deposition transcript could also be used instead of your live testimony should you be unavailable at the time of the trial.

B. Logistics

Q: Do I have to attend the deposition?

A: Yes. Your lawyer has been served with a written notice of your deposition and you must attend. It may be possible for the time and date of your deposition to be changed, and you should discuss this with your attorney if you have any questions.

Q: How long does a deposition take?

A: That depends on the particular case and the lawyer asking the questions. Your lawyer may be able to estimate the time for your deposition. Your schedule should be arranged so that you will not be hurried or rushed for time when you testify.

Q: Will there be any breaks during the deposition?

A: Yes. There will be breaks periodically throughout the deposition, depending on its length. You should be as comfortable as possible at all times. Tell your lawyer about any physical conditions or problems that you have which require special attention. Your lawyer will arrange for any breaks you need during the deposition.

Q: Will I be allowed to drink coffee or water or smoke during the deposition?

A: You will usually be allowed to drink water or coffee or some other refreshment. You may or may not be allowed to smoke. No eating is permitted. If you need a break, let your lawyer know.

Q: Will I get reimbursed for lost wages or transportation expenses?

A: No. You will have to bear those costs as part of your involvement in this lawsuit.

Q: What should I wear to the deposition?

A: You should present your best appearance. Dress as if you were going to appear in court and wear neat, moderate, and comfortable clothing. Your attorney may want you to dress differently; he or she will so advise you.

Q: Will the deposition take place in a courtroom?

A: No. It takes place in an informal setting, frequently in the examining attorney's office, often in the court reporter's office, occasionally in the courthouse, sometimes in the opposing attorney's office, and at times in the deponent's office so that certain documents will be accessible. Your lawyer will advise you as to the exact location of the deposition.

Q: Will there be a "deposition room"?

A: The room will usually be a conference room or library office. There will be a table and several chairs around the table. You will sit in one of the chairs next to your lawyer, and the other people will sit on the other chairs.

Q: Who will be present during my deposition?

A: Your lawyer will be there with you. The lawyer or lawyers representing the party or parties in the case will also be there as will a court reporter-stenographer, who will record what happens.

Q: Will there be anyone else present during my deposition?

A: Ordinarily not. If there will be, your attorney will advise you. Sometimes parties to an action will exercise their right to sit in during depositions.

Q: Can I bring anyone with me to the deposition?

A: Ask your lawyer in advance and he or she will tell you who may or may not sit in with you at the deposition.

Q: Can I object to the presence of someone at the deposition?

A: Probably not. The parties can be there, as can their lawyers. If you expect that someone you do not want to attend will be there, contact your lawyer.

Q: Is the deposition conducted like a trial?

A: Not exactly. There will be no judge or jury present, but otherwise you will be answering questions in somewhat the same manner as you would during a trial. Although a deposition seems less formal than a court hearing, it is important to remember that the deposition testimony can be used in court. So don't let the informal setting make you less careful in answering the questions.

Q: Will my answers be recorded?

A: Yes. Everything said during the formal part of the deposition will be recorded. A court reporter-stenographer will record everything you and everyone else says on a "stenographic machine" or by shorthand or by tape recorder. There may be times when somebody says, "Let's go off the record," and if you see the reporter take his or her hands up off the machine, then that means no real record is being made. This testimony may later be "transcribed" (typed up in a booklet form) by the reporter-stenographer, with copies made available to the court and to the attorneys. Also, the lawyers will be taking notes.

Q: Will my deposition be videotaped?

A: Some courts encourage the use of tape recorders or videotape equipment. If your deposition will be videotaped, your attorney will discuss this aspect with you.

II. THE DEPOSITION ITSELF

A. The Deposition Begins

Q: How does the deposition begin?

A: The reporter-stenographer will ask you to raise your right hand and take an oath to tell the truth. After the oath has been administered or after you have affirmed to tell the truth, the other attorney will ask you questions or may explain some deposition procedures and then begin the questioning.

Q: How should I conduct myself during the deposition?

A: Remain polite and calm at all times. Do not become angry or upset. Be courteous, but do not become overly friendly with, or tell jokes to, the opposing lawyer or the reporter-stenographer. Do not talk at the same time someone else is talking. The reporter will not be able to transcribe two people talking at the same time.

Q: What if I am nervous?

A: You probably will be a little nervous. That's normal, but control it so that you will testify accurately and clearly. The information you give is important, but of almost equal importance is the impression you make on opposing counsel.

Q: Whom should I look at when I give my answers?

A: The other attorney will be asking you the questions, and you should ordinarily look and talk to that attorney. You want to make certain that you speak clearly and loudly enough so that the reporter-stenographer can accurately record what to say. Do not nod your head or use facial expressions or gestures to answer questions. Be certain that you verbalize whatever you do so the reporter-stenographer can record that.

Q: What should I do if I do not understand something that has happened during the deposition?

A: Ask your attorney to explain to you what happened.

Q: May I ask my attorney questions in private during the deposition?

A: Yes. If at some point you're confused, ask to speak to your lawyer. But you should avoid overdoing this. It may look like you and your attorney are planning or changing your answers.

Q: Is it permissible for me to talk to my lawyer during a break in the deposition or when there is a lull in the questioning?

A: If you have some questions or concerns about the deposition, you should discuss them with your lawyer. But be careful not to talk too loudly, or other people will overhear you.

Q: Will I be told anything about the lawyer who will ask me the questions?

A: Yes. Your lawyer will discuss with you the type of questioning usually conducted by an opposing attorney. Your attorney may even tell you something about the attorney's personality, approach, pace, and other factors.

Q: Should I answer differently if the other attorney is friendly or hostile towards me?

A: No. Don't be disarmed by friendliness or intimidated by hostility. Tell the truth, regardless of the disposition of the attorney. Whether he or she is friendly or hostile, the attorney has only one goal, and that is his or her client's best interests, not yours.

B. Types of Questions

Q: What kind of questions will the other attorney ask me?

A: The other attorney will generally ask you questions about what you know and what happened. He may also ask you questions about your personal history and background.

Q: Must I answer every question the opposing lawyer asks?

A: Yes, unless your lawyer objects, or unless you do not know the answer or do not remember the details. Do not make up answers.

Q: What if I consider questions about my personal history and background to be confidential and private?

A: The law usually allows the other attorney to ask you questions about your personal history and background because such information often has a direct or indirect significance to the case or is of importance or interest to the other attorney. If such information is protected by the law, then your attorney will object and advise you not to answer. If your attorney does not object, then you should answer the questions. Your lawyer will protect you.

Q: Do I have to answer hypothetical or "possibility" questions the other attorney asks me?

A: The other attorney may ask you "if" questions, or "assume" questions: "What if this happened?" or "assume that happened?" You do not have to answer such hypothetical or possibility questions and you should not guess at answers. Simply tell the attorney you can't answer and do not want to guess.

Q: What if the other lawyer does not ask me certain questions which I think are important?

A: Do not volunteer facts or answers to questions you have not been asked. The opposing lawyer will ask you questions that he or she wants the answers to. For example:

Q: Where do you live?

A: I live at 1934 Suburban Avenue. My spouse and I live there and we have three children. I work at 3M. My spouse works at Mounds Park Hospital.

Since you were only asked where you live, you should simply give the address and not the other information. If the other attorney wants the other information, he or she will ask for it. If you continue giving details that you have not been asked about, the deposition will become unduly long and disorganized.

Q: What if the other attorney asks me a question that will hurt my case if I answer it?

A: You must tell the truth, regardless of whether your answer will hurt or help your case.

Q: Will the other lawyer ask questions in order, or skip around from subject to subject?

A: Different lawyers ask questions differently. Some follow a pattern, others skip from subject to subject. If you pay close attention, you should be able to answer the questions easily. Remember that you have the right to have a question repeated or clarified if you did not understand or did not hear it. If you tell the truth and stick to the facts as you know them, no amount of skipping around should confuse you.

Q: Will the other attorney ask me any trick questions?

A: You have watched Perry Mason too often. If an opposing lawyer tries to trick you, your attorney will be aware of the situation and will take steps necessary to protect you. Do remain alert, though; otherwise you could become confused.

Q: Will more than one lawyer be asking me questions?

A: That depends on how many parties there are in the case. If each of the parties is represented by a different lawyer, each may ask you some questions.

Q: Will my attorney ask me questions during the deposition?

A: Your attorney may or may not ask you questions after the other attorney has finished asking you questions. Your attorney may ask you questions to clarify some of your answers or to have you give some additional information. This is why you need not volunteer testimony, because your attorney may add information by questioning you later.

C. Specific Questions to Expect

Q: If I am asked, "Did you talk to your lawyer before coming to this deposition?" what should I say?

A: The truth: Yes. There is absolutely no reason for you to hide the fact that you talked to your lawyer before coming to the deposition.

Q: What if the other lawyer asks, "Did your lawyer tell you what to say at this deposition?"

A: Your lawyer will not tell you what to say. Your lawyer will tell you to testify truthfully and to the best of your ability and knowledge. Your lawyer will prepare you for your deposition by referring to reports, notes, and other documents in the file and will review facts in order to refresh your recollection.

Q: What if the other attorney asks, "Do you realize you are testifying under oath?" or "Is that really your sworn testimony?"

A: Some attorneys, by asking such questions, may try to intimidate you or try to insinuate that you are lying. These are usually scare tactics. If you have answered your question honestly, according to the best of your ability, while these tactics may bother you, they should not concern you. Your attorney will protect you if these questions and tactics get out of hand.

Q: Will I be asked if anyone ever sued me or if I was ever a party in a lawsuit?

A: Probably. Answer the questions truthfully.

D. Responses

Q: How should I answer the questions the other attorney asks?

A: Listen to the question. Be sure you understand it before you respond. Take a moment to think about it and make sure that you understand it. Proceed at your own pace. Answer the question asked; don't ramble and don't volunteer any information. Be brief and concise. You are only obligated to answer the question directly. Give only information as to what you saw or heard. Don't speculate as to what other people were doing or what they were thinking. Do not ask questions in answer to questions.

Q: Should I be animated or speak in a monotone?

A: Speak as you normally do. Speak clearly, slowly, distinctly, audibly. Remember also that the court reporter will be taking down everything that is said during the deposition. The court reporter can only take down verbal responses; he or she cannot take down a nod of the head or a gesture.

Q: What should I do if I did not hear a question?

A: Simply say that you did not hear the question asked. The opposing lawyer will then either repeat the question or ask the reporter-stenographer to read the question to you.

Q: What happens if I do not understand the question the other attorney asks me?

A: Speak right up and tell the attorney that you do not understand the question and that you cannot answer it. Before you answer a question, make certain you understand it. You should not and do not have to answer any question you do not understand. Also, if the opposing attorney uses a word that you don't know, don't hesitate to say so. It's important that you not act as if you understood the word and not try to bluff your way through.

Q: Would it be a good idea for me to memorize much of my testimony so I won't forget what to say?

A: Do not memorize your testimony. A deposition is not a memory contest. Your lawyer will prepare you and suggest ways to help you remember answers during the deposition.

Q: Should I conceal any information?

A: No. The lawyer questioning you has a right to certain information. Answer each question as truthfully and honestly as you can. Give a full and complete answer; do not withhold any information. However, do not volunteer additional information.

Q: Can I explain my answers?

A: The attorney will ask you some questions that will require a yes, no, or I-don't-know response. You should answer such questions accordingly. If you cannot answer a question with a simple yes, no, or "I don't know," then explain your answer. The other attorney may nonetheless insist that you answer with a yes, no, or "I don't know." If so, tell the other attorney that you cannot answer the question that way, but only in your own way. Your attorney will protect you if you have difficulty in answering the question.

Q: What if the opposing lawyer interrupts my answer to a question before I'm done?

A: Your attorney will recognize that you have not been permitted to complete your answer. It is possible that your lawyer may not be interested in having you complete your answer. He or she may then do nothing. Your lawyer may ask you if you care to complete your answer or may decide that your interrupted answer is all that opposing counsel is entitled to receive under the circumstances. If your completed answer is vital to your case, your lawyer will make it possible for you to complete your answer. Listen carefully to your lawyer and be guided by his or her instructions to you and by his or her remarks to the stenographer or the opposing lawyer.

Q: What if I do not remember for certain or I am not sure about an answer?

A: There is nothing wrong with an answer that says, "I don't know" or "I don't remember." You will not be expected to remember everything. You should explain what you remember. If you do not remember something for certain or something completely, then you should say so. If you can give a reasonable approximation of something, then you may do so. For example, if you are asked questions about what someone said, and you do not remember exactly what was said, you should respond: "I don't remember the exact words, but he said something to the effect that. . . ." If you are asked about time, speed, or distance, and you are not certain but can make a reasonable estimate, then you may respond: "About one hour," or

"Around 30 miles per hour," or "I am not sure, but I would estimate. . . ." If you cannot make a reasonable approximation or a
reliable estimate, or you do not recall the particular facts, say so.
Use your best judgment. Do not guess or speculate about something. Give only information you have. If the other attorney insists
on an answer or on your best judgment, and you can only guess or
speculate, tell the attorney that you cannot answer the question.

Q: Should I give my opinion about something?

A: If the other attorney asks you for your opinion, then give it. If you
are not asked for it, then do not volunteer your opinion unless you
need to in order to explain an answer fully.

Q: What if the other attorney is dissatisfied with my answer?

A: You are there to tell the truth, not to adapt your answers to satisfy
the other attorney. Most often, because the other attorney will be
representing the other side, your information will not be favorable
to that attorney's position. You should not be concerned whether
you satisfy or dissatisfy the other attorney.

Q: What if I realize during the deposition that I have given an incorrect or inaccurate or incomplete answer to a previous question?

A: You may ask that that particular question and answer be asked or
read again. Then you should think carefully about any change you
wish to make in your testimony. The other lawyer may ask questions
about the change in your testimony in an attempt to discredit your
corrected answer. But it is usually more important for you to correct
an answer than it is for you to leave an incorrect answer on the
transcript. If you have a doubt about what to do, then you should
speak to your attorney about the matter.

Q: What if I feel during the deposition that things are not going well
or that the other attorney is taking advantage of me, what should
I do?

A: Your attorney is there to protect you, and while you may not think
things are going well, your attorney may be satisfied with what is
happening. If you feel strongly that something is wrong, then speak
to your attorney.

E. Objections

Q: What is an objection?

A: If the other attorney asks you a question and your lawyer considers that question improper, your lawyer will say "Objection," or

words to that effect. That word is a signal to you not to answer the question. Do not volunteer to give an answer when your lawyer makes an objection. Your lawyer will make the objection because the question or the expected answer may be improper or confusing or ambiguous. An objection is not a signal for you to explain something. You should remain silent until your attorney no longer objects or gives you permission to answer that question.

Q: Why do attorneys object?

A: The attorney may object because he or she thinks the question is something that really shouldn't be answered. The objection is the only way your attorney can speak to you as well as speak to the other attorney to disagree with the nature and type of question. Sometimes an attorney may object just for the record, so that later on, when the transcript is read, the objection acts as a reminder of a possible error.

Q: Will there be many objections during the deposition?

A: Usually not. The other lawyer can ask you many questions that will be proper for the deposition. These same questions may not be proper for the trial. If those questions were later asked at the trial, your attorney might object. But during a deposition, your attorney probably will not object to such questions because the law allows the other attorney to ask them during the deposition.

Q: Why should I answer if my attorney objects?

A: Your lawyer may object, state his reasons, and then tell you to answer the question. The rules may require this. Do listen very carefully to the objection because it may give you a clue. It may let you know that you're being led into something. Or an objection that the question calls for "speculation" would be a tip to ask yourself, "Am I speculating or do I really know that?"

Q: What if I think a question should not be answered but my lawyer does not make an objection?

A: Answer the question. Your lawyer is there to protect your interests, and he or she knows when to make objections. You may not understand why the other side has asked the question, but you should answer the question unless your attorney objects. If you believe there is no reason at all to answer a question and your attorney does not object, then you might consider conferring with your attorney.

Q: Are there other kinds of objections my lawyer may make?

A: Yes, your lawyer may instruct you not to answer a particular question. Refuse to answer it. If the other attorney asks you whether you will or will not answer the question, tell him or her that on the advice of your attorney you will not answer the question.

F. Exhibits and Documents

Q: Will I have to examine any papers?

A: Maybe. It depends on your case. When an exhibit is handed to you, don't start to answer the question until you have taken time to become familiar with it (i.e., read it, examine it, study it). Take your time.

Q: Will the other attorney ask me to identify certain documents or photographs or objects during the deposition?

A: Perhaps. Before answering questions about a document, make certain that you read the entire segment you are asked about. Even though some documents may contain information or appear to have been signed, read, dated, mailed, or handled by you, do not admit such facts unless you have actual knowledge. If you cannot identify all or part of a document, tell the attorney that.

Q: May I look at documents or papers before I answer a question?

A: If the other attorney asks you a question about a document or a thing, then you should first ask to see that document or thing before you answer. If you do not know an answer, but do know that a document or thing contains the answer, then you can tell the other attorney that. Your attorney may prepare some notes with you to refresh your memory during the deposition. If you need to, you can ask your attorney for these notes.

Q: Should I bring any documents with me?

A: Your attorney will advise you whether or not you need to bring with you any documents or objects or things or papers or materials. You can suggest to your attorney certain documents or materials that may help you in preparation for the deposition or during the deposition. But do not bring anything with you or use any materials without first obtaining your attorney's permission.

Q: May I bring documents with me?

A: No. Do not bring anything to the deposition with you unless told to do so by your attorney. If you bring anything into the deposition room, the opposing counsel may want to look at it.

Q: Can I get the documents back?

A: Yes. Speak to your lawyer about this.

Q: What should I do if the other attorney asks me if I will provide copies of certain documents or look up some facts?

A: Do not agree. Turn to your attorney for advice.

Q: Will the other attorney ask me to make a drawing or diagram during the deposition?

A: Perhaps. You should prepare for this by making some rough sketches for the deposition. You will not be expected to prepare an artist's drawing or draw something to scale. When you discuss preparation with your lawyer, you may do a rough sketch at that time.

TABLE OF CASES

References are to section numbers.

Table of Cases

Table of Cases

Table of Cases

BIBLIOGRAPHY

GENERAL BIBLIOGRAPHY

Barthold, "Negligence" in Discovery: No Paper Tiger, 6 Litigation 39 (Fall 1979).

Barthold, W., Attorney's Guide to Effective Discovery Techniques (1975).

Bishop, Availability and Use of Discovery Procedures in Condemnation Cases, 1977 Planning, Zoning & Eminent Domain Institute 369.

Blair, A Guide to the New Federal Discovery Practice, 21 Drake L. Rev. 58 (1971).

Bruner, Discovery: An Ordered Approach, 30 Fed. Ins. Counsel Q. 205 (1980).

Chandler, Discovery and Pre-Trial Procedure in Federal Courts, 12 Okla. L. Rev. 321 (1959).

Cohn, Federal Discovery: A Survey of Local Rules and Practices in View of Proposed Changes to the Federal Rules, 63 Minn. L. Rev. 253 (1979).

Comment, Civil Discovery of Documents Held by a Grand Jury, 47 U. Chi. L. Rev. 604 (1980).

Comment, Discovery in Aid of Execution and Supplementary Proceedings: Two Weapons in the Creditor's Arsenal, 11 Vill. L. Rev. 601 (1966).

Comment, Discovery Priority Rule under the Federal Rules of Civil Procedure — Friend or Foe? 74 Dick. L. Rev. 103 (1969).

Comment, Masters and Magistrates in Federal Court, 88 Harv. L. Rev. 779 (1976).

Danforth, The 1975 Amendments to the Minnesota Rules of Discovery, 3 Wm. Mitchell L. Rev. 39 (1977).

Developments in the Law — Class Actions, 89 Harv. L. Rev. 1319, 1439-1448 (1976).

Developments in the Law — Discovery, 74 Harv. L. Rev. 940 (1961).

Dobie, The Federal Rules of Civil Procedure, 25 Va. L. Rev. 261 (1939).

Fowler, J., & Sokolow, A., Discovery Proceedings under the Federal Rules (1955).

Frank, Pretrial Conferences and Discovery: Disclosure or Surprise? 1965 Ins. Law Rev. 661 (1965).

Freedman, Discovery as an Instrument of Justice, 22 Temp. L.Q. 174 (1948).

Frost, Discovery and Summary Judgment: The Ascertainment of Truth by Discovery, 28 F.R.D. 89 (1961).

Gardner, Privilege and Discovery: Background and Development in English and American Law, 53 Geo. L.J. 585 (1965).

Glaser, W., Pretrial Discovery and the Adversary System (1968).

Greenwald, What You Don't Know May Hurt You: Effective Pre-Trial Discovery in Medical Negligence Cases, 15 Trial 28 (1979).

Hoey, Discovery Proceedings under the Federal Rules, 9 N.Y.L.F. 517 (1963).

Holtzoff, The Elimination of Surprise in Federal Practice, 7 Vand. L. Rev. 576 (1954).

Holtzoff, Origin and Sources of the Federal Rules of Civil Procedure, 30 N.Y.U.L. Rev. 1057 (1955).

Kaskell, United States and Discovery under the Federal Rules of Civil Procedure, 13 Loy. L. Rev. 1 (1966).

Kirsch, Auto Fuel Tank Fires: Pre-Discovery Techniques, 51 N.Y.S.B.J. 271 (1979).

Kroll & Maciszewski, Pre-Trial Discovery: Change in the Federal Rules, 7 Haw. B.J. 48 (1970), reprinted in W. Treadwell, New Federal Civil Discovery Rule Source Book 205 (1972).

McCullough & Underwood, Uses and Limitations of Some Discovery Devices, 20 Prac. Law. 65 (1974).

McGuire, Defense of Arson in a Suit under an Insurance Policy — Discovery and Trial Preparation, 11 Forum 507 (1976).

Note, Contingent Compensation of Expert Witnesses in Civil Litigation, 52 Ind. L.J. 671 (1977).

Note, Discovery against Corporations under the Federal Rules, 47 Iowa L. Rev. 1006 (1962).

Note, Discovery in States Adopting the Federal Rules of Civil Procedure, 68 Harv. L. Rev. 673 (1955).

Note, Federal Discovery in Concurrent Criminal and Civil Proceedings, 52 Tul. L. Rev. 769 (1978).

Note, Legal Profession — Witnesses — Contingent Fees for Expert Witnesses, 1977 Wis. L. Rev. 603.

Note, Post Judgment Use of Discovery: The "Gap," 9 Cumb. L. Rev. 473 (1978).

Note, Preferential Treatment of United States under Federal Civil Discovery Procedures, 13 Ga. L. Rev. 550 (1979).

Note, Pre-Trial Discovery in Condemnation Proceedings: An Evaluation, 42 St. John's L. Rev. 52 (1967).

Note, Why Not Contingent Fees for Expert Witnesses? 39 U. Pitt. L. Rev. 511 (1978).

Pike & Willis, The New Federal Deposition-Discovery Procedure, 38 Colum. L. Rev. 1179 (1938).

Savell, Discovery Proceedings from the Defendant's Point of View, 26 Ga. B.J. 143 (1963).

Schmertz, Oral Depositions: The Low Income Litigant and the Federal Rules, 54 Va. L. Rev. 391 (1968).

Speck, The Use of Discovery in United States District Courts, 60 Yale L.J. 1032 (1951).

Bibliography

Sunderland, Discovery before Trial under the New Federal Rules, 15 Tenn. L. Rev. 737 (1939).
Sunderland, Scope and Method of Discovery before Trial, 42 Yale L.J. 863 (1933).
Taine, Discovery of Trial Preparations in the Federal Courts, 50 Colum. L. Rev. 1026 (1950).
Underwood, J., A Guide to Federal Discovery Rules (1979).
Weinstein, Standing Masters to Supervise Discovery, 23 F.R.D. 36 (1959).
Weissman, Domestic Relations Litigation Discovery: Auxilliary Aids, Exotic Evidence, and the Duty to Detail, 16 Trial 28 (1980).
Western, The Compulsory Process Clause, 73 Mich. L. Rev. 71 (1974).
Wicker, Tactical Advantages from the Use of Discovery, 27 Tenn. L. Rev. 323 (1960).
Wright, Wegner & Richardson, The Practicing Attorney's View of the Utility of Discovery, 12 F.R.D. 97 (1952).

BIBLIOGRAPHY BY CHAPTER

Chapter One   The Scope
Becker, Modern Discovery: Promoting Efficient Use and Preventing Abuse of Discovery in the Roscoe Pound Tradition, 78 F.R.D. 267 (1978).
Berger & Krash, Government Immunity from Discovery, 59 Yale L.J. 1451 (1950).
Bua, Experts — Some Comments Relating to Discovery and Testimony under New Federal Rules of Evidence, 1977 Trial Law. Guide 1.
Case Comment, Absentee Class Members Subjected to Discovery and Claims Dismissed for Failure to Respond, 1971 Duke L.J. 1007.
Case Note, Work-Product Privilege Extends to Subsequent, Unrelated Litigation, 27 Vand. L. Rev. 826 (1974).
Comment, Ambiguities after the 1970 Amendments to the Federal Rules of Civil Procedure Relating to Discovery of Experts' and Attorneys' Work-Product, 17 Wayne L. Rev. 1145 (1971).
Comment, Civil Discovery of Documents Held by a Grand Jury, 47 U. Chi. L. Rev. 604 (1980).
Comment, Civil Procedure — Discovery of Liability Insurance, 45 N.C.L. Rev. 492 (1967).
Comment, Civil Procedure — Opinion Interrogatories after 1970 Amendment to Federal Rule 33(b), 53 N.C.L. Rev. 695 (1975).
Comment, Civil Procedure — Pre-Trial Discovery of Existence and Amount of Defendant's Liability Insurance Policy, 20 S.C.L. Rev. 85 (1968).
Comment, Discovery of Expert Information under the Federal Rules, 10 U. Rich. L. Rev. 706 (1976).
Comment, Discovery of Expert Opinions and Conclusions in Proceedings in Federal and California Courts, 20 Hastings L.J. 650 (1969).
Comment, Discovery of Expert Opinions in Land Condemnation Proceedings, 41 Ind. L.J. 506 (1969).
Comment, Discovery of Expert Witnesses, 41 Tul. L. Rev. 678 (1967).

Comment, Discovery of Insurance Coverage: Hazy Frontier of the Discovery Process, 35 Tenn. L. Rev. 35 (1967).

Comment, Discovery Priority Rule under the Federal Rules of Civil Procedure — Friend or Foe? 74 Dick. L. Rev. 103 (1969).

Comment, Discovery — The Work Product Protection, 13 Kan. L. Rev. 125 (1964).

Comment, Federal Civil Procedure — Discovery of Existence and Amount of Defendant's Insurance Policy, 17 S.C.L. Rev. 750 (1965).

Comment, The First Amendment Right to Disseminate Discovery Materials: In re Halkin, 92 Harv. L. Rev. 1550 (1979).

Comment, The Potential for Discovery of Opinion Work Product under Rule 26(b)(3), 64 Iowa L. Rev. 103 (1978).

Comment, Work Product Doctrine and Legal Expertise — A Broad Scope of Discovery in Illinois, 1967 U. Ill. L.F. 159 (1967).

Connors, New Look at an Old Concern — Protecting Expert Information from Discovery under the Federal Rule, 18 Duq. L. Rev. 271 (1980).

Cooper, Work Product of the Rule Makers, 53 Minn. L. Rev. 1269 (1969).

Coven, Work Product Exception to Discovery — The New York Experience, 58 Cornell L.Q. 98 (1967).

Degan, The Evidence Law of Discovery: Exclusion of Evidence Because of Fear of Perjury, 43 Tex. L. Rev. 435 (1965).

Discovery and the First Amendment, Wm. & Mary L. Rev. 331 (1979).

Dore, Confidentiality Orders — The Proper Role of the Court in Providing Confidential Treatment for Information Disclosed through the Pre-Trial Discovery Process, 14 New Eng. L. Rev. 1 (1978).

Evans, Civil Litigation — Discovery—Public Interest Immunity and State Papers, 58 Can. B. Rev. 360 (1980).

Fournier, Pre-Trial Discovery of Insurance Coverage and Limits, 28 Fordham L. Rev. 215 (1959).

Frank, Discovery and Insurance Coverage, 1959 Ins. L.J. 281.

Freeman, Production of Statements under Discovery Proceedings in Federal Court, 17 S.C.L. Rev. 529 (1965).

Friedenthal, Discovery and Use of an Adverse Party's Expert Information, 14 Stan. L. Rev. 455 (1962).

Gardner, Privilege and Discovery: Background and Development in English and American Law, 53 Geo. L.J. 585 (1965).

Graham, Discovery of Experts under Rule 26(b)(4) of the Federal Rules of Civil Procedure: Part One, An Analytical Study, 1976 U. Ill. L.F. 895.

—————, Discovery of Experts under Rule 26(b)(4) of the Federal Rules of Civil Procedure: Part Two, An Empirical Study and a Proposal, 1977 U. Ill. L.F. 169.

Gruenberger, Discovery from Class Members: A Fertile Field for Abuse, 4 Litigation 35 (Fall 1977).

Hand, Pre-Trial Discovery of Insurance, 3 Forum 310 (1968).

Hughes & Anderson, Discovery: A Competition between the Right of Privacy and the Right to Know, 23 U. Fla. L. Rev. 289 (1971).

Jayne, Discovery: The New Michigan Rule, 40 A.B.A.J. 304 (1954).

Jenkins, Discovery of Automobile Insurance Limits: Quillets of the Law, 14 Kan. L. Rev. 59 (1965).

Bibliography

Kane, The Work-Product Doctrine — Cornerstone of the Adversary System, 31 Ins. Coun. L.J. 130 (1964).

Keeton, Proprietorship over Deponents, 68 Harv. L. Rev. 600 (1955).

Knepper, Some Suggestions for Limiting Discovery, 34 Ins. Coun. L.J. 398 (1967).

Kyl, Pre-Trial Discovery of Impeachment Evidence: A Need to Reexamine Arizona's New Rule, 7 Ariz. L. Rev. 283 (1966).

LaFrance, Work Product Discovery: A Critique, 68 Dick. L. Rev. 351 (1963).

Long, Discovery and Experts under the Federal Rules of Civil Procedure, 39 Wash. L. Rev. 665 (1964).

Lundquist & Schechter, The New Relevance: An End to Trial by Ordeal, 64 A.B.A.J. 59 (1978).

McCoy, California Civil Discovery: Work Product of Attorneys, 18 Stan. L. Rev. 783 (1966).

McGanney & Seidel, Rule 26(b)(3): Protecting Work Product, 7 Litigation 24 (Spring 1981).

Note, The Availability of the Work-Product of A Disqualified Attorney: What Standard? 127 U. Pa. L. Rev. 1607 (1979).

Note, Civil Discovery Documents Held by a Grand Jury, 47 U. Chi. L. Rev. 604 (1980).

Note, Civil Procedure — Access to Disqualified Counsel's Work Product, 27 Kan. L. Rev. 662 (1971).

Note, Civil Procedure — Discovery — Personal Injury — Plaintiff's Refusal to Submit to Defendant's Medical Examination Before Suit Is Filed, 44 Tul. L. Rev. 174 (1969).

Note, Constitutional Need for Discovery of Pre-Voir Dire Jury Studies, 49 S. Cal. L. Rev. 597 (1976).

Note, Discoverability of Work Product in Diversity Actions, 1 Val. U.L. Rev. 410 (1967).

Note, Discovery: New Jersey Work Product Doctrine, 1 Rutgers Cam. L.J. 346 (1969).

Note, Discovery of an Attorney's Work Product in Subsequent Litigation, 1974 Duke L.J. 799.

Note, Discovery of Expert Information, 47 N.C.L. Rev. 401 (1969).

Note, Discovery of Experts: A Historical Problem and a Proposed FRCP Solution, 53 Minn. L. Rev. 785 (1969).

Note, Discovery of Plaintiff's Financial Situation in Federal Class Actions: Heading 'Em Off at the Passbook, 30 Hastings L.J. 449 (1978).

Note, Improved Definition of Discovery Relevance: A Path Out of the Antitrust Procedural Quagmire, 30 U. Fla. Rev. 751 (1978).

Note, Offering Plaintiff's Deposition in Evidence, 69 Harv. L. Rev. 1503 (1956).

Note, Protective Orders Prohibiting Dissemination of Discovery Information: The First Amendment and Good Cause, 1980 Duke L.J. 776.

Recent Developments, Federal Courts: Recognition of State Work Product Privileges in Diversity Suits, 66 Colum. L. Rev. 1535 (1966).

Slomanson, Supplementation of Discovery Responses in Federal Civil Procedure, 17 San Diego L. Rev. 233 (1980).

Szuch, Protecting the Work Product of Paralegals during Discovery, Natl. L.J., Nov. 24, 1980, at 30.

Tolman, Discovery under the Federal Rules: Production of Documents and the Work Product of the Lawyer, 58 Colum. L. Rev. 498 (1958).

Western, The Compulsory Process Clause, 73 Mich. L. Rev. 71 (1974).

Privilege

Case Comment, Self-Evaluative Reports — A Qualified Privilege in Discovery? 57 Minn. L. Rev. 807 (1973).

Comment, Academic Researchers and the First Amendment: Constitutional Protection for Their Confidential Sources? 14 San Diego L. Rev. 876 (1977).

Gardner, Privilege and Discovery: Background and Development in English and American Law, 53 Geo. L.J. 585 (1965).

Kaminsky, Preventing Unfair Use of the Privilege — Incrimination in Private Civil Litigation: A Critical Analysis, 39 Brooklyn L. Rev. 121 (1972).

Lord, Limitation on the Federal Husband-Wife Evidentiary Privilege, 8 Fla. St. U.L. Rev. 319 (1972).

Louisell, Confidentiality, Conformity and Confusion: Privileges in Federal Courts Today, 31 Tul. L. Rev. 101 (1956).

Moxham, A Comment on the Effect of Exercise of One's Fifth Amendment Privilege in Civil Litigation, 12 New Engl. L. Rev. 265 (1976).

Note, The Attorney-Client Privilege and the Corporation in Shareholder Litigation, 50 S. Cal. L. Rev. 303 (1977).

Note, Privileged Communications under Rule 26(b): Conflict of Laws in Diversity Cases, 12 U. Chi. L. Rev. 705 (1956).

Note, Use of the Privilege against Self-Incrimination in Civil Litigation, 52 Va. L. Rev. 322 (1966).

Chapter Two   Depositions

Comment, Federal Civil Procedure — Rule 30(b)(4) — Trial Judge May Deny Motion for Non-Stenographic Deposition Only When Particulars of Request Do Not Reasonably Ensure Accuracy Equivalent to Stenographic Deposition, 26 S.C.L. Rev. 753 (1975).

Comment, Refusals to Answer at Oral Deposition: A "Relevant" Inquiry? 1979 B.Y.U.L. Rev. 407.

Comment, Tactical Use and Abuse of Depositions under the Federal Rules, 59 Yale L.J. 117 (1949).

Graham, Nonstenographic Recording of Depositions: The Empty Promise of Rule 30(b)(4), 72 Nw. U.L. Rev. 566 (1977).

Miller, Video Taping the Oral Deposition, 18 Prac. Law. 45 (Feb. 1972).

Minnesota State Bar Association, The Video Tape Deposition: "Examining a Medical Witness" (1972).

Note, An Examination of Protective Orders Issued under Rule 30(b), 15 Wyo. L.J. 85 (1960).

Pike & Willis, The New Federal Deposition — Discovery Proceedings, 38 Colum. L. Rev. 1179 (1938).

Salomon, The Use of Video Tape Deposition in Complex Litigation, 51 Cal. St. B.J. 20 (1976).

Bibliography

Schmertz, Written Depositions under the Federal and State Rules as Cost-Effective Discovery at Home and Abroad, 156 Vill. L. Rev. 7 (1979).
Thomas, Changes in the Federal Rules of Civil Procedure Relating to Depositions, 40 J.B.A. Kan. 127 (1971).
Thornton, Extending Video Tape Technique in Pre-Trial and Trial Advocacy, 9 F. 105 (1973).
Valentino, Practice, Procedure and Forms under the Nebraska Video Tape Deposition Statute, 8 Creighton L. Rev. 314 (1974).

Chapter Three   Interrogatories
Comment, Civil Procedure — Opinion Interrogatories after 1970 Amendment to Federal Rule 33(b), 53 N.C.L. Rev. 695 (1975).
Goheen, Changes in Interrogatory Practice, 40 J.B.A. Kan. 133 (1971).
Good, Use of Long Interrogatories in Aviation Cases, 36 J. Air L. Rev. & Comm. 452 (1970).
Schoon & Miner, The Effective Use of Written Interrogatories, 60 Marq. L. Rev. 29 (1976).
Thompson, How to Use Written Interrogatories Effectively, 16 Prac. Law. 81 (Feb. 1970).

Chapter Four   Requests for Production and Physical Examinations
Comment, Discovery of Documents, Books, Records, Etc., for Impeachment Purposes, 22 Baylor L. Rev. 516 (1970).
Fromhold, Discovery, Evidence, Confidentiality, and Security Problems Associated with the Use of Computer-Based Litigation Support Systems, 1977 Wash. U.L.Q. 445.
Hawkins, Discovery and Rule 34: What's So Wrong About Surprise? 39 A.B.A.J. 1075 (1953).
Hughes & Anderson, Discovery: A Competition between the Right of Privacy and the Right to Know, 23 U. Fla. L. Rev. 289 (1971).
Lee, Disclosure of Medical Records, 129 New L.J. 702 (1979).
Morris, Hospital Computers in Court, 1963 Modern Uses of Logic in Law (now Juris. J.) 61.
Nations, Discovery: Motions to Produce under the Texas Rules, 18 S.T.L.J. 49 (1977).
Newport, "Designation" as Used in Rule 34 of the Federal Rules of Civil Procedure on Discovery and Production of Documents, 35 Iowa L. Rev. 422 (1950).
Note, Discovery of Government Documents and the Official Information Privilege, 76 Colum. L. Rev. 142 (1976).
Note, Discovery — Testing — Partially Destructive Testing Is within the Scope of the Illinois Discovery Rule, 26 De Paul L. Rev. 408 (1977).
Note, Limiting the Scope of Litigation: Bills of Particulars, Interrogatories, and Requests for Admission in Illinois and Federal Courts, 1979 U. Ill. L.F. 211.
Note, Rule 34(c) and Discovery of Non-Party Land, 85 Yale L.J. 112 (1975).
Pope, Rule 34: Controlling the Paper Avalanche, 7 Litigation 28 (Spring 1981).
Underwood, Discovery according to Federal Rule 34, 26 Prac. Law. 55 (1980).

Weinstein, Recognition in the United States of the Privileges of Another Jurisdiction, 56 Colum. L. Rev. 535 (1956).

Physical Examinations
Barnet, Compulsory Medical Examination under the Federal Rules, 41 Va. L. Rev. 1059 (1955).
Comment, The Doctor in Court: Impartial Medical Testimony, 40 S. Cal. L. Rev. 728 (1967).
Hausheer, Rule No. 35: A Methodology for Obtaining Medical Examination of Litigants, 46 J.B.A. Kan. 17 (Spring 1978).
Lee, Disclosure of Medical Records, 129 New L.J. 702 (1979).
Note, Discovery and the Doctor: Expansion of Rule 35(d), 34 Mont. L. Rev. 257 (1973).
Note, Medical Discovery in Negligence Actions: Rule 35(b)(2) of Montana Rules of Civil Procedure, 30 Mont. L. Rev. 105 (1968).
Note, Physical Examination of Non-Parties under the Federal Rules of Civil Procedure, 43 Iowa L. Rev. 375 (1958).
Note, Pre-Trial Discovery — Judicial Discretion Determines Whether Personal Injury Plaintiff's Counsel May Attend Pre-Trial Psychiatric Examination Conducted Pursuant to California Code of Civil Procedure Section 2032, 17 Santa Clara L. Rev. 224 (1977).
Note, The Role of Blood Tests in Civil Litigation, 36 S. Cal. L. Rev. 622 (1963).
Urbom, Medical Discovery in the Fifty States Plus Two, 33 Ins. Counsel L.J. 376 (1966).

Chapter Five   Requests for Admissions
Comment, The Dilemma of Federal Rule 36, 56 Nw. U.L. Rev. 679 (1961).
Epstein, Rule 36: In Praise of Requests to Admit, 7 Litigation 30 (Spring 1981).
Finman, The Request for Admissions in Federal Civil Procedure, 71 Yale L.J. 371 (1962).
Kinney, Interpretations of Federal Rule of Civil Procedure 36 — Request for Admission, 1 F. 55 (1966).
Note, Limiting the Scope of Litigation: Bills of Particulars, Interrogatories, and Requests for Admission in Illinois and Federal Courts, 1979 U. Ill. L.F. 211.

Chapter Six   Enforcement of Discovery Rights
Barthold, "Negligence" in Discovery: No Paper Tiger, 6 Litigation 39 (Fall 1979).
Comment, Sanctions Imposed by Courts on Attorneys Who Abuse the Judicial Process, 44 U. Chi. L. Rev. 619 (1977).
Epstein, Corcoran, Krieger & Carr, An Up-Date on Rule 37 Sanctions after *National Hockey League v. Metropolitan Hockey Club, Inc.*, 84 F.R.D. 145 (1979).
Johnston, Appealability and Reviewability of Discovery Orders, 53 Chi. B. Rec. 210 (1972).

Bibliography

Krupp, Rule 37: Sanctions for Discovery Resistance, 7 Litigation 32 (Spring 1981).

McGlinchev, Sanctions Available to Parties in Texas Discovery Procedures, 19 Sw. L.J. 740 (1965).

Note, Civil Procedure — Discovery — Imposition of Sanctions for Failure to Disclose Names of Witnesses, 43 Tenn. L. Rev. 124 (1975).

Note, Civil Procedure: Discovery Sanctions — Gross Negligence in Failure to Respond to Discovery Order Sufficient Justification for Ordering Dismissal, 53 Temp. L.Q. 140 (1980).

Note, Decline and Fall of Sanctions in California Discovery: Time to Modernize California Code of Civil Procedure Section 2034, 9 U.S.F.L. Rev. 360 (1974).

Note, Discovery Sanctions under the Federal Rules of Civil Procedure: A Goal-Oriented Mission for Rule 37, 29 Case W. Res. L. Rev. 603 (1979).

Note, Discovery — The Appealability of an Order Denying Discovery in a Proceeding Ancillary to a Patent Interference, 51 Temp. L.Q. 372 (1978).

Note, The Emerging Deterrence Orientation in the Imposition of Discovery Sanctions, 91 Harv. L. Rev. 1033 (1978).

Note, Expanding Use of Mandamus to Review Texas District Court Discovery Orders: An Immediate Appeal Is Available, 32 Sw. L.J. 1283 (1979).

Note, Federal Rules of Civil Procedure: Defining a Feasible Culpability Threshold for the Imposition of Severe Discovery Sanctions, 65 Minn. L. Rev. 137 (1980).

Note, Imposition and Pretrial Selection of Sanctions in Texas Pre-Trial Discovery Procedure, 31 Baylor L. Rev. 191 (1979).

Note, Recent Innovations to Pretrial Discovery Sanctions: Rule 37 Reinterpreted, 8 Duke L.J. 278 (1959).

Note, Sanctions for Enforcement of Discovery — Constitutionality of Rule 37, 37 Wash. L. Rev. 175 (1962).

Note, Standards for Imposition of Discovery Sanctions, 27 Maine L. Rev. 247 (1975).

Renfrew, Discovery Sanctions: A Judicial Perspective, 67 Calif. L. Rev. 264 (1979).

——————— , Discovery Sanctions: A Judicial Perspective, 6 Litigation 5 (Winter 1980).

Rosenberg, Sanctions to Effectuate Pre-Trial Discovery, 58 Colum. L. Rev. 480 (1958).

Waterman, An Appellate Judge's Approach When Reviewing District Court Sanctions Imposed for the Purpose of Ensuring Compliance with Pre-trial Orders, 29 F.R.D. 420 (1961).

Werner, Survey of Discovery Sanctions, 1979 Ariz. St. L.J. 299 (1979).

INDEX

Index